IPPERWASH

The Tragic Failure of Canada's Aboriginal Policy

On 6 September 1995, Dudley George was shot by Ontario Provincial Police officer Kenneth Deane. He died shortly after midnight the next day. George had been participating in a protest over land claims in Ipperwash Provincial Park, which had been expropriated from the native Ojibwe after the Second World War. A confrontation erupted between members of the Kettle and Stony Point Band and officers of the OPP's Emergency Response Team, who had been instructed to use necessary force to disband the protest by Premier Mike Harris's government. George's death and the grievous mishandling of the protest led to the 2007 Ipperwash Inquiry.

Edward J. Hedican's *Ipperwash* provides an incisive examination of protest and dissent within the context of land claims disputes and Aboriginal rights. Hedican investigates how racism and government practices have affected Aboriginal resistance to policies, especially those that have resulted in the loss of Aboriginal lands and persistent socioeconomic problems in Native communities. He offers a number of specific solutions and policy recommendations on how Aboriginal protests can be resolved using mediation and dispute management – instead of coercive force as was used to such tragic ends in Ipperwash Park.

EDWARD J. HEDICAN is a professor in the Department of Sociology and Anthropology at the University of Guelph. He is the author of *Applied Anthropology in Canada: Understanding Aboriginal Issues*.

EDWARD J. HEDICAN

Ipperwash

The Tragic Failure of Canada's Aboriginal Policy

UNIVERSITY OF TORONTO PRESS
Toronto Buffalo London

© University of Toronto Press 2013
Toronto Buffalo London
www.utppublishing.com
Printed in Canada

ISBN 978-1-4426-4046-7 (cloth)
ISBN 978-1-4426-1013-2 (paper)

Printed on acid-free, 100% post-consumer recycled paper with vegetable-based inks.

Library and Archives Canada Cataloguing in Publication

Hedican, Edward J.
Ipperwash : the tragic failure of Canada's Aboriginal policy / Edward J.
Hedican.

Includes bibliographical references and index.
ISBN 978-1-4426-4046-7 (bound). – ISBN 978-1-4426-1013-2 (pbk.)

1. Native peoples – Goverment policy – Canada.   2. Native peoples –
Canada – Claims.   3. Race discrimination – Canada.   4. Native peoples –
Goverment policy – Ontario.   5. Ipperwash Incident, Ont., 1993–.
6. Race discrimination – Ontario.   I. Title.

E78.O5H39 2013   305.897'0713   C2012-908098-5

This book has been published with the help of a grant from the Canadian
Federation for the Humanities and Social Sciences, through the Awards to
Scholarly Publications Program, using funds provided by the Social Sci-
ences and Humanities Research Council of Canada.

University of Toronto Press acknowledges the financial assistance to its
publishing program of the Canada Council for the Arts and the Ontario
Arts Council.

Canada Council   Conseil des Arts
for the Arts   du Canada

ONTARIO ARTS COUNCIL
CONSEIL DES ARTS DE L'ONTARIO
50 YEARS OF ONTARIO GOVERNMENT SUPPORT OF THE ARTS
50 ANS DE SOUTIEN DU GOUVERNEMENT DE L'ONTARIO AUX ARTS

University of Toronto Press acknowledges the financial support of the
Government of Canada through the Canada Book Fund for its publishing
activities.

To my wife Valentina

Contents

Preface

When the *Report of the Ipperwash Inquiry* was released to the public by the Ontario government, in May 2007, I was busy preparing a second edition for a book on applied anthropology and Aboriginal issues. As I read through this report it became obvious that the Ipperwash Inquiry should become a centrepiece of this revised edition. As I continued reading – the report comprises more than five hundred pages – I was rather startled at the degree of injustice suffered by the Stony and Kettle Point people.

The Chippewas (Anishinabe people) originally ceded title to over two million acres of land to the Crown in the Huron Tract Treaty of 1827. With this treaty, the Anishinabe relinquished 99 per cent of their traditional territory, therefore, retaining less than 1 per cent of their land. All of the signatories to the Huron Tract Treaty – Walpole Island, Sarnia, Kettle Point, and Stony Point – were treated as one large band. Eventually, in 1919, the Kettle and Stony Point Band was created and separated from the Sarnia and Walpole bands.

Beginning in 1912, the Aboriginal people were pressured by an Indian agent to surrender, for recreational development, their beachfront property at the Kettle Point Reserve. Eventually, in 1927, a local land developer purchased the beach property from the Department of Indian Affairs, despite objections by the Aboriginal residents. Additional shoreline property at the Stony Point Reserve was sold to another real estate developer and Sarnia politician in 1928, who later resold some of it as lots for $10,000 a piece, realizing a handsome profit. When Ipperwash Provincial Park was created, in 1936, the chief and council of the Kettle and Stony Point Band notified the authorities of a burial site in the park, but no action was ever taken by the Ontario government to protect or preserve the burials.

In 1942, under the War Measures Act, more land was taken from the band to make a military base that was to be used by army cadets. Despite a promise that the land on which Camp Ipperwash was situated would be returned after the war ended, it was not returned, despite repeated requests by the original Aboriginal residents. The Stony and Kettle Point people, out of feelings of intense frustration, decided to occupy Ipperwash Provincial Park in September 1995. Under directions from Ontario's Premier Mike Harris, the Ontario Provincial Police responded with alarming force, and one of the Aboriginal protesters, Dudley George, was shot and killed by an OPP officer. The OPP officer, Kenneth "Tex" Deane, was subsequently found guilty of criminal negligence causing death for the killing of the unarmed protester and given a suspended sentence and community service. It took until November 2003, with a change of government, for an inquiry to be initiated under Commissioner Sidney Linden.

There are many aspects of the *Report of the Ipperwash Inquiry* that are deeply disturbing. Premier Mike Harris, for example, in a cabinet meeting, is reported by his attorney general in sworn testimony to have used the most egregious profanity when referring to the Aboriginal occupiers of the park. Unfortunately, even several OPP officers, in tape-recorded conversations that were presented to the inquiry as evidence, also used the same vulgar and culturally insensitive terms in reference to the Stony Point people as did Premier Harris.

My feelings of revulsion after reading the report did not stem from a sense of moral outrage. Rather, I felt deep disappointment that our elected officials and police officers should be so imbued with such antipathy and aversion towards the Aboriginal people involved in the protest. Previous to reading the *Report of the Ipperwash Inquiry*, I shared with many of my fellow Canadians pride in our tolerant country, believing that we are among the more unprejudiced, respectful, and charitable people of the world. This report has drastically changed my opinion on these matters, and I now believe that we are probably just as capable of racially oppressive acts as anyone else.

The Ipperwash Report is apt to cause one to reflect on the character of our society, and where it might be heading, and to ask some rather pertinent questions about how dissent is dealt with in Canada. Whatever happened to the right of peaceful protest? Is this not one of the guarantees under our Charter of Rights and Freedoms? Why does it seem that such hateful brutality is directed towards Aboriginal citizens of this country by those in authority, by the very people who should be our paragons of tolerance, respect, and justice? It is sickening to read about the hateful invectives directed towards people whose ancestral lands were taken away from them and who now live, for the most part, in abject poverty. This book is written with the idea that it is about time that a serious academic investigation be taken into the underlying causes of the seemingly interminable First Nations protests and confrontations. The goal is not so much to seek solutions to these intractable issues, but to begin a basis for understanding, such that new Aboriginal policies might be initiated with a sense of respect and tolerance. But, before much meaningful change can take place, first we have to look at the situation as it exists now and at how it became the way it is.

I am indebted to several friends and colleagues for their continued support, especially Stan Barrett (professor emeritus, University of Guelph) and Philip Salzman (McGill University). In addition, a special thanks goes to Jaime Mishibinijima, former director of the Aboriginal Resource Centre, University of Guelph. Victor Gulewitch provided meaningful inside information from his ethnographic studies of the Ipperwash protest and the Stony Point First Nation. My sincere appreciation goes to the anonymous reviewers and to the staff of the University of Toronto Press for their helpful comments on earlier drafts of this manuscript. However, I have learned the most from the many students who have attended my course on Canadian Aboriginal peoples over the past three decades.

Edward J. Hedican
University of Guelph

IPPERWASH

The Tragic Failure of Canada's Aboriginal Policy

Chapter One

Introduction

The ultimate failure to include Indians raises the basic question of how the demands of the Indians at the consultation meetings were presented by the policy-makers inside government. It also requires us to understand how "the Indian problem" was defined by the policy-makers and the public, for defining the problem that a policy is to solve is the first and the most crucial step in policy-making.

– Sally M. Weaver, *Making Canadian Indian Policy* (1981: 11)

The essential argument of this book is that Canada's Aboriginal policy is fundamentally flawed. Patently, this is the case when an unarmed citizen, as was Dudley George, is shot and killed by the Ontario Provincial Police (OPP) while protesting the occupation of his community's land. We would probably all agree that in a civilized society acts of civil disobedience such as land claims protests should not entail the killing of its citizens by the armed representatives of the state. If the basic tenet is accepted that the policy of the Canadian government towards Aboriginal persons is a flawed one, then we are compelled to ask the following two questions: first, how did the policy get this way, and second, what can be done about it?

As a case study, the *Report of the Ipperwash Inquiry* (Linden 2007) provides an excellent opportunity to scrutinize issues associated with the far too frequent instances of Aboriginal political mobilization concerning Native rights and land claims, as well as the overall implications of the report for contemporary Aboriginal policy in Canada. Especially this is true with regard to dispute resolution and the various mechanisms that could be used to ameliorate conflict between Aboriginal and non-Aboriginal people. The overall aim of this book is to use the Ipperwash incident to discuss Canada's policy towards Aboriginal First Nations and to assess its effectiveness. Several approaches are examined that have the potential to mitigate the interminable cycle of Aboriginal acts of resistance to this policy, especially when it comes to land claims and treaty rights in Canada.

Ipperwash as a Case Study

The death of Dudley George, on 6 September 1995, was hardly a national news item at the time.[1] Certainly, the protest by people of the Stony Point First Nation and the ongoing tensions with the Ontario Provincial Police did not compare with the horrific scenes portrayed on television several years earlier at Oka, Quebec. We were not shown Iroquois women bravely confronting tanks, Canadian soldiers firing their rifles at Aboriginal protesters, or the foggy confusion of tear gas and gunshots.

In 1995, few Canadians would have been aware that Ipperwash Provincial Park was anything other than a family campground. They would not have understood the centuries of frustration that lay behind its establishment. Originally, the park was part of more than two million acres of land given up to the British by the Chippewas (or Anishinabe) of the area by the 1827 Huron Tract Treaty. In 1912 and 1928, members of the Kettle and Stony Point reserves were pressured by Indian agents and the Department of Indian Affairs (DIA) to give up their beachfront property, eventually leading to the creation of Ipperwash Provincial Park, in 1936. Aboriginal burial sites on the park property were no longer maintained because of access issues. In 1942, further Aboriginal land was confiscated, and reserve residents evicted, by the Department of National Defence using the War Measures Act to create Camp Ipperwash, a military training base for army cadets.

On Labour Day Monday 1995, a handful of men and women from the Kettle Point and Stony Point reserves waited until the closing of Ipperwash Provincial Park for the season before occupying it with the intention of laying claim to lands which, in their minds, had been unjustly taken away from them. In a confrontation two days later between the Indigenous protesters and the OPP, Acting Sergeant Ken Deane fired three rifle shots at Dudley George, one of the protesters, which killed him. Deane would later claim that Dudley George had aimed a rifle at him, and fearing for his life, he had shot at Dudley George to protect himself. A rifle purportedly belonging to Dudley George was never recovered from the scene, and in fact, fellow officers later testified that they had not seen a rifle in Dudley George's possession. In 1997, Ken Deane was convicted of criminal negligence causing death; Deane subsequently died in a car accident, in February 2006.

It took the Ontario government eight years, until 12 November 2003, to begin an investigation into the death of Dudley George, under the Public Inquiries Act. The mandate of this inquiry was to report specifically on the events surrounding the death of Dudley George, and to suggest recommendations that would serve to prevent similar violent confrontations in the future. The course of this investigation, termed the Ipperwash Inquiry, was headed by the Hon. Sidney B. Linden between the years 2004 and 2006, and its final report was released by Ontario's Attorney General Michael Bryant on 31 May 2007.

The Ipperwash Inquiry was one of the most expensive hearings in Canadian history, costing $13.3 million, but not nearly as expensive as the $63 million (see Hedican 2008b: 140–55) spent on the Royal Commission on Aboriginal Peoples (RCAP), established in 1991. Together, the Ipperwash Inquiry and the RCAP made about five hundred recommendations and interviewed several thousand witnesses. The *Report of the Ipperwash Inquiry* (Linden 2007) alone comprised over five hundred pages, in a complicated arrangement of reports on evidentiary hearings, policy analysis, executive summaries, and a hundred recommendations. The Ipperwash Report was available for but a short time on the Internet and from the Ontario government on CDs, before they rather quickly were sold out; thus, the report was not available for much public scrutiny. It is hard to imagine how, without going to a lot of trouble, concerned Canadians, even those with an above average education, could get to the bottom of the vast historical and contemporary circumstances that contributed to the death of Dudley George.

Dissent and Society

In addition to that of public accessibility, there are wider issues about the Ipperwash Inquiry that are important to Canadian society. One has to do with the suppression of legitimate public dissent in society. As these lines are being written, we are being inundated with horrific media scenes from Syria of brutal beatings and shootings of unarmed citizens. Such news coverage from halfway around the world seems distant from our northern "peaceable" society. But are we, in Canada, any different, when dealing with internal dissent? There has been a history, whether we want to recognize this or not, of using similar force as recently witnessed in Syria and Iran to suppress public dissent in Canada. Salient examples are the government-sanctioned violence in putting down the 1919 general strike in Winnipeg and the brutality with which Aboriginal protests were suppressed at Oka and Ipperwash.

This book is an investigation of the wider issues of how dissent is dealt with in Canadian society, and how peaceful resolutions to such conflicts might be achieved, without a resort to killing and beating Canadian citizens. The question here is: how can Canadians legitimately see themselves to be living in a civilized society if its citizens are pummelled into submission when they have no access to the institutionalized mechanisms to resolve such disputes?

James Tully's (2008) monograph entitled *Public Philosophy in a New Key: Democracy and Civic Freedom*, in terms of how it addresses the relationship between power and governance, is enlightening and informative. "From the perspective of the governed," he writes, "the exercise of power always opens up a diverse field of potential ways of thinking and acting in response" (p. 23). Citizens, as individuals and as groups, may act in a cooperative manner, in accordance with societal rules, or they may challenge a relation of governance and enter into negotiation or deliberation in an attempt to solve the problem(s). However, when institutions of reform are either unavailable or they fail because those who exercise power can subvert or bypass them, the governed may turn to acts of resistance. Resistance may take the form of escape or confrontation, with a strategy of struggle, as a way of challenging domination that is experienced as oppressive.

Tully submits, "In confrontations of this kind (such as struggles of direct action, liberation, decolonization, revolt, revolution, globalization from below), the relations of governance are disrupted and the relatively stable interplay of partners in a practice of governance gives way to the different logic of relations of confrontation among adversaries in strategies of struggle" (p. 24). The goal of the governed in such confrontations and struggles is to attempt to implement new relations of governance and new practices of freedom.

Would it be accurate to characterize Aboriginal protests as acts of civil disobedience? If we follow Burstein's (2008) definition, *civil disobedience* can be regarded as a "deliberate but nonviolent act of lawbreaking to call attention to a particular law or set of laws of questionable legitimacy or morality" (p. 391). It can also refer to "any type of conduct where the offender has intentionally broken the law for the purpose of trying to affect positive social change" (p. 376). According to Burstein, civil disobedience "presents a unique challenge for the justice system, as it involves the actions of normally law-abiding citizens seeking to change public policy by illegal means or, worse, by interfering with the lawful interests of other citizens" (p. 375).

Several questions would seem to follow, such as: Does it matter at all whether a protester's acts have actually led to some social good? Should the courts in such instances consider what alternative means could have been used by a protester with a goal of achieving some social improvement? In the case of Aboriginal protesters, to what extent should the court consider the history of frustration that has ensued over the protracted negotiations over land claims, or situations in which lands were removed from Aboriginal control and possession through illegal or unscrupulous means? There is also the context of the protest to consider: what about when a peaceful protest turns violent or when there is provocation or there are perceived threats during the course of a confrontation? In other words, are there justifications for civil disobedience, and if there are, what might they be? Burstein concludes, "While Canadian sentencing courts have consistently held that the noble motives behind civil disobedience cannot serve to excuse liability, there is much less agreement on how those motives may affect the punishment which follows the finding of guilt" (p. 380).

Whether civil disobedience produces harmful effects on or benefits society at large depends on one's vantage point, on one's convictions or beliefs concerning social justice (Beare 2008: 17–18). Nations can be born out of acts of civil disobedience, but also great social harm may result. Are militants engaged in acts civil disobedience to be regarded as noble heroes or incorrigible villains? Gandhi's philosophy of non-violent resistance might be regarded as an example of the former, and Toronto's G-20 summit protest in the summer of 2010 as a case of the latter. In Canada, high-profile acts of civil disobedience involved the Doukhobors in the mid-twentieth century and, in 1970, civil disobedience in Quebec led to the "October Crisis." Of interest and concern in the present study is the characterization of Aboriginal protests and confrontations, in terms of their legitimacy, and the response to such acts of civil disobedience by government officials, the Canadian army, and Canada's police forces. In such instances, which party is on the high moral, or even legal, ground? The contention here is that this is a nebulous area politically, legally, socially, and morally. When it comes to the courts, how do they balance citizens' rights to engage in acts of civil disobedience against other citizens' rights to be protected by the law (Burstein 2008: 376)?

In the context of Aboriginal and treaty rights, relations between the government and the police are an important matter. When dissent, in the form of protest, is voiced over how the government treats Aboriginal rights issues, and Aboriginal protesters and police interact, pretty much inevitably, there are policing problems to be considered. Aboriginal activists feel they have a right to engage in such protests, under the right to freedom of speech and the right to peaceful assembly. Aside from any Aboriginal or treaty rights that may justify acts of resistance, Aboriginal protesters have a "right to free expression [which] is grounded in a conception of a liberal democracy, and of the conditions necessary for the promotion of values and ideals highly esteemed by those living in and through a liberal democratic structure" (Christie 2007: 156). Indeed, it could be suggested that Aboriginal protesters are exercising their constitutionally protected right to free speech. What then is the appropriate nature of police activity in face of Aboriginal dissent, and what is the nature of the relationship between the actions that the police take and the decisions made by the government? As Christie argues, "Inappropriate police activity in relation to the Aboriginal protest may lead to questions about the relationship between the police and the government in power (especially ... if it appears the government inappropriately directed the police in this matter)" (p. 155).

The Aboriginal mobilization at Ipperwash Provincial Park and the shooting death of Dudley George brings into question the relationship between police activity and decisions made by the provincial government in power at the time. As Beare (2008) explains, "One can trace, for example, the refusal of the Conservative party in Ontario to hold an inquiry into the shooting of Dudley George at Ipperwash and the campaign promise made by the Liberal party that culminated in an inquiry after their election" (p. 19). The Ipperwash Inquiry demonstrated the tensions between social scientific perspectives and a more restricted legalistic view of the events involved in the Aboriginal protest. Concerning the relationship between politics and policing, on the one hand, lawyers are apt to point to case law as an interpretation, while social scientists such as criminologists are more interested in the "working relationship" between the police and government (p. 26). This working relationship that can be found in social scientific research would include such matters as the policing culture and the complex environments in which police operate.

The strategy of investigation taken in this study is to use the seemingly impenetrable *Report of the Ipperwash Inquiry* (Linden 2007) as a case study of Aboriginal policy in Canada, especially as this inquiry reveals aspects of the policing of Aboriginal dissent more generally. After reviewing the history of Aboriginal policy, a brief review of existing Aboriginal conditions in Canada is presented. A synopsis is then given of the events at Ipperwash Provincial Park in September 1995 and a summary of reports, written as a narrative of events, leading to the death of Dudley George. Importantly, several of the more significant recommendations of the Ipperwash Inquiry are discussed that would hold open the possibility of a peaceful resolution of future Aboriginal protests. These are then compared with the earlier RCAP (1996) recommendations, several of which are similar to those presented by Commissioner Linden in the Ipperwash Report (Hedican 2008a).

The So-Called Indian Problem

No doubt many Canadians wonder why Aboriginal peoples seem to be in a constant state of turmoil. Hardly a summer's day goes by when we do not read of a protest over a land claim, the blockade of a railway, highway, or bridge. There are confrontations over burial grounds, pipelines, hydroelectric projects, fishing rights, and seemingly on and on. Some citizens are apt to be asking, "Why doesn't the government do something about this?" The general issue is sometimes simply compressed into a single phrase: "the Indian problem."

Canadians, on the whole, are tolerant people. Indeed, we pride ourselves on our racial and cultural tolerance: is not our official policy in Canada one of multiculturalism? The unfortunate aspect of a phrase such as "the Indian problem" is that it implicitly places the blame for the trouble or problem on the shoulders of Aboriginal people. The idea that "it takes two to make a fight" seems to get forgotten in all the rhetoric. Surely, Aboriginal people are engaging in their acts of civil disobedience not just because they have nothing better to do with their time; surely, they have reasons for their behaviour, and goals that they are trying to achieve with it. But what are these goals? Some people might say, "Why don't they just behave like other Canadians?"

The simple answer to this question is that the Aboriginal peoples in Canada are the Indigenous population of the country. What follows from this fact is that certain rights flow from the various treaties and other agreements that were made by which Aboriginal peoples gave up varying degrees of control over their territories. The colonists needed somewhere to live, and were it not for the treaties there might not have been any land available to build our towns and cities. The treaties with Canada's Indigenous peoples are not "legal issues from the past" – they are what could be called a "living trust."

What was exchanged when the Native land was ceded – small annuities, some preferential rights to fishing and hunting, access to medical care in some instances – has turned out to be a monumental bargain for all Canadians. The problem, in many cases, is that the treaties involved huge injustices. Words were written down that are different from what is recollected in the Natives' oral traditions, and obligations on the government's part were not always maintained. In this wider sense, "the Indian problem" is more of a Euro-Canadian problem, or at least one mutually shared by all Canadians.

It is contingent on Canadians as a whole, or at least their elected representatives, to find equitable solutions to these outstanding problems so that they do not continue to fester, generation after generation. That lives are lost over such issues in a country purporting to abide by democratic ideals is simply intolerable. As numerous writers (e.g., Dyck 1991, 1997; Haig-Brown and Nock 2006; Letkemann 2005) have noted, the Indian problem is one of those political footballs that has been tossed around in Canadian politics since the time of Confederation, and even before.

The issue is such a multifaceted one – with cultural, political, historical, and administrative components – that there does not appear be a rational approach that could be implemented to solve the complex relationships that bind Aboriginal peoples with the wider Canadian society. Most Canadians would perceive that Aboriginals are in a distinctly disadvantageous position. Nevertheless, successive governments, over many decades, have not been able to develop a consistent policy direction. Instead, they have vacillated from one initiative to another such as protectionism, assimilation, or termination. There has been little consistency from one historical period to another or from one government administration to the next, with the result that it has been nearly impossible to even define what is meant by "the Indian problem" or to determine its parameters.

There is the issue of compensation, or at least ameliorative measures, which would serve to restore some balance to the injustices that have been committed by the dominant society. Does the Canadian state accept an obligation to recognize and accommodate the history and culture of the non-dominant Aboriginal groups? According to scholars like Will Kymlicka (1997, 2007), minority cultures have rights of reconciliation in multicultural societies. In his book entitled *Multicultural Odysseys*, Kymlicka (2007: 67) submits, "A multicultural state acknowledges the historical injustice that was done to minority/non-dominant groups by policies of assimilation and exclusion, and manifests a willingness to offer some sort of remedy and rectification for them." The present study of the Ipperwash confrontation, thus, takes as one of its central themes the idea that Canada's aspirations as a liberal democracy place an onus on the state to engage in this process of reconciliation. The point here is that "the Indian problem" is just as much a state issue of national reconciliation as it is one of an expression of minority rights.

Research on Aboriginal Policy

The lack of basic conceptual clarity, even with respect to defining what the Aboriginal "problem" is in Canadian society, suggests that there are fundamental inadequacies in the area of Aboriginal policy research. One obvious difficulty is that those involved are the members of so many different disciplines; they include anthropologists, political scientists, sociologists, economists, criminologists, to name but a few. The members of each of these scholarly fields are apt to view Aboriginal peoples from their own distinctive vantage point, have their own particular methodologies of research, and publish in different journals that are often quite distinct from one another. As a result, within the academic community, there is hardly a coordinated research effort, with probably much duplication – and arguments directed at the esoteric concerns of these disciplines – but without much particular relevance to solving the practical problems of Aboriginal peoples.

Take anthropology, for example. Anthropology is a discipline in which its practitioners have a very long-term association with Aboriginal peoples, at the ground level, as it were. Anthropologists generally conduct ethnographic research over an extended period, usually a year or more, and usually within the confines of a single community. The result is that the problems and concerns of these individual communities then tend to be cast in a broader perspective, whether these generalizations are warranted or not. There is a distinct advantage, nevertheless, in getting to know people over a long period in their home communities, rather than flying in with a handful of questionnaires of dubious local relevance.

Nevertheless, whatever one might conclude about the academic relevance of anthropological research, anthropologists are relative latecomers in addressing issues of public policy. For example, T. Weaver (1985: 97) observes, "anthropologists appear to be confused about the use of anthropology in public policy." The very idea of "policy" in itself is problematic in anthropology. Probably this is because of a deep-seated aversion to ethnocentric practices that could lead to the transferring of Western-based values to the life-ways of people in other cultures and societies. So there is a conceptual bias here or, we could more accurately say, a theoretical quandary in the discipline itself pertaining to the issue of cultural relativism that acts as an inhibiting force when public policy is studied. In this case, internecine academic battles and rivalries get played out in the wider arena of public policy and Canada's legal system.

It would appear that anthropology's position in interpreting Aboriginal rights has given way to that of the legal profession, which at present has taken a leading role in elaborating the historical rationale for the special place of Aboriginal peoples in Canada. Cairns (2000: 175), for example, finds that "the leading role of anthropology as the interpretive community through which Aboriginal realities had been filtered has been ceded to the law faculties, although there is still a significant anthropological presence." Nonetheless, anthropology's enduring strength is in providing a ground-level view gained through long-term fieldwork and research involving participant observation.

The role of anthropology in interpreting "Aboriginal realities" was especially prominent when Aboriginal peoples had limited opportunities to act as their own spokespersons, partly because of linguistic and cultural differences with the dominant society. Today, Aboriginal leaders are able to make articulate arguments on their own behalf, at the political level, with such groups as the Assembly of First Nations, but also within the legal profession itself. In this regard, we can cite the case of John Borrows, a member of the Chippewas of the Nawash First Nation. In 2001, Burrows was appointed to the Faculty of Law as Professor and Law Foundation Chair of Aboriginal Justice and Governance. A graduate of Osgoode Hall Law School, Borrows has also been the director of the First Nations Law Program at the University of British Columbia. His many publications, such as *Canada's Indigenous Constitution* (2010), or *Recovering Canada: The Resurgence of Indigenous Law* (2002), illustrate the major contribution that Aboriginal scholars are making today in interpreting Aboriginal rights in the fields of law, treaties, self-government, and a range of other areas.

According to Borrows (1994), Aboriginal peoples must be active participants in Canadian affairs, and they must take account of the realities of current social and political matters. His premise is that "we cannot ... ignore the world we live in ... In reconstructing our world we cannot just do what we want" (p. 23). The search is for a middle ground where Aboriginal values and identities meet with the surrounding majority society. This search seeks to engage in bridge building between traditional First Nations law and the national and international political systems that have influenced Canadian law that deals with Aboriginal societies. The prospect is that the Aboriginal community will become "a dynamic, relevant, and integral part of Canadian law" (Borrows 1996: 629), aided by a body of First Nations lawyers, which numbered over three hundred at the time that Borrows's articles were written.

The very idea of public policy suggests a comparative basis of understanding. It is not possible, or even practical, for the Canadian government to have a different set of policies for all the myriad ethnic groups in the country or, for that matter, all the varieties of Aboriginal peoples. Even the designation "Canadian Aboriginal people" is in itself a problem, both in terms of our conceptualization of such people and in terms of the practical aspects of administering services and programs to them.

Legal, Cultural, and Social Variability

Using a term such as "Canadian Aboriginal People" suggests a certain degree of uniformity. Indeed, as a consequence, there is one piece of federal legislation pertaining to Aboriginal people in Canada, the Indian Act, suggesting that one policy can be made to apply to all of Canada's Indigenous population. The fallacy of this approach has led to many of the failings of Canada's policy towards Aboriginal peoples because it masks an inherent social and cultural variability.

In fact, the Indian Act refers only to a certain portion of Canada's Aboriginal population – those individuals who hold legal Aboriginal status – which is not even the largest one. In the present work, a preference is given to the term *Aboriginal* as used in the widest sense of the word. This usage follows that given in Section 35 of the Constitution Act of 1982, where it states: "in this act, 'aboriginal peoples of Canada' includes the Indian, Inuit, and Metis peoples of Canada." The usage of the term Aboriginal in the Constitution Act differs from that given in the Indian Act, Section 2(1), where "'Indian' means a person who pursuant to this Act is registered as an Indian or is entitled to be registered as an Indian."

In other words, in Section 2(1) of the Indian Act there is a legal meaning that applies to a certain portion of the Aboriginal population that has special legal rights, as *status* Indians, as opposed to another portion of the Aboriginal population without these rights, who could be termed *non-status* Indians. Obviously, the term *Indian* has a certain ambiguous usage, both legal and otherwise. On the one hand, Indian can be used to refer to Aboriginal peoples in a fairly general sense (excluding Metis and Inuit, of course), and on the other, it refers to a very specific Aboriginal population with special rights not pertaining to all others. One can, therefore, use a variety of terms, such as *legal*, *registered*, or *status* with essentially the same meaning and official connotation, in referring to people for whom the federal government has a special responsibility – but that does not similarly hold for the remainder of the Aboriginal population.

The idea that some Aboriginal people in Canada have special legal rights, while others do not, brings into question the whole area of what constitutes "Aboriginal rights" (Asch 1997). Section 35 of Canada's Constitution Act, for example, makes specific mention of Aboriginal rights, to wit, "the existing aboriginal rights and treaty rights of the aboriginal peoples of Canada are hereby recognized and affirmed." This is an important specification because it counters a perception held by some people that treaties were something that "happened in the past," and therefore are without relevance to today's issues or concerns.

The Royal Commission on Aboriginal Peoples (RCAP 1996) also uses the term *Aboriginal nations*, by which is meant "a sizeable body of Aboriginal people with a shared sense of national identity that constitutes the prominent population in a certain territory or collection of territories" (vol. 1, p. 29). This usage is similar to the term *First Nations*, which has generally replaced the term *band*, as used in the Indian Act (Section 2(1) to refer to a specific population of "Indians who inhabit a common territory and share a similar heritage and cultural tradition." The national organization that represents the status Indian population of Canada is called the Assembly of First Nations. The term *First Nations*, therefore, reinforces a tone of unequivocal founding peoples, the original settlers, who – by implication of this original occupation – have legal rights stemming from this ascendency of prior occupation.

The people who have slipped through the cracks of all this legal terminology are the Metis and Inuit. In the Constitution Act, specific mention is made, for example, of the Metis as one of the three Aboriginal peoples of Canada. There is a certain amount of ambiguity, however, regarding the extent to which Metis have "Aboriginal rights." The term *Metis* is generally used to refer to persons of mixed First Nation and European ancestry. The older term "half-breed" has generally fallen out of use (see, e.g., Campbell 1973). Yet, Metis tend to regard themselves as the only true Canadians, since they actually originated as a "race" on Canadian soil, unlike Europeans or even First Nations people, who are all seen by the Metis as migrants to this country (see, e.g., Adams 1989, Redbird 1980, Sawchuck 1978).

This idea, then, of the only true Canadians, places Metis in a position politically to claim certain Aboriginal rights, especially as land claims are concerned. The Alberta government has apparently agreed to this position because, in 1938, it passed the Metis Betterment Act, which set aside some 1.25 million acres of land for eight Metis settlements, or "colonies." By 1980, it was estimated that approximately four thousand Metis still lived in these Alberta colonies, yet the off-colony populated is probably somewhere between eight and fifteen thousand (Frideres 1998: 36). Today, Metis have a decidedly urban concentration, as about 65 per cent of Metis live in cities (RCAP 1996: vol. 4, 217).

The Metis have attempted to mobilize themselves politically, as they have their own national-level political organization called the Métis National Council. There are also provincial affiliates, such as the Métis Nation of Ontario, which have a more grass-roots orientation. Issues of identity are particularly important to the Metis, because of the public's perception of Metis as occupying an ambiguous position regarding Aboriginal rights (Sawchuck 1982). This is apparent, for example, in commentary in the *Report of the Royal Commission on Aboriginal Peoples*, where a "nation-to-nation" approach is recommended for Metis negotiation with the federal government. The RCAP also called for a Metis governing structure with both national and provincial components (RCAP 1996: vol. 4, p. 203).

Inuit are another Aboriginal group mentioned in the Constitution Act of 1982. Although obviously not "Indians," Inuit have also occupied an ambiguous position with regard to the status–non-status distinction. The Indian Act, for example, does not apply to Inuit. However, in a 1939 Supreme Court of Canada decision, it was ruled that the federal government's powers to make laws which pertained to "Indians, and lands reserved for Indians" be extended to Inuit as well (Frideres 1988a: 91). The Inuit have their own political structure, headed by the Inuit Tapirisat of Canada, which was founded in 1971 and represents some twenty-five thousand persons of Inuit ancestry. More recently, as most people are probably aware, the Inuit have successfully negotiated a very large territory of some 300,000 square kilometres, called Nunavut, established in 1999.

The point to be made from the foregoing discussion is that as far as policy pertaining to Aboriginal peoples is concerned there are complex legal and administrative matters to consider. The term *Indian* now has a restricted legal usage, in comparison with its widespread designation in the past. *Aboriginal* is commonly used today, and is enshrined in our Constitution Act, but it is not specific enough to be used as a cover term when one might wish to refer more specifically to Metis or Inuit people.

Hidden in this plethora of terminology are the social and cultural facts of Aboriginal life not often recognized or understood by the average Canadian. When European settlers arrived in Canada, there were over fifty distinct Aboriginal languages spoken. Some have since died out, while others such as Cree have undergone a recent revival. These Indigenous languages are classified by linguists into a number of language groupings or families. Members of the Algonquian (or Algonkian) language family such as Mi'kmaqs and Ojibways are spread over much of eastern North America. With the advent of the fur trade and the availability of horses, members of branches of the Algonquian family, such as Crees and Blackfoots, moved out into the Plains to act as fur trade middlemen and to hunt buffalo. The Five Nations of the Iroquois family (Mohawk, Oneida, Cayuga, Onondaga, and Seneca) originally lived in western New York State, in the Finger Lakes district, but many moved into southern Ontario in the late 1700s. Led by Joseph Brant, one of their traditional leaders and a general in the British army, the Five Nations Iroquois received a large parcel of land along the Grand River, called the Haldimand Tract, as compensation for their military help during the American Revolution.

The Dene or Athapaskan language family, including Dogrib, Chipewyan, and Slavey, comprises members who live primarily in the western part of the Northwest Territories and the northern parts of the western provinces. Inuit are part of the Eskimo-Aleut language family and include such peoples as the Netsilik, Caribou Inuit, and Iglulik – all of whom speak the same Inuktituk language. The Aboriginal peoples of British Columbia represent a diverse cultural and linguistic mixture.

Salish is the largest language family, comprising such coastal groups as Cowichan, Squamish, and Bella Coola, and the interior Shuswap and Okanagan. Members of the Wakashan family live farther up the coast from the Salish and are represented by the Nootka and Kwakiutl. In addition, there are certain groups whose affiliation is unknown, or a matter of dispute, such as the Haida of Haida Gwaii or the Queen Charlotte Islands.

The 2006 census (Canada 2008) recorded nearly sixty different Aboriginal languages spoken by First Nations people in Canada, grouped into the following distinct language families: Algonquian (or Algonkian), Athapaskan (Dene), Siouan, Salish, Tsimshian, Wakashan, Iroquoian, Haida, Kutenai, and Tlingit. In both 2001 and 2006, about 29 per cent of First Nations people who responded to the census said they could speak an Aboriginal language well enough to carry on a conversation. The figure was higher for First Nations people living on a reserve (51%) than for those living off-reserve (12%). The Aboriginal language spoken by the largest number of First Nations people is Cree. A total of 87,285 individuals reported that they could carry on a conversation in Cree, followed by 30,255 who could speak Ojibway, 12,435 who spoke Ojib-Cree,[2] and 11,080 who spoke Montagnais-Naskapi. The Inuktitut language was strongest in the region of Nunavut, where more than nine out of ten Inuit are fluent in the language (see Canada 2008).

In terms of traditional subsistence economy and political organization, the Aboriginal peoples of Canada represent considerable diversity. Hunters and gathers are found in much of the north, and they are mainly members of the Inuit, Algonquian, and Dene cultures. Their leadership is rather informal and tends to rely on such traits as generosity and hunting prowess. The Iroquois, such as the Hurons and, later, Five Nations people, used to live in large settlements usually consisting of several thousand people, grow their own crops, and have a matrilineal kinship system. The so-called Chiefdoms of the Pacific Northwest also lived in large settlements, afforded by a rich fishing and hunting economy; they also were organized mainly around unilineal kinship groups, both partilineal and matrilineal. Political systems of the Pacific Coast centred on a hierarchical class system in which the potlatch was a pivotal mechanism of resource distribution by which aspiring leaders demonstrated their generosity (Hedican 2012: 188–92).

From the foregoing discussion of linguistic and cultural diversity, it is clear that a broad cover term such as *Indian* is not very appropriate in describing the Aboriginal cultures of Canada. This discussion also suggests that government policy towards Aboriginal peoples is apt to fail unless this diversity is taken into account. Readers more knowledgeable about Aboriginal issues than those with less familiarity in this field and its background material may find the detail in the foregoing discussion of cultural diversity somewhat overly meticulous. Nevertheless, the issue of cultural diversity underlies a very important point concerning Aboriginal policy in Canada. The evident cultural diversity among Aboriginal peoples suggests that a "cookie cutter" approach to policy, or approaches based on a single national policy, will be neither very useful nor effective. The issue of cultural diversity has an important link to policy development at the provincial and federal levels. Let me submit, therefore, that the development of policy cannot be divorced from an appreciation of the significant diversity among Aboriginal peoples in Canada.

Modern Aboriginal Conditions

This section presents a brief synopsis of current social and economic conditions of the Aboriginal population of Canada (see Appendix for further details). The purpose is to give some fundamental background information here on such matters as education, employment, and demographic distribution so that one might better place in context issues that are raised in the following pages of this book. The information discussed here is available from Statistics Canada and is based on an analysis of data on Aboriginal peoples from the 2006 census, which was released in January 2008 (Canada 2008).

Population and Demography

One of the main highlights of the 2006 census is that the number of people in Canada who identify themselves as Aboriginal, that is, First Nations people, Metis, and Inuit surpassed the one million mark (1,172,790) and that over the previous decade there was a substantial increase in the Aboriginal population. In 2006, Aboriginal people accounted for almost 4 per cent of the total Canadian population, an increase from 2.8 per cent in 1996. In the decade 1996–2006, the Aboriginal population increased by 45 per cent, which is nearly six times faster than the 8 per cent growth rate for the non-Aboriginal population of Canada over the same period. Comparatively speaking, Canada has a relatively high Indigenous population, ranking only second to New Zealand where the

Maori account for 15 per cent of the population. In both the United States and Australia, Indigenous peoples make up just 2 per cent of the overall population.

Of the three Aboriginal groups identified in the 2006 census, First Nations people comprise 60 per cent of the Aboriginal population (81% of these persons have "status" under the terms of the Indian Act, while 19% are non-status). The Metis are the second-largest group, accounting for about 33 per cent of Canada's Aboriginal population, while the Inuit comprise 4 per cent. In the 2006 census, 3 per cent of Aboriginal persons identified with more than one Aboriginal group.

Aboriginal people, as a whole, in Canada have become increasingly urban. In 2006, 54 per cent lived in urban areas, up from 50 per cent in 1996. Winnipeg is home to the largest urban Aboriginal population (68,380 in 2006), while Edmonton, Vancouver, Toronto, and Calgary also have substantial numbers of Aboriginal residents. Eight of every ten Aboriginal persons live in either Ontario or in the four western provinces.

In terms of age groupings, the Aboriginal population is much younger than the non-Aboriginal population. In 2006, the median age of the Aboriginal population was 27 years, compared with 40 years for non-Aboriginal people. Children and youth aged 24 years and under make up almost half (48%) of all Aboriginal people, compared with 31 per cent for the non-Aboriginal population. One of the reasons for this age structure is that fertility rates are much higher among Aboriginal women than for other Canadian women. For example, in the 1996 to 2001 period, the fertility rate for Aboriginal women was 2.6 children, compared with 1.5 children among all women in Canada. Relatively high fertility rates among Aboriginal women have a significant effect on family composition. Among Aboriginal families, in 2006, 50.5 per cent included children (under 15 years of age), compared with 37.7 per cent for Canadian families as a whole.

Economy

A significant finding of the 2006 census is that Aboriginal people have nearly twice the unemployment rate (12.3%) than that for the total Canadian workforce (6.6%). Among Inuit workers, unemployment is three times the national average (18.2%). Among all three Aboriginal groups, the Metis (8.9%) are closest to the overall Canadian average. Several factors could account for these differences. Workforce data, for example, provided by Statistics Canada (du Plessis et al. 2002) demonstrate that rural people have lower employment rates and lower incomes than the Canadian average. Thus, a rural to urban continuum could be used to partially account for the unemployment rate. However, an increasing urban Aboriginal population could lead to decreases in unemployment in the future, as Aboriginal persons continue to move to larger population centres where employment opportunities are greater than in rural areas.

A further analysis of employment incomes between Aboriginal persons and the national Canadian average reveals additional discrepancies. Full-time Aboriginal employees earn, on average, almost $10,000 per annum less than their non-Aboriginal Canadian counterparts. Aboriginal workers in the part-time employment category also make significantly less than other Canadians who work part-time. Overall, when both categories of employment are combined, full-time and part-time, the average Aboriginal worker earns about $8,500 on average less per year than do other Canadian workers. These income differences probably have to do with the lesser availability of employment in Aboriginal communities than in other Canadian centres, and the lower rates of pay offered in the jobs that are available.

Education

In terms of educational characteristics revealed by the 2006 census, a significant finding is that 14 per cent more Aboriginal persons are without a diploma or degree than the national Canadian average. In terms of various degrees (Bachelor, Master, and Doctorate) earned, the Canadian average of persons holding such degrees (16%) is over twice that of the average for the Aboriginal population (7%). If the conventional economic wisdom holds true that income levels in a society correspond to the level of skill in the workforce, then increases in income would correlate directly with educational achievement. In this regard, the lower incomes for the Aboriginal groups compared with the Canadian average are at least partly accountable in terms of their lower educational levels.

In summary, the latest census material available (Canada 2008) reveals that the Aboriginal population, as a whole, is now more urban than rural, a trend that has been continuing for several decades and that shows no signs of reversing. The growth rate of the Aboriginal population, at 4 per cent per annum, is well above the national average, increasing by 45 per cent over the decade 1996–2006, which is about six times faster than the 8 per cent growth rate for the non-Aboriginal population over the same period. In 2006, the median age of the Aboriginal population (27 years) was more than a decade lower than what it is for non-Aboriginal people (40 years), suggesting a continuing need for services and institutional support for the much younger Aboriginal population, while the larger Canadian average population continues to age to a significant degree.

Despite various government programs aimed at increasing employment levels, the Aboriginal population suffers from nearly twice the unemployment rate of the overall Canadian workforce, and among those working, income levels continue to be significantly lower for Aboriginal workers than for their non-Aboriginal Canadian counterparts. In terms of educational levels, with regard to degrees earned, Aboriginal educational achievement level lags far behind the national average. The single most important question raised by these recent statistics is why have successive federal and provincial government programs and policies failed to ameliorate the depressing socio-economic conditions among Canadian's Aboriginal population that remain well below national standards of income and educational levels and workforce participation?

The Scope of the Book

The overall purpose of this study is to provide an overview of Canadian Aboriginal policy, protests, and confrontations, using the *Report of the Ipperwash Inquiry* (Linden 2007) as a case study. A historical perspective on Aboriginal policy is presented in Chapter 2 focusing on recent developments such as the Royal Commission on Aboriginal Peoples (RCAP 1996), the creation of Nunavut (1999), and Prime Minister Stephen Harper's historic apology in the House of Commons in 2008.

Chapter 3 studies the nature of Aboriginal rights in Canada from the Royal Proclamation of 1763, through to the Indian Claims Commission (established in 1975). It also discusses the various treaties and surrender as well as a history of Supreme Court of Canada decisions from the St. Catherine's Milling case (1888) to the Kapp decision (2008) regarding fishing rights in British Columbia. Resistance and confrontation is the subject of Chapter 4, which examines such incidents as the confrontation in 1974 between the Ojibway Warrior Society of Kenora and the OPP at Anicinabe Park up to the Akwasasne border dispute in 2009.

Later chapters focus more specifically on various facets of the Ipperwash Inquiry. Chapter 5 describes the confrontation between the people of Kettle and Stony Point First Nation and the OPP, which resulted in the shooting death of protester Dudley George by Acting Sergeant Ken Deane. It also describes the tape recordings of OPP officers that indicate racially and culturally insensitive attitudes of law enforcement individuals and how these same attitudes were reflected in the media's depiction of the protest at Ipperwash Provincial Park.

Chapter 6 discusses at some length the recommendations of the Ipperwash Inquiry, especially in terms of the policing of Aboriginal acts of civil disobedience. In particular, various means are discussed that could serve to facilitate negotiations between activists and police. The focus of Chapter 7 is on the aspects of the occupation of Ipperwash Provincial Park that pertain to the violent suppression of Aboriginal dissent and the institutional or systemic nature of racism in Canadian society. In conclusion, Chapter 8 examines the subject of racism as it pertains to Aboriginal policy and places it in a larger context by posing the question: as a nation, how truly tolerant are the people of Canada? The suggestion emanating from this work is that although there is much to be proud of as far as this country is concerned in comparison with others, Canadians are still not anywhere near what the general perception is regarding the principles of tolerance, justice, and respect. In Canadian society, there is still much work to be done in improving the manner in which dissent is handled by the authorities in power.

Chapter Two

Aboriginal Policy in Canada

Historical Background

Jacques Cartier set sail from France, in 1534, in search of a western passage to the profitable Asian markets. He had previously made voyages
to Brazil and Newfoundland, so he was not a stranger to the so-called
New World. Cartier found the northern coastline of Labrador to comprise a bleak, dismal country, "the land God gave Cain," as he was said
to remark. On his first encounter with Aboriginal people, probably the
Mi'kmaqs, a small amount of trading occurred between the two. On a
later encounter, Cartier felt threatened by a party of about fifty Mi'kmaq
canoes, and he ordered that a warning shot be fired over their heads.
In a third encounter, this time with the St. Lawrence Iroquoians at Baie
de Gaspe, Cartier planted a large cross and indicated that he was taking this territory in the name of the king of France. It was also during
this encounter that Cartier kidnapped two of Chief Donnacona's sons.

The major period of French colonization in eastern Canada began
with the explorations of Samuel de Champlain, sometimes referred to
as "the Father of New France," who founded Quebec City in 1608 and
remained as its principal administrator for the rest of his life. Champlain had a much more involved association with Aboriginal peoples
than did Jacques Cartier. This involvement stemmed primarily from
Champlain's attempts to open up North America to the French fur
trade and colonization.

Alliances were made with the Hurons (or Wendat), Algonquins, and
Montagnais, who lived along the St. Lawrence River and who solicited
Champlain's aid in their conflicts with the Iroquois farther to the south.
In July 1609, a major fight erupted at Crown Point, New York, between

Champlain's party of two French soldiers and sixty Native warriors and about two hundred Iroquois. Champlain used his harquebus to kill several of the opposing Iroquois chiefs. The resulting noise, smoke, and killings resulted in general disarray on the battlefield. The Iroquois warriors subsequently fled the scene, an event that tended to characterize French-Iroquois relationships for the next several hundred years (Morison 1972).

By the end of the seventeenth century, the French had extended their influence through the fur trade and missionary activities throughout the Great Lakes Basin and down through the Mississippi River system. The destruction of Huronia, in 1649–50 changed the patterns of the fur trade. After the defeat of the Hurons by the Iroquois, the fur trade moved towards the northwest, especially along the north shore of Lake Superior where the Ojibways acted as middlemen with other Algonkian-speaking tribes. Famous explorers such as Pierre Radisson and Sieur de Groseilliers were probably the first European traders to reach the western end of Lake Superior. Soon after, in 1679, French traders built posts on the Kaministikwia River and on Lake Nipigon.

Radisson and Groseilliers had a falling out with the authorities in New France and subsequently headed a British expedition aboard the *Nonsuch*, in 1668–69, into Hudson Bay. This expedition eventually led to the formation of the Hudson's Bay Company, which in 1670 received a Royal Charter and trading monopoly over a vast territory of northern Canada called Rupert's Land at the time. The British fur trading influence extended out from posts established on James Bay such as Fort Albany, Moose Factory, and Rupert House. Posts were subsequently built farther inland to compete more effectively with fur traders pushing up from the Ottawa River and Lake Superior who were supplied by Montreal merchants. A major trading enterprise, the North West Company, was founded by Scottish traders in 1807 at Fort William, now Thunder Bay. After a period of intense competition between the North West Company and the Hudson's Bay Company, a merger was completed in 1821, ensuring the virtual monopoly in the fur trade by the British.

The British policy towards Aboriginal peoples began to take shape several years earlier, with the Treaty of Paris and the conclusion of the Seven Years War with France. King George III issued the Royal Proclamation of 1763, sometimes referred to as the "Indian Bill of Rights." The Royal Proclamation established what could be referred to as a *protectionist period* of British colonial policy, stating: "It is just and reasonable, and essential to our interest, and the security of our colonies, that the several nations or Tribes of Indians with whom we are connected, and who live under our protection, should not be molested or disturbed in the Possession of such Parts of our Dominions and Territories as, not having been ceded to or purchased by Us, are reserved to them or any of them as their Hunting Grounds."

The Proclamation stipulated that the British Crown had the sole responsibility for buying or ceding Indian lands.

The British government transferred control of Aboriginal affairs to the Province of Canada in 1860. At this time, the Crown Lands Department assumed control of Indian matters and the commissioner was designated as chief superintendent (Surtees 1969). With the advent of Confederation, "Indians and lands reserved for Indians" became the responsibility of Canada's federal government under Section 91(24) of the British North America Act of 1867. As far as the four original provinces of Ontario, Quebec, New Brunswick, and Nova Scotia were concerned, they simply continued with their existing reserve policy in place at that time. The first federal Indian Act was passed in 1876, which led to the administrative centralization of Indian affairs in Canada (Surtees 1982: 41–2).

The historical dominance of the Indian Act on the affairs of First Nations peoples has been particularly significant. As Frideres (1988a: 25) points out: "The *Indian Act* is the foremost of the legislative Acts that affect Indians in Canada. Its importance cannot be exaggerated nor can its influence be minimized. It is the principal instrument by which the federal government and, indirectly, the provincial governments have exercised control over the lives of Indian people."

However, it was principally the Royal Proclamation that laid the foundation for the Indian Act of 1876, which was a cobbling together of various pieces of existing legislation. The Royal Proclamation of 1763 also laid the basis for the *treaty period*, involving the ceding of very large tracts of land to the British Crown, and later the government of Canada. The Robinson-Huron and Robinson-Superior treaties of 1850, for example, led to the ceding of a vast territory covering the region north of lakes Huron and Superior up to Rupert's Land. Eventually, after Confederation, many more treaties were negotiated during the 1870–1910 period with existing Aboriginal populations of northern Ontario, Manitoba, Saskatchewan, and Alberta.

The colonial heritage in Canada is evidenced by various pieces of legislation that have taken place over the years that have served to undermine Aboriginal autonomy. For example, a 1927 revision to the Indian

Act prevented the organization of Aboriginal political groups beyond the local level. This revision, effectively, prevented Aboriginal peoples from lobbying for their rights or from organizing politically around issues such as land claims. Thus, nation-level political groups did not begin to emerge until the 1960s, with the formation of such organizations as the National Indian Council (1961–68), followed by the National Indian Brotherhood (1968–82), forerunners of the Assembly of First Nations, founded in 1982. A further contributing factor was that Aboriginal people with status were not even given the right to vote in provincial elections until the 1950s and federally until 1960. It is evidently difficult to promote any rights whatsoever without the right to vote.

By the middle of the twentieth century, it was increasingly obvious that previous government Aboriginal policies of protectionism and assimilation were not working. Educational levels among Aboriginal peoples were far below the national average, unemployment in Aboriginal communities was above 25 per cent (compared with about 5–8 per cent for other Canadians overall), and adequate health care was generally not available for Aboriginal people. In an attempt to find out what the conditions were really like in Aboriginal communities, a survey was commissioned by the government, generally referred to as the Hawthorn Report. Researchers conducted profiles on over fifty Aboriginal communities in various locations across Canada, centring on educational, social, and political conditions (Hawthorn 1966–67). The result was a wide array of recommendations, the most famous of which has been referred to as "citizens plus," meaning "Indians should be regarded as 'citizens plus'; in addition to the normal rights and duties of citizenship, Indians possess certain additional rights as charter members of the Canadian community" (p. 13).

Thus, the central idea behind this recommendation is that Aboriginal people in Canada have certain inalienable rights that go beyond those for the average Canadian citizen – rights that emanate from treaty obligations, land rights, and other aspects of their Indigenous status. The term *citizens plus* became the banner of Native organizations in their attempts to fight the assimilationist policy in vogue at the time (Cairns 2000: 36–9).

During the decade of the 1970s, resource issues began to receive widespread news coverage when the Quebec government announced that it was planning on damming the major rivers leading into James

Bay for hydroelectric power purposes. The James Bay Hydroelectric Project was confronted with an alliance of Aboriginal and environmental interests. The Sierra Club, for example, was concerned over the environmental impacts that such large-scale flooding would have on what many considered to be one of the last pristine ecological areas in North America. From the Aboriginal Cree and Inuit perspective, the project demonstrated the arrogance of developers in the wider non-Aboriginal society who refused to acknowledge local-level cultures and ecosystems.

Eventually, the Aboriginal protests over the damming of rivers in northern Quebec led to the negotiation of the James Bay Agreement, in 1975, sometimes referred to as the first "modern" treaty.

Although the Crees and Inuit of Quebec were pressing their environmental concerns in the eastern subarctic, Aboriginal peoples in the Northwest Territories, in particular the Dene, were similarly concerned that their subsistence hunting and fishing activities would be disrupted by construction activities associated with a proposed natural gas pipeline down through the Mackenzie Valley corridor. There were also environmental concerns, since the proposed pipeline would have to be built above ground because of the permafrost in the area. As a result, the Mackenzie Valley Pipeline Inquiry was constituted to examine these matters and was headed by Chief Justice of the British Columbia Supreme Court Thomas Berger. A vigorous debate then ensued over proposals to transport natural gas through the Mackenzie Valley corridor in the Northwest Territories.

Hearings were held in various communities along the Mackenzie corridor, and these tended to raise many other issues besides resource and environmental ones, such as the nature of Native rights and self-determination (Berger 1983). The resulting publication, colloquially called the Berger Report, but more formally entitled *Northern Frontier, Northern Homeland* (Berger 1977) sought a moratorium of ten years on further resource development in the Mackenzie Valley until environmental and Aboriginal resource issues were more fully understood. The Berger Inquiry was, therefore, an important step towards more clearly defining Aboriginal policy concerns, and it served as a sympathetic turning point in recognizing Aboriginal rights. Thus, over the decade spanning the 1970s into the 1980s, Aboriginal resource issues were particularly prominent, but these also led to a focus on related concerns of local autonomy, Aboriginal rights, and self-determination.

The Royal Commission on Aboriginal Peoples (1991–1996)

The Royal Commission of Aboriginal Peoples (RCAP) was established, on 26 August 1991, partly in response to the Oka Crisis in the summer of 1990. It was mandated to investigate the wide-ranging complaints of Aboriginal peoples concerning such matters as the continuing low levels of educational achievement, high unemployment, unresolved land claims, incarceration rates, and health care delivery issues. The commission was co-chaired by George Erasmus, a former national chief of the Assembly of First Nations (1976–80) and Justice René Dussault from the Quebec Appeal Court. The *Report of the Royal Commission of Aboriginal Peoples* (RCAP 1996) comprises five volumes of more than 3,500 pages in total. The RCAP turned out to be the most expensive Royal Commission in Canadian history, costing $63 million (Dickason 2009: 410; Frideres and Gadacz 2008: 373). Over the period during which the RCAP was active, more than 3,500 witnesses were heard. The RCAP published four special reports, – on justice, suicide, land claims, and the relocation of the Inuit. In addition, there were two commentaries on self-government (RCAP 1996, Frideres 1996).

The RCAP made more than four hundred recommendations. It suggested, for example, that the Canadian Parliament issue a royal proclamation in which it would apologize to Aboriginal peoples for harms done and admit to past mistakes. It recommended the establishment of a special Aboriginal parliament, to be called "the House of First Peoples," suggesting that such a parliament would function as an advisory body to the federal government and would be used to represent Aboriginal peoples from across the country. The House of First Peoples would help to ameliorate the virtual lack of Aboriginal interest in government because of the difficulty of electing Aboriginal officials due to the relatively small population levels. This recommendation also envisaged that the many Aboriginal reserves across Canada, now numbering over two thousand, would come together, forming some thirty to fifty Aboriginal Nations. The idea is that these Nations would have powers similar to those presently exercised by provincial governments, but would emphasize the special needs of Aboriginal peoples.

As far as monetary issues are concerned, several of the RCAP's recommendations concerned attempts to simulate local Aboriginal economies and thereby serve to alleviate the pressing poverty in many First Nations communities. It was recommended, for example, that for a twenty-year period (from 1996 to 2016) the federal government be requested to spend some $38 billion above present expenditures in an attempt to resolve outstanding Aboriginal issues. The RCAP Report noted that, in 1996, there was an annual expenditure of $2.5 billion towards dealing with the pressing poverty of Aboriginal communities in Canada. Over a twenty-year period, this annual expenditure of $2.5 billion would amount to $50 billion in any event. It was also noted that at least $1 billion a year is spent on social assistance programs for reserves because of the nearly 80 per cent unemployment in some communities and other abject living conditions.

The RCAP Report points out that nearly 50 per cent of Canada's Aboriginal population is under 21 years of age. Thus, the government's cost for just maintaining the status quo would be about $11 billion by 2016. If the government were to invest in additional social programs, starting back in 1996, the Commission argued that these sorts of expenditures would eventually lead to substantial savings over the twenty-year period ending in 2016. In implementing this suggestion, it was recommended that the federal government increase its expenditures on Aboriginal programs by $1.5 billion per annum for the seven-year period 1996–2002, and subsequently by $2 billion per annum for the remaining thirteen years (2003–16).

When one examines the RCAP's financial proposals, it is evident that they entail a significant "up front" set of expenditures. The strategy proposed by the Commission is that higher expenditures in the beginning, tailing off afterwards, is cost-effective because of the long-term gains using such a method. If we examine the Aboriginal housing crisis, for example, there is the necessity of constructing many more new homes to meet pressing accommodation needs. Many homes on reserves have been poorly constructed, most are not suited to northern environmental conditions, and they have not keep pace with the needs of a growing younger population.

The RCAP recommended that a higher expenditure on housing now would tend to reduce costs in the future. This reduction in housing costs alone, over the following decade after the RCAP findings were submitted, would eventually result in substantial government savings. One could also expect, in turn, increased government revenues because of a more productive Aboriginal population. Increased revenues and savings could be funnelled back into the economic system in the form of new training programs and upgraded Aboriginal economies. In addition, in the long term, such revenues could be used to finance land claims and self-government projects.

Of course, the RCAP was charged with making suggestions for change, not with formulating government policy. The hope was that government personnel in the Department of Indian Affairs (DIA) and associated ministries would take note of the RCAP's findings, discuss them widely, and provide a response. Given that Canadian taxpayers paid over $60 million for this four-year federal inquiry, it could have been hoped, at the very least, that some of the more useful of the Commission's more than four hundred recommendations would have been implemented to help to improve Aboriginal conditions in Canada, and eventually, to rationalize the expenditures of a burgeoning Indian Affairs budget. The lack of a substantial government response has surely been disheartening to many, given the cost and effort involved to produce the RCAP reports.

Cairns (2000: 116–17) sums up the situation: "The *Report* provides the most thorough Aboriginal constitutional vision to have appeared since the defeat of the 1969 White Paper. Although we do not know the inner workings of the Commission, we may reasonably assume that the *Report* reflects an Aboriginal perspective, as four of the seven commissioners, including the co-chair [George Erasmus], were Aboriginal. Further, the basic thrust of the *Report* clearly builds on the prior parallelism thinking of Aboriginal nationalists." As one might expect, the reaction of Aboriginal leaders to the RCAP findings in the various reports was generally quite supportive. The Metis, for example, who are often left out of the Aboriginal debate, were pleased to note the Commission's recommendation for an adequate Metis land base. In Frideres and Gadacz (2008: 376) it is noted that "the president of the Metis National Council also strongly supported the Commission's recognition of the Metis as an Aboriginal people who should have an adequate land base"; see also Cairns (2000: 137–8) on the Metis reaction to the Commission's recommendations.

RCAP co-chair George Erasmus issued a blunt warning: "If the reality is that once more [Aboriginal] peoples' hopes have been dashed, and that this is all for nothing, then what we say is that the people will resort to other things" (Cairns 2000: 139). Erasmus did not elaborate on what these "other things" might be, but we could use our imagination. We are aware, for example, that the Royal Commission on Aboriginal Peoples was initiated, in large part, as a response to the dreadful Oka Crisis of 1990, and so the expectation would certainly have been that the frustrations of Canadian Aboriginal peoples would be addressed in some manner. The RCAP was initiated at a time when the frustrations of Aboriginal peoples were at their highest in decades, and as such, George Erasmus's warnings of dire economic and social consequences if these frustrations were not addressed could certainly be taken as a serious prognostication of future Aboriginal-government troubles.

Since the RCAP Report was released, it is unfortunate to say, the federal government has virtually ignored the many recommendations put forward by the Commission. In life, we can often draw conclusions about people's attitude as much by what they neglect to do, as by their direct actions. In the case of the lack of response to the RCAP findings, one might conclude that the federal government doesn't really care about Aboriginal issues and spent $63 million of taxpayers' dollars not in a constructive manner, but simply as a time-buying "snow job." Even more severe, Aboriginal people are apt to feel that Canadians as a whole do not regard Aboriginal issues as very important.

No doubt, for many Canadians, to read and understand the RCAP Report would seem like an overwhelming job. Many of the recommendations are somewhat esoteric in nature. Partly this is the case because many of the recommendations pertain to specific areas of the country, such as hunting or fishing rights, although they may also deal with more general issues, such as self-government and land claims. While these issues are certainly important, a major criticism of the RCAP Report is that it virtually neglects the urbanized Aboriginal population. For decades, there has been a steady stream of First Nations people moving to Montreal, Toronto, Winnipeg, Calgary, Edmonton, and Vancouver.

In 1966, less than 20 per cent of the registered (i.e., status) Indian population lived off-reserve. The off-reserve population doubled to 40 per cent by 1991 (Frideres and Gadacz 2008: 144). The latest statistics, reported in the 2006 census, indicate that at present over 50 per cent of Aboriginal people with status have left their reserves for an urban environment (Canada 2008). We can draw our own conclusions regarding this urban migration, because they are well known – rural poverty, inadequate housing, lack of educational opportunities, high suicide rates among young Aboriginals, and so on.

The RCAP Report could be faulted for not paying sufficient attention to this contemporary process of urbanization. Despite the large numbers of Aboriginal people moving to urban centres from their reserves, the RCAP Report hardly concerns itself with this significant urban dimension of contemporary Aboriginal life. With the RCAP's preoccupation with such issues as land claims and self-government, its recommendations appear to address an increasingly diminished Aboriginal context. Land claims and self-government are important issues, but the neglect of such a significant process as the reserve to urban migration suggests that the only important Aboriginal issues in Canada are the ones pertaining to government-administered reserves. There is the implication that to leave the reserve is tantamount to relinquishing one's Aboriginal identity.

It would appear, then, that the RCAP had a hidden agenda, one controlled by the registered or status population, which is actually in the minority as far as the overall Aboriginal population goes. Land claims and self-government are not especially important issues in an urban context. What is important here is finding jobs, access to housing, and health care – these are what one could call "meat and potatoes" issues. The homeless Aboriginal man trying to survive on Toronto's Yonge Street might not have much of an opinion on land claims or feel particularly attached to that issue.

The RCAP's main point, as put forth in its report, is that cultural survival for Aboriginal peoples is dependent on an adequate land base. An important criticism, then, is that the RCAP commissioners have virtually ignored the burgeoning growth of the off-reserve population. The Commission's focus, as Cairns (2000: 123) observes, "on a land base as the locus of its hopes for the reinvigoration of Aboriginal culture, inevitably marginalized urban Aboriginals – 45 per cent of the Aboriginal population – as well as many of the additional 20 per cent off-reserve rural Aboriginal population."

It should be pointed out rather quickly, however, that the federal government's minimal attention to the RCAP's recommendations might be justified by noting that the RCAP's suggestions do not apply to urban Aboriginal populations, and thus, this is the basis for the government's inaction on the RCAP Report. The federal government could have commented on the RCAP Report by saying that it did not agree with some of the recommendations, such as the absence of an urban focus, and then make its own recommendations for alleviating urban Aboriginal poverty, housing, health care, and so on. To do nothing on any of these issues – land claims or the urban dimension – shows a remarkable insensitively to Aboriginal issues, especially since the government used millions of dollars of taxpayers' money to implement an inquiry, only to in the end ignore it.

One possible conclusion is that the 1996 RCAP Report does not adequately offer a view of the future that reflects current realities for

Aboriginal peoples. As noted, the Commission's vision does not concern itself with the urban Aboriginal population. One can only wonder what the reasons are behind such a perspective. Perhaps the urban Aboriginal population is too diffuse. Or perhaps in urban society there are high rates of intermarriage with non-Aboriginals and this is seen as problematic. There is also the problem, if one chooses to see it as such, of a diminished use of Aboriginal languages in urban settings. Whatever the case, it is almost as if the RCAP commissioners were holding to the view that the "real Aboriginals" are the ones living in the remote backwoods of Canada, still hunting, trapping, and fishing, and therefore, an adequate land base is promoted as the essential issue for all Aboriginal peoples, regardless of prevailing demographic, social, or economic realities.

Perhaps the powers to be in Ottawa were confused as to how to respond given the RCAP's land base emphasis, on the one hand, and the modern urban realities, on the other. Certainly, whatever credibility the RCAP was apt to muster was not aided by the government's response, which was basically to criticize the RCAP Report, but not offer anything substantial in return. The minister of Indian affairs, for example, noted that the RCAP Report was two years late and that in the meantime Indian Affairs had already begun to act on some of the issues raised in it. In other words, Indian Affairs was essentially saying that it got tired of waiting for the report so decided to act on its own, thus blaming the RCAP commissioners for the government's tardy response. Even more telling, in terms of the government's sentiments, the prime minister was invited to attend an all-chiefs conference to discuss the implications of the RCAP Report but he declined the invitation, citing other commitments.

It is not altogether accurate to say that the federal government ignored the recommendations of the RCAP Report, but rather, we could say that the response was "lukewarm." Indian Affairs did publish a counter-report, two years later, entitled *Gathering Strength: Canada's Aboriginal Action Plan* (Canada 1998). In a poignant comment, Cairns (2000:121) confesses, "It would be reassuring to inform readers that their interpretation of the *Report* can be aided by reading a sophisticated federal government response to the *Report*'s constitutional vision. We are not so blessed." One might surmise that the *Gathering Strength* document was instigated by Minister of Indian Affairs and Northern Development Jane Stewart as a belated response to the federal government's embarrassing silence on the RCAP's recommendations. Unfortunately,

Gathering Strength does not in any specific way address the recommendations of the Royal Commission on Aboriginal Peoples. What it does do is indicate, in a rather vague manner, that the feral government regrets its past actions towards Canada's Aboriginal population, that it would like to build a new partnership, and that it recognizes that certain past government policies, such as the policy of assimilation, were not appropriate. The release of the *Gathering Strength* document, accompanied by much ceremony, was diminished by the prime minister's absence.

Nunavut: A New Land, a New Deal (1999)

The map of Canada was altered for the first time since Newfoundland entered Confederation (1949) on 1 April 1999 with the creation of a new territory called Nunavut. A vast arctic landscape was carved out of the Northwest Territories becoming a new home for the approximately twenty-five thousand residents of Nunavut. The ancestry of this population is mostly (84%) Inuit. Iqaliut, which is a business and government centre of 4,500 people, was named the new capital, and the new premier was Paul Okalik, a 34-year-old lawyer.

In an ironic historical twist, it was Prime Minister Jean Chrétien who presided over the inauguration of Nunavut. Some readers might remember that Chrétien was also the minister of Indian Affairs during the Trudeau era of the 1969 White Paper, when it was proposed that much of the federal government's responsibilities in Aboriginal matters be terminated. As Chrétien reminisced in his speech, "It's personally very important for me because when I started as minister of Indian and Northern Affairs in 1968, we were discussing at that time to establish responsible government in the Yukon and Northwest Territories. For me to be associated with this great step for the Eastern Arctic is extremely important" (Ohler 1999).

The Inuit had been striving for self-government for many decades. In the 1990s, Nunavut came closer to that reality with the signing of a land claims deal that committed the federal government to establish an independent Inuit region in the eastern Arctic (Legere 1998, Mahoney 1999). Despite the initial euphoria and intense pride felt by the Inuit in their achievement, the region nonetheless faces huge challenges. Unemployment is still very high (18.2% in 2006), average incomes compared with other Canadians are low, and significant social issues need addressing in many Inuit communities. Some have taken a pessimistic view of Nunavut's chances for success, such as Anderssen (1998), who has argued that Nunavut might end up as another Aboriginal welfare case.

Premier Okalik, nonetheless, appeared optimistic about Nunavut's future. In delivering his oath of office he said, "Today the people of Nunavut formally join Canada. Today we stand strong and we welcome the changes Nunavut brings." A similar optimistic tone was echoed by Prime Minister Chrétien, who noted the day's historic importance: "Fifty years from now schoolchildren will be reading of this day." This sentiment was echoed by an Inuit elder, who commented, "When we had our historical election of February fifteenth [1999], heaven smiled on us. Heaven is smiling again today" (Ohler 1999).

The inauguration of Nunavut in 1999 probably came as a stunning reminder for other Aboriginal leaders in Canada of how far they have to go before achieving similar results. They must also have been scratching their heads at the seeming facility with which Inuit leaders were able to succeed in reaching their goals. After all, the Inuit were hardly any type of political force until the 1970s, when Inuit Tapirisat was formed. By this time, other Aboriginal groups in Canada had been struggling to achieve some form of autonomy in self-government for hundreds of years, with virtually no success. And so the question is: how did the Inuit achieve their unexpected success in such a short period of time?

Several factors circumscribe the parameters of the answer to this very important question. The first has to do with the characteristics of the Inuit themselves. For centuries, they have been masters of communication, cooperation, and perseverance, all of which are traits that helped them survive in the Arctic's harsh environment. Communication in the Arctic is facilitated immensely by the fact that there is only one language, Inuktitut, spoken among the Inuit. When you consider other Aboriginal groups in Canada, with their more than fifty distinct languages and numerous dialects, the communication of ideas, and the resulting formation of group efforts is going to be difficult to achieve.

The Inuit, unlike some other Aboriginal groups, abhor adversarial politics. They first organized themselves through their umbrella organization, the Inuit Tapirisat, founded in 1971. They then trained their own people in legal, economic, and political matters, and when they were ready, they approached the federal government with a plan from which they would not deviate. Essentially, they said to the government, "We will be responsible citizens; please work with us to achieve our goals of self-governance and eventual economic sufficiency." Thus, the strategy was not one of adversarial politics, so common in other parts of Canada. The Inuit did not engage in confrontations, protests, or other forms of civil disobedience. This is not to say that other Aboriginal groups should be criticized for this, because frustration can certainly lead to such activities, it is just that the Inuit have taken a different tactic – in negotiations, and as they say, it is hard to argue with success.

To be fair, however, to the other Aboriginal groups in Canada, the Inuit did not suffer the debilitating effects of three or four hundred years of colonial administrations, episodes of smallpox and other European-induced diseases, or the loss of their traditional lands and cultures. In fact, at the end of the 1960s, the Inuit in some areas, if we use the Netsilik of the central Arctic as an example, were still living off the land in a traditional manner, building igloos, driving dogsleds, hunting seals through the ice, and so on (Balikci 1970). In other words, the Inuit have been largely spared the catastrophic consequences of contact with European societies that were experienced by other Aboriginal societies. Furthermore, the Inuit were not stripped of their cultural heritage and identity through residential schools, although some Inuit might have attended these on a sporadic basis.

Nevertheless, the modern situation for the Inuit is still fraught with difficulties. Teenage suicide rates among the Inuit are many times higher than for other Canadian teenagers. Alcohol and drug abuse is a major concern in many Inuit communities. Meaningful employment is difficult to find, and so job-training programs have a lack of local relevance (Anderssen 1998, Ohler 1999). One should not get the impression, then, that the Inuit have escaped the significant social trauma resulting from the intrusion into the Arctic of the modern world and its myriad troubles, temptations, and debilitating effects.

Whatever advantages the Inuit have over other Aboriginal groups stem largely from their isolation. As a general rule, it could be said that the least traumatic effects of culture contact are felt by Aboriginal societies that are farthest removed from large-scale European influences. Traditional language retention, for example, is highest among such groups and so is a connection to traditional values and spiritual thought-worlds. What this means is that social and geographical distance from large colonial powers allows for a greater degree of cultural continuity for traditional societies.

The Crees, especially in northern Quebec, could be considered a case that is comparable in some ways to the Inuit. The Crees were hidden away in the forests of northern Quebec, largely unnoticed until the James Bay Project was announced. They carried on a low-impact hunting and trapping economy, with minimal external pressures for change. Language retention among Crees is among the highest in Canada for Aboriginal societies, and there has been a continuation of cultural practices and traditional leadership skills. It has been postulated, for example, that for the First Nations of Quebec, "the issue of ultimate concern to the James Bay Crees, and Canada's Aboriginal leadership in general, is sovereignty, or their rights of self-determination, a concern frequently expressed in a wide range of national and international forums" (Neizen 2004: 120). Geographical distance from centres of colonial power such as that experienced by the Crees and Inuit serves to facilitate self-determination initiatives by Canada's Aboriginal societies.

Ipperwash Inquiry (1995–2007)

The results of the Ipperwash Inquiry, released by the Ontario government on 31 May 2007, are mentioned here to place them in a historical context but the entire case is examined in much more detail farther along in this book. The Inquiry was called in November 2003 by Dalton McGuinty, the newly elected premier of Ontario, under the Public Inquiries Act. The specific mandate of the Ipperwash Inquiry was to report on the events surrounding the death of Dudley George during the September 1995 confrontation at Ipperwash Provincial Park. The Inquiry, however, went on to delve into many other matters relevant to such a case, such as the treatment of Aboriginal dissent, the use of police forces to confront protesters, and recommendations for the peaceful resolution of Aboriginal land claims in the province of Ontario (Hedican 2008a).

What became increasingly evident during the course of the Inquiry is that the type of Aboriginal political mobilization that occurred at Ipperwash in 1995 often has a very long history. In the case of the Stony Point First Nation, Dudley George's reserve near Windsor, Ontario, the origins of the protest can be traced back to the appropriation of reserve lands designated by the Huron Tract (or Amherstburg) Treaty of 1827. In 1928, 377 acres were sold to Mr. Scott and Mr. White who sold this land to the Ontario government in 1936. Previously land surrenders were made in 1912. This involved the surrender of beachfront at the Kettle Point Reserve for recreational development. Reserve lands were appropriated to form Ipperwash Provincial Park, in 1936, and the military Camp Ipperwash in 1942, under the War Measures Act.

Altogether, hundreds of acres of Stony Point, and the adjoining reserve of Kettle Point, were taken without the permission or approval of local reserve residents.

One of the lessons of Ipperwash is that violence tends to occur when non-violent or conventional avenues for the resolution of disputes regarding Aboriginal issues do not exist. Lacking such ameliorative mechanisms, Aboriginal peoples take to protesting, blockading roads, or other disruptive behaviours, which inevitably lead to confrontations with police and local non-Aboriginal residents. There is the issue of the inequities in power in such situations: the police arrive often heavily armed with bullet-proof vests, truncheons, and assault rifles, while typically, the Aboriginal protesters are armed with sticks or rocks.

There are also the consequences of such inequities in power. Dudley George was fatally wounded during the Ipperwash confrontation. The OPP officer who shot him was charged and eventually found guilty of criminal negligence causing death, for which the maximum penalty is life imprisonment. However, Acting Sergeant Ken Deane was, eventually, given a conditional discharge with community service hours. Among the Aboriginal residents, therefore, there is apt to be of a sense of injustice in that a member of their community was killed without any justification and the offending party received what would appear to be the proverbial "slap on the wrist." Resentment is likely to continue in such situations, especially in view of the disproportionate incarceration rates for Aboriginal persons, of whom many spend years in jail for far less serious offences than that committed by Acting Sergeant Deane.

The Ipperwash Inquiry began with a specific incident, the death of Dudley George, but eventually it expanded to include such far-ranging issues as land claims and the inequities in the Canadian justice system. Overall, however, the question that is most important here concerns the lessons learned by such inquiries and the actions taken by the federal and provincial governments to prevent a recurrence of such dreadful circumstances.

Canada Votes against the UN Aboriginal Rights Declaration (2007)

The Conservative government came under heavy criticism in 2007 by Aboriginal leaders, human rights groups, and opposition parties when Canada voted against the United Nations Declaration on the Rights of Indigenous Peoples (see *Toronto Star*, 13 Sept. 2007, from which all of the quotes in this section are taken). Liberal Leader Stéphane Dion said,

"By opposing this declaration the Conservative government has signalled to aboriginal Canadians that their rights aren't worth defending." Similar criticism came from Aboriginal leaders. Grand Chief of the Assembly of First Nations Phil Fontaine declared, "This is a stain on the country's international reputation. It is disappointing to see this government vote against recognizing the basic rights of Canada's First Peoples."

The UN Declaration on the Rights of Indigenous Peoples passed easily, by 143 to 4; only Canada, New Zealand, Australia, and the United States voted against it, while eleven countries abstained. Canada voted against, saying that it could not support the Declaration because its broad wording appeared to give Native communities sweeping powers that could contravene existing law. According to Minister of Indian Affairs Chuck Strahl, "It's inconsistent with the Canadian Constitution, with Supreme Court decisions and with our own treaty negotiations and obligations." Minister Strahl also noted that among many problems with the Declaration are sections that say laws that affect Aboriginals should only be passed with the prior consent of First Nations: "We'd have to consult with 650 First Nations to do that. I mean, it's simply not doable," he said.

Another section of the Declaration states that Aboriginal peoples "have the right to maintain and strengthen their distinct political, legal, economic, social and cultural institutions." This is also unworkable, according to Strahl, who said, "Some people ... say that means we can have our own legislatures, our own council in our own language. But no one's quite sure, and that's the trouble with language like that."

Strahl's critics argued that the UN Declaration is not binding on any country and that it is more of a symbolic commitment to Aboriginal rights. The NDP's Indian affairs critic, Jean Crowder from Nanaimo, British Columbia, said of the Declaration, "It's an inspirational document. It wouldn't contravene laws that are in place. I think [Canada's vote] is a very cowardly and, I would say, un-Canadian approach to human rights."

Aboriginal leaders went even farther in their criticism, arguing that the Declaration was more than just a vague expression of support. "It recognizes who we are, that we have these fundamental rights," said John Paul, executive director of the Atlantic Policy Congress, which represents thirty-five Aboriginal communities. "To us it's like the U.S. Declaration of Independence, because it lays out a number of inalienable truths about us as aboriginal people in the world."

According to Grand Chief of the Assembly of Manitoba chiefs Ron Evans, the vote "doesn't bode well" for relations between Aboriginals and Ottawa. From the position of human rights groups, such as Amnesty International, the vote has given Canada a black eye on the world stage. But Indian Affairs Minister Strahl said the Tories want to focus on concrete measures to improve the lives of Aboriginals instead of symbolic statements. "For First Nations people in Canada, I think we've seen too many years of empty promises," Strahl said. "Our government is taking the approach of 'let's do concrete steps that will actually improve the lives of First Nations.' That's why we're moving ahead on specific [land] claims legislation, on residential schools compensation ... On including First Nations peoples under the Canadian Human Rights Act."

Prime Minister Harper's Apology (2008)

Prime Minister Stephen Harper delivered a speech in the House of Commons, on 11 June 2008, in which he apologized for the harm done to the former students of Indian residential schools. The prime minister said, "The government of Canada sincerely apologizes and asks the forgiveness of the aboriginal peoples of this country for failing them so profoundly." He spoke the exact words everyone was looking for: "we are sorry" (Harper 2008).

If Prime Minister Harper had not said the word "sorry," then the apology would have had a hollow ring to it. The speech would have sounded far less sincere if Harper had said, for example, "the government of Canada regrets the harm done to Aboriginal peoples through its past policies." The text of the speech ends with: "The government of Canada sincerely apologizes and asks the forgiveness of the aboriginal peoples of this country for failing them so profoundly. We are sorry." By using the word "sorry" the apology sounded sincere enough. However, the apology was restricted to the matter of residential schools and the abuse that occurred in them. It was acknowledged, for example, that the "First Nations, Inuit and Metis languages and cultural practices were prohibited in these schools ... The government now recognizes that the consequences of the Indian residential schools policy were profoundly negative and that this policy has had a lasting and damaging impact on aboriginal culture, heritage and language" (Harper 2008).

There was also a hint in Harper's speech of an acknowledgment of wider issues regarding the effect of government policy on Aboriginal societies, especially the policy of assimilation. The prime minister noted, "The two primary objectives of the residential schools system were to remove and isolate children from the influence of their home, families, traditions and cultures, and to *assimilate them* into the dominant culture" (Harper 2008, emphasis added). Furthermore, he acknowledged, "Today, we recognize that this policy of assimilation was wrong, has caused great harm, and has no place in our country" (ibid.).

The question that should be asked with regard to the Harper apology is: does it go far enough? It is a fine thing that the government of Canada has finally begun to take responsibility for its past actions and its injustices towards the country's First Nations. Is it reasonable to assume, although Harper certainly does not mention this, that the government will now enact new policies to replace the older negative ones of assimilation and paternalism? And what of the recommendations of the Royal Commission on Aboriginal Peoples that the federal government virtually ignored, will these now be addressed in some meaningful manner?

Perhaps we should be satisfied with these fine, sincere words. But making amends for past wrongs is also an important step in restoring the balance, although it should be noted that Harper did make reference to an "Indian residential schools settlement agreement," begun in 2007. The prime minister also made reference to "the Indian residential school truth and reconciliation commission," which was formed in 2008 (Harper 2008). Time will await an assessment of the effectiveness of these important initiatives.

Aboriginal Leaders' Reactions

The reactions of Aboriginal leaders from several different organizations to Stephen Harper's apology was that this historic admission of responsibility must now signal the start of a better relationship between Aboriginal peoples and other Canadians. It was recognized that this was the first formal apology *ever* offered by a Canadian prime minister and that a better relationship is hoped for in the future.

Assembly of First Nations National Chief Phil Fontaine told members of Parliament and other observers seated in the gallery, "Our peoples, our history and our present being are the essence of Canada. The attempts to erase our identities hurt us deeply. But it also hurt Canadians and impoverished the character of this nation. We must not falter in our duty now. Emboldened by this spectacle of history, it is possible to end our racial nightmare together ... There are many fights still to be fought" (*CBC News*, 11 June 2008).

As far as the Inuit reaction was concerned, Mary Simon, president of the Inuit Tapirisat and former Canadian ambassador to Denmark, remarked that the prime minister's apology symbolized Canada's commitment to reconciliation and to building new relationships with Aboriginal peoples, echoing Fontaine's sentiments. Simon declared, "I am also filled with optimism that this action by the government of Canada and the generosity in the words chosen to convey this apology will help us all mark the end to this dark period in the collective history as a nation " (ibid.).

Not all Aboriginal leaders agreed with Phil Fontaine and Mary Simon that this apology would pave the way for healing and progress. Some found Harper's statement to be insincere and emotionless. However, many echoed the response of Chief of the Congress of Aboriginal Peoples Patrick Brazeau, who congratulated Harper for being the first Canadian prime minister to formally apologize for the physical abuse that occurred in residential schools, saying that Harper's apology was "humane, moral and the right thing to do" (ibid.).

President of the Métis National Council Clément Chartier spoke after Brazeau, expressing his hope that Harper's sentiments would resonate in the communities of those affected by the residential school system. "I believe," Chartier said, that "those statements made about the dark days and those actions that took place will be addressed and hopefully corrected in the future." President of the Native Women's Association of Canada Beverly Jacobs observed that her own grandmother had been one of the children beaten and sexually abused in residential schools. "We have given thanks to you for your apology," Jacobs said, "but in return, the Native Women's Association wants respect"[1] (ibid.).

Urban Aboriginal Strategy (1997–2012)

In recognition of the fact that, today, over half of the Aboriginal population of Canada lives in urban areas (large cities, metropolitan areas, and smaller urban centres), the Urban Aboriginal Strategy (UAS) was developed, in 1997, to help respond to the serious socio-economic needs of Aboriginal people (see Canada 2005). It was part of *Gathering Strength: Canada's Aboriginal Action Plan* (Canada 1998), a response to the Royal Commission on Aboriginal Peoples. Through the UAS, the government of Canada seeks to partner with other governments, community organizations, and Aboriginal people to support projects that respond to local priorities.

In 2003–4, $50 million was allocated to the Urban Aboriginal Strategy over a four-year period in an attempt to build on existing partnerships and to provide additional funding for pilot projects in a selected sample of cities in order to help find out what could be the most cost-effective use of such funds. In 2007, the government decided to set priorities and make long-term commitments on Aboriginal issues by investing an additional $68.5 million over five years to help respond to the needs of the Aboriginal urban population.

Given the increasingly pressing demographic, social, and economic needs, a strategy targeting urban Aboriginal populations was considered to be a critical dimension to the government's approach. The 2006 census shows that 54 per cent (up from 45% in 1996) of Canada's Aboriginal population now lives in urban areas, and this percentage is steadily increasing. Winnipeg, at the time of the 2006 census, was home to the largest urban Aboriginal population (68,380), followed by Edmonton (52,100), Vancouver (40,310), and Toronto (26,565), with Calgary, Saskatoon, Ottawa, and Montreal also home to relatively large numbers of Aboriginal people. It should also be noted that seven out of ten Metis live in urban centres, and 76 per cent of First Nations people are living off-reserve, making their residence in urban areas (Canada 2008).

The Standing Senate Committee on Aboriginal Peoples has noted that "not only do Aboriginal people constitute a significant percentage of urban populations, especially in the western provinces, but on the whole they have higher rates of joblessness, less formal education, more contact with the justice system, and are in poorer health than their non-Aboriginal counterparts" (Canada 2003). In fact, the Standing Senate Committee also noted that the well-being of Aboriginal people in urban centres has a direct impact on the well-being of the cities themselves. This is especially the case for the provinces of western Canada, where substantial numbers of Aboriginal people reside and who form correspondingly larger proportions of the overall population of these cities compared with eastern areas of the country.

The Urban Aboriginal Strategy has focused expenditures on three critical areas or initiatives. The first, improving life skills, seeks through a close working relationship with partners, for example, Aboriginal communities, municipalities, and school boards, to encourage Aboriginal youth to remain in school, to facilitate the relocation of

Aboriginal learners who have relocated from other communities into urban schools, and to encourage learning enrichment services, such as mentorship programs, summer camps, and leadership programs.

The second initiative is to promote job training, skills, and entrepreneurship. An attempt is being made to bring various partners together at the federal, provincial, and municipal levels to accomplish such goals as identifying gaps in programming and removing access barriers to lasting employment. Specific programs include the development of literacy skills, building more effective linkages between Aboriginal service providers, and increasing the representation of Aboriginal employees at the municipal level.

A third initiative aims at supporting Aboriginal women, children, and families. The attempt is to reduce the number of families living in poverty and prevent women and their families from becoming victims of crime or from entering a life of crime. Specific activities include counselling services for Aboriginal women to build self-esteem, encourage positive life choices, and healing approaches to eliminate sexual exploitation.

The pilot project phase of the Urban Aboriginal Strategy arrived at a number of conclusions in attempting to assess progress to date and address remedial action. The UAS report (Canada 2005) concludes that there is widespread support for the UAS in government among most Aboriginal participants. However, the report also notes the UAS model has been criticized by some Aboriginal organizations (names not mentioned) because it does not devolve control of the Strategy and the funds to what these critics see as representative organizations. Support for the UAS is based on its strategies and innovative aspects, the fact that it is community driven, and the fact that it offers improved collaboration with government.

Another critical issue includes the lack of a commonly understood long-term vision for the UAS among participating government and Aboriginal representatives, the lack of practical guidance for implementing a strategic vision, and what the appropriate time frame might be. At the community level, there was pressure to spend the available funds within the fiscal years to which they were allocated, thus serving to undermine the possibility of the development of a long-term strategic vision.

Finally, while the vision of the UAS is to develop innovative approaches to address specific urban Aboriginal issues, and then leverage resources in support of this vision, there was mixed support for this approach among Aboriginal observers and government officers. In other words, the lack of a commonly shared vision among various participants was a practical barrier to the implementation of the UAS approach. Partly this is a resource issue, since most government departments and programs are already well established; there are very few resources that are currently unallocated and, therefore, available to contribute to the UAS-based initiatives. There would no doubt be considerable administrative and bureaucratic resistance to be faced in attempting to extract new resources from the budgets of already well-established programs. Thus, a major conclusion of the UAS program is the following: "There are historic barriers to the further development of collaboration with Aboriginal communities that need to be overcome, and some bureaucratic barriers that inhibit creative development of the strategies that the UAS envisions. There are also a number of systemic barriers within the federal government that will need to be overcome if the UAS is to advance to the extent envisioned" (Canada 2003: 34).

One cannot also help concluding, in viewing the longer historical initiatives of policy in Canada, that the Urban Aboriginal Strategy suffers from several problems that have become somewhat repetitious. First, the federal government initiates a program or plan of action and then attempts to entice various Aboriginal groups to come on board. For the most part, and one cannot say for certain that this is the case with the UAS, such federal Aboriginal groups as the Assembly of First Nations appear not to be mentioned as contributors or consultants either in the planning stages or the later phases of implementation. This approach sets up an adversarial stance, between government and Aboriginal organizations, and among Aboriginal groups as well. The federal government may argue that such consultation is not necessary, since no one political group represents all of Canada's Aboriginal population. This is, in fact, true; however, there have been cases similar to this in the past in which major Aboriginal political groups and leaders have felt left out of government initiatives, either because of issues of control (who makes the important decisions, government or Aboriginal groups?) or other combative concerns. Then, when funding tends to dry up, the initiative falters and the old blame game sets in.

Assessing Canada's Aboriginal Policy

Covering several hundred years of Aboriginal-settler relationships may appear an ingenuous exercise; nonetheless, such an attempt is no doubt needed. For starters, even though the task is eminently complex at one level, at another level it is not so. This is because government policy has to do with the manner in which people are treated, or in this case, the way that Aboriginal people in Canada have been treated by the settler population.

Indigenous scholar Deborah Doxtator (2011: 31–2) attempts to place this relationship in perspective: "It is very difficult to discuss 'Indianness' with any measure of neutrality. The emotion and experience of both parties in the relationship between 'Indians' and 'Whites' has been such that there is no easy way to discuss the facts. It is impossible to discuss the concept of 'Indianness' without addressing racism and the injustices that have occurred. It is impossible to talk about 'Indianness' without facing the uncomfortable reality of the dispossession of one people by another."

This insightful passage points to several key aspects of the Aboriginal-settler relationship – racism, injustice, and dispossession. More description could be added, such as Taiaiake Alfred's (2011: 3) reference to "colonial stains," such as "Euroamerican arrogance, the institutional and attitudinal expressions of the prejudicial biases inherent in European and Euroamerican cultures." The "colonial stains" are many, and have been at least partly enumerated in the previous historical accounts – for example, the ban on the potlatch and the general suppression of Aboriginal cultural institutions, not to say the dispossession of Aboriginal lands on an unimaginable scale during the treaty period. There was also the unconscionable use of brute force by the Canadian army in quelling the Oka Crisis. More recently, the silence of the federal government concerning the 440 recommendations (Dickason 2009: 417) of the Royal Commission on Aboriginal Peoples (RCAP 1996) and the *Report of the Ipperwash Inquiry* (Linden 2007) is notable.

And, let us not forget what is probably the most egregious act of cultural genocide ever inflicted on Canadian Aboriginal peoples: the residential school system. The Indian Residential Schools Truth and Reconciliation Commission (TRC) was officially established on 2 June 2008. The truth and reconciliation approach is seen as a form of restorative justice, differing from the customary adversarial or retributive justice, which emphasizes fault finding and punishment of the guilty. Restorative justice seeks to heal relationships between offenders, community members, and victims of offences that have taken place. The TRC is part of the court-approved Residential Schools Settlement Agreement negotiated between the legal counsel for former students, church members, government representatives, the Assembly of First Nations, and other Aboriginal organizations. In March 2008, church officials and Aboriginal leaders embarked on a multi-city "Remembering the Children" tour. In January 2009, King's University College of Edmonton, Alberta, convened an interdisciplinary studies conference on the subject of the Truth and Reconciliation Committee.

It did not take long for this worthy enterprise to fall into disarray (*CBC News*, 16 May and 20 Oct. 2008; *Toronto Star*, 29 May 2008). Justice Harry LaForme of the Ontario Court of Appeal, and a member of the Mississaugas of the New Credit First Nation, in southern Ontario, was appointed the first commission chair, but he resigned in October 2008. Justice LaForme cited insubordination by the other commissioners. He also referred to undue political interference by the Assembly of First Nations. Mention was made, in particular, of the interference of Grand Chief Phil Fontaine who, it was claimed, attempted to influence the TRC to abandon the reconciliation approach in favour of one with a more political orientation. Claudette Dumont-Smith, an Aboriginal health expert, and Jane Brewin Morley, a lawyer and public policy adviser, were then appointed as commissioners, but they announced in January 2009 that they would step down effective 1 June 2009. A reconstituted Commission was established in June 2009, headed by Justice Murray Sinclair, the first Aboriginal judge in the Manitoba court system.

It would appear inevitable, then, that politics enters into most facets of government policy involving Aboriginal people and state structures. As Peter Hutchins (2010: 215) argues, "Power and principle frame the portrait of state-indigenous relations – irrespective of era, irrespective of place. With this portrait, Western courts have struggled for a century and a half. Aboriginal litigation of course has one prominent characteristic – almost inevitably it involves the state as plaintiff or defendant. Politics is introduced into the brew, principle is often siphoned off."

We may now offer some suggestions, without the reiteration of more cases, of what does not work. There is abundant literature cited throughout this work that "agreements" reached from a position of power in which one party, usually the Aboriginal one, is in a subordinate position, and another, the Canadian state apparatus, is in a position to exercise coercion, will lead to frustration and discontent. Truly negotiated agreements, in which neither party acts out of desperation, great need, or the exercise of undue influence, have a greater chance of success. Incidents of this type are rare; however, the Nunavut Agreement of 1999 could be counted as an example. This is not to say that the Inuit-government relationship lacked an imbalance of power, yet negotiations appear to have been conducted on a consensual basis, on the basis of nation-to-nation.

Confrontation and disrespect are bred by combative relationships, usually initiated by the injustices that one party perceives have placed it at a disadvantage. Government initiatives also need long-term commitments to succeed. The Urban Aboriginal Strategy, in which millions of dollars have been spent on the conceptualization pilot projects, needs to be followed through with *actual* changes that incorporate power structures within the Aboriginal community. I am thinking, in particular, here of the Assembly of First Nations, which consists of the elected representatives of over six hundred Aboriginal bands: the AFN often appears slighted, or sidelined in government policy initiatives.

The reasons why this might be so are difficult to fathom. Perhaps the Canadian government perceives an inevitable power struggle, or it does not trust that decisions made with these elected officials will be met with satisfaction by leaders at the local level. Of course, there is always the problem of which Aboriginal groups should the government deal with. There are the representatives of the AFN status groups, of the Metis, of non-status Indians, of Indigenous women, and so on. The Inuit appear more cohesive in this regard, suggesting another reason for their apparent success.

This discussion does not lead to a final conclusion as to which government policy is preferable to another, but it does suggest a conclusion concerning which approach has the best chance of success. As human beings, we would all wish to be treated by others with respect and dignity, regardless of our material wealth or position of power. Although it might not be saying much that is altogether new, Aboriginal people wish to be engaged on an equitable basis.

Canada became a signatory to the UN's Declaration on the Rights of Indigenous Peoples on 12 November 2010. As has been pointed out in the postscript to *Racism, Colonialism, and Indigeneity in Canada* (Cannon and Sunseri 2011), Canada's endorsement of the Declaration should be seen "as a noteworthy step toward reconciliation, but only if it is aimed at restitution. It must carry a commitment to ensure that we are able to exercise our responsibility as self-determining peoples, including the rejuvenation and honouring of historic treaty and nation-to-nation agreements ... there is reason to be hopeful because Part VI [of the UN Declaration] repudiates the doctrine of discovery and terra nullius upon which settler-colonial states are premised" (p. 273). This statement seems a fitting summation of the issues involved in possible workable arrangements between Aboriginal peoples and the Canadian state in resolving extant policy and in charting a future course of action.

Conclusion

This chapter traces a lengthy period of Aboriginal policy in Canada. In the early French period, beginning with the voyages of Jacques Cartier in 1534 and later with Samuel de Champlain, the Aboriginal peoples were seen as military allies and people to be converted by Christian missionaries. The subsequent British period of influence saw the Aboriginal people also in a military role, as a buffer with the American colony to the south, and as an important economic asset in the fur trade of the James Bay area. This period of "protectionism" is associated with the Royal Proclamation of 1763 and the negotiation of comprehensive treaties of 1850s, such as the Robinson-Superior and Robinson-Huron Treaties of the Great Lakes area.

With the advent of Canadian Confederation in 1867, the comprehensive treaty approach continued, mainly from Manitoba westward, in the 1870s. The Indian Act was formulated, in 1876, which was mainly a cobbling together of previous British military legislation of the preceding century. The Trudeau-Chrétien era of the late 1960s saw a reversal of the previous assimilation policy, which was an attempt to integrate Aboriginal people into Canadian society. This new "termination" policy, exemplified by the White Paper proposal of 1969 sought to disband the Department of Indian Affairs and hand over its administrative structure to provincial governments. First Nations people, however, fought against this initiative, preferring instead the "citizens plus" proposal of the Hawthorn Report of 1966–67, in which Aboriginal people are seen to have rights beyond those enjoyed by the average Canadian citizen because of their original occupation of this country.

The 1970s saw a focus on resource development issues, especially the hydroelectric proposals of Quebec and the resulting James Bay Agreement (1975). In the Northwest Territories, the Mackenzie Valley Pipeline Inquiry received much attention (Berger 1977); in particular, focus was on the ten-year moratorium on further gas and oil development in the Mackenzie Valley corridor because of the possible detrimental impact on First Nations traditional subsistence economy.

The Royal Commission on Aboriginal Peoples released its report in 1996. To date it has received scant attention from federal or provincial authorities. The creation of Nunavut in 1999 was a much-celebrated event that demonstrates the effectiveness of the Inuit leadership in achieving Inuit goals of self-determination. The Ipperwash Report (Linden 2007) appears to be suffering a fate similar to that of the RCAP Report, although there have been proposals for dealing with the policing of Aboriginal protests that could prove effective in reducing the tension and conflict involved in future standoffs over land claims. Prime Minister Harper's much-anticipated apology to Aboriginal persons who attended residential schools, and an admission that the government's assimilation policy was wrong, was given in a heartfelt manner in the House of Commons in the summer of 2008. However, Canada's vote, in 2007, against ratifying the UN Declaration on the Rights of Indigenous Peoples left some sceptical about the government's sincerity in dealing with extant Aboriginal issues and claims, although Canada did become a signatory to the Declaration in 2010.

Canada's political climate during various periods plays a significant role in whether Aboriginal cultures are accepted in the national fabric of society. In the early years of Canadian Confederation, Kymlicka (2007) points out, "A number of policies were adopted to speed up this process [of assimilation], such as stripping indigenous peoples of their lands, restricting the practice of their traditional cultures, languages, and religions, and undermining their institutions of self-government" (p. 67). This was especially the case with the introduction of residential schools and the enactment of such repressive measures as the anti-potlatch laws (in the 1880s) and the prohibition on Native political gatherings.

In a wider sense, the acceptance of Aboriginal societies is part of the wider acceptance of people who are different from the mainstream of Canadian society. Canada has an official policy of multiculturalism, but support for this perspective has varied during different periods and among those with different political persuasions. Kymlicka (2007: 105) has discussed the bases of political support for multiculturalism: Working on the assumption that multiculturalism reflects a reaction against liberalization in society, the expectation would be that in Canada there would emerge two competing political camps. One camp, the liberal one, would favour reforms that would emancipate individuals, such as gender equality, abortion and gay rights. On the other hand, the conservative camp would favour such "group" issues as immigration, multiculturalism, autonomy for Quebec, and Aboriginal rights. However, Kymlicka argues, the situation in Canada is the opposite of these expectations.

The group that he refers to as the "patriarchal cultural conservatives" not only opposes liberalizing reforms, as could be expected, but equally seems to oppose multiculturalism and Aboriginal rights. Kylicka's (2007: 105) conclusion is that in Canada "there has not been (and is not now) any significant level of public support for any of these forms of multiculturalism among cultural conservatives." This analysis would help to explain the federal government's resistance to the proposals in the RCAP Report (1996) and the recommendations made by the Ipperwash Inquiry (Linden 2007), as well as Canada's 2007 vote against the UN Declaration on the Rights of Indigenous Peoples.

Chapter Three

The Nature of Aboriginal Rights

Despite Canada's constitutional recognition and affirmation of "existing aboriginal and treaty rights," change to the way these rights are understood is sorely needed.

– Michael Asch, *Aboriginal and Treaty Rights in Canada* (1997: xv)

The nature of Aboriginal rights and claims in Canada is a complicated matter. It includes various treaties and other forms of negotiations between Aboriginal First Nations and pre-Confederation powers, mostly notably the French and British, as well as the government of Canada. These various negotiations, in turn, comprise a diversity of cultural, social, legal, political, economic, and religious aspects and interests. Taken as a whole, these various forms of negotiations extend over at least four centuries during which the relationships between Europeans and North American First Nations changed and evolved in various ways. There are also matters of interpretation, often disputed by each party, over what was actually specified in the various treaties and how these were understood. Disputes have arisen over what was said orally in the treaty meetings and what eventually ended up in the written documents.

In describing the nature of the complexities of Aboriginal rights, Franks (2000: 101) writes, "Issues of Aboriginal rights and self-government include problems of individual versus group rights, of the meaning and utility of rights in different cultural contexts, and of conflict between minority and dominant cultures of small versus big." He explains that addressing Aboriginal rights in a comprehensive manner requires of thorough understanding of the complexities of the various arguments about these rights because these rights are essentially contestable concepts. There is no simple agreement on the meaning of Aboriginal rights or how they are to be applied. One has also to take into consideration the context of the various economic, political, legal, and social forces that affect Canada's Aboriginal communities (pp. 102–5).

With an awareness of these various problems of definition and comprehension, the purpose of this chapter is to provide an overview, although admittedly not an exhaustive one, of some of the major facets of Aboriginal claims and rights in Canada.

The Context of Aboriginal Claims

The fur trade provided the first significant basis for the European and Aboriginal First Nations interaction in Canada.[1] In the very first encounters between such French explorers as Jacques Cartier and Samuel de Champlain, the exchange of indigenous furs for European manufactured goods led to an incipient form of trade that eventually evolved into a massive corporate enterprise that lasted for at least three centuries. This corporate enterprise was dependent largely on the good will of both parties, and both profited immensely from the interaction. Both parties learned effective mechanisms of interaction with each other involving their social, cultural, economic, and political characteristics.

Before long, military relationships were also involved in the interaction. Under Champlain, the French colony became embroiled in the long-standing dispute between the Hurons and the Iroquois. The British sided with the Iroquois and came to rely on First Nations peoples in their disputes with the American colonists. The Royal Proclamation of 1763 could be seen as an attempt by the British to consolidate their relationship with the First Nations as military allies, to the extent that the British government was willing to recognize Aboriginal rights to land and would attempt to intercede on the First Nations behalf in any attempt by settlers to dispossess them of their traditional territories.[2]

Eventually, more comprehensive agreements involved the trading of land rights for various benefits such as protection under the umbrella of the British colonial government, annuities, and guarantees of hunting and fishing rights. Soon enough, the Crown became the target for various claims and grievances with regard to land issues, the distribution of resources, and the management of Aboriginal affairs. These various claims, ultimately, resulted from the First Nations position that they possessed certain inalienable rights as the unconquered Indigenous peoples of Canada (Canada 1975).

From this position – of Indigenous occupation – various policies began to be developed that distinguished First Nation societies from other citizens of the country. When the biological mixing of immigrant and Aboriginal peoples began to occur, the boundaries between the two groups started to become less precise, with the result that a bifurcation of policy started to evolve (Brown 1980):[3] there were Indigenous persons upon whom special status was conferred and those in another, non-status category, who did not have special rights. Eventually, this latter category fragmented further with the formation of Metis populations in the western provinces (Driben 1983).

In a historical sense, then, Aboriginal policy evolved into a diversified and not altogether clear set of legal regulations, laws, and administrative units. The implementation of this continually expanding sphere of policy became increasingly complicated and complex, drawing more government resources into the administration of these matters. As a method of containing this administrative quagmire, special residential locations called *reserves* were designated for the status Aboriginal population, yet the problem still existed about what to do with those First Nations people who either chose not to live, or were prohibited from living, on these reserves.

When the proliferation of treaties began, in the mid-nineteenth century, a further fracturing of the Aboriginal population occurred, with treaty and non-treaty populations. What began to develop was a very nebulous jurisdictional and administrative problem. At the time of the Royal Proclamation in 1763, for example, jurisdiction over Indian Affairs was considered to be a military matter under the commander of the forces. In 1860, Indian Affairs was transferred from the imperial domain to the province of Canada, and subsequently, in 1867, the Secretary of State of the federal government assumed control. Over the years, the administration of Indian Affairs was relegated to the Department of the Interior (in 1873), made an independent Department of Indian Affairs (in 1880), made a branch of the Department of Mines and Resources (in 1936), transferred to the Department of Citizenship and Immigration (in 1949), and reorganized (in 1962–64) as the Indian Affairs Branch, which was subsequently transferred to the Department of Northern Affairs and National Resources (in 1965), resulting in the establishment of the Department of Indian Affairs and Northern Development (in 1966), which is also known as the Department of Indian and Northern Affairs (Frideres 1988a: 31–4).

As far as the regulatory apparatus of the Canadian government is concerned, the Indian Act, first passed in 1876, but with a number of revisions since that time, has been the principal mechanism that regulates the lives of the status Aboriginal population. There is also the British North America (BNA) Act, now referred to as the Constitution Act, 1867, the Canadian Bill of Rights, and the Canadian Charter of Rights and Freedoms. The BNA Act stipulates that the federal government exercises exclusive control over "Indian and lands reserved for Indians," through the authority of Parliament. However, the Charter overrides any existing legal statutes that deny individual equality before the law, including the Indian Act. As a result of certain discriminatory sections of the Indian Act pertaining to the status of Aboriginal women and marriage, the Indian Act underwent a significant amendment in 1985 with the passage of Bill C-31.

As far as Aboriginal rights and claims are concerned, it is, therefore, evident that these take place within the context of myriad legislative, administrative, and jurisdictional contexts. From a legal standpoint, Aboriginal claims are also influenced in a significant manner by the various groupings of Aboriginal peoples, such as status versus non-status, treaty versus non-treaty, or reserve versus non-reserve. These categories, in turn, are a major factor in influencing relationships with various government bodies at the federal or provincial level. For the most part, the federal government has been seen to be responsible for the status population, and provincial governments for non-status and Metis Aboriginal peoples, although the demarcations of these lines of jurisdiction and authority are not altogether free from ambiguity. Nevertheless, there is no question that whatever concept of Aboriginal rights might be held by the various Indigenous populations, rights are at the basis of all Aboriginal claims.

The Concept of Aboriginal Rights

A discussion of Aboriginal rights might begin with a wider, more general focus on citizens' rights in general, or what has been termed "modern rights discourse." Franks (2000: 123–5), for example, submits that rights can be classified into three general categories. The first of these categories pertains to what have been termed *negative rights*, that is, rights that citizens are able to claim against their government. These rights would include such aspects as the right to participate in government through elections, voting, or engagement in political activism.

The second category of rights has been termed *positive rights*. These are the rights that citizens are entitled to receive from government, which could include the right to adequate housing, food, education, medical care, or old age pensions. In the third category are rights seen as "procedural." *Procedural rights* define the circumstances by which government is allowed to remove freedoms of the citizen against the state. The most important of these would include the formally established due process and fairness in the courts of law. In fact, given that status Indians were not even considered to be Canadian citizens until the early 1960s, they were also in a dubious position with regard to the second category of rights as well, having to do with pensions, social assistance, housing, medical care, and so on. Various treaties might deal with one aspect, such as the "medicine chest" provision of Treaty Six signed at Forts Charlton and Pitt, in 1876, which eventually became the basis for free health care for Aboriginal peoples. This provision also provided for rations as a strategy of preventing famine when the buffalo on the Plains declined (Leslie and Maguire 1978: 59). In other words, it has never been altogether clear about which treaty provisions applied to which Aboriginal groups beyond the treaty area itself, or if there ever were Aboriginal rights that generally applied across Canada, in all jurisdictions, and all provinces and territories.

At various points in time, any one category of these rights, or combination of categories, has served to define the ability of Aboriginal persons to pursue their rights. In the first category, those First Nations people with status under the Indian Act were denied the right to vote in federal and provincial elections until halfway through the twentieth century. Social and political activism was about the only avenue remaining that Aboriginal people had to express their discontent, because they were denied access to the institutions of power and government.

During various periods, the Canadian government has attempted to place Aboriginal rights in a historical and legal perspective. Ottawa's Indian Claims Commission, for example, attempted to place the concept of Aboriginal rights in Canada in a historical context by noting that "the context of native or aboriginal rights to land stems from a basic fact of Canadian history: that Indian and Inuit peoples were the original, sovereign inhabitants of the country prior to the arrival of the European colonial powers" (Canada 1975: 6).

As far as First Nations people are concerned, their understanding of the legal content of Aboriginal title can be described in the following manner: "Indian title as defined by English law connotes rights as complete as that of a full owner of property with one major limitation. The tribe could not transfer its title; it could only agree to surrender or limit its right to use the land. English law describes Indian title as a right to use and exploit all the economic potential of the land and the waters adjacent thereto, including game, produce, minerals and all other natural resources, and water, riparian, foreshore, and off-shore rights" (Canada 1975: 6).

Voyageur and Calliou (2011: 210) provide a further, more contemporary clarification: "Aboriginal peoples were once distinct and sovereign nations on the land that is now recognized as Canada. They had their own system of laws, religion, and other institutions, all of which supported self-government. Long after contact with Europeans they remained sovereign – so much so that they were not only partners in the fur trade economy but also participated in the wars between the European powers in North America." They place the abrogation of Aboriginal rights clearly on European greed and capricious rationalization, indicating that as "European settlement in North America grew, the Europeans' desire for more land and resources became insatiable. The newcomers justified taking First Nations land by characterizing Aboriginal peoples – their former benefactors and allies – as being less than human" (ibid.). Laws were then made by European powers on the basis of intolerance, which served to dispossess Aboriginal societies of their land and resources, based on a legal protocol that only superficially appeared to be reasonable and valid.

Early colonists in Canada felt justified in encroaching on the lands of First Nations people in Canada out of a feeling of superiority, holding that their more developed technological and agricultural way of life was far superior to the Aboriginal lifestyle largely based on nomadic hunting and fishing. The settlers had difficulty understanding how a people who were seldom seen in one geographical location for any extended period could claim rights to territory that they apparently did not permanently inhabit. What the colonists did not understand was that most Aboriginal populations had a well-developed sense of their hunting territories, that distinguished their use from other neighbouring Aboriginal populations, a topic on which there is a very thoroughly discussed literature in anthropology (see, e.g., Feit 1973, 2004; Hedican

1990; Rogers 1966, 1981; Tanner 1986). Neighbouring families or bands might on occasion be permitted to use the hunting and fishing territory of other groups, but this did not negate the fact that the principal occupants were considered to be the possessors of this territory.[4]

These sorts of misconceptions about Aboriginal land use and occupancy led early government administrators to question the validity of First Nations land rights. In other words, there existed a cultural gap of understanding. If the Europeans believed that the members of Aboriginal nations lacked a concrete concept of land ownership, then this would appear to justify, in the colonists' minds, the dispossession of Aboriginal lands. This attitude on the part of the settlers was largely a self-serving one, as Asch (2002: 23–9) argues, and was used to justify taking property that did not rightly belong to them, on the grounds that the settlers themselves could put the land to better or more productive use than the Aboriginal occupants.

It is evident that legal ideology in Canada relies on what Asch (2000: 149–50) terms the "settlement thesis" as a justification for Canadian sovereignty over Aboriginal lands. The settlement thesis rests on the concept of *terra nullius* ("land without owners"), that is, the territory claimed by the colonists was previously unoccupied territory, or at least not belonging to another political entity. Thus, within the colonial context, it is problematic to assume that there were no Indigenous inhabitants in Canada when the early settlers arrived; nor can it be presumed that such a condition as terra nullius existed for the whole of the territory that was later to become Canada.

Knafla (2010: 2) suggests the term *terra nullius* in reference to Australia, although "at the center of concepts of imperial sovereignty that denied Native title in the nineteenth century, [it] was not actually part of Australian legal discourse until the twentieth century, but that in fact was how the continent was treated." When Captain James Cook, for example, sailed up the east coast of Australia, in 1777, he formed the opinion that the Aborigines were not engaged in any economic enterprises worth investigating and on that basis regarded the continent as uninhabited. However, when later travelling along the coast of British Columbia's Nootka Sound, in 1790, Cook saw commercial possibilities, and on this basis saw the need to reach agreements with the local Aboriginal population (Nettheim 2007: 177–9).

One way to circumvent the difficulties with the settlement thesis is to vary the terra nullius concept so that a justification for occupying Aboriginal lands is based on the premise that "the original inhabitants did not possess political rights or underlying title that required recognition by the colonizers" (Asch 2000: 150). Furthermore, another related rationale against the recognition of Aboriginal title pertains to the view that since Aboriginal peoples in Canada were not Christians at the time of contact their rights did not require recognition. These arguments Asch refers to as forms of "artificial" reasoning that "have been used in subsequent periods to justify the unilateral assertion of sovereignty and underlying title by colonists in the face of indigenous sovereignty" (ibid.).

The terra nullius doctrine, as a further example, was also used in Australia in the 1992 Mabo decision (*Mabo* v. *Queensland*), in which the suggestion was put forth that since the Aborigines did not practice agriculture they could not claim sovereignty over their territory (Russell 2005: 191–218, 247–70). The decisions of the High Court of Australia discredited the terra nullius thesis because it relied on a "discriminatory denigration of indigenous inhabitants, their social organization and customs." Members of the Australian High Court were even more explicit in rejecting the terra nullius doctrine because it treated "the Aboriginal peoples of the continent … as a different and lower form of life whose very existence could be ignored for the purpose of determining the legal rights to occupy and use their traditional homelands" (cited in Asch 2000: 156). As far as the significance of the Mabo case for Aboriginal rights is concerned, Russell (2005: 196) maintains that "the case demonstrates, and herein lies its true importance, that Aboriginal peoples' resort to the highest courts in settler societies can be an opening to a new and worthwhile form of justice. This is possible because the law and the legal process that judges as adjudicators are bound to respect are not the fixed, carved-in-stone entities that conservative legal professionals … are wont to talk about."

The Mabo case in Australia has a counterpart in Canadian jurisprudence because of parallel forms of thinking such that Aboriginal rights are often considered in both countries to be those rights possessed by the original peoples of a region, but which takes into consideration the imposition of power over such peoples by colonizing populations. As Asch (2001a: 1) explains, "The concept of Aboriginal rights has existed since the beginnings of the period of European colonization. It originated in the political and legal system of those who colonized and poses the question of what rights rest with the original population after colonization."

The British used the term *Native rights*, whereas Aboriginal rights were seen to differ from one Aboriginal group to another. The term

Aboriginal rights began to be commonly used from the 1970s, and it is currently somewhat synonymous with *Indigenous rights*, a term that gained ascendency in the 1990s and that may well become the more prominent term in the future. The Aboriginal rights are generally understood to refer to the rights of the original peoples who form a minority population in states that were settled by peoples of European origin. In the legal systems of the dominant society, the term is meant to indicate substantive protections that allow for the continuance of a traditional way of life with minimal interference by the state's population. As the Indigenous populations are apt to interpret the concept, the right is not only to pursue a traditional way of life but to do so on their traditional territories and under self-governing structures. The implication is that Aboriginal rights is a concept implying self-determination, not in the creation of new states for the Indigenous group, but in a reconfiguration of political relationships within states as a system that respects the mutual existence of Indigenous peoples and the settler populations (Asch 2001a, 2001b).

Many future land claims were to emerge over these sorts of issues, ones in which the Euro-Canadian settlers and government administrative apparatus were to take an ethnocentric view of Aboriginal land occupation, and then use this view to justify all sorts of uses of Aboriginal lands to which they were not legally entitled. Over time, if the occupancy was not initially contested by First Nations people, ownership just became "assumed" because of the improvements made to the land, such as house and barn construction, land cleared, and fields plowed.[5] Generations of settlers might pass before a claim is later established with a legal title. The settlers then become bewildered, claiming, "We've always been here." The situation is akin to squatters who might conclude that a long-term occupation of someone else's property somehow justifies a claim to ownership.

It can be noted, however, that despite all these difficulties of cultural conceptions and occupancy problems, the Canadian government has consistently accepted – as a general rule – the concept of Aboriginal title, as did the previous British colonial administration (see Doerr 1975, Cumming 1973, Cumming and Mickenberg 1972). When the transfer of Rupert's Land by the British Crown to the Dominion of Canada occurred in 1870, for example, there was no question that this conveyance would involve a duty on the part of the federal government to recognize Aboriginal claims for compensation when such lands were required for settlement. These Aboriginal claims, it was stipulated, would be "considered and settled in conformity with the equitable principles that have uniformly governed the British Crown in its dealings with the aborigines" (Canada 1975: 7).

The problem was that the further conveyance of the Rupert's Land territory from the Canadian government to various provinces did not consistently practice or honour the concept of Aboriginal title. A major dispute, for example, developed in 1875 when the Canadian government disallowed the passage of the British Columbia Crown Lands Act because of the refusal of this province to recognize Aboriginal land rights. Later, in 1912, with the passage of the Boundaries Extension Act, by which the province of Quebec assumed possession of some 500,000 square kilometres of its present northern provincial area, Quebec agreed to negotiate treaties with the Aboriginal inhabitants but it has never fulfilled this obligation (Moss 1985).[6]

Not until the announcement of the James Bay Project, in 1974, did the issue of the lack of a land settlement with the Cree and Inuit peoples become pressing – and an impediment to the development of the project. It should, of course, be noted that Quebec was only forced into recognizing Aboriginal land claims by a court injunction (the Malouf Injunction in 1972) to the James Bay Hydroelectric Project, otherwise who knows if the land occupancy issues would ever have been resolved. There could not be any quibble, for example, in the Quebec's government's obligation to settle land claims, because it had agreed to do so in taking possession of northern Quebec under the Boundaries Extension Act of 1912, in which it was clearly stipulated that the province would recognize territorial rights "to the same extent, and will obtain surrenders of such rights in the same manner, as the Government of Canada has heretofore recognized such rights and has obtained surrender thereof" (Canada 1975: 7). Furthermore, throughout its entire history since Confederation, the province of British Columbia has consistently refused to negotiate Aboriginal land claims, holding to the position that this matter is a responsibility of the federal government.

Treaties and Land Surrenders

The treaty negotiation process in Canadian history has been part of a concomitant process whereby administrative controls were instituted along with the alienation of Aboriginal lands. Tully (2000) identifies two types or relationships between the Aboriginal and the non-Aboriginal peoples of Canada: treaty and colonial. In the treaty relationship, he explains that "Aboriginal peoples and Canadians recognize each other as equal, coexisting, and self-governing nations and govern their relations with each other by negotiations based on procedures of reciprocity and consent that lead to agreements that are then recorded in treaties or treaty-like accords of various kinds to which both parties are subject" (p. 41). In the second relationship, the colonial one, a relationship was imposed on Aboriginal peoples – without their consent and despite their active resistance. In this relationship, the status of equal, coexisting, and self-governing nations was denied. A structure of domination was established and administered through a series of Indian act and other legislative procedures. These two relationships serve as a useful framework in organizing the following discussion of Canada's historical negotiation process of treaties and surrenders.

The government of Canada published a two-volume set of documents entitled *Indian Treaties and Surrenders* in 1891 (Canada 1971 [1891]). A subsequent third volume was released in 1912. The various treaties and adhesions (amendments to treaties) number 483, from the years 1680 to 1902, and comprise in total 1,044 pages of text. In other words, the various treaties published in these volumes extend over a period of 222 years, averaging just over two treaties per year, and comprising on average just over two pages each.

Considering the millions of acres of land surrendered by these treaties, two pages of detail per treaty would appear rather terse. Keep in mind also that much of the wording in such treaties is taken up with a lengthy preamble, of which that given in Treaty No. 37 of 1834, concerning the "Chippeway" Tribe of London District, province of Upper Canada, would appear rather standard, to wit: "THIS INDENTURE made the fifth day of February in the fourth year of the reign of His Majesty William the Fourth, by the Grace of God, of the United Kingdom of Great Britain and Ireland, King, Defender of the Faith, and in the year of Our Lord, one thousand eight hundred and thirty-four, between Kanatang, John Taicoo" (Canada 1971 [1891]: 90).

Most treaties also included a map based on a survey, but the boundaries are sometimes imprecise, referring, for example, to an oak tree that was well known at the time, having stood for several centuries, but of which there is no evidence of its existence today. Similarly, the vast changes in shorelines, promontories, or other natural features that have occurred over the last several centuries, especially in the more settled areas of eastern Canada, have greatly obscured the boundary markers for treaties.

When perusing the various treaties, one is apt to notice, at least by today's standards, a certain paternalism, or condescension of tone, such as that of Treaty No. 264, signed in 1888, by the Chief and Principal Men of the Chippewas of Lake Huron and Simcoe and the Dominion of Canada, which would appear rather common for the time. After describing the surrender of a certain parcel of land, it is stated: "To have and to hold the same unto Her said Majesty the Queen, Her Heirs and successors forever, in trust, to sell the same to such person or persons and upon such terms as the Government of the Dominion of Canada may deem most conducive to our welfare and that of our people" (Canada 1971 [1891]: 253).

Such wording, common throughout most of these treaties hardly, suggests an agreement between sovereign nations or some other measure of equal standing, but rather that of a subject people – forced to abide by terms more or less imposed by a more powerful party. Some confusion, therefore, was bound to emerge, when one party, the Aboriginal First Nations, were of a mind that the treaties they were signing constituted an agreement to conduct peaceful relations, while the other, the Dominion of Canada, or the British predecessor, saw in such treaties primarily of surrender of territory.

It is, therefore, perhaps somewhat of an understatement, when the federal government itself admits, "The land rights of native peoples in Canada have by no means been treated uniformly" (Canada 1975: 8). It will be up to others to judge whether or not this treatment has also been a fair one. There is no doubt, however, that by the making of the various treaties, Aboriginal persons surrendered most of their territorial rights, in return for various forms of compensation. In British North America (Canada), there developed a fairly consistent body of legal precedent and traditions that were used on the new frontiers at a time when rapid settlement and resource exploitation was being promoted.

The earliest treaties and agreements between the government and First Nations peoples were carried out in the Maritime areas and have been characterized as "Friendship and Peace" Treaties (Frideres 1988a: 99–105). In these pre-Confederation treaties, the important considerations pertained to political and military relationships. Generally speaking, these treaties did not involve any specific land transfers, annual payments, or other forms of compensation for particular rights that were relinquished by the treaties (Sanders 1985).

Before Confederation, treaties with Aboriginal First Nations were made with the British Crown, while after Confederation treaties were made with the Canadian government. At the time of Confederation, the Canadian government assumed all of the terms and responsibilities of the existing treaties. An important question, however, remained and that pertained to the terms of the Royal Proclamation of 1763 and the extent to which the Canadian government was bound by the stipulation of Aboriginal rights specified in this Proclamation. Driben (1983), for example, points out that it is a difficult matter today to determine the boundaries and other terms of reference regarding the "Indian Territory" that was indicated in the Royal Proclamation.

The early treaties of Ontario prior to Confederation were primarily negotiated with the Algonkian-speaking populations north of the Great Lakes, and with those who had migrated south after the Iroquois-Huron War of 1649–50. Ontario, at this time, had a very sparse European settler population comprised mainly of soldiers who were given land after the War of 1812 and other Loyalists who moved north after the American War of Independence. Small amounts of land were purchased from the Mississaugas in the late 1700s to build British forts at York, Kingston, and Niagara. By the early 1800s, prospectors began to move into the Canadian Shield north of Lake Superior. Violence erupted at a mining site in the late 1840s near Sault Ste. Marie, which precipitated negotiation of the Robinson-Huron and Robinson-Superior treaties of 1850. These treaties set a precedent for future negotiations such that subsequent treaties involved relatively large tracts of surrendered land, annuity payments, the establishment of reserves, and usually, a reference to hunting and fishing rights.

Another consideration at the time of Confederation pertained to the transfer of lands held by the Hudson's Bay Company, called Rupert's Land, which was transferred to Canada in 1869. The premise underlying this transfer was that the Canadian government would assume the responsibility for negotiating treaties with the Aboriginal populations of this territory. In turn, when such territory was subsequently transferred to the individual provinces, the assumption prevailed that the provinces receiving this new land would also take on the responsibility of negotiating treaties with the resident tribes, as has been previously discussed, for example, with regard to the Quebec Boundaries Extension Act of 1912.

Shortly after Confederation, the treaty process moved westward into Manitoba and the Prairie Provinces with the so-called numbered Treaties, beginning in 1873. As a general rule, Treaty No. 1 and Treaty No. 2

created reserve lands comprising 160 acres for each family of five individuals. Annuities were paid on the basis of $3 per person, and provisions were made for the construction of a school on each reserve. Treaty No. 3 increased the reserve allotment to 640 acres per family of five. This increased allotment became the standard for all future treaties except Treaty No. 5, which reverted to the 160-acre allotment. Other features of the treaties that became standard terms of agreement included provisions for hunting, trapping, and fishing rights and annual budgets for ammunition and provisions for agricultural supplies such as seed, cattle, and farm equipment. Treaty No. 6 differed from the others in that it included a "medicine chest" provision and the distribution of relief in times of food shortages.

By 1877, Treaty No.1 through Treaty No. 7 were completed allowing for sufficient land for the large-scale settler populations that had begun to enter Canada. The pressure for new lands for settlements and mineral development led to a new round of treaty negotiations after 1899, with the signing of Treaty No. 8 (Athabaska District), No. 9 in northern Ontario, and No. 10 in northern Saskatchewan. Treaty No. 11 was signed in 1921, in the Northwest Territories, after the discovery of oil at Norman Wells. Treaty negotiations returned to southern Ontario with the signing of the Williams Treaties of 1923. Modern treaties include the James Bay and Northern Quebec Agreement (1975) and the Nunavut Agreement (1999). Up until today, most of British Columbia, the Yukon, and Newfoundland and Labrador have not signed treaties with Aboriginal residents.

Aboriginal Claims Policy

Generally speaking, Aboriginal claims fall into two major areas: those relating to treaty grievances and those pertaining to specific Indian bands, now called First Nations. Aboriginal peoples who signed treaties have various claims that emanate from their cessation of lands through the treaty negotiation process. Several of these relate to the contention on the Aboriginal peoples' part that specific treaty terms were not fulfilled. There are instances, for example, with Treaty No. 9 (northern Ontario), in which remembered oral accounts of the Aboriginal persons in attendance at the treaty negotiations differed from the accounts that eventually emerged in the written record (Macklem 1997). Alternatively, as with Treaty No. 7, for example, signed with the

Blackfoot of Alberta, a claim was made that the translator, Jerry Potts, had misrepresented the Blackfoot chiefs' testimony to the government treaty commissioners (Treaty 7 Elders and Tribal Council 1996).

A related area of problems stems from the insistence by Aboriginal peoples that the verbal promises made to First Nations peoples at the time of the treaty gathering were not included in the eventual written texts. As Ottawa's Indian Claims Commission has noted,

> Treaty Indians have a number of claims that relate to the agreements for the cession of their lands through treaty. Some of these rest on an insistence that specific treaty terms have not been fulfilled, and that the broader spirit of the treaties has not been assumed by the government. A frequent claim is that verbal promises made at the time of the negotiations were not included in the written texts. In some areas, Indian people also emphasize in their treaty claims that these transactions constituted inadequate settlements, even if all their terms were fulfilled. These claims involve assertions about the way in which treaties were negotiated, the disparities between the two contracting parties and the alleged unfairness of the terms. (Canada 1975: 5)

With respect to the differences in opinion regarding the terms of the treaties, that is, concerning the Aboriginal signatories and a treaty's written texts, Treaty No. 3 is an important case in point (Daugherty 1985). Treaty No. 3 is an agreement reached in 1873 between various Ojibway (Anishinabe) First Nations and the government of Canada. The territory covered in this agreement comprises a large portion of northwestern Ontario and a part of eastern Manitoba.

One of the most important historical aspects of Treaty No. 3 is that it served as a model for the remainder of the eleven numbered treaties, and as such the previous treaties No. 1 and No. 2 were eventually amended to reflect some of the developments arising out of the negotiations of Treaty No. 3. Moreover, Treaty No. 3 is significant because of the litigation that eventually ensued between the Canadian federal government and the province of Ontario in relation to the responsibility for Aboriginal peoples, an issue discussed further in the section below under the St. Catherine's Milling case (1888).

Second, Treaty No. 3 is historically significant because a written record was kept of the Aboriginal peoples' understanding of the terms of the treaty, commonly known as the "Paypom Document." This document consists of a series of transcripts that were written for Chief

Powasson as the treaty negotiations were being conducted, and it records the promises that were made to the Aboriginal signatories. The importance of the Paypom Document pertains to a number of significant differences between the written version presented by the Canadian government and the Aboriginal version of the agreements that were made.[7]

The signing of Treaty No. 9, often referred to as the James Bay Treaty, could also be used as an example of several of the difficulties mentioned by the Indian Claims Commission (see, e.g., Macklem 1997, Calverley 2006, Long 2006). Treaty No. 9 covers lands in northern Ontario that lie north of the Robinson-Superior Treaty of 1850 and Hudson Bay and James Bay to the north. Treaty No. 9 was negotiated and signed between 1905 and 1906 by Commissioners Duncan Campbell Scott and Samuel Stewart, representing the federal government, Commissioner David McMartin, representing the province of Ontario, and various Cree and Ojibway leaders living in such places as Osnaburgh House, Fort Hope, Moose Factory, and Long Lake. Promises were made to the Aboriginal leaders by these government representatives and subsequently recorded in the written texts of the treaty. These promises were made with the apparent agreement of the Cree and Ojibway leaders, in return for the surrender of certain rights and some 130,000 square miles of territory. The Aboriginal leaders also agreed to relocate to reserves totalling 524 square miles in area. Various adhesions were made to the treaty in 1929–30, covering an additional 128,000 square miles, which extended Ontario's border with Manitoba.

As Macklem (1997: 98) points out, "an examination of the nature, scope, and status of Treaty 9 raises complex questions regarding the relationship between oral and written understandings of the treaty's terms." This treaty also "raises more general questions concerning the constitutional status of treaty rights and the extent to which treaty rights trump governmental and third party activity" (ibid.). When Aboriginal people claim that their oral traditions indicate that certain promises made by government representatives were not included in the written text, or that their traditions indicate a different interpretation of the government promises, it is generally the rule that the written account takes precedence over the oral one. Of course, this is a grave matter as far as Aboriginal peoples are concerned, because they are of the belief that their oral accounts are every bit as accurate as the written ones.

One could cavil over words said or not said at the time, or raise captious objections to the Aboriginal oral accounts, but nonetheless, there is a certain ethnocentrism evident which diminishes one tradition – the Aboriginal one – in favour of the European one. The continuing objections on the government's part that the oral accounts cannot be adequately substantiated does little to instil a sense of fairness in interpreting what took place so many years ago, when all of the principal participants involved are now deceased. These passed individuals ultimately appear as wraiths haunting the present negotiation process.

Among the various stipulations in Treaty No. 9, a significant point of contention concerns the Aboriginal peoples' "right to pursue their usual vocations of hunting, trapping, and fishing throughout the tract surrendered" (Macklem 1997: 109). These rights to fish, hunt, and trap on ancestral lands came with two qualifications. One of these is that the Aboriginal subsistence activities are subject to the various government laws and regulations, and, second, these activities do not extend to tracts of land "as may be required or taken up from time to time for settlement, mining, lumbering, trading and other purposes" (ibid.).

If we just stick to this example of hunting and fishing rights and delve into the matter with further scrutiny and analysis, it soon becomes apparent that the terms of Treaty No. 9 are fraught with disquieting ambiguities and potential misinterpretations. When Treaty No. 9, for example, stipulates that the Aboriginal signatories have agreed to "cede, release, surrender and yield up to the Government of the Dominion of Canada, for His Majesty the King and His successors forever, all ... rights, titles and privileges whatsoever" (in Macklem 1997: 110), it would appear from this statement that the residents of the Treaty No. 9 area have relinquished all of their Aboriginal rights to the Crown. The treaty does recognize the continued right to hunt, trap, and fish. But what determines the treaty's legal effect in this instance? On the one hand, the treaty stipulates that the Aboriginal signatories have agreed to "cede, release, surrender and yield up rights to the land." Yet, on the other hand, the treaty clearly recognizes hunting, trapping, and fishing rights, but without clarifying in any way the nature of these rights, or the conditions under which these rights have any sort of legal basis.

It is evident, therefore, that the terms of the treaty are, in fact, highly misleading, lack clarity, and allow for a number of potentially different interpretations. One wonders, for example, if these hunting, trapping, and fishing rights were actually created by Treaty No. 9, or does the treaty merely reaffirm what would be considered existing or prior Aboriginal rights? If one would side with the latter interpretation, then the Aboriginal signatories did not, in fact, cede or relinquish all of their land rights to the Crown. What follows, then, is that the Aboriginal residents of the Treaty No. 9 area were allowed to continue their hunting, fishing, and trapping rights not so much because these rights were stipulated in the terms of the treaty, but because these rights were recognized as existing prior to the treaty, were merely reaffirmed by the treaty, and therefore, allowed to continue on this basis.

Collateral issues stem from this interpretation. If we consider fishing rights, for example, do these rights imply some control over the water in which the fishing takes place? Moreover, does the right to fish simply refer to this activity alone, or does it further suggest that fishing should be more broadly defined to include some form of regulation of the fishery? How about the supply of fish? Do fishing rights suggest that the Aboriginal residents have a right to fish in quantities that they themselves determine? With regard to hunting and trapping, do these rights imply some protection from non-Aboriginal residents who might also claim access to these resources?

We could continue almost indefinitely laying out potential difficulties with the interpretation of Treaty No. 9. On a comparative basis, Treaty No. 9 is no doubt not unique in this regard to ambiguities and multiple interpretations. There is no need to survey all other treaties searching for ambiguities, for there is a plethora of them, and many of these form the basis for litigation in various forms as Aboriginal peoples search for protection from prosecution and in an attempt to clarify their rights within the various existing treaties.

The Courts and Aboriginal Claims

On a number of occasions, the rights of Aboriginal people have become the subject of adjudication in the Canadian courts. "Although there are exceptions," the Indian Claims Commission submits, "in general the judicial system has not responded positively or adequately to native claims issues" (Canada 1975: 18). The general guiding principal regarding Aboriginal rights has been that when European colonial powers lay claim to lands regarded as previously undiscovered by such powers, then these "newly discovered" lands become the possession of the European society.

When Aboriginal peoples have become litigants in a legal system with which they clearly have little experience, there are social and cultural obstacles that have inhibited their chances of success. An important practical issue concerns the prohibitive legal fees that could result from any possible litigation. In most of the early court cases in the area of fundamental Aboriginal rights, the Aboriginal people involved were not represented directly. The reason for this situation is that most of the early cases were tied to disputes over land and resources between the federal and provincial governments. Aboriginal peoples were only involved to the extent that the federal government sought to strengthen its position that it had an exclusive constitutional responsibility over Aboriginal peoples and their lands. It took many years, almost a century, in fact, before Aboriginal peoples became directly involved to any significant degree in these areas of litigation. In Canadian jurisprudence today, the concept of "existing Aboriginal rights," from which the idea of Aboriginal title emanates, is firmly entrenched in the Canadian Constitution, 1982, under sections 25, 35, and 37; however, it is not an easy matter to determine what is the precise meaning of these terms.

The most significant early case of Aboriginal title in Canada was decided in 1888 by the Judicial Committee of the Privy Council. In *St. Catherine's Milling and Lumber Company* v. *R.*, the ruling made was that Aboriginal title should be regarded as a right to use and occupy, that is, as a "right to possess," or as what might be regarded to be a "usufructuary right." In other words, Aboriginal title was considered in this case to be dependent on the good will of the sovereign and not on any inherent rights developed from treaties, Aboriginal concepts of land use, or other pertinent matters. In fact, the federal government's view of Aboriginal land title was that it was so vaguely defined that it was not feasible to develop a formal policy.

In the St. Catherine's Milling case, the dispute was between the federal government and the province of Ontario over whether or not the government in Ottawa could issue timber licences pertaining to lands in Ontario. The argument of the federal government was that it had acquired title to the lands in question from Aboriginal First Nations. The Judicial Committee of the Privy Council, the highest court in the British Empire, ruled in favour of Ontario on the basis of its opinion that Aboriginal peoples could not be regarded as actually "owning" their land, at least in the sense that Europeans regard the concept of ownership, and therefore, clear title could not be conveyed from the Aboriginal peoples to the federal government via the various treaties in Ontario.

The decision indicated, in effect, that First Nations people relinquished their "personal and usufructuary right" when the various treaties were signed. In effect, then, any interest in their land that Aboriginal peoples had prior to the treaties was extinguished at that time, and the beneficial interest in these lands was transferred immediately upon this signing to the province. It would be many years later that this issue of Aboriginal title would be again considered by the Canadian court of appeal.

In essence, the St. Catherine's Milling case set a precedent in that it led to the adoption of certain fundamental principles in Canadian Aboriginal rights law. The decision of the Privy Council, based on the doctrine of discovery, can be seen to be predicated on the following significant judicial assumptions (Bell and Asch 1997: 47):

1 Sovereignty and legislative power is vested in the British Crown.
2 Ownership of Aboriginal lands accompanies sovereignty over Aboriginal territory.
3 Aboriginal peoples have an interest in land arising from original occupation that is less than full ownership.
4 The British Crown obtained the sole right to acquire the Aboriginal interest.
5 Aboriginal sovereignty was necessarily diminished.

As far as Aboriginal title litigation is concerned, since these presumptions were not challenged, judges sought to clarify the nature and source of Aboriginal title. As such, in matters of litigation, the guiding principles were twofold: the Crown owned the land and had sovereign jurisdiction over it, and Aboriginal occupation of the land was a matter of significant interest, but something less than clear ownership. These entire assumptions stem primarily from the St. Catherine's Milling case and the ruling by Lord Watson that the Aboriginal right of occupancy, based on the Royal Proclamation of 1763, was a "personal and usufructuary right dependent on the good will of the Sovereign."

Over the next eighty-five years (1888–1973), subsequent Canadian court decisions engaged in a debate back and forth about the personal and proprietary nature of Aboriginal title, yet despite this lengthy judicial contemplation, the actual nature of the Crown's interest and legitimate acquisition was never adequately clarified.

The next important court decision regarding Aboriginal title was made in 1973 in the Calder case (*Calder* v. *Attorney General of British Columbia*). The Calder case stems from an attempt by the Nishga First Nation of the northwestern part of British Columbia to assert their Aboriginal claim to traditional lands in the Nass Valley based on their assertion that their land had never been ceded or surrendered by any treaty and their ownership was, therefore, never extinguished. The Nishga began a search through the courts for a judicial declaration that their Aboriginal title that, they claim, had never been relinquished. In 1967, Frank Calder and the Nishga Nation Tribal Council brought an action against the British Columbia government on the basis that their land title had not previously been extinguished and, therefore, the provincial government had no powers over this land.

This action was initially dismissed by the British Columbia Supreme Court in 1969, and again subsequently dismissed by the B.C. Court of Appeal. The case was finally taken to the Supreme Court of Canada, where seven judges ruled four to three against the Nishga claim. Six of the judges supported the idea of Aboriginal title based on "the good will of the Sovereign," but they could not reach an agreement on the fundamental question of how Aboriginal rights might be evaluated.

Three of the Supreme Court judges stood by their decision that Aboriginal title could not be extinguished without compensation or without a judicial judgment removing Aboriginal peoples' right to compensation. Occupation, the judges suggested, was a key element in the Nishga case because there was evidently proof that the Nishga had been in possession of the Nass Valley since time immemorial, and therefore, the Aboriginal rights of the Nishga continued to exist because they had never been surrendered in any agreement with the Crown. Apparently, however, the decision of the Supreme Court was not actually made on the merits of the case, but on a technical point that provincial authorization, which was never granted, was a necessary prerequisite for the Nishga to pursue the matter before a higher judicial authority.

The main issue, then, which is whether or not the Nishga had Aboriginal rights, remained substantially unresolved by the courts. Furthermore, the Supreme Court decision effectively blocked other Aboriginal groups in Canada from pursuing their own claims. The Calder decision was a failed opportunity to clarify many important points regarding Aboriginal title, such as the following: what is the manner in which Aboriginal title can be extinguished? What would be the characteristics of proof necessary to demonstrate an unequivocally valid claim to Aboriginal title? Up until the Nishga case, the federal government had regarded Aboriginal title as far too general and abstract a concept on which to base a claims policy. However, a change of government direction occurred after the Nishga case, in August 1973, when it was announced that the government was prepared to negotiate land settlements in many areas where it had previously been unwilling to consider such settlements. In 1969 (see Weaver 1981: 37–41 on the history of the Indian Claims Commission), a further announcement was made indicating that consultations with Aboriginal leaders had led to the formation of an Indian Claims Commission, thus establishing a basis for the resolution of Aboriginal claims grounded in negotiation, rather than confrontation in the courts.

The Indian Claims Commission may have deflected some of the interest in lands claims away from the previous arena of confrontation; however, the wider issue of Aboriginal rights, of which Aboriginal land entitlement formed a part, continued to be a matter of litigation in the courts. The Calder case led to a much-needed overhaul in the government of Canada's approach to the land claims negotiation process with Aboriginal peoples. However, the basis for Aboriginal title was in need of some expansion, and this expansion was to occur in 1984 with the Guerin case (*Guerin* v. *R.*). This was a landmark Supreme Court of Canada decision on Aboriginal rights, in which the court ruled that the government had a fiduciary duty – of trust or trusteeship, held or given in trust – towards First Nations people in Canada. This court decision also established that Aboriginal title was a sui generis (unique, not classifiable with others) right.

As Russell (2005: 264) explains, "A fiduciary obligation is one that arises from a relationship that is based, at least in part, on trust. It has a long history in relations with North American native peoples, and began with small settler communities trusting the good will of much more powerful Indian nations. When the power relations turned in favour of the settlers, the fiduciary obligation ran increasingly in the other direction." An important aspect of this fiduciary relationship arose, initially with Britain, but subsequently with Canada and the United States, that Aboriginal peoples could only sell their land to the Crown, not to private individuals or other nations. However, the quid pro quo of this restriction, based on the Royal Proclamation of 1763, was that the British Crown had a subsequent responsibility to ensure that fraudulent means were not used to dispossess Aboriginal nations of their land.

The Guerin case involved the Musqueam First Nation, which held approximately 416 acres of valuable land in the Vancouver area. The federal government, acting on behalf of the Musqueam, in 1958, made a deal with the Shaughnessy Heights Golf Club to lease 162 acres of land on which it could build a golf course. Unfortunately, the Musqueam were not made aware of the terms of these negotiations on their behalf. It was not until 1970 that the Musqueam discovered the terms of the agreement and as a result began a protest claiming that the federal government had a responsibility to disclose to them the full terms of the leasing arrangement.

When the case went to court, the First Nation claimed that the Crown was responsible for breaching a trust with them, and on this basis the Musqueam were awarded $10 million. However, the Federal Court of Appeal overturned this ruling, and so the matter went to the Supreme Court of Canada. In a majority decision of the Supreme Court, it was ruled that the Crown holds an enforceable fiduciary duty because of the nature of Aboriginal title. It was also stated that Aboriginal title is an inherent right that is based on the Musqueam First Nation's historical occupation of the Vancouver area, and it is therefore a right that existed prior to the Royal Proclamation of 1763.

The overall significance of this Supreme Court ruling in *Guerin* is that Aboriginal First Nations hold a special right such that Aboriginal title to their land can only be alienated or ceded to the Crown. The onus is also on the Crown to use this land in the interests of the Aboriginal peoples who occupy it. The precedent-setting ruling in the Guerin case, therefore, is that Aboriginal rights in Canada stem from an autochthonous or traditional habitation of the North American continent, as opposed to the previous position of the Crown that these rights derive from, or were created by, the Royal Proclamation of 1763. Thus, the separation of Aboriginal rights from the Royal Proclamation put these rights on a more independent legal basis and set the stage for further litigation as to the nature of these rights and how they might be defined sui generis, or on their own terms. In sum, this principle of "fuduciary duty" was to become a matter of considerable importance with regard to Section 35 of the Constitution Act, 1982, in terms of the protection it provides for Aboriginal rights.

The Canadian Charter of Rights and Freedoms (1982), for example, makes explicit mention of Aboriginal and treaty rights, as in Section 25:

> The guarantee of this Charter of certain rights and freedoms shall not be construed so as to abandon or derogate from any aboriginal treaty or other rights or freedoms that pertain to the aboriginal peoples of Canada.

These rights are further reinforced in Section 35 of the Constitution Act (1982) such that:

1 The existing aboriginal and treaty rights of the aboriginal peoples of Canada are hereby recognized and affirmed.
2 In this Act, "aboriginal peoples of Canada" includes the Indian, Inuit and Metis peoples of Canada.

Another important aspect of the Guerin case is that it "forced the government to clarify its role when negotiating with third parties over Indian land, as well as to obtain informed consent from the band on whose behalf it was acting" (Frideres and Gadacz 2008: 365). In other words, aside from providing a clarification of the nature of Aboriginal rights and the basis on which these rights could be interpreted, *Guerin* also served to redefine the relationship between the federal government, in particular the Department of Indian and Northern Affairs, in terms of the role played by government agencies in the administration of Aboriginal funds and land. In the Guerin case, Indian and Northern Affairs was admonished for neglecting to follow proper administrative procedures, especially in terms of breaching the trust of the Musqueam by not involving them in the leasing arrangement or notifying them of its terms.

The significance of *Guerin* went beyond the mere facts of the case. In the 1973 Calder case, for example, there was disagreement among the judges about what constituted Native title. However, in the 1984 Guerin case, "the Supreme Court of Canada clearly supported the position that native title has its source in pre-contact native society" (Russell 2005: 253).

In 1990, the Supreme Court of Canada, in another landmark decision, attempted to specify definite guidelines for determining the nature of Aboriginal rights. In this particular 1990 decision, *R. v. Sparrow*, the Court ruled that an Aboriginal right, such as fishing, could be established even in the absence of a treaty to support it. The Sparrow decision, ultimately, concerns the application of Aboriginal rights under Section 35(1) of the Constitution Act, 1982. The Supreme Court ruled that such Aboriginal rights as fishing were, in fact, already in existence prior to the passage of the Constitution Act of 1982, and therefore, such rights are protected under the Constitution of Canada. Furthermore, such rights cannot be violated or encroached upon. Harkening back to the Calder judgment, the Supreme Court reiterated the government's fiduciary obligations to Canada's Aboriginal peoples.

The courts became involved in this dispute over Aboriginal rights when Ronald Sparrow, a member of the Musqueam First Nation, was charged under the Fisheries Act with using a drift net much larger than that permitted under the Musqueam's fishing licence. In this case, Sparrow was fishing at the mouth of the Fraser River. Sparrow did not dispute the facts of the case; however, he claimed that the use of his net was justified according to his Aboriginal right to fish under the Constitution Act, Section 35. When the case went to trial, the presiding judge ruled that Section 35 only protects fishing rights under existing treaties. Since the Musqeam had never signed a treaty with the Crown, and it was, therefore, ruled that Sparrow's defence did not apply with regard to his fishing violation.

A series of appeals were dismissed until the issue was eventually brought before the Supreme Court. The specific issue before the Court was whether or not Sparrow's net violation contravened Section 35(1). The judgment of the court was unanimous, stipulating that Sparrow was exercising an "inherent" Aboriginal right that existed prior to the existing provincial fishing laws and that this right was, in fact, guaranteed under the Constitution Act. Taking the wording of Section 35(1) in a literal sense, the Court ruled that the word "existing" was a key element in its decision because this section needs to be "interpreted so as to permit their [rights] evolution over time." In other words, the term "existing" was seen to refer to the Aboriginal rights that were not "extinguished" prior to the Constitution Act.

According to various historical records of Musqueam fishing practices introduced to the Court, the First Nation had a clear and unequivocal right to fish for food. The right of the Musqueam people to fish had never been "extinguished" in any manner, and as such, their fishing could not be seen to violate provincial fishing licensing laws because these are meant simply to regulate fisheries in the province of British Columbia and not to remove or otherwise extinguish Aboriginal rights in this regard.

Additional wording in the Constitution Act, such that Aboriginal and treaty rights are "hereby recognized and affirmed," is also an important aspect of the Sparrow case. The Supreme Court ruling in *Sparrow* held that the words "recognized and affirmed" reinforced the government's fiduciary duty to the Aboriginal peoples of Canada such that the government was obligated to exercise restraint in its application of powers involving Aboriginal rights. *Sparrow* also influenced provincial legislation to the extent that Aboriginal rights could only be limited if appropriate priority was given to these rights, because it was the Court's opinion that Aboriginal rights must be considered as having a different nature from non-Aboriginal rights.

The significance of the Sparrow case lies in the defeat of the "frozen rights doctrine." "This legal theory," according to Arthur Ray (2010: 43), "held that Aboriginal rights only encompassed traditions in place when Europeans had asserted sovereignty – the mythical 'time immemorial' of Canadian law. According to this outlook, cultural practices were considered to be ineligible for legal protection if they had been extensively modified or created as a consequence of interactions with the newcomers. This presumption held sway until 1990 when the Supreme Court rejected this notion in its *Regina* v. *Sparrow* judgement." In other words, the Sparrow case allowed for a breaking away from previous legal concepts of land use based only on traditional patterns (the "frozen rights doctrine"), and opened up new possibilities for interpretations of contemporary practices.

Section 35 of the Constitution Act once again became a point of contention in a 1996 Supreme Court ruling in the *R.* v. *Gladstone* case. In this ruling, the Court provided a somewhat different interpretation of its previous Sparrow decision in that the protection of government commercial fishing rights was given a greater priority. Two members of the Heiltsuk First Nation of British Columbia, William and Donald Gladstone, were charged under the federal Fisheries Act with selling herring spawn. The brothers claimed that under Section 35 of the Constitution Act they had a right to sell herring. During the trial that followed these charges, the Gladstone brothers provided evidence in an attempt to demonstrate that the Heiltsuk (or Bella Bella) people's way of life prior to European colonization involved trade in herring spawn.

In his decision, Chief Justice Antonio Lamer stated his opinion that the Gladstone brothers had an Aboriginal right to sell herring spawn under what was termed the *Van der Peet test*. He also rejected a ruling in the Sparrow decision that limited Aboriginal natural resource use on an a priori basis. Judge Lamer ruled, instead that the distribution of commercial fishing resources should be regarded in a regional sense such that these resources are fairly allocated among all people of an area.

In the Supreme Court ruling of the Van der Peet case (*R.* v. *Van der Peet*), handed down on 21 August 1996, Section 35 of the Constitution Act again played a leading role in interpreting a case on Aboriginal rights. Dorothy Van der Peet, a member of the Sto:lo First Nation, was charged with selling salmon that her common-law husband, Charles

Jimmy, had lawfully caught under a Native food fish licence. However, in this instance, although the salmon were caught legally under existing legislation, the sale of this fish was prohibited. Chief Justice Antonio Lamer ruled that Aboriginal rights allowed for fishing for food and ceremonial purposes, but that this right did not extended to the sale of fish for commercial purposes or for monetary gain.

The legal question at hand was whether or not Dorothy Van der Peet's Aboriginal rights were infringed upon under Section 35 of the Constitution Act under a law that prevented the sale of her husband's salmon. In the opinion of the Court, "In order to be an aboriginal right an activity must be an element of a practice, custom or tradition integral to the distinctive culture of the aboriginal group asserting the right." The judgment further indicated that selling fish for monetary gain was not an integral part of Sto:lo "practice, custom or tradition." The Court then developed ten criteria that could be used as an "Integral to a Distinctive Culture Test" and implemented to define an Aboriginal right under Section 35(1) of the Constitution. Several of these criteria are enumerated below because of their implication in future Aboriginal rights cases, in particular the following:

3 In order to be integral a practice, custom or tradition must be of central significance to the aboriginal society in question.
4 The practices, customs and traditions which constitute aboriginal rights are those which have continuity with the practices, customs and traditions that existed prior to contact.
7 For a practice, custom or tradition to constitute an aboriginal right it must be of independent significance to the aboriginal culture in which it exists.
8 The integral to a distinctive culture test requires that a practice, custom or tradition be distinctive; it does not require that practice, custom or tradition be distinct.
9 The influence of European culture will only be relevant to the inquiry if it is demonstrated that the practice, custom or tradition is only integral because of that influence.

While these "cultural tests" or criteria are, in some ways, a praiseworthy attempt to more precisely define the characteristics of Aboriginal rights so that they are more fully protected by Section 35(1) of the Constitution, they also raise questions concerning the extent to which these "tests" limit an understanding of Aboriginal culture. For example, do these criteria tie Aboriginal cultures unfairly to a past that is now only dimly remembered, or might not have even existed at all? In future court cases, how will Aboriginal people demonstrate these on-going and distinctive "practices, customs and traditions"?

Not surprisingly, these very issues were to emerge as a significant factor in an important Supreme Court ruling the following year, in 1997. *Delgamuukw* v. *R.* is now a famous decision of the Supreme Court in which the most definitive attempt to date was made to delineate the nature of Aboriginal rights in Canada. Court proceedings were initiated thirteen years earlier, in 1984, by the Gitksan and Wet'suwet'en First Nations, whose members claimed ownership and legal jurisdiction over 133 individual hereditary territories and a total of 58,000 square kilometres of northwestern British Columbia in an area larger than the province of Nova Scotia.

A decision was originally made by the Aboriginal people to bypass the Federal Land Claims process, which was thought to be too slow of a venue and which was a process in which the British Columbia Provincial Government would not participate in any event. This land rights case initially went before the B.C. Supreme Court in the *Delgamuukw* v. *British Columbia* case of 1991. The Court judge, Alan McEachern, ruled that the Gitksan and Wet'suwet'en First Nations people did not have Aboriginal rights to the territory in question. This ruling was based on his opinion that the Royal Proclamation of 1763 did not apply to British Columbia. He also ruled that Aboriginal peoples did not own the land in question or have legal jurisdiction over it. Furthermore, the position of the province was that any First Nations land rights that might have previously existed were extinguished when British Columbia became part of Canada in 1871.

The case for Aboriginal land rights in Canada, therefore, suffered a serious setback by this decision. In particular, Chief Justice Alan McEachern's ruling that, in general, Aboriginal rights in Canada existed only because of the "pleasure of the Crown," suggested that these rights could also be extinguished "whenever the intention of the Crown to do so is clear and plain." A controversial aspect of the case revolved around Judge McEachern's refusal to consider evidence from oral history, or from academic researchers such as anthropologists, which he regarded as not objective enough (Culhane 1998, Daly 2005).

In a subsequent decision handed down in the B.C. Court of Appeal, Judge McEachern's decision was modified to the extent that the province changed its position arguing that Aboriginal land rights had not been extinguished after all. When this case went before the Supreme Court of Canada, it was initially decided that a ruling on the land dispute would have to wait.[8] However, for the first time ever, the Court was willing to directly address the matter of Aboriginal title – which the Court judged to be different from rights of land usage. Another important aspect of this decision was that the Court acknowledged the right of Aboriginal peoples to use land in ways in which it had not been used traditionally. This Supreme Court ruling also acknowledged the legitimacy of Aboriginal oral history in demonstrating past land use practices, and ruled that Aboriginal title to land could only be sold to the federal government of Canada and not to private interests.

The Delgamuukw decision left Indigenous groups in Canada still unclear about the acceptance of the role of oral history. Chief Justice Antonio Lamer made reference to Kent McNeil's (1989) *Common Law Aboriginal Title*. However, there were opponents of the decision, who noted in pejorative terms that the court "was swayed by the sophistry of the Royal Commission on Aboriginal Peoples and its coterie of like-minded academics" (cited in Knafla 2010: 7). Justice Lamer's decision is no doubt significant because it held that Aboriginal title was present in both English common law and Native custom. However, Justice Lamer's decision, nonetheless, "placed the onus of proof on Natives who never assented to the view that the underlying title to their lands resides in the crown. The proof of Aboriginal title had to be made in British terms, had to be reconciled with an alien crown sovereignty, and even then was subject to the economic and social needs of the state" (ibid.).

Nonetheless, even though *Delgamuukw* plainly involved Aboriginal title, "the Supreme Court has made clear that indigenous land rights are not limited to the rights of exclusive occupation and use that arise from that title. In situations where Aboriginal peoples do not prove exclusive occupation at the time of crown assertion of sovereignty, they may have site-specific rights to use certain lands for limited purposes, such as hunting or fishing" (McNeil 2010: 153). To Justice Lamer's credit, then, his articulation of the concept of site-specific land rights provides a further clarification to the ongoing debate concerning Aboriginal title.

A statement was issued by the B.C. Treaty Commission, in 1999, concerning the Delgamuukw decision. It recognized that the Supreme Court of Canada ruling in 1997 confirmed that Aboriginal title does exist in British Columbia, that it is a right to the land itself – not just the right to hunt, fish, or gather – and that when dealing with Crown land, the government must consult with and may have to compensate First Nations whose rights are affected. Everyone involved in treaty negotiations recognized that the decision could have major impacts on policies, positions, and mandates. As far as the province of British Columbia is concerned, the most important question remains: will the province now engage in a treaty-making process or will it remain staunchly entrenched in its position, held since 1870 (when British Columbia entered Confederation) that treaty negotiations are a federal responsibility?

The 1999 statement by the B.C. Treaty Commission only hints that treaties with Aboriginal First Nations of the province will now commence in some fashion. The Commission was quite clear in its recognition of Aboriginal title in British Columbia and that Aboriginal people have a right to land. It will take another step, however, for the province to clarify what it means by "Aboriginal title" and, thus, the manner in which this title will be dealt with in the courts. The Commission refers to "mutual recognition," such that "when a First Nation sits down at the treaty table, it recognizes there is some legitimacy to the claims of title, ownership and jurisdiction by Canada and B.C." This statement would appear to imply a less than straightforward recognition of Aboriginal title in the province; British Columbia is hedging its bets, so to speak, while at the same time engaging in platitudes. The Commission also notes "the treaty process was set up as a voluntary process based on political negotiations, *not legal interpretations*" (emphasis added).

Aboriginal people have a right to be sceptical about such a position. Does this mean that they must forgo their right to appeal to the courts for justice? In the past, giving up this right has proved disastrous, especially in British Columbia. Aboriginal people of the province probably have not forgotten what happened in 1906, when Chief Joe Capilano led a delegation of chiefs to London in an attempt to have His Majesty King Edward VII listen to their concerns. The trip to London was largely based on a distrust of provincial and federal policy. The delegation set out a petition complaining that title to their land had never been extinguished, that their appeals to the Canadian government had been in vain, and that they had not voted and were not consulted with respect to the Indian agents (LaViolette 1973: 98–144; Patterson 1972: 145–73).

The appeal to King Edward drew sympathy from the monarch but not much else. In 1909, the premier of British Columbia issued a statement denying the existence of Indian title: "Of course it would be madness to think of conceding the Indians' demands. It is too late to discuss the equity of dispossessing the red man in America" (in LaViolette 1973: 129). It was this attitude that was responsible for the passing of the British Columbia Pre-emption Act of 1870 by which Indians were excluded from claiming Crown land. Further suppression of Aboriginal cultures followed with the 1884 legislation passed by Parliament outlawing the potlatch. By 1927, however, the protest continued to evolve with a parliamentary joint committee hearing of the Senate and the House of Commons. This was the first time that the claim of Aboriginal title made its appearance as a *legal* claim.

The case by the Allied Tribes of British Columbia eventually was sent directly to the Judicial Committee of the Privy Council in London, the highest court in the British Empire at the time. The ongoing distrust of the federal and provincial governments was largely behind this legal initiative. The Allied Tribes were asked to relinquish their claim to the land before a decision was rendered if they would agree to present their case before a Special Joint Committee of Parliament, which the Allied Tribes agreed to do. This was probably done on the understanding, as Patterson (1972: 170) suggests, that the Allied Tribes organization believed that such a move was a preliminary step before going into the courts.

However, they were soon to be disappointed with the result. The Special Joint Committee was composed largely of prominent politicians from British Columbia, who were hardly predisposed to see the Allied Tribes claim in a favourable light. The decision of the Committee was that the Indians had no claim to land in the province, that they were ordered to stop the protest, and they were given $100,000 a year in lieu of treaty money. Of course, there was deep discouragement resulting from this decision and the Allied Tribes organization collapsed soon after. Thus, if we place the B.C. Treaty Commission's 1999 statement in historical perspective, the First Nations people of the province are apt to view the sentiments of "mutual recognition" and "good faith" with a certain degree of distrust. They would also not be inclined, one would suspect, to abrogate their right to legal recourse in the courts to press their land claims in the province, as suggested by the B.C. Treaty Commission.

The Delgamuukw case set the stage for further judicial exploration of Aboriginal rights into the new millennium. In 1999, a Supreme Court of Canada decision (*R. v. Marshall*) ruled that a Mi'kmaq man, Donald Marshall Jr., had the legal right to fish for eels out of season. The

Supreme Court acknowledged that Indigenous people had a right to establish a "moderate livelihood" through trade and the use of natural resources (Coates 2000). The Marshall decision eventually led to an agreement, in 2002, between Ottawa and the Burnt Church First Nation of New Brunswick regarding the Native lobster fishery, worth $20 million over two years.

The Mi'kmaqs were also involved in a leading Aboriginal rights decision in 2005 that pertained to two separate cases in this decision (*R. v. Marshall, R. v. Bernard*). The first of these cases concerned Stephen Marshall (no relation to Donald Marshall) who, along with thirty-four other Mi'kmaqs, was charged with cutting logs on Crown land in Nova Scotia without a permit. Another Mi'kmaq, Joshua Bernard, was charged with the theft of logs stolen from a sawmill in New Brunswick. These logs were also cut from Crown lands. All of the accused, in both of these cases, put forward the argument that because of their Indian status they had the right to cut and possess logs taken from Crown lands and to sell these for commercial purposes according to a previous treaty signed in the eighteenth century.

In the initial trial, all of the accused were convicted of the offences as charged; however, at the provincial courts of appeals, the convictions were overturned. The subsequent Supreme Court of Canada decision is considered a leading Aboriginal rights case because the Court narrowed the test for determining the extent to which Aboriginal practices have constitutional protection. In reference to the Peace and Friendship Treaties of 1760, upon which the Mi'kmaqs based their position, the Court ruled that such treaties did not grant an Aboriginal right to engage in commercial logging, although in the previous *R. v. Marshall* case of 1999 (the Donald Marshall decision) the Mi'kmaqs were granted the right to fish commercially. The presiding Chief Justice of the Supreme Court Beverley McLachlin, in a majority decision, wrote that under the 1760 treaties in support of the Mi'kmaqs' position, no provisions were made for commercial logging by Aboriginal peoples, and furthermore, she indicated that the evidence did not support the conclusion that logging formed a basis of the Mi'kmaqs' traditional culture and identity. Therefore, this Supreme Court decision restored the previous convictions.

Chief Justice McLachlin was also the presiding judge in another important Supreme Court decision in 2008 (*R. v. Kapp*) involving commercial fishing in British Columbia. In this instance, a communal fishing licence was granted to the members of three Aboriginal First Nations, allowing them the exclusive right to fish for salmon for a period of twenty-four hours in the mouth of the Fraser River under a pilot sales program in which they would be allowed to sell their catch. The program was part of the Aboriginal Fisheries Strategy that the federal government initiated in order to enhance Aboriginal involvement in the commercial fishing industry of the west coast.

Non-Aboriginal commercial fisherman were excluded from the fishery for that period and, consequently, alleged that they were the victims of race-based discrimination and, therefore, suffered from a breach of their rights of equality. As a protest, the non-Aboriginal fishers engaged in fishing during this twenty-four–hour period and were subsequently charged with fishing at a prohibited time. The main issue was whether this pilot program was protected under Section 15(2) of the Canadian Charter of Rights and Freedoms. The trial judge ruled that, indeed, the licence granted to the three bands was a breach of the equality rights of the non-Aboriginal fishers under Section 15(1) of the Charter, and as a result, proceedings on all charges were stayed. In an appeal by the Crown, the stay of proceedings was lifted, and convictions were entered against the appellants (non-Aboriginal fishers).

In the Supreme Court of Canada decision, it was ruled that the communal fishing licence issued by the federal government was constitutional and that the appeal of the non-Aboriginal fishers should be dismissed. Furthermore, the ruling indicated that the focus of Section 15(2) is on enabling governments to pro-actively combat discrimination by developing programs aimed at helping disadvantaged groups such as the Aboriginal fishers of British Columbia to improve their situation.

The numerous objectives of the pilot program, such as negotiating solutions to Aboriginal fishing rights claims, providing economic opportunities to First Nations, and supporting their progress towards self-sufficiency are all protected under Section 15(2) of the Charter. In the present case, the means chosen to achieve the purpose, such as special fishing privileges for Aboriginal communities, are therefore, justified because they are part of the process designed towards serving that purpose. In sum, it was ruled that Section 25 of the Charter serves the purpose of protecting the rights of Aboriginal peoples in the event that the protection of the private rights of individuals would serve to diminish the distinctive, collective, and cultural identity of the Aboriginal group. By this reasoning, the prima facie discrimination of the non-Aboriginal fishers was allowed because the pilot program was ultimately aimed at improving the economic conditions of a disadvantaged group. "Section

25 reflects the imperative need to accommodate, recognize and reconcile aboriginal interests," the Court ruled.

Conclusion

Aboriginal rights and claims in Canada involve a long and complicated history extending at least three hundred years. The Royal Proclamation of 1763 is referred to at times as the "Indian Bill of Rights," although it would certainly fall short of that designation by today's standards. Nonetheless, the Royal Proclamation set a precedent in that the British Crown recognized Aboriginal land rights, although the manner in which these rights were determined has been a matter of legal discussion ever since. At the time of the Royal Proclamation, First Nations were seen by the early European settlers to be an important asset, and they were also regarded as an effective military buffer against further American expansion northward. This period, before Canadian Confederation, was also a time of the so-called protectionist phase of British colonial policy, as reflected in the Royal Proclamation's stipulation that Indian lands could only be alienated through the auspices of the British Crown.

The Royal Proclamation is considered to be the foundation of the concept of Aboriginal rights because it recognized that "Indian and Inuit peoples were the original, sovereign inhabitants of this country prior to the arrival of the European colonial powers" (Canada 1975: 6). The Royal Proclamation was also the basis for the Indian Act of 1876, as well as the legal backing for the treaty period during which reserves were created and Aboriginal peoples ceded their right to sole ownership of the territories they inhabited (Morris 1979 [1880]). In the courts, the legal basis upon which the assumptions of the Royal Proclamation were built remained unchallenged until the St. Catherine's Milling case of 1888. This was the leading case on Aboriginal title for more than eighty years in Canada. The Judicial Committee of the Privy Council ruled that Aboriginal title over land was allowed only at the Crown's pleasure and could be taken away at any time. The Royal Proclamation of 1763 was the basis of this decision, as Lord Watson indicated that Aboriginal title existed only as "a personal and usufructuary right, dependent upon the good will of the Sovereign" (Bell and Asch 1997: 47–8).

It was not until the Calder case of 1973 that a serious challenge was mounted in the Supreme Court questioning the assumption that Aboriginal title "was allowed only at the Crown's pleasure." This case was the first time that Canadian law acknowledged that Aboriginal title existed prior to the colonization of North America and, as such, prior to the Royal Proclamation. This decision forced the government of Canada to overhaul its land claims negotiation process, because Aboriginal title was now seen as an inherent right, not one existing "at the pleasure of the Crown." In later Supreme Court decisions, such as in *Guerin* (1984), *Sparrow* (1990), *Van der Peet* (1996), *Gladstone* (1996), *Delgamuukw* (1997), *Marshall* (1999), *Marshall* (2005), and *Kapp* (2008), the basis of Aboriginal rights was further expanded and clarified, not only with regard to land title, but also into areas of resource use for ceremonial and commercial purposes.

Would it be accurate to conclude then that the Canadian judiciary has advanced the process of Aboriginal self-determination? Dalton (2006) has argued quite strongly to the contrary. Although it is commonly thought that the watershed Supreme Court of Canada cases represent a gradual trend wherein Aboriginal peoples have gained increasing protection under Canadian common law, an alternative interpretation is suggested. Dalton's argument is based on the suggestion that, ultimately, the Canadian government has tended towards higher levels of support for more extensive rights for Aboriginal peoples than has the judiciary, and most notably the Supreme Court of Canada, despite the destructive treatment of Aboriginal peoples by the Canadian state. The reasoning behind this assessment is that judges have introduced and applied various legal tests that have ultimately resulted in further impediments to the expansion of broad Aboriginal rights under Section 35(1) of the Constitution Act, 1982.

If the Canadian judiciary can be seen to be an impediment to Aboriginal self-determination, and the Canadian state as generally not predisposed to expanding these rights, then there can be an understandable expectation that frustration would mount among certain sectors of the Aboriginal population – leading to further protests, resistance activities, and confrontations. While land claims were being pursued in the courtrooms of the nation, Native activism, primarily beginning in the 1960s, brought Aboriginal claims to the attention of the wider Canadian public.

Chapter Four

The Politics of Resistance and Confrontation

I'm personally pissed off – a helluva lot of my fellow Indian people are pissed off, but you know what that does – it builds up a feeling inside to fight.
> – Andrew Nicholas, *The Only Good Indian* (1970: 42–3)

> This Piece of Land
> We Stand on, is Our
> Flesh n Blood,
> Bone n Marrow
> Of Our Bodies, This
> Is Why we Choose
> To Die Here at
> Anishinabe Park
>> – Sign posted at Anicinabe Park, Kenora, Ontario, 1974

The Indian Land Claims, not only in Kenora, but throughout the whole of Canada, are absurd and should not even be discussed by the government. Every Canadian has the opportunity to work and buy land, but no one is entitled to a free hand-out.
> – Eleanor Jacobson, *Bended Elbow: Kenora Ontario Talks Back* (1975: 14)

Many Canadians no doubt wonder why in this country there are so many protests and confrontations involving Aboriginal peoples. Hardly a month goes by, especially in the summer, when one does not read about a highway, bridge, or border crossing being blockaded. There are confrontations with police over burial grounds, over land

claims of various sorts, and over construction sites. Some of the protesters are armed with rifles, and police retaliate with their own heavy
tactical equipment. At times shots are fired – both police and protesters
have been killed in such skirmishes. This is hardly, one might think, the
peaceable country that many Canadians think, or wish, Canada to be.

The wider question in these acts of resistance is why there are not
adequate means of conflict resolution in this country so that such violent confrontations that endanger people's lives are not necessary or
can be brought to a more amicable solution. Canada's political leaders,
both at the provincial and federal levels, appear reticent about becoming involved, at least until the confrontation goes too far with property
damage and personal injury. Why, also, are the officers of the various
police forces placed in harm's way, without adequate guidelines as to
their proper conduct in such instances? Why is there not the political
will in Canada to deal with the issues before they become violent and
out of control?

The purpose of this chapter is to examine various Aboriginal conflicts from the mid-1970s to more recently. We are particularly interested in the ultimate nature of these conflicts, how they played out, and
if they were finally resolved in some satisfactory manner. What have
we learned, if anything, over these past few decades about dispute resolution regarding Aboriginal protests and confrontations? But first, a
brief discourse about resistance follows.

Contested Ground: The Nature of Resistance

In an article discussing "strategies of resistance," Allahar (1998: 338)
defines *resistance* as "any action, whether physical, verbal or psychological, and whether individual or collective, that seeks to undo the
negative consequences of being categorized for racial reasons ... Resistance [can] be seen as a political act ultimately tied to the wider cultural
forces that frame it." Allahar's approach is an attempt "to understand
some ways in which the concept of race can be used or manipulated to
resist or mollify the deleterious consequences of racism" (ibid.).

Three different strategies of resistance can be identified (Allahar 1998:
338–52). The first, which is not commonly thought of as resistance, is
multiculturalism. Multiculturalism is seen as a means of resistance because it involves a strategic retreat. In this case, there is a rejection of the
means to achieve acceptance into the majority group, by integration or
other sociocultural means, and a rejection by minority group members

of the dominant group's culture and value system. The retreat is into the original or traditional culture, its norms and values. This strategy could be seen as a form of accommodation, as it is often portrayed in the sociological literature, and involves separate or culturally parallel institutions such as schools, churches, or community centres.

A second strategy involves the politics of assimilation, that is, a strategy whereby members of the minority group accept the normative value system of the dominant society and attempt to "pass" into it. In a sense, this is a strategy by which the path of least resistance is followed, and it conforms to the definition of resistance quoted above because it is a strategy that seeks to undo the negative consequences of racial categorization, even though it is a rejection of the policy of multiculturalism. This strategy is political to the extent that an attempt is made to negotiate the terms under which the minority group is accepted into the social structure of the dominant one. "In Canada today," as Alfred and Corntassel (2011: 140) observe, "many Indigenous people have embraced the Canadian government's label of 'aboriginal,' along with the concomitant and limited notion of postcolonial justice framed within the institutional structure of the state ... 'aboriginalism' is a legal, political, and cultural discourse designed to serve an agenda of silent surrender to an inherently unjust relation at the root of the colonial state itself."

A third strategy of resistance involves neither accommodation nor assimilation, and it is the most commonly thought of approach that involves the violent or physical engagement of the oppressor. Typically, this form of violent resistance is not particularly well planned or coordinated, if at all. Also, there is generally lacking a clearly articulated vision of the new social order that the group hopes to achieve. This resistance is often uncoordinated because of its predominately spontaneous nature and a lack of effective leadership that is able to control the violence. Indeed, the violence may turn inward, as the minority group members jostle for positions of control and argue over strategy and the means to achieve group goals. It is not only the interstitial "ground" between dominant and minority group that is contested, but also the coordination, visions, and strategic means of addressing wrongs are in dispute.

This is the sense in which Frantz Fanon's *The Wretched of the Earth* (1963) argues that decolonization is a violent process by necessity, but in the early phase of resistance, the colonized are sometimes unable to direct their frustration and anger at the colonizer. Instead, the anger is directed inwards, against their fellows. In time, however, as the struggle builds, there is the realization that the settler is not any more inherently superior to the Native, and this "discovery shakes the world in a very necessary manner" (p. 45). In Fanon's resistance scenario, violence and colonialism are inseparable phenomena.

Frantz Fanon also poignantly captures the ironies of the resistance to colonialism, especially in terms of reinvention. The "new Natives" are forced to find their own way along a path that is neither tribal nor Western since, as Emma LaRocque (2010: 157) states, "We cannot accept that human progress begins and ends with European culture. Because it does not." For Fanon, there is a certain inevitability of reinvention with resistance, in a mobilizing of human creativity. LaRocque, however, counters with, "I believe we must reinvent ourselves." She continues, "our country, our Americas, our world. By reinvention, I do not mean prefabrication or myth-making, I mean, among other things, throwing off the weight of antiquity, and, by doing so, offering new possibilities for reconstruction" (p. 158).

Resistance to oppression can, therefore, take many shapes, either through passive forms of non-compliance or through violent confrontation, with various blendings of these extremes in between. LaRocque begins her book on Native resistance discourse, in the opening chapter on "Representation and Resistance," by explaining that her work is about "the inevitable Aboriginal contrapuntal reply to Canada's colonial constructs. What will emerge is a resistance born from the contested ground upon which we, the Canadian colonizer-colonialist and Native colonized, have built our troubled discourse" (p. 3). Aboriginal resistance in Canada is rooted in the colonizer-colonized complex, and the power that is maintained by the colonizer over the colonized.

LaRocque (pp. 4–16) points to a significant issue concerning the nature of cultural representation and its relationship with acts of resistance. She refers to "the devastating impact of White-written judgement on Native peoples," such as the portrayal of Indigenous peoples as savages or other dehumanizing characterizations. Thus, "this developing counter-discourse may best be understood as a resistance response to gross misrepresentation. This misrepresentation is no benign cross-cultural misunderstanding, though there was and is certainly that, but rather it was and is a war of words, words that have animalized and demonized Aboriginal peoples" (p. 4). The texts of various writings relating to European colonization have served the various material and ideological ends of the settler population, justifying the exploitation of the colonized.

Resistance can be understood as a form of racial politics, at least to the extent that it is a fight against racist constructions. Resistance, at one level, is a power struggle and engagement for control over the colonial discourse. Early on in the Native-settler encounter, Aboriginal peoples who had learned the rudiments of Western literacy began to challenge or retaliate against the way in which they were portrayed, which was usually in a stereotypical manner. Robert Berkhofer (1978), for example, in *The White Man's Indian* traces the history of stereotypes and legal designations, especially relating to the term *Indian*, the White man's invention. If words are power, then control over the lexicon of oppression is an important fact of resistance.

In Canada, as Indigenous scholars Voyageur and Calliou (2011: 206–7) explain, "Aboriginal peoples resisted control by the Canadian state in many different ways. They made – and continue to make – persistent attempts to exercise independence through political, economic, and self-governing initiatives." Resistance has taken the form of protesting the Indian Act from the beginning, and opposing the long history of the government's assimilation program. The courts have been used to resist the dispossession of Aboriginal lands. In the political arena, resistance has been expressed by the growing numbers of Aboriginal lawyers, judges, and professors. We are also reminded of Manitoba MLA Elijah Harper's 1990 resistance to the passage of the Meech Lake Accord constitutional amendments, on the ground that it did not adequately deal with Aboriginal rights.

Going back farther in history, the Red River Rebellion was the first act of Aboriginal resistance that the new government of Canada faced following Confederation in 1867 (Madden 2008: 327–31). The Metis, led by Louis Riel, initially opposed the surveying of the land they occupied following the 1869 transfer of Rupert's Land from the Hudson's Bay Company. The Metis created a provisional government and undertook to negotiate directly with the Canadian government to establish a new province, which they called *Assiniboia*. Riel's men also arrested Thomas Scott, a member of the pro-Canadian faction against the provisional government, and subsequently executed him on charges of treason.

A military force, known as the Wolseley Expedition, was then sent to the new province of Manitoba, created in 1870, to enforce federal authority. As the expedition approached the Red River, Riel fled to the United States. In his absence, he was elected to the Canadian Parliament three times, but never took his seat. He eventually returned to Canada in 1885 and led the ill-fated North-West Rebellion, was subsequently tried, convicted of treason, and executed by hanging.

The Metis were consistently a presence in Canada's nation-building process, although "it is eventually important to note," Madden (2008: 330) asserts, "that Canada's response [or in some cases lack thereof] to Metis collective actions underlies many of the current challenges that exist between the Metis nation and Canadian governments. For example, while Canada proceeded to deal with Indians as collectives through negotiating treaties and setting aside land bases – that is, reserves – for them, its policy towards Metis was substantially different. By and large, the Metis were dealt with as individuals rather than as an Aboriginal people with collective rights and interests." However, defeat at the Battle of Batoche in 1885 did not prevent the Metis from continuing to organize and gather politically into the future in an attempt to have their rights and lands recognized by the government.

Disputes over land continued throughout Canadian history as a focal point of Aboriginal protest and resistance to unjust treatment. In the political arena, resistance was expressed in the strong opposition to the 1969 White Paper, in which an attempt was made to abolish the Indian Affairs Department and devolve federal responsibility to the provinces. Aboriginal resistance led to the violent and highly publicized crisis in 1990 at Oka, Quebec, over lands that the Mohawks claimed were the site of a traditional burial ground. Gufstafson Lake in British Columbia was the site of another armed conflict, in 1996, in which a heavy exchange of gunfire ensued. Gunfire also led to the death of Dudley George, in 1995, during the dispute over a land claim at Ipperwash, Ontario.

The source of these conflicts and Aboriginal resistance, as Indigenous scholar Bonita Lawrence (2011) remarks, is revealed in "the historical record of how [Aboriginal] land was acquired – the forcible and relentless dispossession of Indigenous peoples, the theft of their territories, and the implementation of legislation and policies designed to affect their total disappearance as people" (p. 69). The problem is that history is written outside Indigenous perspectives, with the result that "we cannot grasp the overall picture of a focused, concerted process of invasion and land theft" (p. 70). It is necessary, therefore, to "decolonize history," to the extent that the dominant perspective that sees the colonization process as essentially a benign one be counterbalanced with the accounts of the members of Native communities and their experiences of racism and genocide.

These are the perspectives that most people gain through the reading of Canadian history and from the contemporary media focus on "images of aggressive and bloodthirsty savages [which] continue to pervade Canadian society – images that date back to the European's first arrival in North America and that are seen daily in movies and TV programs" (Belanger 2010: 174). The images that most North Americans, therefore, have of Aboriginal peoples are of warriors. Belanger does note that although warrior societies continue to operate in First Nations communities, he cautions against making generalizations since not all First Nations claim to have such groups (pp. 174–7). An added caveat is that, despite the name, most warrior societies were actually for the most part intended for peacekeeping forces. There was an attempt to inculcate in the young men a greater sense of self-control.

The Aboriginal warrior as peacekeeper has not fared well in recent media imagery because of self-proclaimed warriors who have initiated confrontations with Canadian authorities. These may not be members of traditional warrior societies, but individuals acting on their own out of frustration with what they perceive have been injustices inflicted on their communities. Statistics on resistance activities may be difficult to obtain.

Nevertheless, Wilkes (2004) has conducted a study of band-level political mobilization in Canada. During the period from 1981 to 2000, there were 266 instances of active resistance nationally, involving more than 120 First Nations communities. Wilkes found that one-fifth of bands in Canada had at least one or more such events. The tactics most often used were blockades, marches, demonstrations, and protests (more than 70%). Rates of mobilization were higher in Saskatchewan, British Columbia, and the Maritimes than for bands in the other provinces, probably because of the higher number of bands in the former areas.

The criteria for band-level mobilization in Wilkes's study were that such events were non-routine and non-institutional. This would exclude from analysis annual cultural events and challenges before the courts, but would include mobilizations around issues such as band rights to resources and land or band rights to education. This analysis did not include Indigenous mobilization at the pan-tribal or supra-tribal level. It is significant to note that of the 558 bands (First Nations) in Canada during the time of the study, 436 (78%) had no political mobilization event.

In terms of frequency of such events, there were very few in the early 1980s, although there were an unusually high number in the late 1980s and, particularly, in 1990. The rise of band-level political mobilization in the late 1980s could be at least partly explained by the passage of Bill C-31, in 1985, and the strain on band resources created by the doubling of the annual growth rate of the registered Indian population after this date. The Meech Lake Accord was drafted in 1987, for which the federal government failed to include consultation with First Nations, thus galvanizing bands into political action. Moreover, it could be surmised that many of the band-level political mobilizations in 1990 were in support of the Mohawk warriors from Kanesatake during the Oka Crisis. By the late 1990s, there were very few such events at the band level in any given year.

The most frequently used tactic was a blockade, with almost 50 per cent of events falling into this category. Marches, demonstrations, and protests are the next most frequent, accounting for over 20 per cent of the 266 cases. Occupations of land and buildings comprise another 8 per cent, and other, infrequent types included boycotts, fish-ins, and log-ins. It is significant that a very small minority of band-level political mobilizations, less than 2 per cent, used violence or destruction of property as the sole tactic (Wilkes 2004: 451–4).

More research is needed to further investigate the factors leading to acts of Aboriginal resistance, including the impact of provincial and national economic differences.

The literature draws a strong connection between a coalescence of factors contributing to unrest in Aboriginal communities, such as colonial policies of oppression and racial intolerance by settler populations, and resistance as a mechanism to cope with or otherwise counteract these negative influences. In "Decolonizing Resistance, Challenging Colonial States," for example, Sharma and Wright (2008–9) point to the problem of defining in the first place the identity of the settler population(s): "We challenge the conflation," they assert, "between processes of migration and those of colonialism. We ask whether it is historically accurate or analytically precise to describe as *settler colonialism* the forced movements of enslaved Africans, the movement of unfree indentured Asians, or the subsequent Third World displacements and migrations of people from across the globe, many of them indigenous peoples themselves" (p. 121, original emphasis).

This comment was made in reaction to an article by Lawrence and Dua (2005) entitled "Decolonizing Antiracism," in which the claim is made that Aboriginal people "cannot see themselves in antiracism contexts and Aboriginal activism against settler domination takes place without people of color as allies" (p. 122). Furthermore, Lawrence and Dua contend that postcolonial critiques of national liberation strategies serve only to secure the colonization of Indigenous peoples by contributing to "the ongoing legitimization of Indigenous nationhood" (p. 128). Such attacks, Lawrence and Dua maintain, are "are *attacks* against both the pre-colonial identity of indigenous people and of their contemporary efforts at achieving sovereignty" (cited in Sharma and Wright 2008–9: 120, original emphasis).

The exception that Sharma and Wright make with Lawrence and Dua's contention – that people of colour have not helped the cause of Aboriginal rights – is with the implication of non-whites within the colonial project. For example, Lawrence and Dua's central argument is "people of color are settlers. Broad differences exist between those brought as slaves, currently working as migrant laborers, are [sic] refugees without legal documentation, or émigrés who have obtained citizenship. Yet people of color live on land that is appropriated and contested, where Aboriginal peoples are denied nationhood and access to their own lands" (2005: 134).

Clearly, there are differences of opinion concerning alliances within a political mobilization movement, alliances that one group may forge, or not forge, with another such group. Resistance is a matter of achieving the goals or objectives of one's own group first, regardless of broader bonds that may be perceived, for example, in the colonial context. For the Aboriginal populations of Canada, access to ancestral lands is a key aspect of asserting their nationhood and advancing their sovereignty project. Other oppressed groups, such as people of colour or Asian immigrants, may well be lumped in with white settlers when these other groups may also be seen by First Nations people as complicit in the appropriation of Aboriginal lands or in impeding Aboriginal goals of sovereignty and nationhood.

Sharma and Wright (2008–9), in rebuttal, even go so far as to question whether efforts at decolonization that rely on ideas of "nationhood" have any chance of success, either in Canada or elsewhere. They ask, for example, "Are critiques of naturalized nationhoods and nationalisms tantamount to support for colonialism? Are there other more transformative and more effective paths to liberation than through the national sovereignty projects?" (p. 121). These are important considerations in the context of resistance struggles. Surely, one would think, Aboriginal peoples in Canada would prefer not to have their efforts in achieving nationhood construed as in the end supportive of the very colonialism that their struggles are attempting to overcome. Nevertheless, it would appear to be a particularly disingenuous act on their part if their emphasis on a land base as a cornerstone of Aboriginal rights actually served to sever ties with other struggling groups and if it also served to lump people of colour in with the oppressing settling populations.

Our discussion in this section draws to a close with the comments made by political philosopher James Tully (2008) on "internal colonisation and arts of resistance" (pp. 258–71). Tully begins this discussion by pointing to a fundamental problem concerning the *"development of Western societies and the pre-existence and continuing resistance of Indigenous societies on the same territory"* (p. 259, original emphasis). It is appropriate that Tully refers to "territory" (or land) since that is such a fundamental aspect of Aboriginal rights in Canada and the continuing source of the tension among the authors discussed above in the dialogue over who are the settlers? or put differently, who is oppressing whom?

For Tully (2008) "this general problematic" revolves around relationships commonly called the "internal colonisation" of Indigenous peoples and how these relationships become interwoven with the "arts of resistance." Internal colonization is, first of all, a reference to the historical processes that have spawned structures of domination over Indigenous peoples, and the territories in which they live, without their consent. Such historical processes, in turn, have led to resistance as a response to these structures. The structures of domination that have been instituted over time become "relatively stable, immovable and irreversible vis-à-vis any direct confrontation by the colonized population" (p. 259).

Domination of the Indigenous peoples takes the form of "incorporation" and "domestication." Structures of incorporation refer to the wide array of techniques used by the national government both directly and indirectly that serve as mechanisms of response to Aboriginal peoples' resistance. The struggles of Indigenous groups in North America have had more to do with attempts to modify the techniques of government in such a way that more control over their territories might be gained, and a degree of self-government achieved, than they have with finding solutions outside these historically developing structures. Internal colonization serves to deflect any direct confrontation away from these background structures of domination, as Tully suggests. However, "there is not a sharp distinction between structures of domination and techniques of government in practice, as what appears to be part of the immovable background to one generation can be called into question and become the object of struggle and modification by another, and vice versa ... the processes of internal colonisation have developed in response to the struggles of Indigenous peoples for freedom both against and within colonisation on the one hand, and in response to overriding objectives of the settler societies and the capitalist market on the other" (p. 260).

Our attention is now turned to specific examples of resistance among Aboriginal groups in Canada. The purpose of this examination is to afford a comparative view of various political mobilizations with the idea of drawing attention to similarities and differences in the response to colonization over time. It will also allow for a return later on to the foregoing discussion of the nature of resistance, especially in terms of Tully's reference to "strategies of extinguishment" (p. 262).

The Ojibway Warrior Society, Kenora, Ontario (1974)

The 1974 tourist season around Kenora, in northwestern Ontario, should have been well under way by the summer months, but there was an unusual interruption. About 150 members of the Ojibway Warrior Society,[1] of which an unknown number were armed with rifles and shotguns of unknown vintage, took possession of Anicinabe Park on 22 July, in an attempt to back their claim to a land title. One Ojibway Warrior rested his rifle on his hip as he bent down to talk to the driver of a sedan that had just pulled in for camping. He explained that there would be a delay in the opening of the park until the title to the park was settled.

At issue was a dispute between the town of Kenora and local Aboriginal residents over the ownership of a fourteen-acre park. The Ojibway Warrior Society contended that the park was illegally sold to Kenora in 1959 by the Department of Indian Affairs. Minister of Indian and Northern Affairs Judd Buchanan issued a ruling that the park property, purchased by the department in 1929 from a Kenora resident, never constituted an Indian reserve. On this basis, Minister Buchanan indicated that there were insufficient grounds to support the Ojibways' claim to the park (*Times-News* [Thunder Bay], 25 April 1975).

There was a nervous tension among all who were involved. The members of the Ojibway Warrior Society realized that a fight could break out at any time. Poised to enter the park were 143 members of the Ontario Provincial Police, reinforced by a contingent of Kenora policemen. Most of the OPP officers had been flown in from Toronto and Thunder Bay on chartered flights. Inspector Walter Mychalyshyn of the Kenora police explained, "This is different – this is a confrontation situation and we don't want a shootout" (ibid.).

The local, non-Ojibway residents of Kenora were less than sympathetic about the Aboriginal people's reasons for occupying the park. For them, the summer was their one chance to make some money to last them through the winter. They depended on the tourist dollars that came in from southern Ontario and the northern United States, after which many probably go on employment insurance, as the town of Kenora practically diminishes by half after the fishing and moose hunting season ends. Local sentiments were apparently described by Eleanor Jacobson, a nurse, in her publication entitled *Bended Elbow: Kenora Ontario Talks Back* (1975). She quotes a police officer, who she claims was heard saying, "Look, a white group couldn't pull this crap so why should they?" The officer continued, "Pointing firearms to start discharging weapons and unlawful assembly are all matters dealt with severely under the Criminal Code" (p. 3). She goes on to say that "the white population of Kenora is just fed up. They're talking of water-bombing the Indians to force them out of the park and chasing them out of the town with tear gas" (p. 5).

As far as the tourist industry was concerned, the Ojibways said it didn't matter to them because they didn't profit from it much as they were seldom hired by the local white businessmen. Jacobson states, "Local businesses have hired Indians, but they found that they are not reliable. They will show up for a few days or a couple of months at the longest, but when they get their pay cheque they get drunk, disappear and forget they ever had a job" (p. 5).

Louis Cameron was one of the leaders of the Ojibway Warrior Society. He was joined by Dennis Banks and a few associates who arrived from Wounded Knee, South Dakota, to lend their support. The term "pan-Indian" was just coming into use, implying that cultural differences among the Aboriginal peoples of North America are a secondary consideration to the shared experiences of colonial suppression and dispossession of their ancestral lands. Jacobson calls them "these misfit

Indians from the U.S.A." (p. 4), and Louis Cameron is referred to as "this young thug" (p. 2).

In an ironic twist, it was Jacobson's *Bended Elbow* booklet that drew outside attention in Thunder Bay and Toronto newspapers, and ultimately in Queen's Park, to the Anicinabe Park occupation. I was conducting ethnographic fieldwork in the Armstrong area of northwestern Ontario, about two hundred kilometres east of Kenora, during 1974–75 and had an opportunity to collect many of the letters to the editor and items of news coverage, especially in Thunder Bay's *Times-News*. The residents of Thunder Bay were concerned that all the people of northwestern Ontario would be branded as racist hicks. "We have a university here [Lakehead University], a symphony orchestra, libraries and a museum – there is more to the north than just rednecks" was the sentiment generally expressed.

In Kenora itself there was a backlash against the *Bended Elbow* portrayal. The local Ministerial Association had two meetings on the issue and planned a joint statement. Pastor Leon Linquist of the Lutheran Church delivered a stinging criticism to his congregation one Sunday morning. He called Jacobson's publication "a pornographic, racist, libellous, slanderous, repetitious, angry coarse book littered with half-truths" (*Times-News*, 23 April 1975). Over at the Anglican Church, the Right Rev. James Allen, Bishop of Keewatin, asserted that "the really unfortunate thing about the book, is the tremendous hurt it does to the many Indian people who do care and who bear such hurt already ... it will help no one if stupidity, anger and prejudice reign supreme. Acts of violence accomplish nothing but greater hostility" (ibid.).

It did not take long before the initial reasons behind the occupation of Anicinabe Park were virtually forgotten. Various Ontario Aboriginal organizations soon became involved, such as the Union of Ontario Indians, Grand Council of Treaty No. 3, and Treaty 4 Tribal Council, as well as the Association of Iroquois and Allied Indians, who requested that the province set up a joint committee at the ministerial level to examine the situation. In fact, representatives of the four Aboriginal groups met with Premier William Davis and the Ontario cabinet to seek a mechanism for continuing discussions with the provincial government. Three briefs were presented to cabinet showing that while Aboriginal peoples in Ontario are not included in the constitutional framework of the province, the policies of the government nonetheless do affect them. Among the topics that Aboriginal people wanted to talk about were land issues, fishing and hunting rights, pollution and conservation, and the harvest of wild rice in the Lake of the Woods area (*Times-News*, 1 May 1975).

Louis Cameron and other members of the Ojibway Warrior Society agreed to end their occupation of Anicinabe Park when weapons charges against them were dropped and proposals for a negotiated settlement of the land claim were instituted. Peter Kelly, president of Grand Council of Treaty No. 3, stated that there would not be another occupation of Anicinabe Park. Kelly indicated that there were ongoing discussions between Indian Land Claims commissioners and the Indian chiefs of the Lake of the Woods area. The chiefs of the Grand Council asked that the Ojibway Warrior Society refrain from taking up arms and that the Warrior Society's leader, Louis Cameron, agree to honour the request. However, the chiefs rejected Indian Affairs Minister Judd Buchanan's ruling that the Aboriginal people of the area do not have a claim to the park. The minister was asked by the Grand Council of Treaty No. 3 to settle the land claim and use the Indian Land Commission as an avenue to reach a settlement. Kelly made an announcement that Buchanan's statement "had not finalized the matter" (*Times-News*, 25 April 1975).

The chiefs also passed a resolution condemning the *Bended Elbow* publication by Eleanor Jacobson. "We are not hung up on the book," Grand Council President Kelly stated, "The most important thing in the town is for people to get on with the business of getting along together" (*Times-News*, 25 April 1975).

Meanwhile, as most members of Cameron's party were from the nearby White Dog and Grassy Narrows reserves, they became preoccupied with the debilitating effects of minimata disease, a result of the mercury pollution emanating from the Reed Paper Company mill in Kenora. To avoid lawsuits, Reed Paper closed its plant and pulled its operation out of the province. As far as the *Bended Elbow* publication is concerned, it was still generating interest over three decades after it came out, as evidenced by a lengthy article on the subject in the *American Indian Quarterly* in 2007 (Anderson and Robertson 2007).

The Teme-Augama Anishnabai Logging Blockade (1988)

Members of the Teme-Augama Anishnabai (Temagami) First Nation, or "People of the Deep Water," in northern Ontario, set up a blockade on 1 June 1988, on a road that was under construction by the Ontario government. This road was to provide access to logging companies who intended to cut down one of the last stands of ancient white pine forest in the province. The two camps of the 1988 road blockade were named Wendaban and Misabi, after two traditional family hunting grounds, thus establishing links with their ancestors and cultural way of life. Chief Gary Potts (1990: 201) explains the reason for the blockade: "If our land dies, we die. This land is our Crown. This land, along with the seasons affecting it, is our touchstone to past life and the gateway to future life, both human and non-human."

The Teme-Augama Anishnabai political mobilization is based on their claim that they were omitted from the 1850 Robinson-Huron Treaty when it was signed. The Robinson-Huron Treaty covers a vast area of Aboriginal lands north of Lake Huron, and the Teme-Augama Anishnabai have laid claim to about four thousand square miles (10,000 km) of land surrounding Lake Temagami situated about a hundred miles (160 km) northwest of North Bay. By about 1875, Chief Tonene began to request that his people become part of the treaty in order to gain protection from the encroachment of timber companies and settlers who had already begun to invade the Lake Temagami area (Hodgins and Benidickson 1989, McNeil 1990: 185–221).

In 1884, the federal government surveyed, a hundred square miles in area, at the southern end of Lake Temagami; however, the Ontario government refused to transfer the land, apparently because of the rich timber within the proposed reserve. Logging began in the Temagami forest in 1920, and in the 1960s an all-season road was constructed. The logging operations during this period were of the "clear-cutting" variety, leaving little of the original forest standing. Then, in 1972, proposals were under way to construct an $80-million resort in this area.

The Teme-Augama Anishnabai responded by filing land cautions in 110 townships within their traditional territory, in an attempt to assert Aboriginal ownership. This action effectively froze development of all Crown lands; however, the government allowed the logging to continue. It took until 1989 for the matter to reach the Ontario Court of Appeal, with the intention that the case would eventually reach the Supreme Court of Canada (Hodgins, Lischke, and McNab 2003).

While these legal proceeding were before the courts, the Teme-Augama Anishnabai decided to continue their blockade because they reasoned that there would be little left of their forest if they waited for a court decision. The loggers, however, felt that they had the right to continue their work on the ground that there had never been an injunction issued preventing logging of the Lake Temagami area. Thus, two sides, the Aboriginal First Nations and workers from the surrounding area, both felt justification and frustration by the situation, which was in a jurisdictional limbo. Clearly, the Ontario government had a responsibility to adjudicate this matter in a speedy manner or, at least, to cease all logging, lest violence break out between the conflicting parties.

Chief Potts (1990: 207) explains, "The flashpoint that brought about our road blockades in 1988 was the decision of the Ontario government to extend logging into the so-called Wakimika triangle, which lies at the very heart of n'Daki-Menan. In the centre of this area is what we call the Conjuring Rock, among our most sacred sites, one of the places to which we have always retired, alone or in groups, to make contact with the spirits."

Eventually, on 8 December 1988 – 191 days after the blockade was established – the Ontario Court of Appeal ordered that the blockade be taken down and that no further work take place in the disputed area other than surveys. Eventually, on 27 February 1989, the Appeal Court of Ontario issued a unanimous decision rejecting the appeal of the Teme-Augama Anishnabai. Three reasons were given for the decision that the Aboriginal title claim of the Teme-Augama Anishnabai was not legally valid: (1) Taigawene (another chief in the area) signed the treaty on behalf of the Teme-Augama Anishnabai in 1850 at Sault Ste. Marie, (2) acceptance of treaty money in 1883 constituted an adhesion by the Teme-Augama Anishnabai to the treaty, and (3) "the Sovereign" intended to take the lands of the Teme-Augama Anishnabai.

The first point was disputed on the ground that there was no evidence that Chief Taigawene represented any band at the treaty negotiations other than his own. On the second point, it was countered that the Royal Proclamation of 1763 provided protection against the surrender of Aboriginal lands by deception, and the Teme-Augama Anishnabai – who did accept government money – would certainly have had no idea that they were doing so as a validation of their participation in an existing treaty. The third point was disputed on the ground that it has never been made clear what the intentions of "the Sovereign" ever were. Thus, as far as the Teme-Augama Anishnabai are concerned, their land was unjustifiably taken away from them by deceit and government fiat. "We are not giving up our struggle," Chief Potts (1990: 227) explains, "we are now focusing on public education."

Eventually, a Supreme Court of Canada decision was reached, on 15 August 1991(*Ontario [Attorney General]* v. *Bear Island Foundation*). In this case, the Bear Island Foundation and Gary Potts, etc. are the Appellants and the attorney general for Ontario is the respondent. Also listed as respondents are, among others, the attorney general of Canada; the attorneys general of Quebec, British Columbia, Alberta, and Newfoundland; and the Union of Ontario Indians, the Association of Iroquois and Allied Indians, and the Assembly of First Nations.[2]

The decision, in part, reads:

> In particular, the Indians exercised sufficient occupation of the lands in question throughout the relevant period to establish an aboriginal right.
>
> It was unnecessary, however, to examine the specific nature of the aboriginal right because that right was surrendered, whatever the situation on the signing of the Robinson-Huron Treaty, by arrangements subsequent to the treaty by which the Indians adhered to the treaty in exchange for treaty annuities and a reserve. The Crown breached its fiduciary obligations to the Indians by failing to comply with some of the obligations under this agreement; these matters currently form the subject of negotiations between the parties. These breaches do not alter the fact that the aboriginal right was extinguished.

One can only speculate, at this point, on the reasons why such Aboriginal groups, for example, the Union of Ontario Indians and the Assembly of First Nations that one would normally expect to support the Teme-Augama Anishnabai cause acted against them. We only can only assume these large Aboriginal political organizations felt that their interests were better served by supporting the Ontario government – and not risking a challenge to the legal basis of the Robinson-Huron Treaty of 1850 – than by siding with such a small First Nation as the Teme-Augama Anishnabai who, one would think, would be dismayed by such a lack of support from "their own people."

The Innu and the Goose Bay Air Base Occupation (1988)

The jet noise from the low-level flights of the NATO exercises out of Goose Bay, Labrador, for some time were terrifying to the Innu hunters and their families in their territory which they call *Nitassinan* or "our land." A researcher on a field trip with the Sheshatshiu Innu during May 1988 provides the following account of this experience: "as if hit by an abrupt, incredible blast of noise. The tent canvas shook. I fell back on the floor, ears rang, and I felt my heart begin to pound painfully. Before I had time to recover I heard Janet scream my name ... Another blast of noise struck, and the recorder's volume meter jumped crazily in the split second it took another jet to fly over us. I felt shaken and stood up unsteadily. My initial fear changed to anger ... The twenty-tonne jet bomber had swooped just thirty meters above our heads, flying at 900 kilometers an hour" (Wadden 2001: 36).

In his ethnographic study, Georg Henriksen (1973) describes the Innu, or *Naskapi* to use an older term, as living "on the edge of the white man's world." The Innu have always highly valued their life as caribou hunters; the white world is seen as a sometimes useful source of medicine and material goods, but not as a world in which they would wish to live permanently. In a postscript, entitled "The Future of the Naskapi," Henriksen presents a not altogether bright picture of what the Innu can expect in their future relations with Western societies: "in this confrontation [with industrialized nations], they are fighting a losing battle for their social and cultural integrity. In my opinion, a most important problem is how to protect these cultures from disintegration and at the same time help them to attain an effective bargaining position *vis-à-vis* the outside world" (p. 115). As it turns out, the Innu could not depend on anyone else to "protect" them from the disintegrating effects of the outside world on their hunting way of life.

The Innu have traditionally followed a nomadic way of live, travelling between the Barren Ground of Labrador to hunt caribou in the winter and the Davis Inlet area to fish in the summer. Traders and missionaries attempted to influence their lifestyle when the Innu were living on the coast, but for the most part, this influence was fairly minimal. In 1927, a border was established between Labrador and Quebec, which divided the Innu into two groups under different government jurisdictions. More significant changes resulted in 1941, with the construction of a government-built military base in central Labrador, which became the city of Happy Valley–Goose Bay. Then, in the 1960s, the Innu were forcibly removed from their traditional territories in the Labrador interior to the coastal areas of Sheshatshiu and Davis Inlet. This removal of the Indigenous population enabled the government to act unimpededly in implementing various government projects (Ryan 1988).

One of these concerned the Churchill Falls hydroelectric project in 1972, which diverted major waterways and caused flooding to over four thousand kilometres of Innu hunting and burial grounds. By the end of the 1970s, the federal government had given permission for NATO to use the military base at Goose Bay for low-level test flights. Next, in 1994, nickel deposits were discovered at Voisey's Bay, an area that the

Innu claimed belonged to them, and subsequently in the later 1990s the construction of a highway was begun between Churchill Falls and the Labrador coast (see Alcantara 2000, Armitage and Kennedy 1989).

The Innu had felt overwhelmed by all these projects occurring in their hunting territories and, as a result, decided to take an initiative to make their plight known to the outside world and, if possible, to play a role in further developments. Their initial actions were focused on the low-level flights out of Goose Bay, and so the Innu planned an occupation of the Goose Bay base in September 1988 (Ashini 1990).

Prior to this occupation, Innu leaders engaged in a series of actions in an attempt to express their dissatisfaction with the military flights. A delegation of Innu leaders, for example, travelled to West Germany in 1983 to seek the support of the Green Party. The German Green Party was interested in this visit because, in an ironic twist, the West German government had been promoting the low-level flights in Labrador as a means of protecting the German environment (Lackenbauer 2007). The Green Party, in turn, provided resources to the Innu in the form of contacts with other environmental and Aboriginal support groups capable of bringing the Innu protest to the attention of a wider audience.

Matters escalated rapidly in 1988, with the proposal for the construction of a new $555 million flight facility at the Goose Bay Air Force Base. The Innu leadership wanted to meet the NATO team that was to arrive at Goose Bay to discuss these plans but such a meeting was refused. The Innu community realized then that they had to take more direct action, so on 15 September 1988, about seventy-five members of the Sheshatshiu community began an occupation of one of the Goose Bay airstrips, resulting in the arrest of two leaders (Cox 1990a).

After the arrests, about two hundred Innu people set up a protest campsite outside of the fence surrounding the main runway. By now, the protest was receiving national and international attention, and by December the bombing flights were suspended due to cold weather – so the Innu ended their occupation. In the spring, Innu attempts at an occupation resumed, resulting in more arrests, prosecutions, and jail sentences for five people (*Globe and Mail*, 2 Oct. 1990). However, a trial judge eventually overturned four of the convictions on the ground that the protesters who were charged had believed that they were not trespassing because the Innu had never surrendered the land on which the air base was built (Cox 1990b).

In May 1990, it was announced that the NATO facility would not be built after all, although at the time, low-level flights continued over

Innu territory. Over the ensuing period, from 1992 to 1994, the Innu resumed their protests and periodic occupations of the air base. After that there was a general reduction in the number of low-level flights, and these tended to avoid Innu caribou hunting areas with the use of a satellite monitoring system. The reason given for the decrease in the number of low-level lights was that new strategic approaches were now being used, which resulted in the obsolescence of low-level bombing; thus, the military facility at Goose Bay had become less important to NATO than it had been in previous times.

It will be left to future analysts to determine the extent to which the tactical training facility was abandoned due to the Innu protests and occupations, or due to larger international factors, such as reduction of tensions in the Cold War. Certainly, one can say that the Innu political mobilization demonstrated the effectiveness of bringing their plight to a wider audience and that this action was pivotal in bringing attention to Aboriginal issues in Canada. One can, therefore, say that the Innu were largely successful in protecting themselves and the surrounding wildlife from the debilitating effects of the low-level flights. The protests had internal effects on the Innu as well, to the extent that more effective leadership strategies were developed that could be used in the future should such confrontations emerge again. As Daniel Ashini (1990: 70) states in his article entitled "David Confronts Goliath": "The Innu will continue to use civil disobedience and will continue the fight for our rights in Nitassinan. We will continue to appeal to Canadians' sense of justice. We will not simply disappear off the cultural face of this world without a fight."

The Lubicon Lake Cree Confrontation (1988)

The Crees of Lubicon Lake, in northern Alberta, established a blockade of roads leading into their traditional territory on 15 October 1988, after many years of frustrated negotiations over their land claim. The blockade was into its fifth day when a force of fifty RCMP officers arrived, removed the barricade, and arrested twenty-seven of the Aboriginal protesters. Within two days, Lubicon Chief Bernard Ominayak and Alberta Premier Don Getty agreed to the establishment of a reserve of 250 square kilometres (95 square miles). This agreement was conditional on the approval of the federal government. As with many such political mobilizations over land claims, there is often a lengthy history involved (see Smith 1988, Richardson 1990, Goddard 1991, Martin-Hill 2008).

For many centuries, the Lubicon Crees maintained a traditional hunting-and-trapping lifestyle in the forests of northern Alberta, within about a seventy-mile radius of Lubicon Lake. There was not really any sort of permanent contact with the outside world until 1954, when a missionary built a school at nearby Little Buffalo Lake, where the English language was learned. Even before the missionary school, as far back as 1939, the Lubicon Crees had been attempting to have a reserve settlement established in their area. This initiative stems from an even earlier one, when they learned in 1899 that other Crees in the area had signed a treaty with the government.

Since the Lubicon Crees were not a party to this treaty, they undertook what turned out to be a long-term project, indeed, to find out what their treaty status was. What they learned was that several Lubicon representatives had been "signed up" by the government to the existing Treaty No. 8. While attempts were being made to ascertain the Lubicon Crees' treaty status, a significant portion of their population was lost during the flu epidemic of 1916–18, reducing their numbers from 2,500 to about 200 persons. In 1939, the Lubicon Crees succeeded in gaining legal recognition as a band (Goddard 1991, Martin-Hill 2008).

Over the ensuring decades, encroachment on the Lubicon territory continued, and this provided impetus to settle their land claim. In 1942, an official of the Department of Indian Affairs, Malcolm McCrimmon, apparently removed many names from the registered lists for northern Alberta, including ninety from the Lubicon band roll. He even refused to acknowledge that the Lubicon population qualified as a band: "If my recommendation is approved by the Minister, the number of Indians remaining on the membership list at Lubicon Lake would hardly warrant an establishment of a Reserve" (cited in Martin-Hill 2008: 16).

The Lubicon Crees elected their first chief, Walter Whitehead, in the 1970s and began immediately to conduct a census of the Lubicon membership, which was uncertain because of residents moving back and forth between several settlements. About this time, oil exploration began in the area as well, leading to a sense of urgency for the Lubicon people. One of the initiatives of Chief Whitehead and his council, working with the Alberta Indian Association, was to file a caveat with the Alberta Land Registration Office; however, this caveat was refused by the Alberta government.

Over the next decade, the plight of the Lubicon Crees became increasingly severe. Between 1974 and 1985, welfare dependency increased at an alarming rate. In 1981, according to the band records, only 9 per cent of band members received social assistance; however, by 1985 this proportion had increased to 95 per cent. In addition, by 1980, at least ten major oil companies had taken up positions on Lubicon land and had drilled over four hundred wells. The impacts of these oil and gas developments began to negatively affect the wildlife in the area and the Crees' ability to secure a living from the land, turning many hunters and trappers to welfare dependency. Trapping income declined from a per capita average of over $5,000 in 1979 to just $400 by 1984. In 1979, moose production stood at two hundred but it had declined to nineteen in 1984, with corresponding increases in Lubicon Cree members receiving social assistance (welfare).

It would, therefore, appear from these various statistics that the Lubicon road blockade perhaps had less to do with an outstanding land claim than it did with calling attention to the appalling social and economic conditions that were taking place as a result of outside intrusions into their territory. Unable to make a living in the traditional manner, and unable to stop the oil and gas companies that were causing so much environmental instability, the Lubicon Crees found themselves in a very precarious position. As one fieldworker noted, "The band reported a marked increase in social breakdown at this point [1984–85]" (Martin-Hill 2008: 19).

Chief Ominayak describes the community stress in the following account: "The change in diet, influx of outsiders brought our health down. The T.B. outbreak in the eighties was just the first sign that development was having an impact on our health. There are no sure studies to show exactly the kind of impact. However, we have witnessed a marked increase in alcohol consumption, violence and even suicide. We never had these social problems before. All the development, welfare, nothing to do, nothing to hunt, changed our traditional structure of men having pride in providing for their families" (cited in Martin-Hill 2008: 19).

Matters became even worse in 1988. The provincial government announced that a pulp mill would be built near Peace River, which would involve the granting of a timber lease of eleven thousand square miles, including four thousand square miles of traditional Lubicon territory (Goddard 1991). In February 1989, a series of meetings were held in Edmonton between government representatives and Lubicon band members. These band members wished to take advantage of a clause in Treaty No. 8 that allowed for land to be "held in severalty," meaning that certain families could obtain land if they lived apart from the band. What this essentially meant was that a dissident band had become organized, calling themselves the "Woodland Crees," securing land around Cadotte Lake. The result of this initiative was that the Lubicon land claim was undermined because of a reduction in its membership. Then, in 1992, the Woodland Crees struck a land claims deal, signing up about sixty former Lubicon people to the new band.

In 1998, an agreement in principle was reached with the federal government on a Lubicon determination of membership. However, in the following year, talks with the federal government were suspended as the Lubicon were pressured to include the provincial government in the negotiations. Three neighbouring bands in 2001, including the Woodland Crees, began clear-cut logging within the Lubicon traditional territory. On January 2009, it was announced that TransCanada Pipelines was proceeding with the construction of a controversial pipeline. Then the Lubicon announced, on 8 April 2009, the launching of a "National Lubicon Petition Campaign," calling on the federal government to resume negotiations with the Lubicon First Nation.

The Mohawk Warrior Society, Oka, Quebec (1990)

The most famous clash between Aboriginal protesters and police took place near Oka, Quebec, during the summer of 1990. The so-called Oka Crisis was ostensibly a dispute over a relatively small piece of land designated for the expansion of a golf course. However, as with many of these sorts of disputes, the history behind this one is long and involved (see York and Pindera 1991, Ciaccia 2000, Frideres and Gadacz 2008: 240–5).

The Mohawks were originally located in the Finger Lakes region of upper New York State. By the seventeenth century, some of the Mohawks had converted to Catholicism and moved north into settlements in New France. The dispute between the Kanesatake Mohawks and the residents of Oka can be traced to a land grant that had been made by the governor of New France in 1717 to the Catholic Seminary of St. Sulpice of Montreal. Several years later, in 1721, the Sulpicians founded a community of converts, which included the Mohawks and Algonquian-speaking peoples.

The Mohawks' claim is that the purpose of the original grant for the seminary was intended to be held in trust for the Mohawk First Nation, and that the seminary should not have assumed sole ownership rights. By 1787, the Mohawks had already begun to protest the Sulpician claim to sole ownership of the property but received no satisfaction. The Mohawks of Oka continued their claim well into the next century. Shortly after Confederation, in 1868, Chief Joseph Onasakenrat, the leader of the Mohawk people, wrote a letter to the Sulpician missionaries informing them that they were illegally holding Mohawk land and that the dispute could be settled if the land in question was returned to the Mohawks. When they received no answer to their request, the Mohawks took over possession of the land, in 1869, with a small, armed force; however, the standoff ended when the Mohawks were forced from the property by local authorities.

The dispute continued into the next century. Legal action, in 1912, went all the way to the Judicial Committee of the Privy Council, then the highest court of appeal for Canada. The decision of the Privy Council was that the Mohawks' claim was to be denied because they could not prove that they had occupied the property in question "since time immemorial." There was also the issue of a lack of a treaty, which would have indicated that the land was held in trust for the Mohawks. Essentially, the ruling was that the Mohawks had a right to use and occupy the land but only up until such time as the Sulpicians decided to sell it.

Sale of the property by the Sulpicians occurred in 1936, under protest by the Mohawk community, and the seminary vacated the territory. In 1945, the federal government attempted to resolve the conflict by purchasing some of the remaining Sulpician lands with the intent to forge several such purchases into a reserve for the Kanesatake people. As could be expected, the controversy emerged again, when, in 1961, a golf course was built on some of the disputed land by the municipality of Oka. Despite a Mohawk legal protest to cease construction, most of the land was cleared and a parking lot was constructed close to the Mohawk cemetery. Later, in 1977, the Mohawks filed a claim with the federal Office of Native Claims but it was eventually rejected on technical grounds. These grounds, among several, were that the Mohawks had not maintained sole possession of the land, which at various times was also occupied by both the Algonquin and Iroquois peoples. Another matter was that the Iroquois did not occupy the territory in question before the European possession of this land, and in fact, the Mohawks did not even arrive in the disputed area until after the Sulpician mission was established in the early 1700s. In turn, the Mohawks argued that these details did not negate the fact that the territory in dispute had been occupied by some Aboriginal peoples before the arrival of Europeans and that the specification of occupancy by Mohawks or Algonquins, among the members of other tribes, was merely a legal ruse to invalidate the Aboriginal peoples' claim.[3]

The dispute simmered away into the latter part of the 1980s, but the Mohawks lacked the monetary and legal means to continue to press their claim before the courts. Matters came to a head in 1990, when the town of Oka decided to expand the existing golf course into the disputed area, consisting of some thirty-nine hectares of land. This area is the site of the Mohawk cemetery and a portion of a pine forest. The dispute emerged in full force when the Mohawks, after centuries of frustrated legal action and inaction, decided to barricade the location, on 11 July 1990. Almost immediately, Oka's mayor, Jean Ouelette, asked the Quebec Provincial Police (QPP) to intervene in the dispute. In an interesting twist, Quebec's Minister for Native Affairs John Ciaccia (2000) wrote a letter in support of the Mohawks' cause, stating, "These people have seen their lands disappear without having been consulted or compensated, and that, in my opinion, is unfair and unjust, especially over a golf course." One might speculate from Ciaccia's statement that the interests of the province of Quebec, and the municipality of Oka, were becoming divergent.

The Mohawks were intent on following their own constitution (of the Iroquois Confederacy), which required that the Mohawk women, who were considered to be caretakers of the land, be consulted. The Mohawk women decided that the weapons that the warriors had assembled should be used for defensive purposes, or if the police proceeded to fire on the barricade. The QPP did attempt to storm the barricade but were repulsed by the Mohawk protesters. During the attack on the barricade, tear gas canisters were directed at the Mohawks and a series of shots rang out – it was never determined from which side – and during the barrage of bullets, 31-year-old Corporal Marcel Lemay was shot and killed. The police withdrew at this point, abandoning several of their cruisers.

The Mohawks behind the barricade were joined by supporters from other Aboriginal communities in Canada and the United States. Before long, the QPP established their own blockade, which served to curtail access to Kanesatake and Oka. Other Mohawks set up a blockade at the Mercier Bridge to the Island of Montreal, causing huge traffic difficulties and disgruntled drivers. Even as far away as British Columbia, the Seton Lake Band supported the Mohawks' cause by blockading the B.C. Rail line, provoking a confrontation with officers of the Royal Canadian Mounted Police.

The federal government attempted to ameliorate the situation at Oka by agreeing to spend $5.3 million to buy the property in question, thus preventing further development of the site. The Mohawks, however, did not approve of this move because they felt that their original concern was not being addressed by this purchase and that the land ownership question was simply being shipped around from the provincial to the federal level of government. This move did not resolve the issue in any way, and the QPP, feeling that they were losing control of the situation called in the RCMP to intervene between the disputing parties. The Mohawk warriors soon overpowered the RCMP, and fourteen officers were sent to hospital in the middle of August.

Robert Bourassa, the Quebec premier, then invoked the National Defence Act in an attempt to send federal troops to Oka, arguing that the same sort of situation had occurred two decades earlier, when the Canadian army was used to quell the October Crisis. When the troops from the Canadian brigade groups arrived, on 20 August, the situation was very tense, but unlike the earlier confrontation with the QPP, no shots were ever fired between the Mohawks and the army. On 29 August, the Mohawks agreed to end the Mercier Bridge blockade; however, once the traffic was moving again, the Quebec government refused to engage in any further negotiations.

The Mohawks eventually dismantled their blockade at Oka, on 26 September, and returned to their reserve. Meanwhile, the armed forces and QPP arrested and charged several of the protesters. Ronald Cross, also known as "Lasagna," was sentenced to four years and four months in jail, and Gordon Lazore, also known as "Noriega," was sentenced to serve twenty-three months. Later, thirty-nine other Mohawks were brought to trial but all charges were eventually dismissed. Altogether, the Oka standoff lasted seventy-eight days. The monetary costs of the police and military actions were high. The decision to bring in the Canadian army cost $83 million, and altogether the expenditure for the province of Quebec amounted to $112 million; the total cost was, therefore, estimated to be about $200 million (Dickason 2009: 322, 524).

The expansion of the golf course, which precipitated the Oka Crisis, was eventually cancelled. Given the loss of the life of Corporal Marcel Lemay, the $200 million in costs borne by Canadian taxpayers, and the

lingering ill will and animosity that is bound to last for decades between the Mohawks and the surrounding Oka population, and between
the Mohawks and the Quebec and federal governments over their handling of this affair, one is forced to ask about what was learned from the
Oka Crisis. Why did it take almost three hundred years for a dispute
over this relatively small parcel of land that had such important symbolic importance to the Mohawks, because the site was situated on their
burial grounds, to have to be dealt with in such a horrific manner? Are
Canadians as a whole proud of the way their governments, both provincial and federal, dealt with this matter? Could the issue have been
handled in a more effective manner rather than through armed confrontation? Given the death of Aboriginal protester Dudley George at
the hands of a heavily armed force of the Ontario Provincial Police, just
five years later, we can well wonder whether any concern was given
by government authorities in effectively resolving Aboriginal protests
now and in the future.

In the decade following the Oka Crisis, the federal government
seemed to be forming a policy committing increased expenditures and
funding for land claims settlements. It would also appear that the federal government is pursuing a policy of ad hoc purchasing of properties involved in Aboriginal disputes, which should have the effect of
reducing confrontations. The federal government, for example, signed
an agreement with the Mohawks, in June 2000, giving them legal jurisdiction over some 960 hectares of property. Further negotiations are
continuing in the area of self-government structures for the Mohawks
of Quebec (*CBC News*, 10 July 2000).

First Nations Policing Policy (1992)

One of the unsettling aspects of the Oka Crisis was that the confrontation between Mohawk warriors and the Quebec Provincial Police resulted in the death of QPP Officer Marcel Lemay. It became obvious
to many observers that changes were needed in Canada's treatment
of policing issues in Aboriginal communities. A positive result of the
Oka Crisis was the development of a First Nations Policing Policy, introduced by the federal government in 1991. An important initiative in
this regard was the formation of the First Nations Chiefs of Police Association (FNCPA), in 1992, to help coordinate ideas from the various
Aboriginal police forces across Canada and to create a wider awareness
of the special policing needs among Aboriginal people.

First Nations police forces have been created because of the need for greater sensitivity in the criminal justice area pertaining to Aboriginal communities. One of the goals of Aboriginal police forces is to reduce the conflict often created between the people living in Aboriginal communities and non-Aboriginal police forces. Aboriginal police officers often speak the local Aboriginal language and have a familiarity with the special social characteristics, such as local family conflicts and the tensions that might exist within such communities.

Several models have been used, for example, integrating Aboriginal officers into existing police departments or creating stand-alone, autonomous Aboriginal police forces. An example of the first initiative is the First Nations Police (FNP) of Ontario. The FNP is a collective of Aboriginal police forces responsible for duties pertaining to reserves in Ontario. The commissioner of the Ontario Provincial Police appoints the First Nations constables, who have the same powers as other police officers in the province. Examples of such FNP agencies are the Treaty Three Police Service (Kenora), Tyendinaga Mohawk Police (Shannonville), Six Nations Police (Ohsweken), and the Nishnawbe-Aski Police Service (Thunder Bay).

The Nishnawbe-Aski Police Service (NAPS) is an organization representing thirty-five First Nations communities in the Nishnawbe-Aski Nation Territory of northwestern Ontario. The officers of this police force are spread across a very large area covering about two-thirds of the province of Ontario, stretching from the Manitoba border in the west, up to the James Bay coastal communities, and over to the Quebec border. Although NAPS is relatively new, it has grown considerably in recent years, and it is now the second-largest First Nations police service in North America. To give an example of the activities of NAPS, on 16 July 2009, the Nishnawbe-Aski Police Enforcement Unit conducted a search at the Thunder Bay Airport and seized about $7,200 worth of Percocet prescription drugs and charged a 31-year-old Eabemetoong First Nation resident (formerly known as Fort Hope, situated about 385 km northwest of Thunder Bay) with possession for the purposes of trafficking).

The Dakota Ojibway Police Service (DOPS) of Brandon Manitoba, established in 1977, is an example of a stand-alone police force, and it is one of the longest-operating First Nations police forces in Canada. Policing services are provided to five First Nations communities in southwestern Manitoba, such as Birdtail Sioux (Birtle), Canupawakpa Dakota (Virden), and Sioux Valley (Brandon). DOPS investigates all major crimes including murder and aggravated and sexual assaults, while enforcing various federal and provincial band by-laws and statutes (www.dops.org).

On 29 November 1999, The Manitoba government established the Aboriginal Justice Implementation Commission. One basis for this Commission is that Manitoba has the highest proportion of Aboriginal people relative to its total population of any of Canada's provinces. For example, in the 1996 census, it was reported that of the 1.1 million people living in Manitoba, about 77,500 are members of First Nations, with an additional 57,000 Metis and non-status Indians (www.ajic.mb.ca).

Before this, in April 1988, the Manitoba government created the Public Inquiry into the Administration of Justice and Aboriginal People, commonly known as the Aboriginal Justice Inquiry. The Aboriginal Justice Inquiry was a response to several incidents. One was the much-publicized trial for the 1971 murder of Helen Betty Osborne of The Pas. The CBC's *Fifth Estate* program reported that at the time of the murder the identities of four people present at the killing were widely known in the community but that local people would not speak out, suggesting racial overtones to this incident.

The other incident was the death, in March 1988, of J.J. Harper, who was a director of the Island Lake Tribal Council, after an encounter with officers of the Winnipeg Police Department. There were complaints in the Aboriginal community that the police services internal investigation left too many questions unanswered.

The report of the Aboriginal Justice Inquiry was issued in the fall of 1991. Created, in 1999, to develop a plan of action based on the Aboriginal Justice Inquiry's recommendations, the Aboriginal Justice Implementation Commission issued its final report in 2009.

The Gustafsen Lake Standoff (1995)

A sign tacked above a makeshift cabin at Gustafsen Lake reads "Sovereigntists *Not* Terrorists."

Gustafsen Lake, in northern British Columbia, was the site of an Aboriginal land dispute involving the Secwepemc (Shuswap) First Nation that began on 15 June 1995 and lasted until 17 September 1995 (see Milloy 1995, Lambertus 2003, Platiel 1996). The dispute had its origins back in 1989 when a local rancher, Lyall James, was asked if the Secwepemc Sundance Society would be able to hold its ten-day ceremony on his ranch. For the next four years, the Society was allowed to hold their

ceremony on James's property; after that, however, a different group
held the Sundance ceremony, for the next two years, and moved to another nearby location.

At the end of the ten-day period in June 1995, during which the Sundance ceremony was normally held, the new group, called the Defenders of the Shuswap Nation, refused to leave the property. The claim
of this group is that the ceremony was being held on Crown land and
the Defenders were asserting a claim of Indigenous rights to unceded
British Columbia territory. James attempted to evict the group, which
would not leave, and as a consequence the matter was brought to the attention of Attorney General of British Columbia Ujjal Dosanjh, who declared that the occupation constituted a strictly criminal action, rather
than a land claim dispute.

What was to occur over the ensuing summer months of 1995 was one
of the largest police actions ever conducted in Canadian history. The
RCMP confronted the Shuswap group with several hundred officers
(estimates range from two to four hundred) with tactical assault training, two helicopters, and nine armoured personnel carriers. By contrast,
the Defenders, led by Jones William ("Wolverine") Ignace, consisted of
about twenty men and women armed with several hunting rifles.

The British Columbia government, which has consistently refused
to negotiate Aboriginal land claims or treaty rights ever since Confederation, claiming that this is a responsibility of the federal government
rather than the province, assessed the occupation as a "law and order"
issue. Attorney General Dosanjh and Premier Mike Harcourt claimed
from the outset that the Defenders do not have any claim to the Sundance site. As a spokesperson for the attorney general indicated, it is
the British Columbia government's position that the occupation is regarded "as a problem for the RCMP, and we have complete confidence
in their sensitivity and care in this issue." In addition, it was asserted
that, "they [the Defenders] have no legal right to be there, and there is
no land claims process for that area. This is simply a law enforcement
issue." Staff Sergeant Peter Montague, the local RCMP commander for
the region, offered his opinion that the Defenders were nothing more
than "terrorists, criminals and thugs" (Milloy 1995: 1).

The RCMP cordoned off the area to the Gustafsen Lake site with a
barricade. A lawyer for the Defenders, Bruce Clark, was refused access.
Two officers were shot while attempting to move a log in order to reinforce the barricade but were uninjured because of their chest protec-
tors. Opinion was divided about the importance of the land claim. The

Caribou Tribal Council, a local band council, suggested that there was no particular significance to the cattle ranch land. In the meantime, Assembly of First Nations Grand Chief Ovide Mercredi visited the camp and appealed for calm from both parties. He rejected all uses of violence to resolve the conflict, and denied the RCMP and B.C. government's characterization of the Defenders, saying, "The individuals are not terrorists, they are people with strong convictions ... They are not criminals" (Milloy 1995: 3).

The legal issues, according to the lawyer for the Defenders, are complex, and not as simple as representatives of the British Columbia government would have the public believe. Bruce Clark indicated that, unlike in most other areas of Canada, the territory of British Columbia had never been ceded by treaties negotiated with Aboriginal societies. Until Canadian Confederation in 1867, the Royal Proclamation of 1763 was the legal basis in force for Aboriginal claims, which indicated that Aboriginal nations retained all of the title to their lands until they were relinquished by treaties. Since such treaties were never negotiated in British Columbia, the Aboriginal societies retain a right to the legal title of their lands and territories. So, as far as the Gustafsen Lake property is concerned, the Shuswap have a rightful claim to this land as unceded Crown land. This is a claim that should not, therefore, be dismissed outright.

It follows, furthermore, that since this is unceded territory, the government does not have the right to exercise power or influence in this area, and it is therefore illegal for such powers as the RCMP to exert their authority over Aboriginal societies. The Native position was that the RCMP constituted an illegitimate force, and was trespassing on Aboriginal land. Clark further explained, "My clients' intent at Gustafsen Lake is to save many lives at the risk of their own. That is heroism not terrorism" (Milloy 1995: 4).

Apparently, the RCMP did not agree with these legal "subtleties." After a standoff that lasted nearly four months and involved a shootout with the police, Ignace and his Defenders were persuaded to give up their occupation by a Stoney medicine man named John Stevens. In all, eighteen Aboriginal and non-Aboriginal persons were cited following the occupation on various weapons charges, fifteen of them received jail terms of six months to eight years. Three of the defendants attempted to appeal their convictions on the ground that Canadian courts did not have jurisdiction over the Gustafsen Lake property since this was considered to be unceded Aboriginal land, but the Supreme

Court of British Columbia refused to hear the appeal. The occupation and subsequent standoff apparently cost taxpayers $5.5 million (Milloy 1995).

Since the Gustafsen Lake occupation was the first armed confrontation since the Oka Crisis, comparisons between the two conflicts were bound to be made (Platiel 1996). On the whole, the assessment was that significant differences existed between Oka and Gustafsen Lake. As far as the Mohawks of Oka were concerned, the disputed property had special spiritual significance for their people and they had occupied the area in the vicinity of the dispute for over two hundred years. By contrast, at Gustafsen Lake, local and regional chiefs claimed that the territory did not have any special historical significance; the use of the area for Sundance ceremonies, they stated, was only a recent development, not a long-standing cultural one.

The Burnt Church Fishing Dispute (2002)

The Burnt Church First Nation is a member of the Mi'kmaq people, who reside on the east coast of Canada in the provinces of Nova Scotia, New Brunswick, and Newfoundland and Labrador, as well as several other locations. Archaeological research indicates that the Mi'kmaqs have inhabited this region for over ten thousand years (Robinson 2005). With the arrival of Europeans, the Mi'kmaqs suffered significant depopulation from such imported diseases as smallpox and influenza, as well as a disruption of their traditional subsistence activities due to settlers clearing the land and competing with Mi'kmaq fishing and hunting activities (McGee 1984).

The Mi'kmaqs depended on a wide-ranging foraging strategy prior to the arrival of Europeans. They followed the seasonal migration patterns of such animals as moose, caribou, and bear. However, for the most part, "although they depended on a variety of natural resources for subsistence, the Mi'kmaqs gathered the largest percentage of their diet from the sea. They used a number of technologies to harvest seafood, including harpoons, weirs, traps, and hook and line" (Robinson 2005: 21). In January the Mi'kmaqs hunted seals, while in March with the fish spawns they fished for smelts, followed by herring, sturgeon, salmon, eels, and cod from April through to the end of September.

During the post-contact period, in the seventeenth to the late eighteenth centuries, the Mi'kmaq people faced a serious source of resource competition with the arrival of French trappers, traders, and missionaries, who all combined to undermine the stability of the traditional Mi'kmaq culture. As historical studies for this period show, "after the British takeover, the Indians were a defense problem. The alliance between the Indians and the French continued to be a threat ... the British resorted to engaging the Mohawks against the Micmac and other Indians allied with the French" (Patterson 1972: 62).

In order to compete with the Europeans, the Mi'kmaqs began to change their more traditional stewardship approach to subsistence production to one based on increasingly more market-driven enterprises. The Mi'kmaqs did not fare well in this competition because of their declining numbers due to disease and because of their less mechanized or technologically driven approaches than those of the French and British. The result was that by the twentieth century the Mi'kmaqs were forced into the more marginal areas of the east coast, where resources were less abundant.

The Mi'kmaqs and the British signed a number of treaties between 1725 and 1779 that recognized the Mi'kmaq entitlement to land. The expansion of Halifax, which was established in 1749, resulted in a Mi'kmaq relocation to wilderness areas that were considered unfavourable for development by European settlers (see MacFarlane 1938; Upton 1975, 1979). This pattern of encroachment on traditional lands by European settlers continued until, by the beginning of the 1800s, it was almost impossible for the Mi'kmaqs to maintain their traditional means of subsistence.

By the 1940s, various licensing programs were put into place with the increasing commercialization of game, fish, and forestry resources. For the Mi'kmaqs, the purchasing of these licences was prohibitive because of their impoverished condition and lack of financial means. At one time, the Mi'kmaqs were granted hunting and fishing permits in accordance with various treaty agreements, but these permits were eventually withdrawn. It, therefore, became illegal for the Mi'kmaqs to engage in their traditional subsistence activities without these licences (Bock 1966).

Over the following decades, frustration grew among the Mi'kmaqs because of their inability to adequately feed themselves using their traditional resources and the increased competition and commercialization of hunting and fishing. Chief Donald Marshall Sr. (1990) describes in detail the source of this frustration. For example, on 17 September 1988, over a hundred Mi'kmaq harvesters and their supporters arrived at Hunter's Mountain in Nova Scotia to mark the beginning of a two-week Treaty Moose Harvest. A short distance away, hidden from view, dozens of game wardens and RCMP officers were waiting. The Moose Treaty Harvest had recently been declared "unauthorized" by Nova Scotia's Minister of Lands and Forests. The Mi'kmaqs were proceeding with their harvest because of a 1985 decision of the Supreme Court of Canada (CBC News, 8 May 2004), which ruled that the 1752 treaty between the Mi'kmaq Nation and the British Crown, which allowed for Aboriginal subsistence harvesting, was still valid. This treaty of 1752 states in unequivocal terms: "It is agreed that the said Tribe of Indians shall not be hindered from, but have free liberty of hunting and fishing as usual" (Marshall 1990: 91).

The game wardens and RCMP officers then proceeded to search the Mi'kmaqs' vehicles and seize hunting weapons. Six of the harvesters were subsequently charged with provincial game law infractions. This isolated event is just one in a series of attempts by the Mi'kmaqs to exercise their Aboriginal rights under existing treaties. The issue at stake was not only about securing access to traditional subsistence resources, but of holding on to the very essence of Mi'kmaq identity (Larsen 1983).

The Burnt Church fishing dispute can be seen as a continuation of the Mi'kmaq First Nations' attempts to assert its rights to traditional resource harvesting, as guaranteed by various treaties in the past. These treaties, in a legal sense, can be considered "living documents," as opposed to the thinking of many Canadians that Aboriginal treaties are merely historical curiosities with no relevance to today's world. The assertion that existing treaties are still relevant in a legal sense even today was reinforced by a Supreme Court of Canada decision in 1999 called "the Marshall Decision" (see Coates 2000).

Donald Marshall was originally convicted in Provincial Court of three counts of fishing for eels out of season, fishing without a licence, and fishing with an illegal net. These convictions were subsequently upheld by the Nova Scotia Court of Appeal. Marshall then took his case to Canada's Supreme Court, where he argued that the treaties of 1752 and 1760–1 released him from the current fisheries regulations and gave him the right to catch fish for sale. The Supreme Court agreed with Donald Marshall's argument, indicating in its decision that "nothing less would uphold the honour and integrity of the Crown in its dealings with the Mi'kmaq people to secure their peace and friendship." The Supreme Court also ruled that Aboriginal people had a right to establish a "moderate livelihood," and through a use in resources to obtain trade items (*R. v. Marshall*; see also *CBC News*, 9 May 2004).

As a result of this decision, thirty-four bands (First Nations) of the Maritime Provinces and eastern Quebec began fishing for lobster out of season on the ground that the Supreme Court decision gave them complete and unregulated fishing rights. Problems resulted because all of the parties affected by the Marshall decision tended to interpret the ruling in a different manner. The non-Aboriginal fishermen, whose livelihood was also directly influenced by the Marshall decision, were concerned that the lobster catch would suffer a significant decline, and so they demanded that the government put a ban on the catch.

On 3 October 1999, trouble began when about 150 boats belonging to non-Native fishermen headed out into Miramichi Bay, New Brunswick, which is one of Canada's most lucrative lobster fishing areas, as a protest against Native lobster fishing out of season. A serious confrontation ensued after hundreds of Native lobster traps were destroyed and three fish plants were vandalized. In response, Mi'kmaq warriors established an armed encampment on the wharf in Burnt Church in an attempt to protect Native lobster fishermen in Miramichi Bay.

Within days, federal Fisheries Minister Herb Dhaliwal intervened in an effort to diffuse the tensions. After a period of negotiations, all but two of the thirty-four First Nations agreed to a voluntary moratorium on lobster fishing. The two dissenting bands – Burnt Church and Indian Brook – refused to accept government regulation of the fisheries. Later, in October 1999, the West Nova Scotia Fishermen's Coalition applied for a rehearing of the appeal in an attempt to have the judgment set aside. As a consequence, that November the Supreme Court released a new ruling, known as Marshall 2, which stipulated that the government still had the power to regulate Native fishing where the issues of conservation were concerned.

As a result of this revised ruling, the Department of Fisheries and Oceans (DFO) ordered the Mi'kmaqs to reduce the number of their lobster traps used, which left the Burnt Church community with a total of forty traps for the whole band. As one could expect, some of the Mi'kmaqs resisted this decision, claiming that they already used their own conservation measures, which they considered adequate to prevent the depletion of the lobster stocks. In February 2000, negotiations began between fishermen of First Nations communities in the Atlantic Provinces and the DFO.

Over the next several months, negotiations continued with the various Mi'kmaq First Nations, which resulted in thirteen bands signing deals with Ottawa and others making agreements in principle. Various

First Nations made different deals, as the characteristics and interests of these bands differed from one another. In general, the deals gave Aboriginal people the same access as non-Aboriginals to commercial and food fisheries. It was reported in the news media (*Halifax Daily News*, 3 June 2001; *Telegraph Journal* [New Brunswick], 24 Aug. 2002) that some bands had incorporated these new deals into the existing Aboriginal Fisheries Strategy (AFS), while others decided to keep their deals separate from any existing arrangements. The Aboriginal Fisheries Strategy was established, in 1992, in an attempt to stabilize existing fishery management, and it was a response to a Supreme Court of Canada ruling in 1990, called "the Sparrow Decision," which allowed Aboriginal peoples the right to fish for food and to use this resource for social and ceremonial purposes (see *R. v. Sparrow*).

Fisheries Minister Herb Dhaliwal then promised a plan that would decide how non-Native and Native fishermen would share in the coastal fishing resources, but the negotiations over this deal bogged down. Meanwhile, members of the Maritime Fishermen's Union were critical of the DFO for its go-slow approach, and furthermore indicated that some of its members were willing to sell their licences and get out of the fishing business. By February 2000, the federal government announced that it would be willing to buy back more than a thousand commercial fishing licences, including boats and gear, and that it would expand the Native lobster fishery. In all, by the end of the summer, about fourteen hundred fishermen had been offered the licence buyback plan that would retire some five thousand licences. The federal government also announced that it was willing to set aside $160 million that would pay for the retired licences and economic development initiatives, with the goal to bring more First Nations people into the fishing industry.

Between 2000 and 2001, tensions mounted which led to a standoff between the Aboriginal people and the Royal Canadian Mounted Police, during which sixteen arrests were made, including the chief of the Burnt Church First Nation. During the altercations that followed, several DFO officers were injured by rocks thrown in the course of a confrontation with Mi'kmaq fishermen. DFO officers then launched a raid on Native lobster traps, and two Native boats were swamped and sank. Three non-Natives were also arrested and their firearms seized after it was reported that shots were fired, although no one was injured.

In May 2001, a Native man, Rayburn Dedam, was fined $170 resulting from assault charges during the confrontations of the previous fall.

Also that month, two other Burnt Church men were fined $1,000 each for obstructing DFO officers. Tensions escalated throughout the summer, and in September at least thirty gunshots were fired during a confrontation between Native and non-Native fishermen in chase-and-dodge actions around the reserve. In October, a jury acquitted Leigh Morrison, a non-Native fisherman, of three charges of assault with a weapon stemming from incidents that had occurred in 1999.

Further convictions followed, in 2002, when a Native fisherman, John Dedam, was sentenced to three years in prison for aggravated assault for attacking a DFO officer during a confrontation on Miramichi Bay in August 2000. Lobster and treaty rights issues resulted in ten Mi'kmaq men from Burnt Church facing trial in September of that year for allegedly breaching Fisheries Act regulations. Eventually, on 1 August 2002, an agreement in principle was reached between the Burnt Church First Nation and Ottawa worth about $20 million over two years.

The agreement allows members of the Burnt Church community to fish for subsistence purposes but not to sell their lobster catch for commercial purposes. What this means is that Burnt Church fishermen are allowed a fall fishery of 25,000 pounds of lobster for food and 5,000 pounds for ceremonial use, but the sale of lobster is prohibited. In addition, funding will be provided for upgrades to existing fishing vessels, and a provision will be made for the replacement of lost gear and equipment.

Since the Marshall Decision, the federal government has spent about $425 million on Aboriginal fishing agreements with the First Nations in Atlantic Canada. Ottawa also expected to spend another $143 million in 2003 to facilitate Native access to fisheries (*Telegraph Journal*, 24 Aug. 2002) on the east coast. As Bob Allain, regional director of the DFO's Fisheries Management Branch points out, "Negotiated agreements aren't the be-all and end-all. If there is no support whatsoever in a community – never mind whether it's aboriginal – if there's no support for a management plan of any kind in a community, you can expect to see some problems. In the case of Burnt Church, there is support; there are some significant benefits that are taking place for the community" (ibid.). These sentiments were echoed by Robert Thibault, federal minister of Fisheries and Oceans, who believes that reaching a consensus will be a positive development for the entire region: "I am hopeful this agreement will mean peace on the water this fall in the Miramichi Bay" (Cox 2000: A7; Hamilton 2000; *Globe and Mail*, 23 April 2001).

Caledonia and the Grand River Land Dispute (2006)

The defeat of the Huron Confederacy by the Iroquois of Upper New York State, in 1649–50, left a population vacuum in the area south of Lake Huron to the north shores of lakes Eire and Ontario. Slowly, the Mississaugas who had been settled in the Sault Ste. Marie area began to drift southwards down to Lake Ontario. In 1781, they signed a treaty with the British, alienating a section of land on the west side of the Ottawa River, and then eventually other areas of what is now southern Ontario.

These land cessations allowed for a large area of land along the Grand River to be transferred to the Six Nations Iroquois (Seneca, Onondaga, Cayuga, Oneida, Mohawk, and Tuscarora) as compensation for their loss of land during the American Revolution and in appreciation for their military support of the British Crown. This land transfer was known as the Haldimand Grant, named after Sir Frederick Haldimand, governor of Canada from 1778 to 1786. The proclamation of the grant was made on 25 October 1784, and it included six miles on either side of the Grand River from its source (vaguely thought of today as near Fergus, Ontario) to its mouth on Lake Erie: "I do hereby in his Majesty's name authorize and permit the said Mohawk nation, and such other of the Six Nations Indians as wish to settle in that Quarter to take possession of, and Settle upon the Banks of the River commonly called Ours (Ourse) or Grand River, running into lake Erie, allotting to them for that Purpose Six Miles deep from each Sidè of the River beginning at lake Erie, and extending in the Proportion to the Head of said River, which them and their Posterity are to enjoy forever" (Johnston 1964: 50–1; Patterson 1972: 82).

Shortly after this Proclamation, their leader Joseph Brant led about sixteen hundred of his followers to settle in their new territory. There were difficulties, however, from the beginning over several issues. One of the most important of these was that this territory had not been adequately surveyed at the time of transfer, so nobody was very sure of the area's exact boundaries. The other problem was that Brant insisted on selling some of the property, the proceeds of such sales he claimed were needed to buy cattle, building supplies, and so on to equip the new settlers since they had come to the Grand River with almost nothing to support their new farming life.

At issue were Brant's claims that the land in question belonged exclusively to the Six Nations people and, therefore, could be disposed of by them in any way they wished. The government of the time did not agree with this point of view, especially Lieutenant Governor Simcoe opposed the sales. Eventually, the Crown withdrew its opposition, probably not wanting to antagonize its Six Nations allies who might still be needed in any war with the Americans, or who might even rise up against the nearby settlement at York (Toronto).

Beginning in February 1798, various land sales were officially registered, which reduced the original land grant from about 570,000 acres down to about 190,000 acres, as nearly 380,000 acres had been sold, thus resulting in the sale of two-thirds of the Haldimand Grant. The sold land was mainly from the northern part of the grant; however, the land speculators who had bought the land had difficulty in selling the lots, with the result that by 1801 all of the speculators had fallen in arrears of their payments. The problem was exacerbated by the large number of white settlers who moved in the Grand River area and who began to squat on lands owned by the Six Nations.

An attempt at a resolution of these various issues was made in 1841, when it was agreed that the Indian Affairs Office of the colonial government would take responsibility for administering the Six Nations land. This included all the land currently under cultivation by then, in addition to another twenty thousand acres, all of which would comprise a reserve. All additional land above this acreage was to be sold and the proceeds deposited into a Six Nations account.

In later depictions of this transaction, Six Nations leaders claimed that they had only agreed to the lease of this land, and not to its sale. Further difficulties of this nature arose in 1825, when an agreement was reached with Six Nations leaders to lease land of one-half mile in extent on either side of a proposed road, which became Highway 6, but not to the surrender of this land. Later, in 1845, Sir Francis Bond Head, lieutenant governor of Upper Canada, ignored this previous arrangement and sold the lands on which this road was situated to another party.

In his opinion, such moves were necessary so as not to impede "progress" and in order to "protect" the Aboriginal Nations. As Bond Head told an assembled group of Ottawas and Ojibways of Manitoulin Island, in August 1836, when they signed a treaty alienating their land: "as an unavoidable increase in white population as well as the progress of cultivation have had the natural effect of impoverishing your hunting grounds it has become necessary that new arrangements should be entered into for the purpose of protecting you from the encroachment of the whites" (Patterson 1972: 86). Apparently these "new arrangements" would include reneging on existing agreements to the detriment of the Aboriginal Nations for their own good.

The preceding discussion is necessary to understand what transpired in the 1990s and beyond. In 1992, for example, a company called Henco Industries purchased forty hectares of land that would to be called the Douglas Creek Estates but later, in 1995, the Six Nations sued the federal government over this land, claiming that it had never been surrendered. In February 2006, members of the Six Nations reserve set up tents and a wooden building on the property. Eventually, a local sheriff attempted to deliver an eviction notice to the protesters but they burned it in open defiance of Justice Matheson's order to vacate the premises.

Various other court orders were issued, including a contempt of court charge that led eventually to the OPP arresting twenty-one Aboriginal persons. With these arrests, even more protesters arrived on the scene, and a barricade of burning tires and dumped gravel was erected blocking off the main road into Caledonia, a small town situated about twenty kilometres southwest of Hamilton. Meanwhile, tensions escalated as residents of Caledonia held their own rally, demanding an end to the occupation.

News media flocked to Caledonia in 2006, providing coverage of another of the summer Aboriginal protests and occupations in southern Ontario. Many television viewers at the time, on 25 April, might remember Mayor Marie Trainer's interview on the CBC, in which she commented that residents of the town were being hurt economically by the occupation as these residents, presumably non-Aboriginal ones, did not have money flowing automatically into their accounts, but had to work for it. The Aboriginal protesters took this as not only a very insulting comment, but racist as well, as it would apparently presume that the Aboriginal protesters were all on social assistance. Within days, the former premier of the province, David Peterson, was appointed to help negotiate a settlement to the dispute.

In May 2006, the blockade of the Caledonia road into town was partially removed to allow emergency vehicles to enter. Then a group of townspeople, calling themselves the Caledonia Citizens Alliance, confronted the Aboriginal protesters at the site of the blockade, trading insults and punches with them before the OPP arrived to break up the skirmish. Confrontations continued throughout the day, with injuries being sustained by all parties, including OPP officers. The escalation of violence continued when vandals sent a burning truck into a hydroelectric power substation, causing a power outage and substantial damage. Later a state of emergency was declared.

Several altercations ensued into the month of June, one involving Aboriginal protesters and Caledonia residents in the downtown area after a police cruiser drove through a line of protesters. At about the same time, news camera operators were assaulted by protesters when they refused to relinquish their video tapes. In another incident, a U.S. Border Patrol vehicle, which had attempted to intervene in what the Border Patrol observed to be an assault on OPP officers, was attacked by Six Nations protesters. Eventually, six protesters were issued warrants involving fourteen charges ranging from attempted murder to theft of a motor vehicle (*Toronto Star*, 12 June 2006).

These actions resulted in Ontario Premier Dalton McGuinty calling off negotiations with the Aboriginal protesters. In the meantime, the government of Ontario announced that it had negotiated the purchase of the disputed Douglas Estates property from Henco Industries for $21.1 million and would provide $1 million in additional compensation for the Caledonia businesses that had suffered losses as a result of the protest (*CBC News*, 16 June 2006). In a further announcement the following year, on 29 March 2007, the federal government said that it was contributing $15.8 million to Ontario's purchase of the property.

With the disputed property now in the hands of the provincial government, its fate is at present unclear. Aboriginal protesters claim, on the basis of an unofficial archaeological excavation, to have uncovered the remains of a previous First Nations settlement including a burial ground and a section of a longhouse. Caledonia residents apparently fear that the digging is an attempt to undermine their water supply. On 15 October 2006, about 750 Native and non-Native supporters gather at the disputed site for a "Potluck for Peace" rally. On 15 June 2009, some residents of Caledonia announced that they were forming unarmed "militias" that would attempt to enforce laws they think the OPP has not been willing or able to enforce (*Globe and Mail*, 22 May 2006; *Toronto Star*, 14 Sept. 2007; Ferguson 2007).

Grassy Narrows: Mercury Poisoning and Forest Management Protest (2006)

When members of the Grassy Narrows First Nation, in northwestern Ontario, attempted to blockade Trans-Canada Highway 17 near

Kenora, on 13 July 2006, they were hardly newcomers to protests and confrontations. Many of their members had been involved in the occupation of Anicinabe Park, in the summer of 1974, an event that garnered international attention in the news media. Later, it was discovered that the pickerel they were eating out of the Wabigoon River system were contaminated with mercury emanating from the effluent of a local pulp and paper mill in Dryden, Ontario, which caused neurological disorders among the Aboriginal residents. Grassy Narrows leaders showed their media acumen by forging links with such groups as Amnesty International, eventually causing forestry giant AbitibiBowater to surrender their cutting licence in the area. Even though they are a relatively isolated population, there is much that can be learned from the Grassy Narrows forging of media connections, protests, confrontations, and negotiations as they attempt to achieve their goals.

Mercury Pollution

Grassy Narrows is an Ojibway First Nation situated about eighty kilometres north of Kenora, Ontario. Their reserve, English River 21, is also situated on the Wabigoon-English river system into which a chlor-alkali processing plant, the Dryden Chemical Company, had been discharging mercury-contaminated effluent for years. Eventually, it was bought out by Reed Paper Ltd., a British multinational corporation, which continued to discharge the harmful effluent into the river system.

Reed Paper purchased an old pulp mill in Dryden, Ontario, in 1961. Mercury pollution was first detected downstream from the mill at Dryden in 1969. Altogether, it is estimated that about ten tons of mercury is known to have leaked or been dumped into the Wabigoon-English river system, while up to fifteen tons was never accounted for. Some controls were finally introduced in 1970, but the commercial fishery of the river system had been terminated the previous year. Sport fishing was allowed to continue, and most tourist camps continued to operate in the area despite the high contamination levels (Michalenko and Suffling 1982).

The members of Grassy Narrows and White Dog First Nations had depended on the commercial fishery in the Wabigoon-English river system for food and employment income. During the 1970s, a Japanese health researcher, Masazumi Harada, diagnosed eight Grassy Narrows residents with "Minimata disease," a neurological disorder that causes shaking and poor muscle coordination, slurred speech, blurred vision, and numbness in the limbs. One study, reported in the news media, found that from a sample of sixty First Nations people who were examined at the Grassy Narrows and White Dog reserves, 42 (70%) showed symptoms of a neurological disorder (Bueckert 2003).

The response of the Ontario government was to tell the local residents to stop eating fish from the river system and to close their commercial fishery, yet no alternative forms of employment or source of food were offered. For the local residents, fishing provided a much-needed source of protein, and the reserve suffered from 90 per cent unemployment at the time, so closing the fishery caused great nutritional and economic hardship.

In 1985, the Grassy Narrows and White Dog First Nations received a settlement from the Canadian government and Reed Paper of $16.6 million in compensation. However, the contamination of the river system remains a problem, as the mercury was never removed from the water. Thirty years after his initial discovery, Harada returned to the area in a follow-up study that concluded that the mercury problem has not been resolved and may be getting more severe. It had been hoped that the level of mercury pollution would improve once the pulp mills shut down and stopped discharging the harmful effluent into the Wabigoon-English river system, but the problem seems to have gotten worse, rather than better, Harada concluded as a result of these findings. Health Canada has begun to conduct a new study to find out if mercury levels have increased (Bueckert 2003).

One theory, as yet unsubstantiated, is that today's mercury pollution problem is linked to clear-cut forestry practices. The idea is that coal-fired power plants and incinerators are a source of airborne mercury that would normally be held intact in the forest foliage, but with the large-scale logging in the area, the mercury accumulates in the form of runoff into the local waterways. Thus, the issue of mercury contamination is not seen as an isolated phenomenon, but as coincident with forest-cutting practices.

Forestry Protest

Discussions between the Grassy Narrows First Nation and the Ontario government over forestry-related issues began on 8 September 2007. Previous to this, in 2002, Grassy Narrows residents had conducted a blockade of logging roads in their territory to protest the clear-cutting by Weyerhauser and AbitibiBowater, which the First Nations people regarded as "an assault on our culture, our way of life, and indeed our very existence" (*Toronto Star*, 5 June 2008). Aboriginal residents then staged a blockade of Trans-Canada Highway 17 near Kenora, on 13 July 2006.

One of the most effective political mobilization strategies of Grassy Narrows and White Dog residents has been to enlist the aid of large international organizations such as Amnesty International. On 5 June 2008, Amnesty International Canada posted the following message on their web page, from Grassy Narrows Elder Bill Forester: "Six years ago when we blocked the main logging road near our community people told us we were crazy to take on two of the largest logging companies in the world. We weren't crazy, we were just fed up with watching our livelihood, our culture, our medicine, our children's future – our forest – being carried off our land right before our eyes" (www.amnesty.ca/themes/inidgenous_grassy_narrows.php).

Shortly after AbitibiBowater announced it would surrender its licence to harvest trees in the Whiskey Jack forest because the company was not able to wait for the negotiations which were estimated to take four years. The Whiskey Jack forest is part of a million-hectare forest that is on land claimed by the Grassy Narrows First Nation. This forest has been the subject of a five-year blockade by Grassy Narrows residents, backed by various environmental and human rights groups. Until the announcement, AbitibiBowater had been licensed to cut 700,000 cubic metres of wood a year from the Whiskey Jack forest until 2023.

Along with Amnesty International, the Rainforest Action Network (RAN) has also been a strong supporter of the Grassy Narrows blockade. A RAN spokesperson for this San Francisco–based environmental organization indicated that the AbitibiBowater withdrawal sends a clear message to large corporations working in the north that they cannot conduct their business without local consent and participation: "all companies operating in the boreal forest should take this as a wake-up call. This is proof that communities can say 'no' and enforce their rights to control development in their territory" (RAN 2007). The province of Ontario, meanwhile, has been negotiating several forestry agreements in northern Ontario backed by First Nations, industry, and other communities. Ontario's Natural Resources Minister Donna Cansfield has said that they are working towards an agreement for the Whiskey Jack forest area, which "shouldn't take four years, it's their [AbitibiBowater] decision, not mine" (*Toronto Star*, 5 June 2008).

A lesson here from the Grassy Narrows experience for other Aboriginal communities engaged in disputes over their territory is that non-Indigenous support groups can be enlisted to help meet local objectives. These groups can also be used in conjunction with media relations support, which in turn, serves to mobilize international and national networks. Although we have mentioned Amnesty International and the Rainforest Action Network, there is also the Sierra Legal Defence Fund (now called Ecojustice), which can provide legal advocacy. Such groups are useful in providing funding, public education, and information flow through websites and press releases, all of which can provide the basis for campaigns that put pressure on large corporations and serve to counteract the asymmetrical power relationships involved in many Aboriginal disputes.

The Akwesasne Border Confrontation (2009)

The Jay Treaty of 1794 formalized the border between the United States and British North America (Canada). Border crossings, as Johannes Fabian (1993) notes, involve acts of "submission' – the border [is] a place and time of dominance/submission" (p. 49). The image that Fabian evokes is that of boundary crossings as matters of control and power, of borders as places of ambiguity and liminality.

For the Mohawks of Akwesasne, the Jay Treaty served to criss-cross their community with powerful new rules of submission, control, and, ultimately on their part, of defiance. Border disputes have been a problem since the enactment of the Jay Treaty because of the borders that transverse their territory, and the need to travel from one part of their community to another, necessitating at times the crossing of both international and provincial boundaries (Bemis 1962).

The territory of the Akwesasne comprises various islands in the St. Lawrence River and portions of both the north and south shores of the river. Located not far from Cornwall, Ontario, the southern part of Akwesasne lies in the United States, which is under the jurisdiction of the U.S. federal government and New York State. The Akwesasne community does not recognize these borders.

The problem for the Akwesasne pertains to their need to transverse these various boundaries in an unimpeded manner. Indeed, the Jay Treaty apparently recognized this right. Lieutenant Governor John

Graves Simcoe explained to the Six Nations Iroquois, in 1795, at Fort Erie:

> Brothers:
>
> By the present [Jay] Treaty your rights are guarded, and specifically placed on their ancient footing ... you have the right to go to the British Settlements, or to those of the U. States, as shall suit your convenience, nor shall your passing or repassing with your own proper goods and effects of whatever nature, pay for the same any impost whatever. (Mitchell 1990: 113)

Over the ensuing years, the provisions of the Jay Treaty pertaining to unfettered Aboriginal border crossings have apparently fallen into disuse, or become otherwise not recognized, as each government has attempted to exercise control. The Mohawks of Akwesasne are caught in the middle of the Canadian and American powers. In attempting to assert what they see as their rights under the Jay Treaty, they have had to engage in protests and confrontations meant to attract attention to their grievances regarding the border issues.

One of these political mobilizations occurred in 1968, when the Mohawks of Akwesasne blocked the Seaway International Bridge (Three Nations Bridge), near Cornwall, and fifty persons were arrested. The issue in this incident was about Canada's decision not to recognize the rights of Aboriginal people at its border crossings. Over the years, further disputes and confrontations developed between the Mohawks and Customs officials. In March 1988, Chief of the Mohawk Council of Akwasasne Michael Mitchell was arrested when he attempted to bring a truckload of groceries across the international border, from one part of Akwesasne to another. In the same year, on 13 October, some 250 police officers from Ontario and New York State invaded Akwesasne territory armed with helicopters and patrol vessels in a search for duty-free cigarettes allegedly taken illegally across the international border from the United States into Canada. In 1989, a firebomb was thrown at a chartered bus, and in another incident, a shotgun was fired at a bus in the Customs area.

From the police perspective, and that of the government authorities, the issue here is not one of transporting groceries, but of smuggling, especially contraband cigarettes. Apparently, cigarettes are taken into Akwesasne territory on the Canadian side, and then later into Canada proper. Canadian cigarettes are initially exported to border towns in the United States tariff-free, and then bought in large quantities to be smuggled back into Canada through Akwesasne.

It is important to point out here that the Mohawk leadership at Akwesasne has not condoned the smuggling of cigarettes. Grand Chief Michael Mitchell (1990: 130) has stated, "Our people in Akwesasne have shown that they are against smuggling; they have co-operated with police, and our own Mohawk police have made a number of drug busts. Cigarettes are perhaps the least of our worries. Drugs, liquor, and automatic weapons, all of which are harmful to our people, have been brought into the territory in great quantities." So there exist within the Akwesasne community two divergent views of the border issue.

On the one side are those who are involved in smuggling, and their opinion is that there is no border as far as they are concerned, therefore, they feel free to bring anything, anywhere, to sell to anybody. This faction at Akwesasne has made life difficult for those in the Mohawk community who do not support smuggling. For this latter group, the smuggling interferes with their right to bring "ordinary" goods across the border. From this group's perspective, it is unfortunate that the smuggling issue has become confused with the right to cross the border with personal goods. Even though Canada has not officially ratified the Jay Treaty, it has nonetheless unofficially recognized the Mohawks' right by establishing a separate lane so that they can cross the border at Cornwall Island without the usual questions and inspections. There is an issue of trust involved here, one in which it is implicitly recognized that the Mohawks' travel through the border, from one side of their territory to another, will not involve a corresponding attempt to smuggle other goods along with one's personal items.

The police raids in 1988 brought to the forefront the divisions among the Mohawks of Akwesasne over the smuggling issue. Many residents at Akwesasne resent the smugglers because they feel that their activities not only contravene Canadian laws and, therefore, place all residents at risk, but also that Mohawk laws are broken, as well, border or no border. However, the Mohawks also feel that it is the Canadian laws that have allowed this smuggling to occur. It is furthermore obvious that the Canadian authorities have not been successful in dealing with such a large-scale operation.

Many in the Mohawk community feel that they need to take control of their own affairs and not depend on Canadian or American authorities to handle matters for them. However, the Mohawks have been stifled in their attempts. For example, a Mohawk Justice Conduct Society was formed. They then formed the Akwesasne Mohawk Police Service (AMPS), a law enforcement agency trained by the New York State Police. The Ontario Provincial Police arrested an AMPS officer, charging him with unauthorized possession of a restricted weapon, even though his service revolver was part of his uniform. The charge went through various court levels, first dismissed, then appealed, then dismissed again (Mitchell 1990: 126).

A final event should be mentioned here, which occurred on 1 June 2009, to show that border issues continue to take place. A protest occurred in the summer of 2009 when Akwesasne Mohawk residents set up an encampment across the road from the Customs facility at Cornwall because of the arming of officers of the Canada Border Services Agency (CBSA). The CBSA officers then walked off the job in response to this protest, citing safety concerns. The CBSA was created in 2003, amalgamating the former Canada Customs with the Department of Citizenship and Immigration. CBSA officers are currently armed with Beretta 500 mm Storm pistols.

The port of entry was left vacant when the CBSA officers who had left at the end of their shift were not replaced by incoming officers. The Cornwall police then blocked access to the Three Nations Bridge, while the New York State Police also denied access from the United States side of the bridge. Akwesasne residents were, therefore, denied access into Canada and within their territory until a temporary border post was instituted, on 13 July 2009.

Several hundred Mohawks set up a camp in the vicinity of the border as a protest of the new gun policy. Signs were set up reading "This Is Mohawk Land" and "Honk for No Guns." The Mohawks were angry about the border agents carrying guns because they believe that carrying guns is apt to increase the likelihood that violent confrontations will occur. They also expressed that the whole issue violates their sovereignty. The sovereignty issue is an ongoing one, as the Mohawks' position is that they have been at this Akwesasne territory, which straddles Quebec, Ontario, and New York State long before these provinces or countries came into existence, therefore, they have prior, Indigenous rights (i.e., sovereignty) of occupancy.

The Mohawks are resentful that their territory was arbitrarily divided up by this criss-crossing of borders and that now they have to

pay the price of an inconvenienced lifestyle along with the subjuga-
tion that is inflicted upon them. Akwesasne Elder John Boots told a
CBC reporter on the scene that the border guards are "nasty" to his
people, at times handcuffing them and subjecting them to other forms
of humiliation. "They're so nasty and harassing our people that we can
almost feel ... their finger being itchy on the trigger. That's how bad
those people are. The customs officers." Boots also indicated that he
did not expect his people to back down from this protest: "If they say
they're going to arm the guards, we're going to stay here, and we're
going to stop them whenever we see them coming" (*CBC News*, 1 June
2009).

   As far as the safety issue is concerned, a district chief of the Mohawk
Council of Akwesasne, Cheryl Jacob, pointed out that "their biggest
fear is that because of the animosity that exists right now, that one of
them young people that has guns in there [and] three weeks of training,
probably no psychological testing either – that one of them is going to
lose it in there and kill one of our people" (ibid.).

   The two positions, those of the Mohawk protesters and the border
guards, appear to be deeply entrenched with no sign of any form of mediation or negotiations in sight. Public Safety Minister Peter Van Loan
has stated that the gun policy is one that is being applied to all of Canada's borders without exception. Meanwhile, the Cornwall police have
indicated that as long as the dispute lasts, residents of the Akwesasne
Territory who wish to leave will be allowed to do so, but they will not
be allowed to return (ibid.).

Patterns of Resistance: Comparative Perspectives

This chapter is not meant to provide a comprehensive account of Aboriginal political mobilization in Canada, but to furnish a basis for a
comparative overview of cases so that some preliminary observations
may be cast over the similarities and differences of Aboriginal resistance. All of the events discussed range across Canada in space and
time from British Columbia to Nova Scotia and over a thirty-five-year
period from the 1970s to 2009. Three involved armed Aboriginal protesters (Kenora, Oka, and Gustafsen Lake), although there were violent
confrontations in several other instances (Burnt Church, Caledonia,
and Akwesasne). The tactics of resistance employed were primarily the
occupation of property or the blockade of roads or other transportation

routes. Disputes over land were the apparent cause of most of the protests, although resource issues figured prominently as well such as forestry management in the case of Grassy Narrows, in northern Ontario, or resource harvesting among the Mi'kmaqs of New Brunswick and Nova Scotia.

Another significant aspect of the confrontations was the direct involvement of the various police forces, not just there to keep the peace or uphold the rule of law, but whose members engaged in shootouts with protesters. A key issue in the present study, therefore, concerns the role of police forces in dealing with incidents of Aboriginal political mobilization so that a closer examination in particular cases is warranted. Our question concerns the appropriateness of the level of force used by the police, and whether the use of this force was in its own right a precipitating factor in the escalation of violence or at least potential violence. Furthermore, we are also led to ask if such use of force could be considered a positive or negative factor in eventually resolving the particular issues at hand. The wider issue, of course, is the question of the effectiveness of the armed suppression of dissent in a democratic, liberal society, as opposed to other means of dispute resolution and reconciliation.

We note, for example, that the occupation of Anicinabe Park in Kenora, Ontario, involved about 150 members of the local Ojibway community with additional support from several persons belonging to the American Indian Movement (AIM). An unknown number of protesters, but probably only a handful from what one can gather from the local news coverage at the time, were armed with hunting rifles and shotguns, of an antiquated vintage. The authorities responded with 143 members of the Ontario Provincial Police, in addition to a contingent of the Kenora police. The OPP officers were mostly flown in from Toronto and Thunder Bay, so that one may presume that the knowledge possessed by these officers of local conditions and of local Aboriginal people was probably limited at best.

Police action does not appear to be a significant factor in the Teme-Augama Anishnabai or Lubicon Cree blockades or the occupation of the Goose Bay Air Base, although there were a small number of arrests in each of these instances. It was not until the Oka Crisis of 1990 that one of the largest police actions in Canadian history took place in response to an Aboriginal protest. In dispute were thirty-nine hectares of land whose ownership had been a matter of unresolved controversy for several centuries. When plans were announced by the town of Oka,

Quebec, to utilize the disputed land for a golf course, the Mohawk of Kanesatake barricaded the road leading to this land. Oka's mayor then asked the Quebec Provincial Police to intervene in the dispute. Despite support for the Mohawk position from Quebec's Minister of Native Affairs John Ciaccia, the QPP attempted to storm the barricade but were met with armed resistance by members of the Mohawk Warrior Society.

In the ensuing barrage of gunfire, Corporal Marcel Lemay was mortally wounded, although it was never determined which side was responsible for his death. The confrontation escalated when a contingent of RCMP officers intervened, resulting in fourteen members of this force being sent to hospital with various injuries. Next, troops from the brigades groups of the Canadian army arrived to further fuel the confrontation, although no shots were ever fired by either side in this encounter.

The Oka Crisis was at least partly responsible for the institution of the First Nations Policing Policy of 1992 in an attempt to coordinate activities by the various Aboriginal police services across Canada. Also at this time, the First Nations Chiefs of Police Association was formed to further facilitate awareness of the special needs of policing among Aboriginal residents. The intention behind these initiatives was that Aboriginal police would be more sensitive to the special problems of policing in Aboriginal communities, would be conversant in the local language, and would ultimately serve to reduce the conflicts that often arise between Aboriginal communities and non-Aboriginal police forces. The creation of Aboriginal police services would appear to function as an effective mechanism for diffusing Aboriginal political mobilization since they would be prone to use persuasion and negotiation, rather than force in ameliorating local problems.

A dispute at Gustafsen Lake in northern British Columbia, in 1995, however, brought to the forefront once again the escalating nature of violence when armed protesters are pitted against the police. The standoff lasted nearly four months and resulted in one of the largest police actions ever conducted in Canadian history when several hundred (200–400?) RCMP officers with tactical assault training, two helicopters, and nine armoured assault personnel carriers confronted an Aboriginal contingent of about twenty men and women, several of whom were armed with hunting rifles. Two officers were shot attempting to remove a log that was part of a barricade. The "Defenders" were eventually persuaded to surrender by a Stoney elder. Eighteen Aboriginal and non-Aboriginal men and women were subsequently cited on various weapons charges; fifteen of them were sentenced to jail terms of between six months to eight years.

Seven years later, violence once again was precipitated in a fishing dispute involving the Mi'kmaqs of the Burnt Church First Nation, in New Brunswick. In 1999, about 150 boats belonging to non-Aboriginal fishermen in Miramichi Bay led to the destruction of hundreds of Aboriginal lobster traps and the vandalization of three Aboriginal fish plants. In response, Mi'kmaq warriors established an armed encampment on the wharf of Burnt Church, in an attempt to prevent further destruction of their property. Between 2000 and 2001, tensions again mounted leading to a standoff between Aboriginal fishermen and officers of the RCMP during which sixteen arrests were made. When Department of Fisheries and Oceans officers launched a raid on Native lobster traps, two Native boats were swamped and sank. Several officers were injured by rocks thrown at them during the altercation. In addition, three non-Natives were arrested and their firearms seized when shots were reportedly fired. Further convictions followed when Burnt Church men were charged with assault and obstructing DOF officers. During the same summer and early fall, at least thirty gunshots were fired during a confrontation between Aboriginal and non-Aboriginal fishermen in additional altercations.

The town of Caledonia, Ontario, was the site of armed violence involving Six Nations protesters, the police, and local non-Aboriginal residents, in 2006. The Six Nations people claimed that a forty-hectare piece of property intended for a housing development had never been surrendered. After the erection of tents and a wooden building on the disputed land, eviction notices were served on the protesters, resulting eventually in the OPP arresting twenty-one Aboriginal protesters. The arrests brought on even more protesters, who then constructed a barricade of burning tires and gravel on the main road leading into Caledonia. The barricade was partially removed to allow emergency vehicles to enter the town. However, non-Aboriginal townspeople engaged in a confrontation with the protesters at the site of the barricade, resulting in a skirmish of insults and punches. The escalation of violence continued with the injury to several OPP officers and other parties in the dispute, the burning of a truck at a hydroelectric power substation, and the declaration of a state of emergency in the town.

The following month, further altercations developed as a police cruiser attempted to drive through a line of protesters. A news cameraman was assaulted by protesters during this incident, and surprisingly, a U.S. Border Patrol vehicle was attacked by several protesters. Six Aboriginal protesters were eventually cited on fourteen charges ranging from attempted murder to theft of a motor vehicle. Finally, in 2007, the dispute was diffused when Ontario Premier Dalton McGuinty announced the purchase of the controversial property by the provincial government. In a subsequent development, in 2009, non-Aboriginal citizens of Caledonia announced the formation of local "militias" to enforce the laws that they believe the OPP are unwilling or unable to enforce.

The Akwesasne Border Confrontation of 2009 was a further case of a violent confrontation between Aboriginal protesters and the members of several police forces. For the Mohawks of Akwesasne, daily life is a complicated matter because their territory is divided in various ways between Ontario, Quebec, and New York State. A significant issue for the Mohawks is the traversing of the various borders in order to get to different sections of their territory. The Jay Treaty of 1794, according to the Mohawks, allows for their unimpeded crossing of the international border.

Protests began as early as the 1960s, when the Mohawks blocked the Seaway International Bridge (Three Nations Bridge) near Cornwall, Ontario, and fifty protesters were arrested. Ten years later, the chief of the Mohawk Council of Akwasasne was arrested while attempting to bring a truckload of groceries across the international border. According to the authorities, it is not the transport of groceries that was at issue, but smuggling. For example, in 1988, 250 police officers from Ontario and New York State invaded the Akwasasne reserve armed with helicopters and patrol vessels in a search for duty-free cigarettes. In 1989, a firebomb was thrown at a charter bus and in a later incident a shotgun was fired at another bus.

Later, in 2009, a further confrontation developed when the Mohawks set up an encampment near a Customs facility at Cornwall in response to the arming of border guards. The Mohawks felt that there was no need to arm these officers and that doing so would only escalate the potential for violence, given the long history of such events. As of the time of this writing, there has not been a resolution to this issue, and no signs of mediation or negotiation are evident.

Returning now to a question posed at the beginning of this discussion concerning how important police actions have been in resolving Aboriginal protests, the cases reviewed thus far would indicate that the use of force by the police leads only to a further escalation of violence.

In every case reviewed here, it has *not* been the use of force that eventually led to a resolution of conflict. On the contrary, negotiation and mediation have shown the best results.

Ironically, it has been our first case, the occupation of Anicinabe Park in 1974 that may be taken as a model of dispute resolution. Before the occupation of the park exploded into acts of armed violence, Ontario Premier William Davis, and members of his cabinet, intervened. They were joined in their efforts by the federal minister of Indian and Northern Affairs, various Aboriginal organizations, such as the Union of Ontario Indians, Grand Council of Treaty No. 3 and Treaty 4 Tribal Council, and the Association of Iroquois and Allied Tribes. A request was then made that the province set up a joint committee at the ministerial level to examine the dispute. Aside from the specific issue of the occupation of Anicinabe Park, local Aboriginal residents were also allowed to bring into the discussion larger issues in the area such as land, hunting and fishing rights, and pollution and conservation concerns. Eventually, the land issue of Anicinabe Park was referred to the Indian Land Claims Commission, which also involved discussions with the Aboriginal chiefs of the Lake of the Woods area.

In the case of the Teme-Augama Anishnabai logging blockade, a resolution of the dispute was sought through the courts, first through the Ontario Court of Appeal, and then eventually in a Supreme Court of Canada decision. The Supreme Court ruled that Aboriginal title had been extinguished by the Robinson-Huron Treaty of 1850; however, it did place the Teme-Augama Anishnabai in an adversarial position with other Aboriginal organizations, principally the Union of Ontario Indians and the Assembly of First Nations, laying groundwork for possible future animosity between these various Aboriginal political groups.

The Innu occupation of the Goose Bay Air Base in Labrador was apparently resolved when NATO decided to discontinue their low-level flights for reasons that were not made clear. Effective leadership strategies were, however, developed by the Innu which may be used in the future should further confrontations develop. Issues underlying the Lubicon Cree confrontation, in northern Alberta, have not been satisfactorily resolved, at least from the First Nation's perspective, as it was announced in 2009 that the TransCanada Pipeline would begin construction.

The dispute at Oka, Quebec, was eventually resolved when plans for the proposed golf course were cancelled. In 2000, the Mohawks were given legal jurisdiction over 960 hectares of property in an agreement signed with the federal government. Similarly, the Grand River dispute at Caledonia was resolved, at least partially, with the purchase of the disputed property by the provincial government, with a financial contribution by the federal government. Resolution of the Burnt Church fishing dispute was the result of a negotiated settlement in conjunction with a Supreme Court of Canada decision ruling that Aboriginal people were entitled to establish a "moderate livelihood" through the use of local resources. The federal government also participated in a plan by which more than a thousand commercial fishing licences were bought, thus reducing competition between non-Aboriginal and Aboriginal fishermen. In addition, an agreement was reached between the Burnt Church First Nation and Ottawa worth $20 million paid out over two years. One could conclude, then, that a resolution of the east coast fishery dispute, which at one time involved widespread violence, was eventually resolved by non-confrontational tactics and the active participation by federal and provincial ministries in tackling the fundamental issues that have historically placed Aboriginal peoples at a disadvantage in their attempts to secure adequate subsistence resources.

The forest management dispute in northern Ontario involving the Grassy Narrows First Nation was also resolved through a negotiation process involving band members, various levels of government, and decisions by multinational corporations. It is also interesting that in this case the Aboriginal groups received support by international lobby groups, such as Amnesty International and the Rainforest Action Network, support reminiscent of that received by the James Bay Crees from the Sierra Club in the 1970s.

Each of the aforementioned cases of Aboriginal resistance is unique in its own right, and yet they are all the same in that confrontations emerged between Indigenous protesters and elements of the Canadian state. When police forces have been involved in such confrontations, there has been a tendency for violence to escalate leading in some instance to the death of both protesters and police officers. How can such deaths be avoided in the future? How can conflict be resolved without engendering animosity and loss of life? What role does negotiations, among various parties such as Aboriginal residents and their political organizations, government officials and associated ministries, and policing authorities play in reaching reconciliation and dispute resolution? These are the sorts of questions that frame the following discussion.

Aboriginal-Police Relations: Resistance and Reconciliation

This discussion begins with the assumption that little is to be gained by simply suppressing Aboriginal dissent by brute force, since inevitably any particular dispute will only arise again in another place and time. In other words, conflicts and differences between Aboriginal peoples and the Canadian state are most effectively resolved in a non-confrontational manner, using techniques of negotiation, mediation, and reconciliation, rather than through the exercise of force, manipulation, and intimidation.

Gordon Christie (2007: 147), law professor at the University of British Columbia, has commented, "Contextual analysis is critical to making sense of the appropriate relation between the police and the Canadian government when these two bodies intersect with the interests of both Aboriginal nations and Aboriginal individuals within Canada. It is also critically important when attention is turned to particular disputes, for no scenario played out in the arena of Canadian-Aboriginal relations can be adequately understood outside its place within the larger legal, constitutional, historical and political landscape." These "contextual" variables of history, politics, and constitutional aspects make state-Aboriginal relations a particularly complex matter in terms of policing acts of confrontation and resistance.

Police officers who are involved in Aboriginal confrontations over land claims, resource issues, or other similar contentious matters cannot be expected to have much familiarity or training in the "legal, constitutional, historical or political" aspects of such disputes. The role of the police is more specifically engaged in exercising the rule of law, rather than attempting to act as constitutional lawyers, political scientists, or legal experts in the fiduciary aspects of Aboriginal land claims. Leaving the police with an increase in discretionary powers in these disputes would also only lead to further confusion over what their role should be in Aboriginal confrontations. "It can be extraordinarily difficult," Pue (2007: 132–3) suggests, "to mark precisely where one constitutional right – freedom of expression or Aboriginal entitlement, for example – must give way to another – the preservation of the peace, perhaps. Such boundaries fuzzily demarcate the frontier between lawful and unlawful police conduct." When gunfire is exchanged between Aboriginal protesters and the police, one would hope that such "fuzziness" is kept to a minimum for the safety of all concerned.

There is evidently, then, a lack of clarity in Aboriginal-police relationships that hinders the execution of the proper role of the police when disputes arise in the context of Aboriginal rights. According to Christie (2007: 159), "What this means in the context of police-governance relations should be clear. While some discretionary leeway around the exercise of decision-making power will remain unavoidably present, in broad terms the decisions of the government about how to set appropriate police policy must be by and large settled." The conclusion that could be reached, therefore, in the context of our previous analysis of Aboriginal-police involvement from Anicinabe Park to Caledonia is that both the provincial and federal governments could exercise more effective involvement by intervening more actively in formulating stricter rules of engagement between the conflicting parties in order to reduce future harm to both.

This also means that in the context of Aboriginal and treaty rights the government is not "free to develop and implement policy as it sees fit" (Christie 2007: 158). The Crown has "legally mandated fiduciary duties [which] serve to place the debate [over appropriate police-government relationships] itself in a particular and unique context" (ibid.). There are, therefore, unique fiduciary obligations on the Crown that even predate the arrival of the Crown in present-day Canada. As such, "until the process of reconciliation has run its course in a fair and just fashion the Crown cannot treat Aboriginal peoples as nothing more than groups of citizens within society, their rights contained entirely within the ambit of the social contract forming the nation state. In a sense, a fully formed social contract (which will complete the process of welcoming Aboriginal peoples into Canadian society) would be the outcome of this process" (pp. 158–9).

The Crown, therefore, has a fiduciary obligation to protect the rights of Aboriginal peoples. It also has discretionary control over the legal and other interests of Aboriginal peoples as beneficiaries. This obligation places the Crown in a unique position because of its fiduciary duties and the Crown's discretionary ability to influence Aboriginal interests in either negative or positive ways. The Crown is under an obligation to protect the (Aboriginal) beneficiaries' interests, and while there may be some discretion available in the workings of the fiduciary obligations, there are, nonetheless, "strong guiding principles laying out general restrictions on how the fiduciary can act, and guiding the fiduciary towards a narrow range of acceptable options. Ranging over the particular principles and guideposts is one over-arching fiduciary principle: the fiduciary must act in the best interests of the beneficiary" (p. 159).

The exercise of fiduciary responsibilities is, therefore, a significant aspect of Aboriginal-police relationships in managing confrontations because the police, as a representative of the Crown, share in these responsibilities of protecting the beneficiaries' interests, whether the police see this as their role or not. These fiduciary responsibilities not only constrain the government in its exercise of power, but by extension, also constrain the police when they are engaged in policing particular disputes about Aboriginal rights. What this would appear to mean is that when it comes to Aboriginal issues, the police have an obligation that goes beyond simply exercising their discretionary powers in administering the rule of law. Aboriginal peoples must trust that the state will deal with them in a fair and honourable manner and that their interests will be protected by the rule of law – however that might be interpreted – as Aboriginal peoples must submit, correspondingly, to the power of the government.

These various government-police-Aboriginal relationships, of course, also take place at the same time as the debate continues over the role of Aboriginal peoples in Canadian society. In fact, the very relationship between the state and Aboriginal First Nations is, in itself, a particularly contentious issue. This debate is also about the role of the judiciary in conceptualizing state-Aboriginal relationships because not all Aboriginal peoples are willing to accept the premise that they a priori fall under the sovereignty of the Crown. While the state and the courts may assume that this is the case, it is a problematic matter in Aboriginal communities.

There are Aboriginal people who dispute the jurisdiction of the state in their internal affairs and who, likewise, would not agree that the dialogue concerning their sovereignty rests solely on the contention or presumption that such dialogue is necessarily a matter internal to Canadian society. In terms of jurisdictional matters, it is not altogether clear how much of a right the police have when it comes to enforcement on Aboriginal lands, especially when such lands are part of, or situated on, disputed territory that is the subject of a claim. Furthermore, if the position of the Crown's sovereignty over Aboriginal peoples is seen to be an unquestioned fact, then surely, reconciliation attempts are particularly one-sided. This is especially the case, as a form of neo-colonialism, where Aboriginal and treaty rights are controlled by the state and its courts, while simultaneously purporting to act in the best interests of First Nations people; thus, reinforcing the subordinate position of Aboriginal communities in Canadian society (Christie 2007: 166–8). In the matter of police governance, for example, we are, therefore, confronted with fundamental questions "arising from Canada's history of imperial colonisation and contemporary practices of internal colonization" (Williams and Murray 2007: 172).

At the heart of the issue of jurisdiction is that Canada's relationship with Aboriginal peoples remains unresolved. Moreover, the liberal democratic assumptions upon which this relationship appears to be founded are also a matter of contestation and dispute among Aboriginal First Nations. Since the Canada-First Nations relationship remains a contested one, the matter of police governance also remains problematic in terms of the force that the police might feel justified in using in their involvement in Aboriginal protests and confrontations, regardless whether that justification stems from the rule of law or not. Christie's (2007) analysis, for example, clearly disputes the legitimacy of the Canadian state in determining the relationships of its institutions, such as the courts, police, or governments, to Aboriginal peoples according to the logic of the liberal democratic order.

Police governance in Canada, as it relates to Aboriginal peoples, can be most accurately described in terms of Kent Roach's (2007) "democratic policing" model. Although this model allows for "quasi-judicial" police independence, "the democratic policing model affirms the importance of the minister being informed about important cases lest they reveal policy issues or structural defects that should be reformed. The democratic policing model sees ministerial responsibility for policing matters as a fundamental feature of responsible government and as a necessary means of ensuring that the police do not become a law unto themselves" (pp. 59–60).

This model suggests that the responsible minister would be informed about ongoing criminal investigations if such investigations raise more general policy matters. It is also based on the assumption that there will be a general understanding among the various participants that an important distinction is drawn between the seeking of information so as to influence the conduct of an investigation, and seeking information because of such an investigation's relevance to policy matters. This matter of seeking information by non-police personnel into an ongoing investigation raises a matter of faith that such conduct has legal merit, and that each party, a minister and the police, for example, are not placed in a position of determining the course of an ongoing investigation. This matter of faith may be too much for some to swallow. As Roach (2007: 61) explains, "If the democratic policing model is based on what some might see as a nostalgic faith in the integrity of politicians and their willingness to accept responsibility for making difficult policy decisions for the police, it is also based on a more limited faith in police expertise and professionalism than the model of full police independence."

These matters relating to the democratic policing model become particularly important when it comes to policing confrontations with First Nations people because there is so much policy ambiguity in the area of Aboriginal land and treaty rights. At present, there is not a lot of direction given to police forces. The relationship between the Crown and Aboriginal peoples is a constantly evolving one, as processes of reconciliation take place and as a position in the fabric of Canadian society is accorded Aboriginal peoples. The role of the police in the reconciliation process is not entirely clear at this point, yet "this task will require in turn that direction be provided to police forces. The police must be directed away from actions that potentially interfere with Aboriginal (and treaty) rights and towards actions that promote the reconciliation envisioned" (Christie 2007: 157).

It is inevitable, then, that our present discussion about how police interact with Aboriginal peoples should be directed towards wider issues, such as those involving institutional structures, rather than on specific instances that have been analysed previously in this chapter concerning cases of political mobilization. In this regard, Williams and Murray (2007: 176) have arrived at a particularly reasonable conclusion: "Ultimately, the development of a structure to govern how the police interact with Aboriginal peoples will not turn on details of institutional design but on an honest and sincere commitment to a decolonizing framework of action, a framework that embodies the core values identified by Aboriginal peoples: truth, reconciliation, reparation, and the reconstruction of the relationship between Aboriginal peoples and the Canadian state."

The Canadian state and Aboriginal First Nations are currently engaged in what Bashir and Kymlicka (2008) have termed "the politics of reconciliation." This process is based on the recognition in modern democracies that the older practices of exclusion and marginalization of minority groups have become increasingly discredited, although the effects of these ideologies have had a lingering effect (see also Kymlicka and Bashir 2004). Reconciliation is the basis upon which a new framework is constructed for developing new relationships between the Aboriginal peoples and the Canadian state (Penikett 2006). Walter (2008) also explores how the idea of reconciliation and the larger jurisprudence of Aboriginal rights in Canada merge or fit together.

Walter (2008) compares two modes of reconciliation – the political and the legal. He points out that reconciliation in the context of Indigenous peoples and European settler states is often seen as a political process rather than a legal doctrine. As he suggests, "It is usually assumed that reconciliation offers to political discourse something that the liberal concepts of democracy, justice, equality, and the rule of law cannot – in particular, ideas of repentance, forgiveness, healing, and harmony. But the features of reconciliation that make it a powerful political ideal also makes it controversial." (p. 165). The reason that reconciliation can be considered a controversial topic is that it might be seen to undermine liberal values that could occur when justice is seen to be sacrificed in favour of amnesty and truth, or, as Philpott (2006: 25–33) observes, when personal moral convictions are allowed into the domain of public institutions.

Goals of reconciliation such as truth telling, healing, forgiveness, and nation building are usually considered to be best achieved as a political process, rather than through the use of formal legal doctrines, even if the rule of law needs to be sacrificed in order to achieve these goals. However, Walter (2008) argues that the law is a critically important aspect of reconciliation, especially as efforts are made to reconcile legal traditions of the state with those of Indigenous societies. He further suggests that while the "use of law as an instrument to help achieve the end of reconciliation is frequently acknowledged ... little attention seems to be given to the possibility that reconciliation may be ... an intrinsic part of what law is – or, to be more precise, what the ideal of legality or the rule of law requires. Of course, if some conception of reconciliation really does form an intrinsic part of what we mean by the rule of law within liberal democracies overcoming past conflicts, then concerns that reconciliation and liberalism conflict may prove to be unfounded" (pp. 165–6).

We are left, therefore, with the suggestion that certain attempts at reconciliation may be in conflict with the democratic values of liberalism. The conception of reconciliation within liberal democracies, one could therefore suggest, needs to be more clearly defined, especially in terms of whatever role reconciliation may play in the application of the rule of law, which would be a means of ameliorating or resolving the possible reconciliation-liberalism opposition. John Hatch, in *Race and Reconciliation* (2008), offers further insight into the process of reconciliation in the context of jurisprudence and restorative justice. Hatch notes, "Reconciliation puts *justice* into play with the exercise of rhetorical *judgement*" (p. 51, original emphasis). He then quotes the work of Erik Doxtader (2003: 270) in support of this idea with the comment that "reconciliation precedes, enacts, and follows a critique of law, the laws that govern both the state [apartheid] and struggle [against apartheid]. It generates a productive uncertainty about the nature of justice as well as the ways and means of establishing the common good" (quoted on p. 51).

We return, then, having traversed through Bashir and Kymlicka's (2008) "politics of reconciliation" and Walter's comments on the "jurisprudence of reconciliation," to James Tully's (2008: 258–76) discourse on the "arts of resistance" in the context of internal colonization. In particular, we are concerned here with what Tully (2008) refers to as the "structures of domination" that have resulted from the historical processes that "have been set in place on Great Turtle Island (North America) over the Indigenous peoples and their territories without their consent and in response to their resistance both against and within these structures" (p. 259). These "structures of domination" have been aptly illustrated by our previous case studies of Aboriginal resistance, from Anicinabe Park in 1974 to the Akwesasne Border Confrontation in 2009, and all the other protests and confrontations in between.

Canadian police forces have been employed to one degree or another in all of these instances in response to Aboriginal resistance, suggesting that an important aspect of the Canadian state's methods of dealing with dissent is through the use of force, rather than through processes of reconciliation, healing, and nation building. The use of such force is usually justified by the dictum that the "rule of law" must be upheld. The problem is that the very colonial structures that have led to the acts of resistance in the first place are contested by Indigenous peoples, and as such the very laws that have been designed to uphold these structures (of domination) are also in dispute. Of course, this all brings into question the legitimacy of the use of force, and the employment of police forces in a combative manner, to quell acts of Aboriginal resistance in Canada. Certainly, one can question whether the use of such force, in cases such as land claims that are clearly matters of civil litigation, has any chance to result in the achievement of goals of reconciliation that the federal government purports to desire through the establishment of such apparently noble ventures as the Truth and Reconciliation Commission. One could very well argue that the Canadian government is at a cross-roads in its treatment of the Aboriginal population. Will government continue to use force and "rule of law" to suppress dissent and resistance, or will it attempt another approach, one more tempered towards negotiation, reconciliation, and eventual healing?

Conclusion

The core of this chapter has focused on various contestations of Aboriginal land and treaty rights in Canada. Many more protests and confrontations could be presented, but the ones discussed are perhaps the most prominent ones, extending over at least three decades. There has been a wide historical and geographical basis to this discussion, ranging from the 1960s to those still going on today. Geographically, the disputes have ranged from Gustafsen Lake in British Columbia to the shores of Miramichi Bay on the east coast. Culturally and linguistically speaking, these disputes have ranged across the Ojibway (Anishinabe), Mi'kmaq, Mohawk, Shuswap, and Innu nations, among others. The disputes have involved fishing and hunting rights, land claims of various sorts, forestry issues, burial grounds, and border problems, to name some of the more prominent ones. In other words, there would appear to be no part of this country that has not been affected by Aboriginal disputes, protests, and confrontations, nor many First Nations that have not been involved. A discussion of more of these situations would serve little purpose except, perhaps, to magnify the endemic and perdurable nature of such disputes. It is necessary, therefore, to step back and attempt an overview, one that goes beyond the specific details of any one of these troubles.

Ultimately, the disputes emanate from the frustration that Aboriginal peoples hold, and the manner in which these frustrations are dealt with by those empowered in our society at the government level to deal with them. One would think that the normal process would be that disputes should be brought initially to a member of the federal Department of Indian Affairs, such as a district superintendent. However, these individuals are not equipped to deal with such legal issues as land claims because they are essentially administrators whose problems are primarily budgetary and accounting ones. At the local reserve or First Nation level, there is not available a nearby mechanism for dealing with land and treaty issues. This causes Aboriginal peoples to seek other methods to bring attention to their problems, which usually involve making the issue public in some manner, in the hope of attracting attention through the news media.

In other countries, people have dealt with their problems using different methods that probably would not work well with Aboriginal populations. Take the Gandhian way, for example, of going on a hunger strike. An Aboriginal person in a far out-of-the-way place in Canada's north is not going to attract much attention by going on a hunger strike since there are few people around to notice, and in any event, everyone else is hungry all the time anyway. How about the methods of the civil rights movement of Martin Luther King? The fact is that these methods are more suited to very large urban centres where hundreds of thousands of people could attend mass rallies. Aboriginal peoples in Canada do not have this sort of large population base for this method to be effective.

The demographics of Aboriginal life in Canada are such that many live in out-of-the-way rural or isolated areas where matters of linguistic fluency are an issue in communicating their concerns to a wider public. In the southern areas, the population base is still not very large – the largest reserve in Canada, the Six Nations of the Grand River Reserve, still only has slightly over 20,000 people (22,924 in 2004, according to Frideres and Gadacz 2008: 67). Next in population size are the Mohawks at Akwesasne (at 10,013) and Kahnawake, Quebec (at 10, 201). The largest non-Iroquois Aboriginal settlement in Canada is the Blood Reserve of Alberta, with a population of 9,956. The population concentrations, therefore, are not conducive to large-scale political mobilization. In any event, the mobilizations as a whole, are primarily parochial in nature, concerning local disputes over land, fishing and hunting, and so on. There are not usually large-scale gatherings to protest, for example, injustice, poverty, discrimination, unemployment, or other more prominent social issues.

The primary conclusion that could be made in this chapter regarding Aboriginal acts of civil disobedience is that they should be thought of as essentially political acts. They are attempts to bring attention to a particular issue or problem that exists in the relationship between First Nations people and the wider Canadian society. It is true that many of the disputes have an economic dimension to them, such as in the case of hunting, fishing, or other resource use. The primary characteristic is political in nature because there is an attempt to influence or even force the outside society to understand or agree to an Aboriginal perspective in situations where there does not exist an intermediary or ombudsman role that could serve to ameliorate such disputes.

The police are unfairly thrust into a situation that they do not perceive as essentially political. As far as the police are concerned, they are apt to see Aboriginal confrontations as attempts to usurp their authority, or the authority of the state, which they are compelled to uphold. This is especially difficult when you have politicians referring to land claims as essentially a criminal matter, as in the Gustafsen Lake occupation. One suggestion that could be made here is that the police in the future should resist the tendency to march in with full force and start making arrests. In most cases, the defendants are released of the charges in any event. What the police should do is attempt to contain the situation, by not posing a threat, and keep recalcitrant or belligerent non-Aboriginal citizens from becoming involved, as happened at Caledonia.

The police should also realize that any aggression towards them on the part of Aboriginal protesters has more to do with attracting media attention than an attack on the police's authority. If a confrontation breaks out with a police force, then the media quickly takes notice, and we then see coverage on the *CBC News*, or printed stories in the *Globe and Mail*, the *Toronto Star*, or the *National Post*. Aboriginal protesters realize that politicians are not apt to take notice of a protest or confrontation unless it is written up in a national newspaper; their strategy is aimed at putting pressure on politicians to act to resolve the dispute. Such acts are meant to persuade and influence, not to harm or coerce, although many would appear to be of that nature on the surface. Where would the Oka Crisis be without the startling images played out before the cameras on the nightly news of 1990?

Aboriginal acts of resistance share aspects in common, as a process. First, there is an initial blockade, for example, and then the police intervene. Next, local citizens become angry that arrests are not made; there is pushing and shouting, and insults are hurled at the various participants. Sometimes shots are fired. The news media arrive to record the trouble. Politicians arrive and attempt to appease and ameliorate with promises of negotiations. Eventually, an inquiry might be called. Sometimes, the issue is forgotten and, at other times, it is remembered like a festering sore. Time goes on, with new disputes emerging on a regular basis, in different geographical locales, over apparently different underlying issues. Everyone is dancing to a different tune that they have in their heads, oblivious to the music the other is hearing.

Most of the civil disobedience discussed in this chapter involves complicated situations – the disputes often differ at many levels of background, participants, levels of violence, efforts at negotiations, and so forth. There is the risk, then, of inadvertently drawing gratuitous or invidious comparisons concerning what are essentially incommensurate examples. At one level, all of the Aboriginal confrontations are the same, at least to the degree that they involve an assertion of rights and claims of unresolved issues. They are all, of course, inherently different, as well, reflecting the multifaceted dimensions of treaty negotiations, hunting and fishing rights, or cultural tendencies either towards negotiation or conflict.

It is helpful to attempt to place the foregoing discussion of Aboriginal resistance in a wider perspective. We can examine, for example, the works of such political philosophers as James Tully (2008), in his study of *Public Philosophy in a New Key: Democracy and Civic Freedom*. According to Tully, Aboriginal resistance in Canada stems from the pressures of internal colonization and from the "structures of domination" which precipitate resistance and dissent. These dominating structures are the result of historical processes that have led to the loss of Indigenous territory without the consent of the Indigenous people. One might argue that the various treaties that resulted in this loss of territory were "negotiated" and that compensation was provided. However, looking more objectively at the treaty process, it is evident that the Aboriginal leaders who signed the treaties were often unsure about the implications involved – were they signing a peace treaty between nations, for example, rather than alienating their right to their land forever?

After a treaty was signed, before the Aboriginal population knew what was happening, their appropriated land was settled by newcomers who began to displace the Aboriginal population, which was becoming rapidly diminished by disease and loss of habitat. The remaining population was relocated to small reserves, while their former territory was subjected to the ravages of an industrial economy, as forests were denuded for agriculture, logging, and mining enterprises. The process of internal colonization was augmented by government structures, such as the Department of Indian and Northern Affairs and its various forerunners, which consolidated administrative control over the Aboriginal population.

The Aboriginal population became increasingly fragmented by these administrative structures and legislative initiatives such as the Indian

Act, resulting in competing subgroups, such as reserve versus non-reserve populations, treaty versus non-treaty, status versus non-status, Metis, Inuit, and so on. The end result is that a formerly politically independent, economically self-sufficient Indigenous population became largely dependent on meagre government handouts and suffered from inadequate housing, high levels of unemployment, and substandard health and educational facilities.

Options for resisting this downward spiral were few in number, because of the lack of resources to fight for rights in the courts or to lobby the government politically; remember that status Indians did not even have the right to vote until the mid-twentieth century. Resistance took the form of blockading roads, railways, and other transportation routes. Band offices and government buildings were occupied, and at times violent clashes broke out between police and protesters. Government representatives and leaders of Aboriginal organizations were often reluctant to intervene, blocking avenues for negotiation and dispute resolution. Land claims commissions were established, but it might take generations for particular land disputes to be resolved, if at all.

As Tully (2008: 261–2) remarks, "The essence of internal colonisation ... is the appropriation of the land, resources and jurisdiction of the Indigenous peoples, not only for the sake of resettlement and exploitation (which is also true of external colonisation), but for the territorial foundation of the dominant society itself." In external colonization, the imperial society and the colony exist on different territories, leading to the possibility that at some future date the colony may be free to establish its own state which is independent geographically from the dominant one, as Canada itself has done. This is not possible when the colonization is an internal one: "The problematic, unresolved contradiction and constant provocation at the foundation of internal colonisation, therefore, is that the dominant society coexists on and exercises exclusive jurisdiction over the territories and jurisdictions that the Indigenous people refuse to surrender" (p. 262).

A pattern of push and pull is established in which the Indigenous populations resist the enforced assimilation and pressures to conform to the dominant group, while the larger, dominant one exerts increasingly greater measures of force and suppression in an attempt to quell the dissent. Reconciliation appears only as a distant goal because the two competing pressures – one to conform through the structure of domination as a whole, and the other to resist in the name of sovereignty and self-determination – never seems to lead to the freedom as self-governing peoples that the colonized Indigenous societies so desperately struggle for. This "unresolved contradiction" that Tully refers to in internal colonization cannot be resolved by the eradication or disappearance of the freedom sought by Aboriginal peoples or by the suppression of their rights to their territories and pre-existing governments.

Chapter Five

The Ipperwash Confrontation[1]

The occupiers saw the OPP dressed in "riot" gear, standing should-to-shoulder in rows and stretched across the road ... The police officers were equipped with bulletproof vests, shields, batons, helmets, and guns. The Aboriginal people had no protective clothing and had simply stockpiled rocks and sticks and stones on the inside border of the park fence ... Acting Sergeant Deane discharged his semi-automatic gun. He fired three shots in rapid succession at Dudley George.[2]

          – Hon. Sidney B. Linden, *Report of the Ipperwash Inquiry* (2007: 66, 71)

Aboriginal Origins in Ontario

The history of human habitation by the Indigenous peoples of Ontario extends back at least eleven thousand years, beginning soon after the retreat of the ice sheets of the Wisconsin Glaciation period. In the Palaeolithic period of big-game hunting, called the Clovis Culture, the Brohm site near Thunder Bay was occupied from at least ten thousand years ago. On Manitoulin Island, a quarrying area called the Sheguindah site was occupied for the last nine thousand years. A similar site, called Bronte Gap, was discovered near Hamilton. Copper artefacts were manufactured in the Great Lakes area from around six thousand years ago and traded as far south as the Gulf of Mexico. These objects included an array of tools such as spear points, knives, adzes, and scrapers, as well as pendants and bracelets for personal adornment (Quimby 1967, Wright 1972). The point to be made here, as far as land claims are concerned is that there is no doubt that Aboriginal peoples have resided in Ontario for over ten thousand years, and any quibbling about the occupation of particular locations or particular cultural groups, for example, whether they be Algonkian or Iroquoian, is apt to lead to misleading conclusions about the Indigenous habitation of the province.

The first direct contact between the Algonkian- and Iroquoian-speaking peoples of southern Ontario with Europeans came in 1615 with the Jesuit missionary activity. Samuel de Champlain became actively involved in the wars of the Algonkian and Iroquois tribes, forming a close relationship between the French and the Huron-Petun. The War of the Iroquois in 1649–50 caused a widespread dispersal of the Huron peoples and a large-scale reduction in the human habitation of southern Ontario for nearly the next century, until about 1760.

The Chippewas, or Ojibways or Anishinabe,[3] had made contact with the French in the early 1600s along the eastern shores of Georgian Bay (Rogers 1978, Schmalz 1991). The Jesuits made their way to Sault Ste. Marie, in 1641, and subsequently opened a mission on Manitoulin Island in 1648. After the dispersal of the Hurons, the Chippewas appear to have maintained their territories along the shores of Georgian Bay and Lake Huron. During the 1690s, the Chippewas began moving south into Ontario and soon were replacing the Iroquois who were settled along the north shores of lakes Erie and Ontario. Chippewas destroyed several Iroquois villages at the mouth of the Humber River, in 1702–4, and began to push them farther south into the Niagara region by 1707.

By the early part of the eighteenth century, the Chippewas, and other namesakes such as the Ojibways, Odawas, and Mississaugas, were well established in the country down as far as the north end of Lake St. Clair and Detroit. The southeastern Chippewas began to cede their lands to the British after about 1760. The first British purchase of land in Ontario occurred in 1764, although a treaty recognizing this purchase was not signed until 1781. Further land sales continued, until by 1830 the Chippewas had ceded most of their lands to the British Crown. As their territory diminished because of these land deals, the Chippewas were encouraged to settle upon a series of relatively small reserves that had been set aside "for their benefit" (Surtees 1969). During this period, the Chippewas also became involved in various military enterprises, such as the nearly successful attempt by Pontiac to oust the British from the Upper Great Lakes area in 1763, and they had significant involvement in the War of 1812, under Tecumseh.

Many Chippewas began to adopt farming in the extreme southern portion of Ontario between 1820 and 1840, raising wheat, hay, oats, peas, corn, and potatoes. However, the initial enthusiasm for farming does not appear to have been sustained to any great degree, as hunting, fishing, and trapping began to increase again in economic importance (Rogers and Tobobondung 1975).

Kettle and Stony Point First Nations

Wiiwkwedong, which means "by the bay," is the Anishinabe name for Kettle Point. The sister community of Stony Point is called *Aashoode-nong*, or "the other side of town."[4] Both communities are situated on the shore of Lake Huron between Sarnia and Grand Bend, with a hunting territory from Blue Point to Goderich. The traditional economy involved seasonal movements, from the fishing camps along the Lake Huron coast during the summer to inland hunting locations during the fall and winter months. Maple sugar was prepared during the spring, while berries, medicines, nuts, and other useful plants were collected according to their seasonal availability.

The Kettle and Stony Point[5] Chippewas formerly lived in a more northerly location, but at the time of the destruction of Neutral and Huron communities in 1649–50, they moved farther south as the Iroquois withdrew or were driven out of southern Ontario. The Chippewas played a significant role in defending southern Ontario (called Upper Canada, and then Canada West from 1841 until Confederation) during the conflict between the British and Americans from 1776 to 1814. The Treaty of Niagara, in 1764, secured an alliance between the British Crown and the more than fifteen hundred Anishinabe chiefs and warriors gathered at Niagara Falls.

One of the founding chiefs of the Kettle and Stony Point First Nation, Oshawnoo (a descendant of Tecumseh), was awarded a silver Chief's Medallion by King George III in recognition of his contribution to the War of 1812. Oral history relates that Chief Oshawnoo and his brother Shignobick participated in the Battle of the Longwoods, in which Tecumseh died, and that they participated in his secret burial to prevent his body from falling into the hands of the Americans. A second silver medal was also presented to Oshawnoo in 1860 during a Royal visit to Sarnia (Gulewitsch 1995).

Land Cessions

The Anishinabe of Kettle and Stony Point, in 1827, ceded some 2.1 million acres of land to the British Crown with the signing of the Huron

Tract Treaty (Treaty No. 29). The British Indian Department treated the Chippewas who had signed the Huron Tract Treaty as one large band that had a shared interest in four reserves; namely, Walpole Island, Sarnia, Kettle Point, and Stony Point.[6] Between 1860 and the 1880s, the various reserves began to separate from one another.

Further land surrenders followed. During the early part of the twentieth century, in 1912, the Kettle Point Reserve was pressured into surrendering its beachfront property for recreational development. Under similar circumstances, a portion of the Stony Point Reserve was surrendered, in 1928, under pressure from the Indian agent and the Department of Indian Affairs, on the rationale that such property had little value because it could not be used for agricultural purposes. Subsequently, in 1936, some of the surrendered land was used to create Ipperwash Provincial Park. A year later, the chief and council of the Kettle and Stony Point Band indicated that a burial ground was situated on park property and asked that the burial sites be protected. There were apparently never any steps taken by the Ontario government to protect the burial site. Human remains were discovered at Ipperwash Provincial Park in 1950 and photographed by the park superintendent's wife.[7]

Further expropriation of Chippewa lands took place when the Department of National Defence decided during the Second World War that it should establish an army training facility on the site of the Stony Point Reserve. Despite protests by the residents of the Kettle and Stony Point Band, and a vote of 82 per cent against the proposal by eligible voters, 2,240 acres of Stony Point Reserve property were appropriated on 14 April 1942, under the War Measures Act. Residents of the Stony Point community were consequently evicted from their land, many houses were bulldozed over, and others were removed by flatbed trucks or hauled on skids by tractors to locations on the Kettle Point Reserve.

The Chippewa people were forcibly relocated to the much smaller Kettle Point Reserve, which was not prepared to house its reluctant guests. Aboriginal soldiers returning home after the war were shocked to find that their homes were gone and their community had disappeared. The main problem with the relocation was that the land at Kettle Point lacked the resources necessary to sustain the additional families. The residents of both the Kettle and Stony Point reserves suffered great emotional and physical hardship as a result. It was not long before tension arose between the two communities, which prior to the relocation had had a mutually harmonious relationship.

The Stony Point people had expected that after the war the federal government would return their land, as promised in the original appropriation order of 1942.[8] However, over the next several decades, numerous attempts were made by the Chippewas to negotiate the return of the Stony Point Reserve, but the Department of National Defence insisted that it continued to need the camp for military training (of army cadets[9]). Since all attempts to persuade the federal government to return the reserve had failed, the former residents of the Stony Point Reserve, out of a growing sense of frustration, decided to occupy the military ranges of Camp Ipperwash in May 1993.[10]

The Occupation of Ipperwash Provincial Park

The depiction of events concerning the confrontation between the police and Aboriginal protesters, as reported by the Ipperwash Inquiry (Linden 2007) is a common enough one, at least as far as Canada is concerned. However, what is perhaps unique about the standoff at Ipperwash Provincial Park is the preponderance of power wielded by the Ontario Provincial Police over the Aboriginal protesters. As the events unfolded leading up to the death of Dudley George, a group of Stony Point people entered the military camp through the main gate and set up tents and a trailer. Their intention was to push forward the negotiation process and to reclaim their land. Members of the Stony Point First Nation also marched to Ottawa, in September 1993, in protest over the military's persistence in remaining on the Camp Ipperwash land. First Nations people continued to occupy the military camp into the summer of 1995, although since the summer of 1993 the camp was no longer in use as a cadet training facility. This summary is derived from the *Report of the Ipperwash Inquiry* (2007).

After several altercations between the Aboriginal occupiers and the military police, the military eventually left the camp on 29 July 1995. The Department of National Defence made no attempt to re-enter the military camp after this date. However, a dozen officers of the OPP Emergency Response Team (ERT) travelled to the area. Four of the officers were assigned to the park disguised as campers. Apparently, the OPP were of the opinion that the Aboriginal people planned to assume control of Ipperwash Provincial Park, in addition to the military camp, which they already were occupying.

A meeting of senior OPP officials took place on 28 August 1995. Tactics were discussed with regard to the possible occupation by Aboriginal people of the Ipperwash campground. On 4 September 1995, Labour Day, First Nations people entered Ipperwash Provincial Park. The park closed at 6:00 p.m., and by 7:30 p.m., Aboriginal protesters had begun to cut back a fence and move vehicles onto the park property. The reason for the occupation stemmed from the belief that the provincial parklands were part of the Stony Point traditional territory. Stony Point people also believed that they had a right to this land because their interests had not been adequately represented by the Indian agent when the land for the park was purchased from them in the 1920s. Another reason for the occupation of the park was to protect the sacred burial sites that had been neglected since the creation of the park.

As far as the OPP were concerned, the occupation came as no surprise to them because there had been threats to occupy the park by Kettle and Stony Point residents since the previous May. The OPP had developed a strategy at this time to co-occupy the park with First Nations protesters. A contingency plan was formulated by the police called "Project Maple," which stressed a peaceful resolution to the protest and proposed that a team of two negotiators be placed on call, although there is no evidence as to the identity of these negotiators or if their services were ever used.

During the evening and night of 4 September 1995, several imbroglios developed between the OPP and the Aboriginal protesters. A car door made contact with a police cruiser causing minor damage. Flares were thrown in the direction of the officers by an Aboriginal person. The rear window of a police cruiser was smashed with a stick. Tension escalated into the next day. Around 11:00 a.m., Ministry of Natural Resources and OPP personnel attempted to serve legal papers on the occupiers, who refused to accept the documents.

Throughout the day of 5 September 1995, First Nations people arrived at the park to support the occupation. They included Stony Point people, who had been living at the military camp, residents of the Kettle Point First Nation, and people from other reserves and communities such as Oneida and Walpole Island. The OPP were attempting to arrange for the transport of armoured vehicles to the area for defensive purposes. The occupiers were being monitored from the air by helicopters, from Lake Huron by boat, and in the dark with night-vision goggles. There was a noticeable increase in the number of OPP cruisers and general police surveillance.

Also on this date, the day after Labour Day, Ontario Conservative MPP Marcel Beaubien contacted the police as well as the office of

Premier Mike Harris in an attempt to pressure the government to intervene and stop the protest. Beaubien testified at the Ipperwash Inquiry
(on 19 January 2006) as follows: "Well, basically I'm giving him [pre-
sumably Premier Harris] a heads up that there's a press release that's
going to go out. And, you know, when you – you give somewhat of a
quote/unquote, I guess, 'ultimatum,' to somebody in the Premier's office, they may not like it. But I felt, hey, I got to get some attention here"
(Linden 2007: 21).

OPP officers marched into the park the next day, Wednesday, 6 September 1995, in a hubristic posture – protected by body armour, shields,
and guns. Evidence indicates that the numbers of Aboriginal park occupiers fluctuated from between ten and forty people, including women
and children. From all reports at the time, the protest was a peaceful,
non-violent one, with no weapons visible in the hands of the Aboriginal protesters, except for a pile of stones, sticks, and several baseball
bats. There did not appear to be any risk to public safety by this demonstration because the demonstration was being held after the Labour
Day weekend and there were not any non-Aboriginal campers left in
the park. Aboriginal leaders stated that they had planned the protest
at that time so that the general public would not be inconvenienced by
any demonstrations.

The Ontario Government's Response

Provincial government representatives later claimed that they had little
specific information on the grievances of the Aboriginal occupiers other
than their claim that a sacred burial ground existed in the park. This
lack of information as to the reasons behind the Aboriginal protest was
to play a crucial role in the general lack of communication between the
Aboriginal residents and government authorities, including the OPP.
What was crucially needed at this time was a go-between so that each
of the parties – the Aboriginal protesters and the Ontario government
representatives – could be made aware of the other's position and intended course of action. Thus, an extremely important aspect of the
Ipperwash Inquiry Report (Linden 2007) concerns the inner workings
and decision making of government personnel with regard to Aboriginal political mobilization – information that could profitably be compared with an earlier study of the Trudeau government's 1969 White
Paper in Sally Weaver's ground-breaking work entitled *Making Canadian Indian Policy: The Hidden Agenda 1968–1970* (1981).

Meanwhile, on that Wednesday, which was the day Stony Point resident Dudley George was shot, Attorney General Harnick told Deputy Attorney General Taman that Premier Mike Harris wanted an injunction immediately and the Aboriginal occupiers removed from the park within twenty-four hours. Apparently, this decision was made that morning during a twenty-minute meeting at the Ontario Legislature Building, in a "dining room" next to the premier's office. The meeting was attended by Premier Harris, various ministers, and their support staff.

Attorney General Harnick testified during the Ipperwash Inquiry, under oath, that while he was taking his seat for the meeting, he heard Premier Harris say in a loud voice, "I want the fucking Indians out of the park." Harnick further testified at the Inquiry that he was "stunned" by Premier Harris's "insensitive and inappropriate" remark. Premier Harris denied that he had uttered the words reported by Harnick and that he considered such words to be a racist statement (*CBC News*, 14 Feb. 2006).[11] Harris did, however, acknowledge that he could think of no reason why Harnick would fabricate or concoct such a statement. Nonetheless, although the government officials cavilled over the precise words uttered at the meeting, the general tenor of Premier Harris's comment (even if he did not use the exact words testified to by Harnick) would appear to have set a certain tone or attitude regarding the precipitous actions to follow at Ipperwash Provincial Park on that fateful day.

Moreover, it could be suggested with a reasonable degree of certainty that it would not have been in Harnick's best interest to offer false information to the Ipperwash Inquiry or to testify that he had heard such a statement by Premier Harris if he had not so heard. More than ten years had elapsed since the former premier reportedly made this derogatory statement. Furthermore, there was no evidence that the statement had had any influence on the OPP operation on the night of Dudley George's death. However, as Commissioner Linden (2007) states in his summary of this situation, "In my view, Premier Harris's comments in the dining room, and generally the speed at which he wished to end the occupation of Ipperwash Park, created an atmosphere that unduly narrowed the scope of the government's response to the Aboriginal occupation. The Premier's determination to seek a quick resolution closed off many options" (p. 49).

A wider issue pertains to the attitudes towards Aboriginal political mobilization held by individuals with authority – either in government or the police. A revealing seventeen-minute tape, for example, emerged during the Inquiry. This tape involves a conversation between OPP Inspector Ronald Fox and Inspector John Carson, the commander overseeing the standoff at Ipperwash Provincial Park. Because of his secondment to the Ministry of the Solicitor General, even though he remained a police office, Inspector Fox was in attendance at "the dining-room meeting" at Queen's Park, Fox continued to report to a senior officer at the OPP for administrative matters. Recorded on this tape is a discussion of Premier Harris's view that the government has "tried to pacify and pander to these people far too long" and that the use of "swift affirmative action" is needed to remove the protesters from the park. As he left the Ontario Legislative Building after the dining-room meeting, Officer Fox was frustrated with comments made by Premier Harris which Fox took as criticism of the OPP. Fox then phoned Inspector Carson, the Incident Commander at Ipperwash, to share his agitation and to explain: "John, we're dealing with a real redneck government ... [T]hey are fucking barrel suckers; they just are in love with guns ... [T]here's no question they couldn't give a shit less about Indians" (p. 50).

Another especially perplexing question concerns who was actually in charge of the decision making emanating for the Premiere's Office after the dining-room meeting. Mike Harris, for example, confirmed that his aide, Deb Hutton, had the authority to speak on his behalf and on the behalf of the Premier's Office (p. 42). However, Deb Hutton repeatedly testified, on 23 November 2005, that she could not remember any specific conversations. One cross-examiner pointed out that she had used phrases such as "I don't recall," or "I don't specifically recall," a total of 134 times. There is, however, evidence that Hutton played a direct role in the crucial decision leading to the deployment of the OPP when Hutton testified that she said: "The Premier feels the longer they occupy it, the more support they'll get – he wants them out in a day or two" (p. 39).

This sense of urgency, whether truly reflective of the premier's wishes on the matter or not, placed particular pressure on any attempts to negotiate an end to the confrontation. Of course, all of this sort of testimony does not place the Harris government in a propitious light in terms of its handling of the Ipperwash Crisis, leading Commissioner Linden to write: "In my opinion neither Deb Hutton nor Michael Harris fully appreciated at that time the power of the Premier and the Premier's Office. They were a new government and did not understand that Ms. Hutton's forceful personality and her strong statements made on behalf of the Premier at the IMC [Inter-Ministerial Committee] meetings has the effect of halting the exchange of important ideas and recommendations by other members of the Committee who very much wanted the occupation at Ipperwash to be resolved peacefully" (p. 42).

Some months after the death of Dudley George, on 1 April 1996, his family filed a wrongful death lawsuit. Premier Mike Harris is named as one of the accused, based on allegations that Harris initiated and ordered the raid that killed Dudley George (*CTV News*, 13 Feb. 2006). Testifying at the trial, on 21 November 2001, Mike Harris denied that he had ordered the OPP to conduct the raid on the protesters; however, more than a year earlier, on 20 December 2000, Harris had confirmed that on the day Dudley George was killed he had met with OPP Commissioner Thomas O'Grady, as evidenced in a memo validated in the Legislature. On 21 November 2001, Mike Harris reversed his position that he had met with Commissioner O'Grady on the day of the raid. Premier Harris then launched a $15 million libel suit, on 19 February 2002, against the *Globe and Mail* regarding an article that discussed the way Harris allegedly reacted to the Ipperwash standoff. The Harris statement of claim says that the article, printed on 14 December 2001, a date that marks his last appearance in the Legislature as premier, implied that he took part in a homicide. Harris continues to deny accusations that he or his government ordered the use of force in the incident.

The family of Dudley George settled a civil suit against former Premier Mike Harris and several members of his former cabinet, on 2 October 2003. The George family also accepted a $100,000 settlement from the Ontario Provincial Police plus undetermined legal costs. A few weeks later, on 12 November 2003, the new premier of Ontario, Dalton McGuinty, kept his election promise and announced that his government had launched an inquiry into the death of protester Dudley George at Ipperwash Provincial Park.

In a statement released on the same day as the *Report of the Ipperwash Inquiry* (Linden 2007), Mike Harris declared that he believes that the Inquiry completely absolves him and his government of directing or interfering with the OPP's handling of the occupation of Ipperwash Provincial Park, meaning that he had "no influence" on the death of Dudley George. Harris also referred to allegations that he and his government were responsible as "false and politically motivated accusations," which were "malicious and petty" (*CBC News*, 31 May 2007).

Racial and Culturally Intolerant Attitudes

What is alarming with regard to the attitudes towards the Aboriginal protesters held by those in power, such as the attitudes apparently held by Premier Mike Harris, is the hardened racist disposition of several OPP officers. In a tape recording made the day before Dudley George was killed, OPP Sergeant Stan Korosec, who was in charge of the OPP Emergency Response Team at Ipperwash, is heard saying, "We want to amass a fucking army. A real fucking army and do this. Do these fuckers big-time" (Linden 2007: 27).

Such attitudes towards Aboriginal peoples would appear not to be unusual. On the morning of 6 September 1995, Mayor Fred Thomas approached Inspector Carson at the OPP command post, in Forest, to convey his concern that his community felt "terrorized" by the events at Ipperwash Provincial Park. No reason was given by the mayor for this heightened level of concern, aside from the information that Native people were involved in the occupation and perhaps the mayor felt threatened by this fact. Also visiting the command post that Wednesday was MPP Marcel Beaubien who conveyed to Inspector Carson that the "Premier is in constant touch. Good communication" (Linden 2007: 33).

In testimony to the Inquiry, OPP Commissioner O' Grady voiced the opinion that it was not appropriate that politicians, including MPP Beaubien and Mayor Thomas, attended at the command post. He also expressed that some topics of conversation between the Incident Commander and the MPP were "regrettable," especially the references to the premier's personal views and wishes. What is also regrettable is the perception, founded in fact or not, that white politicians have an inside track on the information flow of what occurred on 6 September 1995.

During the previous evening (5 September), tensions had escalated, as park occupiers moved about a dozen picnic tables to the Ipperwash parking lot in an attempt to control access to the area. Shortly after, officers in three OPP cruisers approached the parking lot, and one of the cruisers rammed into one of the picnic tables, on which some Aboriginal people were sitting at the time, causing it to break up under the impact of the collision. Aboriginal protesters then flung the broken table onto the hood of the cruiser amid much yelling and commotion.

Aboriginal witnesses testified that several OPP officers made racist comments during this altercation, referring to the occupiers as "wagon burners" and "wahoos." Apparently, one of the officers then pointed at Dudley George and said, "Come on out, Dudley. You're going to be the first." An OPP officer then pulled out a can of pepper spray and sprayed it at some of the protesters, who in turn threw sand in the officer's face (p. 27).

In addition to the aggressive and culturally insensitive remarks made by OPP officers, several of them designed and circulated racist items on 5 and 6 September – even after the death of Dudley George. OPP officers procured T-shirts and related "memorabilia" as mementos or souvenirs of the events of 6 September. On the day of Dudley George's funeral, 11 September 1995, his sister, Pam George, discovered that mugs and T-shirts with the OPP insignia, mixed mockingly with Native symbols, were being sold in a local convenience store.

Such items included a coffee mug with an OPP shoulder flash with an arrow through it, and on the other side, an OPP shoulder flash with the words "Team Ipperwash '95" written below. One of the T-shirts depicted a feather on its side below an OPP crest. The implication portrayed by the image of the feather on its side presumably represented the death of the local Aboriginal culture. Remarkably, the OPP officers involved in the distribution of this anti-Native memorabilia testified that they "believed these images and the objects themselves were benign and that it was not inappropriate to possess or sell them" (p. 30).

It is certainly hard to believe that OPP officers would not regard the T-shirt as portraying racist imagery. The Inquiry also learned of a second souvenir T-shirt that was produced during the course of the Inquiry hearings – almost ten years later – depicting a TRU symbol, that is, a sword, breaking an arrow in half over an anvil, which represented the Emergency Response Team. As the Ipperwash Report notes, "The use of the broken arrow imagery targeted a distinct group of people by their race through the use of violent imagery. It is a negative, stereotypical symbol of the Aboriginal people in the context of the TRU and ERT teams exercising their power over the occupiers" (p. 30).

The Ontario Provincial Police Association (OPPA 2006) made a submission to the Ipperwash Inquiry, on 28 July 2006. The OPPA states that "the existence of the t-shirt has only recently come to its attention and the Professional Standards Branch of the OPP was conducting a formal disciplinary investigation into the conduct of uniform officers involved in the creation, distribution, or possession of the t-shirt" (p. 10). It is certainly hard to believe that the T-shirt issue only came to the attention of the OPP eleven years after the incident. So far, there has been no word on what disciplinary action, if any, was taken against the officers involved.

Elsewhere in its submission, it is revealing that the OPPA believes that "the names and identifying information of police officers who were involved in the OPP discipline investigation and deposition in respect of certain mugs and t-shirts, and other items ... are not relevant to the mandate of the Commission, since none of the police officers had any involvement in the events from September 4–6, 1995" (p. 5). In other words, the OPPA does not feel that it is any of the public's business to know the identity of the officers who perpetrated these racist acts, nor does it feel that the public should be privy to its internal investigation of the matter. One has to wonder how such a blunt and defensive stance on such egregious and culturally insensitive acts by OPP officers will do anything towards improving their image when it comes to future Aboriginal protests.

Racial and culturally intolerant attitudes are conveyed in the flow of conversation between the officers themselves, thereby reinforcing commonly held perceptions that negatively portray the Aboriginal oc-cupiers. An OPP sergeant, for example, who was responsible for coor-dinating the ERTs, and who therefore serves as a role model for other ERT officers, continually made inappropriate and degrading comments about Aboriginal people. While speaking to another officer responsible for the OPP's Marine Unit, on 5 September 1995, this sergeant said that he was going to give his overtime pay "to the government ... so that they can give the Indians more stuff. Like you know, all this stuff we keep giving them doesn't come cheap. Somebody's got to pay for it." Later, in a recorded call to the OPP Dispatch, the sergeant was involved in the following conversation (p. 28):

SERGEANT: And we just pay more taxes so that we could afford to build houses for them.
OPP DISPATCH: Oh, come on ... Now we're going to give in to them with houses?
SERGEANT: Yeah. Don't you think that's right? Because you and I stole that land from them?

Of the recorded conversations, probably the most sarcastic and de-rogatory remarks about Aboriginal people were made by members of the OPP Intelligence Team on 5 September – one day before the shoot-ing (pp. 28–9):

OFFICER 1: No, there's no one down there. Just a big, fat, fuck Indian.
OFFICER 2: The camera's rolling.
OFFICER 1: Yeah. We had this plan, you know. We thought if we could ...
    five or six cases of Labatt's 50, we could bait them.
OFFICER 2: Yeah.
OFFICER 1: And we'd have this big net at a pit.
OFFICER 2: Creative thinking.
OFFICER 1: Works in the south with watermelons.

As outrageous as it sounds, these are the very individuals on whom the public – including, presumably, Aboriginal peoples as well as all other Canadians – rely for protection of their rights and freedoms. It is, of course, incredibly disappointing to hear of such intolerance from people who we expect to be paragons of virtue and models of excellence in Canadian society. As with the mugs and T-shirt issue, the OPPA's reaction to these tapes was handled in a similar manner (2006: 269): "When the OPP discovered the recorded impugned remarks, its Professional Standards branch conducted an internal discipline investigation. The investigators interviewed those OPP members who were identified on the tape recordings to have made inappropriate remarks. The OPP then informally disciplined or counselled its officers and civilian members who made inappropriate remarks. Most of the OPP members who made the remarks or comments were neither present at the Ipperwash Incident from September 4 to 6, nor were they called as witnesses at the Inquiry."

Here, again, the public has not, as yet, been informed of what sort of "informal discipline" took place. Meanwhile, in the OPPA submission, it states, "Sgt. Korosec testified that he did not recall the conversation" (p. 271). A fellow officer, Constable Jacklin, testified that the comments by Sargeant Korosec were made "just out of frustration ... I didn't put any significance on it ... I put absolutely no interpretation of any sort of malice coming from Stan." According to Constable Jacklin, Sargeant Korosec "was just venting and needed sleep. He didn't take the comment seriously or believe that Sgt. Korosec meant what he said" (p. 272). So, presumably, the public also should not take these obviously racist comments "seriously"; if we are "just venting," we are allowed to say just about anything we wish, and such comments, no matter how hurtful or spiteful, are not to be taken seriously. Perhaps Constable Jacklin and Sargeant Korosec should be reminded of the laws against slander, libel, and defamation of character, which are the making of false and malicious statements damaging to a person's reputation. Surely, when an OPP officer makes such slanderous statements when on duty it is a matter of some "significance."

The Shooting of Dudley George

Dudley George was a 38-year-old Aboriginal man from the Stony Point Reserve near Windsor, Ontario. He was one of a number of Aboriginal people, including men, women, and children, who gathered at Ipperwash Provincial Park on Labour Day, 4 September 1995, to protest the refusal of the federal government to return the Stony Point Reserve to its original inhabitants.

The conditions of this occupation have previously been briefly summarized; however, it will suffice here to indicate that under the War Measures Act the federal government had conducted an appropriation of the Stony Point Reserve to be used as a military training base, with the promise that the confiscated reserve lands would be returned to the Aboriginal residents after the Second World War ended. Over the ensuing five decades, the appropriated reserve lands were not returned to the Stony Point people. As a result, frustration among the Aboriginal people grew, as their persistent attempts to persuade the Canadian government to return their land were not successful. A confrontation developed between Aboriginal people outside Ipperwash Provincial Park and the Ontario Provincial Police, at which time Dudley George was shot and killed by the police.

According to testimony at the Ipperwash Inquiry (Linden 2007: 65) from the Aboriginal occupiers of the park, the evening of 6 September 1995 was a terrifying and unsettling one. At approximately 9:00 p.m. the OPP closed the roads leading to the park. Thirty-two OPP officers from the Crowd Management Unit (CMU), an additional eight officers assigned as an arrest team, two canine teams, and two prisoner vans assembled at the park boundary. The CMU commander and his force marched in darkness to the park. Members of the CMU were dressed in "Hard Tac" equipment – shin guards, thigh guards, forearm guards, helmets and visors, and bulletproof vests, and carried batons and guns. The arrest team wore the same equipment as the CMU but did not carry shields. In turn, the Aboriginal occupiers, numbering about 20 to 25 people after the departure of women and children; collected rocks, stones and sticks, and a few carried baseball bats. OPP officers testified that they believed, mistakenly as it turned out, that the Aboriginal protesters were armed with "a number of assault weapons ... AK-47s, hunting rifles, and Molotov cocktails" (Linden 2007: 65).

This crucial information on firearms was provided by a councillor of the Kettle and Stony Point First Nation named Gerald George, a man who had not agreed with the occupation of Camp Ipperwash and Ipperwash Provincial Park. In a letter to the editor of the *Forest Standard* newspaper, he had criticized the occupiers for taking control of the barracks at Camp Ipperwash, referring to them in derogatory terms such as "animals" and "army camp Indians." Gerald George approached the OPP officers at a checkpoint and indicated that the park occupiers were in possession of "AK-47s with a 30 round mag duct taped to the back, Mini Ruger 14s, and hunting rifles" (p. 55).[12]

Provided with this information concerning firearms, by Gerald George, at 10:27 p.m., the forty-officer unit, canine teams, and prisoner vans moved towards the park in a tight "box formation." The Aboriginal people wore no protective clothing, body armour, or head protection. They had stockpiled some rocks and sticks near the park fence. By accounts given at the Inquiry, the Aboriginal people "felt greatly outnumbered. As the police officers marched towards Ipperwash Park, the First Nations people were anxious and terrified" (p. 66).

The first casualty was a protester's dog, kicked by an officer as it was barking, sending the creature spinning in the dirt. One of the occupiers, Cecil Bernard George, began to approach the police. The protesters said that the approach of Cecil George was made with peaceful intentions, although according to police reports the approach was made in a violent manner. Cecil George was then taken down, surrounded by police, and arrested. A number of Aboriginal occupiers attempted to rescue Cecil George from the assault by the police units, which then resulted in a riotous scene.

The Aboriginal occupiers began yelling that the officers were standing on sacred ground; grandfathers were buried on this property. One of the CMU officers yelled "punchout" – a tactic used to intimidate and frighten protesters – and the police, beating on their shields, quickly advanced towards the Aboriginal occupiers. An Aboriginal man struck an officer on the edge of his helmet with a steel pole, breaking the Plexiglas shield in half. The officer responded by striking the man's shoulder area with his baton. A number of confrontations broke out in the near-darkness. A school bus and car driven by Native protesters then came out of the park in an attempt to assist the occupiers.

Acting Sergeant Ken "Tex" Deane claimed that he saw a muzzle flash from the interior of a bus driven by a 16-year-old boy. Suddenly, a car swerved towards about ten CMU officers. A number of the officers then opened fire on the approaching vehicle, firing several rounds into the driver's side. Bullets hit the school bus, shattering a window, and wounding two of the Native occupants. Acting Sergeant Ken Deane claimed that he saw two muzzle flashes coming from the bush area. He then saw a man he thought was responsible for the muzzle flashes walk onto the roadway. Deane claimed that the man, Dudley George, was shouldering a rifle in a half-crouched position, aiming it at several OPP officers. Ken Deane then fired three shots at Dudley George in rapid succession. Dudley George dropped to the ground immediately and was then carried away by Aboriginal people who had come to his rescue.

The OPP Response

Ken Deane claimed, at a preliminary hearing prior to the Ipperwash Inquiry, that Dudley George's gun had fallen to the ground after the shooting. However, he did not attempt to retrieve the rifle but left it on the road, he testified. In the Ipperwash Report, it states, "Ken Deane claimed that Dudley George's gun fell to the ground after he shot him. Deane testified that he did not attempt to retrieve the rifle" (p. 71). Other officers could not corroborate Deane's version of the events, as they did not see a firearm carried by Dudley George. At no time, in fact, during the confrontation was any Aboriginal occupier reported by the police to have been seen carrying a firearm. Deane later claimed that he had mistaken the brown, elongated stick carried by Dudley George for a rifle. Sometime later, on 18 September 1995, investigators combed the scene of the standoff but were unable to find any evidence that the protesters had been armed.

Of course, it was a puzzling matter to the Ipperwash Inquiry that Acting Sergeant Deane did not attempt to retrieve the rifle that was allegedly in Dudley George's possession, especially since there was a danger that other protesters could have used this gun to threaten other OPP officers. Also, the supposed rifle would have been an important piece of evidence that the Aboriginal occupiers of the park had weapons. Officer Deane also did not report over the police communications system that an Aboriginal occupier had tried to shoot at the police officers; he simply reported that an individual was down and that an ambulance was needed. The Inquiry did not accept Acting Sergeant Deane's version of the events, concluding unequivocally: "Dudley George did not have a rifle or firearm in the confrontation with the police on the night of September 6, 1995" (p. 72).

On 28 April 1997, Ontario Provincial Court Judge Hugh Fraser ruled that OPP Officer Deane knew Dudley George was unarmed when he shot him. Deane received 180 hours of community service, with no house arrest. Deane was convicted of criminal negligence causing the death of Dudley George. The judge rejected Deane's defence that he believed Dudley George was carrying a rifle, and sentenced him to a conditional sentence of two years less a day to be served in the community, not in custody. On 25 February 2006, Deane died in a car accident – shortly before he was scheduled to testify at the Ipperwash Inquiry. According to the police incident report, Deane had been speeding and driving in multiple lanes when he crashed into a truck.[13] The Inquiry concluded that, besides Acting Sergeant Deane and Inspector Carson (the OPP commander), "the OPP, as an institution, also needs to be accountable and take some responsibility for the tragedy that resulted on September 6, 1995" (p. 77).

Even after Ken Deane's conviction by Judge Fraser in 1997, he continued to profess his innocence. Lawyers acting on his behalf announced, in September 1999, that they had new witnesses who could prove that the protesters were armed during the raid. However, in 2001, the Supreme Court of Canada rejected an appeal by Deane, upholding his conviction. Later, in 2002, Deane was removed from duty after a meeting of the Police Services Board in London, Ontario. Adjudicator Loyall Cann gave Deane seven days to officially submit his resignation. Deane appealed this decision, but in September 2002, Deane resigned from the force and ended the appeal of his dismissal.

Even though it was reported over the OPP communications system by Acting Sergeant Deane that an individual was down, and that an ambulance was needed, Dudley George was transported to the Strathroy Hospital some fifty kilometres away, not by ambulance, but in a car accompanied by his brother Pierre and sister Carolyn. The attempt to bring Dudley George to hospital for treatment was delayed for over an hour because his brother and sister were arrested by the OPP. Dudley George was declared dead at 12:20 a.m. on 7 September 1995, at Middlesex General Hospital in Strathroy, Ontario.

The George family was not satisfied with the conviction of Acting Sergeant Deane and spent years attempting to initiate a fuller investigation by the Ontario and federal governments into the events at Ipperwash Provincial Park. As long as the Conservative party under Premier Mike Harris held power in the provincial legislature, the Ontario government strongly resisted pressure for an inquiry. Finally, with the defeat of the Conservatives by the Ontario Liberal party in the 2003 election, a public inquiry was launched on 12 November 2003.

Although the Inquiry was funded by the government of Ontario, it was conducted by a neutral third party, presumably as an attempt to avoid accusations of a "witch hunt" by the Liberals. The investigation was conducted under the Public Inquiries Act (of Ontario), with a specific mandate to report on the events surrounding the death of Dudley George, although it became obvious from the onset of the Inquiry that other important matters would come into play, such as the role of the police in Native acts of political mobilization, as well as the larger issue of policy in Canada regarding Aboriginal rights and claims. As such, the Inquiry was asked to make recommendations that could serve to avoid similar violent circumstances in the future involving Aboriginal occupations and protests.

The submission of the Ontario Provincial Police Association (OPPA 2006) to the Ipperwash Inquiry contains some 1,023 items in a document comprising a lengthy 271 pages. On the cover of the document are listed six attorneys from a Toronto law firm. It is obvious that each word in this document has been chosen carefully, in a parsimonious manner, but also with an ultimate purpose in mind. The tenor of the document is primarily defensive, in which the intent is to justify or rationalize the OPP's behaviour during the events surrounding the death of Dudley George. Although the Ipperwash Inquiry was not initiated to pursue criminal charges, but as a broad-based attempt at information gathering, nonetheless, the wording of the OPPA document suggests the utmost care in avoiding any possibility that such charges might occur and that the OPP, other than Officer Ken Deane, be free of any culpability or further inculpation of fellow officers in the death of Dudley George and in the treatment of other Aboriginal protesters.

Of primary interest, then, in the OPPA submission is the treatment of the issue of Dudley George's shooting. There are at least thirty-five items in this document pertaining to the behaviour of Dudley George prior to his death. For example, the items begin with the observations of two OPP officers disguised as campers, assigned to the "camping detail," during the summer of 1995. The officers claim to have witnessed the following:

> *Item 91*: On the evening of July 31 [1995] ... a blue Trans-Am carrying Dudley George and two male natives parked along the fence that separated the Park from Matheson Drive. They were drinking alcohol. Dudley George taunted people on the Ipperwash Park beach and told them to get off native land. He said they would soon be taking over Ipperwash and Pinery Parks, and swore at an elderly couple, telling them to "get the fuck" off their land. Dudley George then urinated on the beach. (p. 35)
>
> *Item 96*: [Later, on August 11,] Cst. Parks interviewed a man who reported two incidents on the Port Franks beach where persons were chased off the beach by Dudley George in a car. (p. 37)
>
> *Item 98*: On September 2, two officers noted a car stuck on the beach on the road allowance that separated the military beach from Ipperwash Park. Dudley George and another male native were drinking beer by the car ... Dudley George threatened to throw the officers "off their land." (p. 37)
>
> *Item 99*: Tina George was present during this incident and described Dudley George as being in the face of the police officers, spit flying and telling them to get out. She was with Russ Jewell at the time, who she says tried to make the police think he had guns in the trunk of his car. (pp. 37–8).
>
> *Item 100*: On September 3, 1995, D/Cst. Drew witnessed Dudley George, who was drunk, kicking children off the beach. (p. 38)

On the issue of Dudley George and other Aboriginal people being in possession of firearms:

> *Item 104*: According to Marlin Simon, between May 1993 and July 1995, he generally has between 8–10 guns, including shotguns, 22s and high-powered rifles. The guns were usually kept at his trailer in the Army Base. (p. 39)
>
> *Item 106*: Carl George ... told S/Sgt. Bouwman about a high-powered rifle in Dudley George's trailer. (p. 39).
>
> *Item 108*: Marlin Simon testified that he frequently went hunting with Dudley George and others. Dudley George would borrow a gun to

hunt. According to Marlin Simon, Dudley George was a good shot. (p. 40)

Item 110: D/Cst. Speck testified that he and others heard automatic gunfire in the Army Camp. On one occasion, on April 20, D/Cst. Speck saw Dudley George in the doorway of his trailer holding a rifle. (p. 40)

Item 113: As part of the Ipperwash investigation, D/Sgt. Richardson interviewed a number of Department of National Defence members who were posted at the Army Camp between 1993 and 1995. Out of the 38 persons interviewed, a number recalled incidents involving weapons and occupiers: R.G. Saw Dudley George shoot out a hydro transformer by his trailer.

- M.B. was chased by Dudley George in a vehicle and there was a gun in the vehicle. On another occasion, his patrol vehicle was rammed and guns were seen in the suspect's vehicle.
- C.P. observed occupiers with guns and observed Dudley George point a gun at this location.
- S.D. had a scoped rifle pointed at him by Dudley George. (p. 41)

There is no need to go further with this enumeration of events and situations. The OPPA submission offers no analysis, so one presumes that readers are supposed to draw their own conclusions, based on the "facts" as presented. We should bear in mind that while some of the accounts are based on sworn testimony, there has been no cross examination of these observations, and none of them have been established with regard to their veracity.

The question, then, is what conclusions, if any, could be drawn from the information presented, and how does it relate to the shooting of Dudley George by Acting Sergeant Ken Deane on the evening of 6 September 1995? For one thing, it is evident based on the OPPA's submission that Dudley George would appear to have been an aggressive, belligerent, "pain in the ass" sort of person. He also would appear to have owned firearms himself, and was a "good shot." It is obvious that the OPP have presented this information in order to establish in the reader's mind that Dudley George was frequently in possession of firearms, and therefore, it would be a reasonable expectation that he would have a firearm in his possession on 6 September 1995. In addition, given Dudley George's often threatening gestures, one could also expect that he would be prepared to use such a firearm, although none of the information indicates that Dudley George actually acted on his threats and actually fired at anyone.

The trouble with this copious information pertaining to Dudley George's character, personal propensities, and use of firearms is that it is all circumstantial in nature. It perhaps established that Dudley George *might* have had a firearm in his possession on 6 September 1995, but it does not establish that he actually did have a firearm, nor that he was prepared to use it. Suspecting that a person has a firearm in his or her possession is insufficient reason for a trained police officer to draw his or her own gun and shoot at an individual, regardless of the extenuating circumstances, and this was the reasoned conclusion of the Ipperwash Inquiry (Linden 2007).

A Framework for Police Preparedness

Towards the end of the Ipperwash Inquiry, the OPP (2006) presented its *Framework for Police Preparedness for Aboriginal Critical Incidents*, a document said to be a key element of the OPP strategy to improve the policing of First Nations protests and blockades. In that document, the OPP asserts that it had been applying the principles of the *Framework* for several years before formally adopting them as policy early in 2006.

Release of the *Framework for Police Preparedness* document was timely because, although the mandate of the Ipperwash Inquiry was to inquire into the circumstances of the killing of Dudley George, a more general concern was to investigate the policing of civil disobedience by First Nations people in Ontario. As such, the mandate of the Inquiry was to make recommendations directed at avoiding violence in similar circumstances in the future. However, Commissioner Linden expressed concern about the sustainability of the *Framework*, adopting a wait-and-see approach to the possible effectiveness as an OPP policy initiative.

Perhaps the most important concern about the *Framework* document is whether or not the OPP sincerely intends to adopt the principles as set out in the document as an official policy proposal for handling Native political mobilization, or is this a document developed as window dressing to appease public concerns and deflect criticism? The proposals set out in the *Framework* (2006: 2) are certainly worth noting. In case there was any question of the matter, the document begins by stating, "The Ontario Provincial Police (OPP) is committed to safeguarding the individual rights enshrined within Federal and Provincial laws, inclusive of those specifically respecting the rights of Aboriginal persons of

Canada as set out in the Canadian Charter of Rights and Freedoms. The OPP recognizes that conflicts may arise as Aboriginal communities and the various levels of government work to resolve outstanding issues associated with matters such as land claims, self-determination and Aboriginal and treaty rights, which may relate to education, hunting and fishing."

The *Framework* notes that "critical incidents are often unavoidable" and outlines several significant approaches that would serve to diffuse or ameliorate such incidents. Moreover, the *Framework* points out that "disputes may, and often do, originate with government agencies other than the police, [and] this framework applies to the negotiation and mediation of police-related issues surrounding a dispute" (p. 3). In other words, the OPP attempts to make it quite clear that an important caveat is that it is up to the government and Aboriginal communities to solve their problems themselves, and that these parties should not expect the OPP to do such work for them.

The position of the OPP during Aboriginal protests is, therefore, seen as an intercalary role: one facilitating negotiations but not one in which the OPP is responsible for the outcomes of such a process. This process would be facilitated by an Aboriginal Liaison Operations Officer who is a member of the OPP reporting to the Office of the Commissioner. The purpose of this role (Linden 2007: 3) is to:

- Foster trusting relationships between the OPP and Aboriginal communities
- Assist in facilitating communications during any Aboriginal related dispute, conflict or critical incident.[14]

There is also mention of a Critical Incident Mediator who:

- Meets with Aboriginal representatives and communicates police interests
- Listens for and identifies key issues and interests of the Aboriginal representatives
- Develops in concert with the incident commander a mutually acceptable and lasting resolution strategy. (p. 4)

The *Framework* seeks to "build positive trusting relationships with members of the community, First Nations police officers and other agencies" (p. 5).

Chiefs of Ontario Response to the Framework

The First Nations Chiefs of Ontario (COO) organization met in 2006 to formulate a critical response to the OPP's *Framework* document (Chiefs of Ontario 2006). In this response, it was made clear that "the Chiefs of Ontario do not endorse the framework; rather, it is our intent to provide constructive suggestions." The COO response focuses on the "Critical Incident procedures" proposed by the OPP. The COO recognize, as indicated in the *Framework*, that disputes may, and often do, originate with government agencies other than the police. Therefore, the *Framework* is limited to the negotiation and mediation of police-related issues surrounding a dispute.

A crucial aspect of this negotiation or mediation process focuses on the newly created Aboriginal Liaison Officer, the Aboriginal Relations Team, and the Incident Commander, and their ability to work in collaboration with one another. The COO point out, however, that the *Framework* only reflects this collaboration at the critical incident level. Just as important, the chiefs suggest, is what happens at the pre-critical incident level, that is, the crucial events leading up to a crisis point. As the First Nations chiefs submit, "Local First Nation police service must play a lead role pre-critical as they will be in the best position to prevent conflicts from arising. What to look for and what can be done are further articulated with the framework document" (COO 2006). In other words, the Chiefs of Ontario are proposing a much more enhanced role for Aboriginal police officers than has hitherto been the case in dealing with Aboriginal acts of political mobilization.

Another important aspect not discussed in the *Framework*, the chiefs suggest, is what they term the "Post Critical Incident," which is outlined as follows: "At this stage it is important to reflect on what has just occurred and promote discussion among all parties involved regarding the lessons learned and identify peace-building actions. Attention must be given to those who require action in terms of emotional and physical exhaustion. What to look for and what can be done are further articulated with the framework document" (COO 2006).

Another significant point pertains to the problematic interpretation of Ontario law. The First Nations chiefs indicate in the event that an incident occurs on First Nations territory a problem arises over jurisdiction and interpretation because First Nations governments and the government of Ontario may have different perspectives regarding Ontario law. For example, if the OPP is to be an effective mediating presence, its officers will need to consider both provincial and Aboriginal and treaty rights – and the potential conflicts that stream from these various interpretations.

The problems inherent in these various legal interpretations could be enhanced, the chiefs suggest, if the OPP Commissioner's Office would be required to create a direct dialogue process with the Chiefs of Ontario. This step would act as a starting point for an improved relationship between the OPP Commissioner's Office and Ontario First Nations communities. In the event that this more direct dialogue would be established, the Chiefs of Ontario would be in a position to facilitate a common voice in responding to a number of concerns that Ontario First Nations have with OPP initiatives. In summary, the Chiefs of Ontario would like to see a more prominent role for First Nations police officers when Aboriginal protests or disputes occur, and a more direct dialogue between the OPP Commissioner's Office and the Chiefs of Ontario organization. The First Nations chiefs suggest that if these suggestions are implemented, along with the proposals of the OPP's *Framework*, then lines of communication would be improved at the ground level, between Aboriginal protesters and OPP officers, and the higher levels of command between the Commissioner's Office and the Chiefs of Ontario, First Nations leadership body.

Did the OPP Forget the Lessons of Ipperwash?

In 2008, the *Toronto Star* published an article with the headline "OPP Forgets Lessons of Ipperwash" (30 July 2008). The article notes that one of the main conclusions of the Ipperwash Inquiry is that "the single biggest source of frustration, distrust, and ill-feeling among aboriginal people in Ontario is our failure to deal in a just and expeditious way with breaches of treaty and other legal obligations to First Nations." However, when Aboriginal peoples attempt to regain control over their traditional lands through blockades, occupations, and protests, federal and provincial governments have resorted to the criminalization and incarceration of First Nations people defending their land claims.

According to that *Toronto Star* article, "Fantino's threats ignored an emphasis on negotiation and building trust during aboriginal occupations," as presented in the OPP's *Framework for Police Preparedness* document of 2006, an approach recommended by the Ipperwash Inquiry (Linden 2007). A test of the OPP's new strategy towards Aboriginal protests came on 29 June 2007, when First Nations people held a "National

Day of Action." Tyendinaga Mohawks, a community situated on the Bay of Quinte in southwestern Ontario, blockaded both Highway 401 and the main railway line between Toronto and Montreal. The spokesperson for the Mohawks, who himself participated, Shawn Brant, was subsequently arrested on a number of charges related to the blockades.

Brant objected to the arrests. During a November 2006 Tyendinaga reclamation of a gravel quarry – allegedly stolen by the Canadian government – Brant was charged with making death threats to Canadian army personnel. On 14 April 2008, Brant was cleared of the charge by Justice Charles Anderson, who described the police and provincial roles in the affair as "problematic" and "troubling." In an interview with the Aboriginal Peoples Television (APTN) Brant voiced his exasperation: "This is it? Justice for First Nations communities: lock us up. Anybody who speaks out, lock 'em up. K16, Bob Lovelace, lock 'em up. That's what it's about: lock 'em up. Don't fix the problem, lock 'em up."

A preliminary hearing into the charges against Brant was held in August 2007, with a trial scheduled for a later date. In testimony at this preliminary hearing, which attracted much interest, OPP Commissioner Julian Fantino described how the OPP would proceed in this post-Ipperwash era. According to the *Toronto Star* article, Commissioner Fantino said that with regard to the Aboriginal blockade of the CN rail line, "The OPP would go in with everything they had, whether or not there were women and children." Other transcripts presented at the hearing report on conversations held between Commissioner Fantino and Shawn Brant based on OPP wiretapping of Brant's phone.

Among the statements Fantino made to Brant, as revealed by the transcripts, were the following: "I don't wanna get on your bad side but you're gonna force me to do ... everything I can within your community and everywhere else to destroy your ... reputation [and] your whole world's gonna come crashing down on this issue." Fantino also urged Brant to 'pull the plug' on the blockades or 'suffer grave consequences.'"

Brant's lawyer, Peter Rosenthal, criticized Fantino for the wiretap and his controversial statements. Rosenthal called on Ontario Premier Dalton McGuinty to investigate whether Fantino was appropriate for the commissioner's post. As Rosenthal warned, "If somebody does read that transcript, who's aware of Ipperwash, they would recognize that there's danger in allowing Fantino to be head of OPP and the danger we talk about is life and death."

Commissioner Fantino then issued the following statement in response: "Consistent with the recommendations from the Ipperwash Inquiry, the OPP continues to work collectively with legitimate First Nations leadership and communities to ensure that both the interests of participants during lawful protests and public safety can be served in the best way possible" (Petersen 2008).

One can only hope that this prepared statement by Commissioner Fantino will represent his police force's true policy for dealing with Aboriginal protests and blockades, and not the impromptu threats by the commissioner levelled at Shawn Brant during the OPP's wiretapping.

Amnesty International Is Watching

Soon after the *Toronto Star* news article appeared concerning the actions of Commissioner Fantino, and which questioned whether the OPP were actually prepared to follow its own suggestions in the *Framework for Police Preparedness* document, Amnesty International Canada released the contents of a letter of 12 November 2008, to the Honourable Rick Bartolucci, minister of Community Safety and Correctional Services. In this letter, Amnesty International (www.amnesty.ca/resource_centre/news/view) calls for the province of Ontario to immediately:

- Publicly affirm its support for the Ontario Provincial Police (OPP) *Framework for Police Preparedness for Aboriginal Critical Incidents* and commit to ensuring that officers are held accountable for any breaches in the *Framework*.
- Work with Indigenous peoples' organizations to establish a timetable and process for an independent evaluation of the OPP *Framework* and appropriate codification of the *Framework* in provincial laws and policies.

The Amnesty International Canada (2008) news release outlining this call for action stems from the OPP response, it indicates, to the land rights protest of the Tyendinaga Mohawk Territory in June 2007 and April 2008. It urges the province of Ontario to establish an independent, impartial probe into OPP actions on these dates and to make the findings of such an investigation public. What is particularly vexing from Amnesty International's perspective is OPP Commissioner Fantino's assertion made during cross-examination in a provincial court that the *Framework* is "not a firm and fixed mandated way of doing business." "The Commissioner's response," Amnesty International asserts, "raises serious questions about the amount of discretion being exercised by the OPP with respect to the *Framework* and whether the OPP is being appropriately held to account for full and consistent implementation of the *Framework*."

Ipperwash Inquiry Backlash

Since there are two sides to every story, conventional wisdom informs us, it could be expected that not everyone in Ontario is pleased with the recommendations of the *Report of the Ipperwash Inquiry* (Linden 2007). There are various websites, such as Voice of Canada (www.Voiceof-Canada.ca), which promulgate the opinion that such inquiries as Ipperwash further incapacitate the OPP's ability to carry out their duties. They also holds to the view that Aboriginal protesters are allowed to break the law with impunity.

The Voice of Canada website reports on a news conference in the Media Studio at Queen's Park, held on 14 March 2007, in which an announcement was made concerning the release of *The Ipperwash Papers* by Mark Vandermass (2007).[15] This publication of over four hundred pages of documents purportedly "reveal[s] the suffering of innocent Ipperwash residents at the hands of native criminals, and by Department of National Defence and OPP." These papers, it is contended by Voice of Canada, also "expose the shameful secret of how the Ipperwash Inquiry prevented residents from testifying and suppressed all evidence of their suffering. Out of 139 witnesses called, only one was a full-time resident." The website goes on to impugn the credibility of the Ipperwash recommendations and lashes out against the "land claim lawlessness by native protesters." "How can anybody," it continues, "government or police – use the Inquiry's recommendations as justification for abandoning the innocent victims of native extremism?"

A personal opinion is also volunteered: "As we were going through the thousands of pages of documents [of the Ipperwash Papers, not the *Report of the Ipperwash Inquiry*], I broke down in tears of rage when I realized that the failures of the Ipperwash Inquiry meant that more innocent people – in Caledonia and other towns in the future – were destined to be sacrificed on the altar of political-correctness."

Of course, in Canada, people are entitled to their opinions, and they can express them in a free press. The Voice of Canada site includes a political "cartoon" from the *London Free Press* (26 May 2007) depicting a large book in the centre entitled *Canadian Law: As Applied to the Majority of Canadians*, and in the lower right is the caption "And for native protesters: a Get out of Jail Free Card." It also reports on other newspaper articles critical of the Ipperwash Inquiry such as one report in the *Sudbury Star* (6 June 2007) with the caption, "Ipperwash Inquiry Folly; It's Inconceivable that Natives Were Found to Have No Part in the Problems." There are others, such as those appearing in the *National Post* (2 June 2007), "Native Violence Becomes Blameless," and "For Natives, a Legal Free-for-All."

Ipperwash and the Media

The involvement of Canada's news media in the Ipperwash affair became such a convoluted matter that Aboriginal Legal Services of Toronto commissioned a study of this phenomenon by John Miller (2005), professor of journalism at Ryerson University. Media coverage of the confrontation at Ipperwash Provincial Park was a problematic matter right from the start, Miller contends. He notes, for example, that of a sample of "435 news and opinion articles that were written by journalists ... there was only one that mentioned the role of the media in the tragic events" (p. 5). There were also no reporters present on the night of 6 September 1995, when about forty riot police marched on a group of First Nations protesters, with the result that "the public was left with widely conflicting accounts of what happened, without independent verification by media witnesses" (ibid.).

Media coverage at the time of the shooting of Dudley George took quite divergent points of view. Some newspapers saw the incident as an example of police brutality against Aboriginals engaged in a legitimate dispute over a burial ground. Other journalists took the view that the Kettle and Stony Point protesters were a bunch of thugs and lawless criminals. Only one article, Miller noted, saw the issue as a land claims problem, rather than as primarily an Aboriginal-police confrontation, and that was not even a Canadian newspaper but the *New York Times*. Clyde Farnsworth put the Ipperwash occupation in context as a land claims issue, pointing out, "It is taking place at a time when the Canadian government and the country's 1.2 million aboriginal people ... are trying to seek new approaches to an often troubled relationship" (*New York Times*, 27 Aug. 1995). Nevertheless, not even one Canadian newspaper, Miller (2005: 58) notes, ran this story.

As an example of the divergent opinions that emerged shortly after the Ipperwash confrontation, George Mathewson, under the caption "FOREST – The Cops Are Everywhere," wrote, "Community goodwill for a native occupation of ancestral Camp Ipperwash seemed to crumble when it spread to the provincial park. The shooting of Anthony 'Dudley' George and the disputed versions of how it happened have hardened attitudes on racial lines" (*Sarnia Observer*, 13 Sept. 1995).

Miller (2005) found that there were many editorials and opinion columns in which the writers rushed to a judgment on the significance of the confrontation, and these were generally not sympathetic to the Stony Point protesters. He observes that only three of a total of ninety-two opinion articles were written by journalists who actually went to Ipperwash and did their own reporting. One of the most extreme examples of the sort of ill-informed opinions that appeared shortly after the confrontation was by a Canadian columnist writing from Singapore: "One of the best things about being 12 time zones away from Canada is that I no longer have to cover obscure and occasionally bloody Indian standoffs such as those at Camp Ipperwash ... No longer do I have to travel hundreds of miles down bad roads with scores of other journalists to dusty mosquito-infested villages for a media opportunity with a bunch of unkempt and menacing thugs who are eager for their moment of fame" (Matthew Fisher, *Toronto Sun*, 17 Sept. 1995, in Miller 2005: 9).

These were the sorts of opinions and analyses that were being published in Canadian newspapers within two weeks of the Dudley George shooting. Most articles accepted the OPP's versions of events, which was that the Ipperwash occupiers had attacked the police and fired first. As time when on, this interpretation of events gained a solid footing in the public's mind, and also served to discredit the Aboriginal account. This latter account was that the protesters had no guns at Ipperwash, but if it was mentioned at all, it was well after the OPP's interpretation of events. Because of this media bias in "framing" the Ipperwash story, the news commentaries were generally unsympathetic to the Stony Pointers and their Aboriginal allies. The protesters were called "warriors," but reporters did not bother to define what this term meant, reinforcing in the public mind an image of the occupiers as "armed and dangerous." To the credit of the *London Free Press* (8 Sept. 1995), it ran an article entitled "Two versions of the same event: who fired the first shot?" in an effort to sort out the divergent points of view – OPP versus the Aboriginal protesters – in the shooting of Dudley George.

The "framing" of the Ipperwash story, as Miller (2005: 8–10) indicates, was "most frequently one about violent, lawless First Nations people causing a fuss, instead of one about people who believe they have a legitimate right to their land." The events at Ipperwash were also frequently linked in the same story to other First Nations disputes, especially to the contemporaneous one happening at Gustafsen Lake, British Columbia, where occupiers had guns and did fire upon the police in an armed confrontation. The implication, although never demonstrated, was that Canada was on the brink of a bloody nationwide Aboriginal revolution. However, hard evidence that this upheaval was about to occur was completely lacking.

What was also completely lacking from the news coverage at the time was an appreciation of the legal dispute involving the Kettle and Stony Point First Nation, caused by the displacement of Stony Pointers in 1942 under the War Measures Act. In fact, the Aboriginal people occupying the military base and later the provincial park were not seen as having any legitimacy in the Kettle and Stony Point community, but rather, were regarded as a bunch of "rebels" or a "splinter group of hotheads." Once the occupation was under way, whatever links the protesters had with the news media began to dissipate completely, in part, no doubt, because the protesters regarded the media as being inimically hostile to their interests.

The Ipperwash protesters were also cast in the role of common stereotypes promulgated and reinforced by the media, "framed" with racist dialogue – First Nations people were characterized as troublemakers, as unruly and violent.[16] Aboriginals were portrayed as benefiting from double standards of justice, as seen, for example, in the London Free Press (26 May 2007) depiction of a Canadian lawbook "as applied to the majority of Canadians," and the Native protesters' "get out of jail free" card. For example, Rory Leishman in the London Free Press expressed the following view: "Canada is supposed to be a democracy in which the rules of law apply equally to every citizen, regardless of race, creed, colour or any other extraneous consideration. However, in recent years ... [government] routinely allows lawbreaking Indians to get away with crimes that would land the rest of us in the slammer" (in Miller 2007: 44). Expressed in even stronger terms is the opinion of William Johnson in a column for the Montreal Gazette: "The real problem is the threat of fascism growing in some native communities. This should be a real concern for everyone, native and non-natives alike ... A flagrant case of fascist thuggery occurred on the weekend at Camp

Ipperwash, in Ontario ... A self-appointed group of Chippewas have made a power grab of its own" (ibid.).

The result of this sort of overdramatization of events was an ever-increasing intolerance for First Nations people, who are seen as lawbreakers, regardless of any validity that might adhere to their particular land claims or treaty rights. As a result of this media viewpoint, the public is drawn into complicity with a perspective that sees land claims and treaty rights as something to do with "way in the past," but of little relevance to what is happening in "today's real world." The perspective that sees First Nations people as possessing legitimate grievances is largely ignored or not considered by the news media.

There was the odd writer of letters to the editor, however, who questioned the dominant perspective, and who was generally supportive of the First Nations point of view. Here is an example, published in the *London Free Press* (6 Oct. 1995), that directly challenged such conclusions: "I suggest your paper should try to find someone from the reserve who might be willing to tell their side of what the events of the last few weeks have done to them and their families" (in Miller 2005: 10). Similarly, a reader wrote to the *London Free Press* (16 Sept. 1995), stating, "I am disturbed that people have found in the banner 'Canadian Law and Order' a refuge for their anti-native racism. But I guess I'm not surprised. After all, the law reflects the fundamentally racist conditions under which Crown land was acquired in the first place" (in Miller 2005: 46).

Such views in support of an Aboriginal perspective were extremely rare, as most of the opinion in the print media was critical of the Stony Point occupation. The news coverage of the occupation – before the death of Dudley George – may at one time have had its roots in a land dispute, but after the shooting it became a much bigger story. The media coverage became less and less about a land dispute between a band of Chippewas and the Canadian federal government, and more and more about a police investigation into troubling events caused by First Nations protesters. Canadian newspapers were also quick to pass judgment, framing the Stony Point people and their activities in a critical or derogatory perspective.

There is no doubt that Ipperwash was a complicated story to cover. There was a peaceful protest that eventually turned violent in a dramatic fashion on the evening of 6 September 1995. Few reporters covering the story had any appreciation of the important historical context of the protest, which pertained to the broken promises of the federal government to return land seized in 1942, which examined the anger and frustration of the Stony Point First Nation members. Clearly, in this context, Miller's (2005) assessment that "all in all, the Ipperwash crisis was not journalism's finest hour" (p. 15), would appear to be entirely justified.[17]

Conclusion

The *Report of the Ipperwash Inquiry* (2007) reveals many startling statements of a racially insensitive and discriminatory nature by political leaders of the province and members of the armed police force. We could also add to this mix of racist discourse coverage in the news media, views expressed in Internet web pages, and the comments of the local citizenry.

According to evidence presented at the Ipperwash Inquiry (Linden 2007) by Attorney General Harnick in sworn testimony, on the morning of 6 September 1995, Ontario Premier Mike Harris in an informal meeting said, "I want the fucking Indians out of the park." Premier Harris denied that he ever made such a statement, but he could not give a reason why the attorney general would perjure himself.

Latter in the day, OPP Sergeant Stan Korosec, head of the Emergency Response Team (ERT) was recorded by OPP Dispatch as saying, "Do these fuckers big-time," referring to the Aboriginal protesters. Fellow OPP officer Constable Jacklin, in his testimony, dismissed these comments by saying that they were made "just out of frustration," one should not "put any significance on it," or "take the comment seriously." Also recorded on dispatch tapes was a comment by another officer, who was a member of the OPP Intelligence Team, saying, "There's no one down there. Just a big, fat, fuck Indian." Later that evening, Acting Sergeant Ken Deane fired three shots at protestor Dudley George in the mistaken belief that George had aimed a firearm at him. Acting Sergeant Ken Deane maintained until his death that he had acted appropriately under the circumstances. On the day of Dudley George's funeral, his sister discovered anti-Aboriginal T-shirts, mugs, and other "memorabilia" produced by OPP officers for sale at a local convenience store. One cannot help but wonder about the source of such deep-seated hatred for other human beings and from which such truculent and bellicose animosity emerges.

How is one to place this information in a reasonable context? For starters, a basic tenet of sociological theory is that beliefs and attitudes underlie people's behaviour. These beliefs and attitudes do not result from a certain genetic predisposition but are learned by the passage of information from generation to generation (enculturation) or by other socializing mechanisms such as learning from peers and other cultural influences. In this context, the inculcation of certain prejudicial and discriminatory attitudes towards others in a society is a learned phenomenon, passed on from person to person, and it is not to be understood as a "natural" process.

We note, therefore, the context and prejudicial influences that led to the shooting of Aboriginal protester Dudley George which was preceded, it could be suggested, by certain discriminatory attitudes and beliefs shared by a sector of the Canadian population. Unfortunately, the effects of these discriminatory and culturally insensitive attitudes of this sector of the population were magnified because those individuals holding these malevolent views were in very important influential positions in Ontario, such as the premier of the province, or were members of an armed force such as the Ontario Provincial Police. The obvious conclusion is that there does exist, or at least did exist in the fall of 1995, at the very highest levels of power and authority in Ontario society what could be termed a "culture of racism and prejudice."

At a personal level, what is perhaps the most disheartening of all is the complete denial of any wrongdoing and the utterly defensive stance taken by those responsible for killing Dudley George. Neither the premier of the province, nor the OPP commissioner, ever apologized to the George family or the Stony Point First Nation community. The implication, of course, is that these powerful individuals believe that the killing was perhaps unfortunate but not unexpected "under the circumstances."

What would be wrong, from one human being to another, by a statement that said "Members of the Ontario Government and the Ontario Provincial Police regret our involvement in the shooting of Dudley George and give our heartfelt regrets for this loss of life and the harm done to the First Nations community of Kettle and Stony Point." It is unfortunate that all the Aboriginal community ever got were defensive rationalizations and denials of responsibility to this very day. The lack of such a statement implies that Mike Harris and the OPP officers, people empowered to "serve and protect," were not at all sorry that Dudley George was killed, believing perhaps given their attitudes that he deserved what happened to him. Even the smallest act of contrition on the OPP's part would have gone a long way towards building the trust with Aboriginal communities that will surely be needed when future political mobilizations inevitably occur at later points in time.

Chapter Six

Ipperwash Inquiry Recommendations

Police officers, like the rest of society, are not always perfect.
  – Ontario Provincial Police Association (OPPA) submission to the Ipperwash Inquiry regarding the shooting of Dudley George (2006: 14)

Royal Commissions provide politicians with space to avoid confrontation and conflict.
  – R. Darnell, *Anthropologica* (2000: 171)

The Ipperwash Inquiry was initiated by the government of Ontario, on 12 November 2003, under the Public Inquiries Act. Its mandate was to inquire into and report on events surrounding the death of Dudley George, who was shot in 1995 during a protest by First Nations people at Ipperwash Provincial Park. The Inquiry was also asked to make recommendations that would help all parties avoid violence in similar circumstances in the future.

The Hon. Sidney B. Linden was appointed commissioner. The Inquiry was separated by the commissioners into two phases, which ran concurrently. The first phase dealt with the events surrounding the death of Dudley George (the evidentiary hearings), and the second phase (the policy and research part) was concerned with the issues related to avoiding violence in future Aboriginal protests. The hearings began in Forest, Ontario, in July 2004 and ended in August 2006. The Inquiry's final report, containing the findings and recommendations pertaining to both phases, was released to Ontario's Attorney General Michael Bryant and made public on 31 May 2007 (*CBC News*, 31 May 2007).[1]

Ipperwash Inquiry Recommendations

The recommendations of the *Report of the Ipperwash Inquiry* (Linden 2007) fall into three broad areas. The first area, "Investigation and Findings," deals with matters principally pertaining to police planning for responding to Aboriginal civil disobedience. The second area, "Policy Analysis," is concerned with suggestions relating to settling land and treaty claims in Ontario. The third area delves into the nature of public inquiries and will not be discussed here because it is not particularly pertinent to the subject of Aboriginal issues per se. Although the Inquiry report contains a hundred recommendations, the majority (78) fall into the "Policy Analysis" area.

Policing Aboriginal Acts of Civil Disobedience

Since the mandate of the Ipperwash Inquiry was focused specifically on the circumstances surrounding the death of Dudley George, it would be expected that a major thrust of the Inquiry's recommendations should deal with the policing of Aboriginal acts of civil disobedience, or political mobilization. In other words, the question is how police involvement in such events could be handled more effectively in the future. A related issue pertains to the manner in which police involvement in such confrontations could serve to ameliorate the situation rather than inflame it further. In this regard, two of the "Investigation and Findings" recommendations, while rather lengthy in detail, are particularly worthy of enumeration and analysis (p. 95):

2 Police planning for responding to an Aboriginal occupation or protest should include:
   a. a communication strategy for important messages that ought to be conveyed to the occupiers
   b. the technical aspects of how the police would communicate with the occupiers, and
   c. specified people outside the police service who could effectively communicate with the occupiers.

3 Police services should ensure:
   a. that the intelligence unit of the police service is engaged and operating and has adequate resources and procedures for collection, collation and evaluation of information

b. that reports are reduced to writing in a timely manner whether initially transmitted verbally or not

c. that intelligence data is subject to analysis and reliability assessment

d. that there is a single repository through which intelligence data flows to the Incident Commander

e. that the leader of the intelligence unit or his or her designate reports directly to the Incident Commander, and

f. that the Incident Commander and other senior personnel receive training in intelligence.

Perhaps the most salient point made by the *Report of the Ipperwash Inquiry* is that the manner in which "Aboriginal occupations and protests are policed is important to Aboriginal protesters, Aboriginal communities, and the police, but the issue affects all Ontarians" (p. 86). In other words, Ipperwash, Caledonia, Oka, and other similar incidents are not only "Aboriginal issues" – they are just as much Canadian issues, too. In one sense, it matters little that the protesters involved in a social or political issue in Canada are Aboriginal persons because the way these protests are handled has a bearing on how other protests, involving non-Aboriginal persons, are handled as well. Non-Aboriginal persons in Canada cannot afford to be so smug as to think that the way Aboriginal protests and occupations are dealt with is a factor solely inherent to their ethnic identity.

Although far removed in time and space from Ipperwash, a few words should be mentioned concerning the Winnipeg General Strike of 1919 (Fudge and Tucker 2004). This was certainly one of the most influential strikes in Canadian history, and it led to many future labour reforms. Probably the main impetus for the strike had to do with dismal wages and working conditions, but the strike was also about the rights of average working people. Particularly relevant is the egregious manner in which the strike was suppressed. Granted, there were a few extenuating circumstances, such as the recent Bolshevik Revolution which had frightened many Western governments, yet the utter vehemence with which a demonstration by workers was handled has certainly gone down in memory for its shocking brutality and violence. The Royal Commission that investigated the strike concluded with the famous statement: "if Capital does not provide enough to assure Labour a contented existence ... the Government might find it necessary to step in and let the state do these things at the expense of Capital." Ultimately, how the strike was handled turned the labour movement against the Conservatives and led indirectly to the formation of the New Democratic Party (p. 112).[2]

The point here is that collective political mobilization involving strikes, protests, and occupations, regardless of the particular cultural or ethnic group, has important implication for all Canadians. If an unarmed Aboriginal protester can be shot to death in a recent occupation of a provincial park, is it then inconceivable that non-Aboriginal people might suffer the same fate?

There would seem to be an impression held by certain sectors of the Canadian population that anyone protesting and confronting the police is somehow inherently in the wrong. What is mistaken about this captious attitude towards authority is that Canadians have a democratic right to peaceful assembly; this right is guaranteed under Section 2 of the Charter of Rights and Freedoms. If the government permits the police to carry arms, then it is contingent upon the members of such a force to exercise restraint in the discharging of their duties. At all costs, violent confrontation needs to be avoided and replaced with attempts at peaceful resolution of conflict.

It is certainly unfair to place the entire onus for peaceful resolution on the police. Each officer tends to take his or her orders from superiors in command. The OPP, as a whole, takes it direction from the Ontario government, particularly from the Premier's Office. In the Ipperwash incident, Premier Harris, whether he used the f-word or not, nonetheless did use strident and inflammatory language to convey his wish for the immediate removal of the protesters. It is appropriate, therefore, for the Ipperwash Inquiry to have made a recommendation regarding the manner in which the executive office of the Ontario government becomes involved in Aboriginal political mobilizations. As noted in the Inquiry's report, "The responsibility for promoting a peacekeeping approach does not rest with the OPP alone. The provincial government should develop a policy to govern its own response to Aboriginal occupations and protests" (Linden 2007: 88).

The risk of violence is reduced considerably when each party in the dispute does not necessarily see the other as adversaries to be confronted or defeated. As such, the above recommendations pertaining to the sharing of information are relevant. The OPP evidently did not know why the Aboriginal protesters were engaged in their action. The information about a burial site in Ipperwash Provincial Park only came to light during the initial charge of the OPP. It becomes evident that the education of police force members regarding the nature of Aboriginal civil disobedience should be a key element in the communications process. Police need to know why Aboriginal people are engaging in this collective action; the police need to know why they are taking such desperate action as to put members of their own communities in harm's way.

The police must also be made aware that Aboriginal protesters are not, for the most part, gangs of disaffected malcontents bent on destruction. One of the purposes of the lengthy review of Aboriginal acts of resistance in previous chapters is to demonstrate that most such acts have very long-term origins and implications, sometimes involving centuries of smouldering issues that could not apparently be concluded in any other manner. That the federal government has been largely unwilling or unable to resolve land claims issues makes it culpable in the resulting protests as well.

Facilitating Negotiations

Of the nineteen recommendations in the "Investigation and Findings" section, recommendations 5 and 19 appear to be particularly significant. Recommendation 5, for example, focuses on facilitating negotiations (Linden 2007: 96):

> 5. The Ontario Secretariat for Aboriginal Affairs, in consultation with Aboriginal organizations, should compile a list of available negotiators and facilitators who could assist the government to quickly and peacefully resolve Aboriginal issues that emerge.

As the *Report of the Ipperwash Inquiry* states, "Failed intelligence and miscommunication led to tragic consequences ... The OPP's lack of communication in this operation was a very serious failing" (p. 61). The police were largely unaware of the underlying reasons for the occupation of Ipperwash Provincial Park by First Nations protesters. The OPP were apparently also not aware that the occupiers were in the park to protect a sacred burial site and that this was a deeply felt emotional and spiritual issue for the Aboriginal occupiers. All the police were aware of was that Aboriginal protesters were in the park illegally and that the Ontario premier and his cabinet wanted the occupiers removed in an expeditious manner. A facilitator or go-between could have communicated to the OPP – and the government representatives – the reasons for the occupation of the park and, in turn, could have set in motion a series of actions that might have defused the situation before it led to such disastrous results.

The Ipperwash Report did point out that negotiators were apparently available. The base commander at Camp Ipperwash, Captain Smith, had made contact with Robert Antone, a First Nations negotiator trained in conflict resolution and crisis management. Antone had previously been involved in the 1990 Oka Crisis in Quebec. Along with Bruce Elijah, Antone had also facilitated a cross-cultural awareness training session with the military, as recently as on 12 and 13 July 1995, with the purpose of attempting to build a better relationship between the Stony Point people, who at the time were occupying the artillery range, and military personnel. Elijah was also a First Nations negotiator as well as a peacekeeper from the Oneida First Nation. Captain Smith made it quite clear that he did not want a physical confrontation with First Nations people, and so with the assistance of Antone and Elijah, the military left the camp on 29 July 1995 (p. 12).

It was also pointed out in the Inquiry testimony that OPP Inspector Carson did not make an attempt to contact representatives of the Assembly of First Nations, the Chiefs of Ontario, or the Union of Ontario Indians for assistance. He also did not ask Chief Tom Bressette if anyone on the band council could help with initiating negotiations with the park occupiers. Furthermore, Inspector Carson did not seek out the assistance of the OPP's First Nations Police Branch in an attempt to open communications with the Aboriginal protesters. Carson did, however, approach local OPP officers, but they lacked the appropriate negotiation skills (p. 25).

The question therefore remains: why were these two trained negotiators not employed to ameliorate the tensions during the confrontations at Ipperwash Provincial Park after Labour Day 1995? The Inquiry report notes that Cyndy Elder of "Approaches Mediation" called the OPP at about 4:00 p.m. on 6 September to offer her assistance to Inspector Carson. This First Nations mediator explained to Sergeant Drummelsmith that she had had contact with Inspector Carson that August 1995, after the army camp occupation. At the time, Elder was also involved with the Gustafsen Lake protest in British Columbia, and on that basis her services might have been used to diffuse the tension at Ipperwash Provincial Park. Sergeant Drummelsmith promised to convey her message to Inspector Carson. Testimony reveals that Inspector Carson was "too busy to return Ms. Elder's call that day." "The best I can do is some time tomorrow," said Inspector Carson, but tomorrow was too late, and a significant opportunity to establish lines of communication with the park occupiers was lost. Meanwhile, on September 6, Inspector Carson left at 7:00 p.m. for a dinner at the private home of friends in Forest, with orders to those left in charge to "basically sit tight" (pp. 36, 37).

The Ontario Provincial Police mounted a vigorous rebuttal to the charge that its members were negligent in enacting the role of peacekeepers or negotiators in the Ipperwash dispute (OPPA, 2006). In particular, the OPP Association vehemently objected to the intercalary role in which its members had been put between the Ontario government and the Aboriginal activists. OPP officers see their role as peacekeepers, but not as land claims negotiators.

This role of dispute negotiator is one for which the officers have no training and which is inherently dangerous to its members and to the protesters given the fact that members on one or both sides carry firearms. As the OPPA (2006: 14) points out: "Many of the police officers who testified expressed their displeasure with the role assigned to them as interveners in what was and continues to be a civil dispute over property rights between First Nations people and the federal and provincial governments."

Project Maple: Crisis Negotiation

In a meeting of senior OPP officers, on 1 September 1991, "Project Maple" was developed to deal with the possibility of an extended standoff at Ipperwash Provincial Park (OPPA 2006: 46–9). The primary objective of Project Maple was "to contain and negotiate a peaceful solution." The plans included an organizational chart setting out a structure involving the incident commander, senior officers, and other various police units including the Emergency Response Team and Tactical Rescue Unit. Each of the various components of this structure was asked to develop a logistical plan should their participation be required.

The OPPA (2006: 46) makes quite clear that their use of the term "crisis negotiation" has a specific meaning as far as Project Maple is concerned: "Police crisis negotiation is not synonymous to land claims negotiation. Rather, police crisis negotiation applies only in very specific, limited situations. Crisis negotiators may only respond when directed to do so by an Incident Commander."

In such events, the incident commander will involve the crisis negotiating team under situations that fit the following criteria: first, there must be a threat to life, such as when a person is barricaded or in a hostage situation, and second, the individual refuses to attorn[3] to the local police. Crisis negotiators are not deployed short of a threat to life. According to the OPPA, the criteria for the use of crisis negotiators were not met during the events at Ipperwash Provincial Park and, therefore, crisis negotiators were not deployed.

According to this submission, then, the OPP have a specific set of terms of reference when it comes to "crisis negotiation," and these do not apply to land claims negotiations because there is not (usually) a threat to life. However, what is evident in the Ipperwash confrontation, on 6 September 1995, is that there exists a lacuna between the rather strict usage of the OPP's term "crisis negotiation" and a less circumscribed view of what constitutes a crisis. If the OPP were led to believe that on that evening the Aboriginal protesters were armed, then one would suppose that such a situation posed "a threat to life." That it was never proven that the Aboriginal occupiers were armed in any manner, save for baseball bats, sticks, and stones, does not diminish the fact that the OPP had grounds to believe that someone's life would be threatened under such circumstances. Otherwise the OPP's use of such "Hard-Tac" equipment (see above) as well as their own firearms hardly seems justified in the face of unarmed opponents. Moreover, it is very unfortunate that such a highly structured OPP organization for dealing with crisis management was not, therefore, utilized, regardless of the strict terms of reference under which the negotiation team could be deployed. Given that an Aboriginal protester was eventually fatally wounded during the confrontation, it would seem highly reasonable in the future that the terms of reference regarding "crisis negotiators" be subject to some flexibility and good judgment.

Certainly, what is not at fault here is the intent of the crisis negotiation process, as articulated by the OPPA (2006: 97), which is "to develop trust with the subject ... an effective negotiator receives information directly from the subject of the negotiation process as part of the process of building trust and rapport." What remains to be done, then, is to incorporate these laudable objectives into realistic terms of reference so that in the future unarmed land claims protesters are not shot and killed by the very authorities seeking their "trust and rapport."

Redressive Action

Recommendation 19 of the *Report of the Ipperwash Inquiry* (Linden 2007: 97) focuses on redressing identified grievances:

19. The federal government should immediately return the former army camp to the peoples of the Kettle and Stoney Point First Nation and guarantee that it will assume complete responsibility for any appropriate environment cleanup of the site.

Had the appropriated lands belonging to the Kettle and Stony Point First Nation been promptly returned – as initially promised – to the original owners of the Ipperwash military camp shortly after the Second World War, decades of grief, frustration, and wasted mental anguish would have been saved. Instead, the federal government, in particular the Department of National Defence, went back on its promise to return the disputed lands, resulting in the eventual death of Dudley George following sixty years of needless disputing between band members and the forces of the Canadian military and the Ontario Provincial Police.

Eventually, on 20 December 2007, the Ontario provincial government announced a plan to return the Ipperwash Provincial Park to its original owners, the Chippewas of Kettle and Stony Point. Aboriginal Affairs Minister Michael Bryant explained that, initially, the land comprising the park will be "co-managed" by the province and the Kettle and Stony Point First Nation with a gradual assumption of control in the hands of the Aboriginal people (*Toronto Star*, 21 Dec. 2007). Ipperwash Provincial Park was officially signed over to the Chippewas on 28 May 2009.

There is obviously much that could be said here under the topic of "lessons learned." Suffice to say that a through "thinking through" of the issues surrounding land claims is essential in order avoid the loss of life and long-term ill-will that the Ipperwash confrontation provoked. What was gained by all this trouble? The park was eventually returned to its original owners in any event. Could not our elected representatives have moved forward to that eventuality sooner, in a more expeditious manner, without the acrimony that resulted from nearly a century of needless suppression of a protest over such an obvious injustice?

Treaty Commission of Ontario

In the second set of recommendations set out in the *Report of the Ipperwash Inquiry* (Linden 2007: 99), dealing with "Policy Analysis," three are particularly important because they have far-reaching implications for Aboriginal land claims in the province of Ontario:

1. The provincial government should establish a permanent, independent, and impartial agency to facilitate and oversee the settling of land and treaty claims in Ontario. The agency should be called the Treaty Commission of Ontario.

2. The Treaty Commission of Ontario should be established in a provincial statute as an independent agency reporting directly to the Legislative Assembly of Ontario. The Treaty Commission of Ontario should have permanent administrative, legal, and research staff and should be fully independent from the governments of Canada, Ontario, and First Nations. The statute should specify that the purpose of the Treaty Commission of Ontario is to assist Ontario in discharging its treaty responsibilities.

3. The provincial government should create a Ministry of Aboriginal Affairs. This ministry should have a dedicated minister and its own deputy minister.

The *Report of the Ipperwash Inquiry* did not discuss the practical details of establishing a Treaty Commission of Ontario or of the proposed Ministry of Aboriginal Affairs. As far as a Treaty Commission of Ontario is concerned, this would be an effective mechanism for resolving land claims disputes, which are in most cases, essentially, local ones. This Treaty Commission would have the benefit of focusing on regions of Ontario, and the various treaties involved, with a degree of familiarity that is simply not possible with the unwieldy responsibility of such ineffective agencies as Ottawa's Indian Claims Commission.

The present mechanism for resolving land claims is far too expensive and cumbersome. Since the focus is at the federal level, dealing with all First Nations communities in Canada, the Indian Claims Commission has little hope of effectively dealing with so many claims, or establishing priorities for the claims as they come in to the agency. The federal government, for example, made a commitment to spend $355 million on resolving land claims between 1991 and 1995, which amounts to four times the amount spent in the late 1980s (Frideres and Gadacz 2008: 237). Proposals were made to help "streamline" land claims that amounted to less than a half-million dollars. As an example of this streamlining, the Department of Indian and Northern Affairs was given complete authority by the Treasury Board to approve settlements up to $7 million without the Board's approval.

The hope was that in the first few years of the new millennium about 250 outstanding claims could be settled under the new guidelines. Unfortunately, by 2008 fewer than thirty of these land claims had, in fact, been settled, with a backlog of new cases mounting in an almost exponential manner. Clearly, the present approach to settling land claims in Canada has little chance of success, guaranteeing further frustration, discontent, and a disaffected Aboriginal population.

As far as the land claims process in Ontario is concerned, the track record is not much better. Ontario takes an average of 6.5 years to review a land claim, once all research has been completed. On average, to settle a claim takes fifteen years. If an allegation is made that Ontario has acted illegally in some manner, then a claim takes an average of 19.2 years to be resolved. In the five years prior to 2005, Ontario received twenty-one new claims, but only four of these had been settled in that period (Coyle 2005).

If we look historically at the federal government's attempts to deal with land claims, there was initially a degree of hope when the Indian Claims Commission was established in 1991. The Commission noted that the Crown became the target of grievances and claims respecting land, resources, and the management of Native affairs by First Nations people because of "their insistence on continuing special status as the original people of Canada. These claims are based on aboriginal rights or on agreements which were made with government which were based on the Indians' position as unconquered indigenous occupants of the land" (Canada 1975: 3). The implication is that the federal government had developed and implemented a policy such that dealings with Aboriginal peoples were handled differently from those of other citizens. Of course, Aboriginal peoples themselves insisted on dealing directly with the Crown through their Indigenous leadership structure and then by proxy with the government of Canada through such national-level organizations as the Assembly of First Nations, on the presumed basis of one nation negotiating with another. This process largely left the provincial governments out of this negotiation dyad.

When it became evident that the recommendations of the Indian Claims Commission were not working being implemented in an effective manner, a task force was struck in 1985 (Canada 1985) to review the government's claims policy and to submit a report to the minister of Indian and Northern Affairs. The approach of the government was that in the negotiation of land claims the goal should be to extinguish all Aboriginal claims once and for all. Aboriginal peoples vehemently objected to this philosophy. The result was that negotiations and settlements stalled once again over this philosophical impasse. As such the Task Force to Review Comprehensive Claims Policy recognized that a new approach to settling land claims needs to be formulated. The task force's articulation of the problem is worth noting: "Much is at stake in working towards consensual settlements with those Aboriginal peoples who have never entered into agreements concerning the destiny of their traditional lands within Canada. In the deepest sense, what is at stake is our identity as a nation that revolves its internal differences not through coercion or domination by the majority, but through agreements based on mutual consent" (Canada 1985: 101). Partly in response to the 1985 vision of the task force, the prime minister announced plans to establish a Royal Commission on Aboriginal affairs in Canada, and finally did so in 1996.

The preceding discussion provides important contextual information regarding the proposal of the Ipperwash Inquiry (Linden 2007) regarding the establishment of a Treaty Commission of Ontario and a Ministry of Aboriginal Affairs. There is much to be said in favour of such a proposal but will the present political climate allow for its implementation? The major impediment is that First Nations people have, historically, been distrustful of provincial government intentions. We have reviewed, for instance, the situation at some length regarding Native-government relations in British Columbia. Aboriginal people have greater trust in the federal government because of a perceived notion that it is a more effective and prestigious government body than that existing at the provincial level.

Of course, if the truth be known, many First Nations people would have preferred to deal directly with the British Crown and were bitterly disappointed at the time of Canadian Confederation when Canada assumed the Crown's responsibilities for Indian Affairs. Such a proposal, therefore, is unlikely to receive large-scale acceptance from First Nations people until such time as provincial governments become more effective players in resolving disputes. At present, the provincial governments are not seen by Aboriginal peoples as negotiators with a compassionate interest in resolving land claims, but are seen as acting in their own interests, to the detriment of Aboriginal ones. However, since the provinces control the vast majority of lands in Canada, sooner or later, one might suggest, a triad needs to be formed such that provincial governments become effective negotiating partners, along with the federal government and Aboriginal First Nations, in resolving the long-standing land claims disputes. That so many Supreme Court of Canada cases have taken place with Aboriginal groups, on one side, and provincial governments, on the other, has also not done much to engender a sense of mutual interest and trust.

A major issue in terms of dispute resolution, therefore, is that "First Nations claimants do not perceive the current Ontario process as fair. Since there is no independent review of claims, the Ontario government is in an inherent conflict of interest when it decides on whether a claim is valid" (Coyle 2005: 1). This conflict of interest stems, in large part, from Ontario's lack of a dispute mechanism for negotiated claims. Such a dispute mechanism could be used to settle various matters such as the validity of a claim, the amount of compensation, or the determination of responsibility between Ontario and the federal governments. Thus, as far as the Ipperwash Inquiry's recommendation for the establishment of a Treaty Commission of Ontario is concerned, it is evident that such a commission cannot operate in isolation from similar processes operating at the federal level. It is also evident that First Nations communities who are contemplating submitting a claim would need assurances that the processing of their claim will be done in a fair and timely manner.[4]

Wider Considerations of the Ipperwash Inquiry

Every year, across Canada there are numerous acts of Aboriginal political mobilization. Roads and railways are blockaded. Marches to Ottawa take place. Buildings and parcels of land are occupied. In various instances, protests lead to confrontations with local police forces, the OPP, the RCMP, the Canadian army, and even with local non-Aboriginal citizens. These protests sometimes lead to injury or even death on the part of the protesters or those who confront them. Hardly ever during these episodes do proper rules of engagement or conduct appear to be followed.

When emotions run high and frustration mounts, the gathered assembly begins to appear like a mob out of control. Why do the same unfortunate scenarios play themselves out in Canada over and over again without order or resolution? Why have our Canadian legislators, who are empowered to provide structure and coherence for such events, turned a blind eye to these catastrophes? In the civil society that Canada purports to be, there should be ways to resolve such disputes other than by the use of armed troops to pummel protesters into submission, reminiscent of the 1919 Winnipeg strike almost a century ago.

The recommendations quoted from the "Policy Analysis" section of the *Report of the Ipperwash Inquiry* (Linden 2007) proposing to establish a Treaty Commission of Ontario and to create a Ministry of Aboriginal Affairs have the potential to deal with Aboriginal land claims and other areas of grievance in a constructive manner without resorting to violence. It is unfortunate, and not often recognized, that Canada has a long history of suppressing Aboriginal cultural practices and political dissent. The reader is reminded of the potlatch ban in the 1880s, in which some of the Aboriginal practitioners were incarcerated. There was also the 1906 petition to King Edward VII over the lack of land settlements in British Columbia, led by Chief Joseph Capilano of the Squamish Delegation, which was subsequently denied. A national ban on Aboriginal political organizations was legislated in 1927. Aboriginal people were denied the right to vote in provincial elections until the 1950s, and in federal elections until 1960. The Trudeau government can be remembered for its White Paper of 1969, which an Aboriginal leader in Alberta called a "thinly disguised programme of extermination through assimilation" (Cardinal 1969: 1). In the late 1960s, the OPP used armed force to suppress a burial ground protest at Anicinabe Park near Kenora, Ontario.

It took the Quebec government sixty-five years to fulfil its treaty and land obligations to the Crees, Inuit, and Innu people, as specified under the Quebec Boundaries Extension Act, 1912, and finally acted upon in the James Bay Agreement of 1975. It took until 16 July 2007, another thirty-two years later, for the federal government to reach a $1.4 billion settlement with the Crees over outstanding land claims. Some of the sexist and discriminatory practices of the Indian Act were not eliminated until the Bill C-31 amendment of 1985, an amendment that created a new Aboriginal population possessing second-class Indian status.

Government laws and other legal initiatives have fragmented the First Nations of Canada into a myriad of competing interest groups – treaty versus non-treaty, status versus non-status, and reserve versus non-reserve. There are diverse political groups set against one another, such as the Métis National Council, the Assembly of First Nations, the Aboriginal Congress of Canada, and the Inuit Tapirisat.

It can be difficult to identify which First Nations peoples are protesting and to understand what their claim is about. Aboriginal acts of political mobilization seemingly occur without warning. The issues are apt to appear as inscrutably difficult to comprehend, even to insiders in the field. They are frequently quite diverse and complex in nature and might involve the desecration of burial sites, unsettled land claims, intrusions on hunting and fishing rights, resource development issues, or concerns over transportation initiatives involving highways, railways, or bridges.

Many people are familiar with such names as Oka, Caledonia, Ipperwash, Burnt Church, and Gustafsen Lake. The public might well wonder how long such Aboriginal acts of civil disobedience will continue, sometimes with deadly results. The recommendations of the Ipperwash Inquiry, if acted upon by the government of Ontario, would lead to constructive changes in the laws and public institutions of Ontario. In turn, such legislative changes would diminish the need for mobilizing protests and lead to the building of peaceful relations between Aboriginal and non-Aboriginal people over the ownership and control of land. As the *Report of the Ipperwash Inquiry* (Linden 2007: 80) reiterates, "Nearly all of the lands and inland waters in Ontario are subject to treaties between First Nations and the British and Canadian governments. These treaties are not, as some believe, relics of the distant past. They are living agreements, and the understandings on which they are based continue to have the full force of law in Canada today."

The experience of the people of the Kettle and Stony Point First Nation serves to illustrate the deeply felt anger and frustration that results when provincial and federal governments fail to deal constructively with extant treaty obligations. The proposal of the Ipperwash Inquiry to establish a provincial Treaty Commission and a Ministry of Aboriginal Affairs has the potential to deal constructively with disputes over treaty rights and other unresolved issues concerning burial and heritage sites. First, however, trust must be regained by Aboriginal peoples that the various federal and provincial governments are acting in their interests or on their behalf, and not just as land claims adversaries, as has been the case in much previous litigation. Implementation of the Ipperwash proposals would also help to mitigate the deleterious consequences of a failure to take seriously Canada's legal obligations towards First Nations people and, it is hoped, prevent further needless loss of life such as the tragic death of Dudley George.

It should also be noted that Royal Commissions and other public inquiries are expensive, so one always hopes that their costs are justified. A cynical view might see such commissions as a waste of money designed to give governments some breathing space in times of crisis and to deflect criticism away from them. As anthropologist Regna Darnell

(2000: 171) has observed, "Royal Commissions provide politicians with space to avoid confrontation and conflict. Extremists on both right and left are wont to mutter about the 'anesthetic' quality of the always numerous and broad-ranging recommendations." A similar perspective is offered by James Frideres (1996: 251), "Royal commissions ... can be used as a 'stalling' process to deal with issues politically embarrassing to the government in the hopes that the issues will 'go away'" (see also Doern 1967).

The Royal Commission on Aboriginal Peoples (RCAP) of 1996 cost Canadian taxpayers, which of course include Aboriginal peoples as well, $63 million and produced four hundred recommendations. As far as has been reported in the literature (Cairns 2000, Frideres 1998: 229), the federal government has virtually ignored all of the Commission's recommendations. Since the RCAP is reputed to be the most expensive federal inquiry in Canadian history, one is entitled to ask: what was the point of this huge financial undertaking, and how has it benefited Aboriginal people in Canada? The RCAP has been described as the embodiment of "the politics of ambivalence, shifting identities and elusive borders ... most Canadians and all politicians found the recommendations to be unrealistic even to inspire backlash" (Darnell 2000: 171). The failure of the RCAP to get a response from the federal government has been described as "disturbing and astonishing" given the massive expenditure and historical importance of the inquiry (Cairns 2000: 5).

The Ipperwash Inquiry (Linden 2007), on the other hand, cost a more modest $13.3 million; a relatively low price tag compared with the RCAP, and made one hundred recommendations. It is too soon to tell if the Ipperwash Inquiry will suffer the same fate as the RCAP. The Ipperwash recommendation to create a Ministry of Aboriginal Affairs for Ontario is similar to the RCAP's recommendation to institute an Aboriginal parliament, or "House of First People," which would act as an advisory body to the federal government.

Either of these proposals would seem justified given the lack of intermediary links between local reserves and the higher levels of provincial and federal governments. Lacking such links, communication to appropriate government agencies of Aboriginal peoples' concerns about such matters as employment, land claims, housing, or breaches of treaty agreements is often not effective. Aboriginal political organizations, such as the provincial-level Union of Ontario Indians or the federal-level Assembly of First Nations, are often not very effective in the communicative role because they tend to serve a limited Aboriginal constituency and, at times, take an adversarial position vis-à-vis federal and provincial governments. In any event, one wonders whether the $76.3 million spent on these two inquiries alone might not have been put to better use in improving the housing conditions of the Aboriginal population, or in job-creation efforts – anything rather than have these precious assets gobbled up by commissioners and their witnesses for plane fares, car rentals, hotel accommodations, and dining at expensive city restaurants.

Perhaps some would regard it as unfair to single out social scientists for neglecting to comment on such commissions and inquiries, and thereby failing to influence the formation of public policy. After all, we are reminded that academics themselves also serve on royal commissions, so that academics who criticize the recommendations they help to formulate appear to have a conflict of interest (Darnell 2000: 170–1). There are many in the social sciences who would no doubt welcome a more proactive stance on public issues, such as Aboriginal rights, so that the redress of social injustice could be seen as an increasingly important goal, aside from the more traditional academic concerns of theory and internecine debates over arcane and esoteric intellectual matters of limited practical, public importance. If such a transformation were to begin to occur in the academic community, it would be "bound to have a lasting impact on our ability and willingness to engage in research which might depart from the rather narrow scope circumscribed by the job-description of a well-meaning 'advocate'" (Scheffel 2000: 185).

Update: Return of Land and Settlements

In 1998, a land claim was settled with a $26 million agreement. Each member of the Kettle and Stony Point First Nation received between $150,000 and $400,000. The land of the Camp Ipperwash military base was eventually cleaned up and returned to the band members. On 20 December 2007, the Ontario government announced its intention to return the fifty-six-hectare Ipperwash Provincial Park to its original owner, namely, the Chippewas of Kettle and Stony Point First Nation (*Toronto Star*, 21 Dec. 2007). On Thursday, 28 May 2009, Ontario Aboriginal Affairs Minister Brad Duguid formally signed over control of Ipperwash Provincial Park to the Kettle and Stony Point First Nation (*London Free Press*, 28 May 2009).

Conclusion

Although not everyone in Canadian society would agree, the protesters at Ipperwash Provincial Park should be given credit. They stood up to injustice, as they saw it, and were willing to suffer the consequences. Their plight was a moral one as much as anything else. It was perhaps also a harkening back to a past, in which the Chippewa men as warriors stood up for what they believed in and were willing to fight for it. They may view themselves as warriors once again, but today the odds are overwhelmingly against them.

The Ontario Provincial Police were armed, and the occupiers knew they could be hurt physically by standing up to the police. The white community was also against them – from the Premier's Office in the highest levels of the Ontario government, down to their "neighbours" in the local community of Forest. Yet, despite these odds, the First Nations people stood their ground and did not flinch from their ancestral duty to brave the forces of oppression.

For those who wish to think about such matters, if we look beyond Ipperwash and all the other Aboriginal acts of political mobilization, then we inevitably confront a large issue, that is, the extent to which citizens of a modern democratic state should engage in civil disobedience in the face of injustice. There are obvious parallels here with the American civil rights movement of the Martin Luther King era and the question of appropriate tactics. Similarly, students during the 1960s protested the war in Vietnam, and four were shot to death at Kent State University. If Canada purports to be an enlightened democratic country, it must allow for the expression of dissent without the fear of armed suppression used as a mechanism to forcibly oppress those engaged in acts of political resistance.

Chapter Seven

Ipperwash as Racial Oppression

Racial oppression produces antagonism.
  – B. Singh Bolaria and Peter S. Li, *Racial Oppression in Canada* (1988: 25)

The *Report of the Ipperwash Inquiry* (Linden 2007) reveals in the starkest manner possible the utter, ineffable failure of Canada's Aboriginal policy. The report lays bare several reasons for this failure. Perhaps the most disturbing of these pertains to the intolerant racial and cultural attitudes towards First Nations people that apparently pervade the political system, from the premier of the province of Ontario down to the officers at the local OPP headquarters. Canadians, no doubt, see themselves as a nation of affable people, more socially and culturally tolerant than many of their global neighbours, and sensitive to social and political injustice. Unfortunately, the Ipperwash Inquiry reveals a different sort of people – perhaps outwardly friendly, but internally harbouring deep-seated resentments for the minorities and economically deprived in their midst. Worst of all, the term *racist* may be an apt description of many Canadians, whether they wish to admit it or not.

Anti-Native Prejudice

The subject of anti-Native prejudice in Canada is certainly a sensitive one. Aboriginal people are saying that the reason they do not have jobs is not because they are lazy or drunks, but because there exists in Canada a structured system of inequality that denies them employment. Without adequate employment, it is difficult to provide decent housing for their families or to seek higher education for their children.

Such a system traps them in a cycle of poverty and despair, a cycle that is almost impossible to break out of. This is exactly the suggestion that James Frideres (1988b) makes when he argues that Native people in Canada suffer from economic deprivation because of institutional structures that lead to a high degree of dependence, which in turn, forces them into a position of marginality. Moreover, this dependency relationship is fostered by an assimilationist government policy, "to the extent that they [Aboriginal people] would become wage earners and domestic consumers of various goods produced by capitalist entrepreneurs" (p. 88).

The literature on anti-Native prejudice extends back at least four decades. For example, at about the same time as the occupation of Anicinabe Park, David Stymeist (1975) was conducting fieldwork just north of Kenora, in the railway town of Sioux Lookout, referred to as "Crow Lake" in his ethnography. His study, entitled *Ethnics and Indians: Social Relations in a Northwestern Ontario Town*, is an examination of social relations, especially as these relate to the interaction of Aboriginal and non-Aboriginal peoples. This is one of his conclusions: "Prejudice and discrimination are important to the community, for whether or not the people of Crow Lake are fully aware of it, the town as a whole is heavily dependent upon the existence of a separate, unequal, and adjacent native population" (p. 9). Anti-Native prejudice is enacted through a variety of control mechanisms that serve as a boundary maintenance system separating Aboriginal peoples from employment opportunities, adequate housing, health care (there was a separate "Indian or Zone hospital" in Sioux Lookout) as well as other social services. Stymeist argues "that active discrimination against Native people largely prevented them from taking a full and active part in the social and economic life of the town" (ibid.).

In another study of northern Ontario, undertaken decades later, Thomas Dunk (2007) portrays the city of Thunder Bay in *It's a Working Man's Town*. Dunk echoes Stymeist's earlier observations, when he writes, "For many white people in Thunder Bay and in northwestern Ontario as a whole, the most important racial and ethnic distinction today is between whites and Indians. The Indian is perceived as an inferior other against whom whites define themselves ... The whites' understanding of their own subordinate position in the broader society is refracted into a racist perspective against Native people" (pp. 102–3).

Dunk supports his conclusions concerning Aboriginal discrimination in Thunder Bay and the surrounding area with the following statistics:

"The most deeply affected [by economic boom-and-bust cycles] are Native communities where unemployment may run as high as ninety per cent, and the social pathologies associated with deplorable economic conditions are taking a heavy toll" (p. 58). "Whereas in 1985," he continues, "median male income in the city of Thunder Bay was $24,396 ... across the river on the Fort William Indian reserve it was only $12,624 ... The unemployment rate for both sexes between the ages of fifteen and twenty-four years was 15.1 per cent in the city of Thunder Bay, and 56.3 per cent on the adjacent [Fort William] reserve ... the situation of Native women in the city: 76.9 per cent were unemployed; the source of income for 63.1 per cent of these women was social assistance; 66.9 per cent had a monthly income of less than $1,000 a month; and the mean annual income was $8,902.68, nearly $9,000 below the National Council of Welfare's poverty line for a family of four" (pp. 59–60). How does one account for these egregious socio-economic disparities?

Understanding Racial Oppression

It is apparent from the social scientific literature on racism that racial oppression is a very complex issue, with various points of view concerning its fundamental properties, sources, and dimensions (see, e.g., Mullings 2005, Carter and Virdee 2008). There are those, for instance, who hold to the belief that humankind has a "natural" predisposition towards racism (Kallen 1982: 22). Others, such as Banton (1977) and Stepan (1982), have attempted to demonstrate that the idea of race has not been a universal phenomenon in history, that the Greeks and Romans, for example, were free of colour prejudice. However, Isaac (2006) disagrees, and proposes that we use the term *proto-racism* in reference to Graeco-Roman antiquity. Moreover, it is useful to distinguish between ethnocentrism – the idea that one's own group is superior to others – and racism, which involves antagonism and discrimination towards people of another colour or religion. In other words, ethnocentrism is more of an attitude, while racism usually involves overt acts of a prejudicial or discriminatory nature.

Even in the history of the social scientific community, there has been a certain tendency towards what has been referred to as "scientific racism" (Dewbury 2007, Gravlee and Sweet 2008, Mevorach 2007, Shanklin 2000). A strong case can be made for an academic complicity in promulgating racist ideas under the guise of acceptable "science." Billig (1979) has presented a convincing argument that Western science

over the last several centuries has provided a consistent source of racist mythology. One cannot dismiss racism, he maintains, as a phenomenon only embraced by the uneducated, and that racism is compatible
with science is unjustified. Racists assume that there is a correlation
between biological, cultural, and intellectual development, with the
"white race" leading the way, and that they are the least apelike in the
human community. Anthropology apparently provided the intellectual
schema for this rationalization with its brainchild of evolutionary development, designating the categories of "savage," "barbarian," and
"civilization," as if there was a scientific validity to these groupings
(Jahoda 2009: 27–51).

There are arguments to be made suggesting academic complicity in
perpetuating outmoded concepts of race and as such, implicitly, promoting racist concepts. As Mevorach (2007: 239) explains, "Perhaps
the most insidious aspect to the shameful legacy of the science of race
... is that the concept of 'race' continues to underwrite the biologization of difference within the academic community from undergraduate
classrooms to biogenetic research laboratories and think tanks." Thus,
"race" should be regarded as a metaphor, as a social construct, and as a
human invention, as a way of managing difference.

Even though most scientists agree that race is a bogus concept, this
message is not getting through to the general public. The message that
is not being translated from the academic community to the general
population is that when it comes to differentiating one racial group
from another, it is only the most overt phenotypical (physical criteria) characteristics that are used for comparisons, such a skin colour or
amount of body hair, and it is these limited criteria that are at the "biologization of difference" (Gibel Azoulay 2006). Furthermore, as soci-
ologist Paul Gilroy (2001: 29) observes, "Whether it is articulated in the
more specialized tongues of biological science and pseudo-science, or
in the vernacular idiom of culture and common sense, the term 'race'
conjures up a peculiarly resistant variety of natural difference."

Racists suggest that anthropologists – presumably the *inventors* of
race – have "proven" the inherent superiority of Caucasoids, especially
Europeans, in their cultural and scientific development. Sociobiology
is the latest preoccupation of the scientific racists, interpreted by some
to suggest that whites are more adaptable to the challenges that the
world offers and are capable of making more intelligent responses to
change than others. Sociobiology is an acceptable scientific approach;
it is just the misuses of this perspective that are objectionable. There is

no scientific justification for assuming that one group of people is any more "inferior" than another, as the racists assume. Biology, certainly, has a role to play in our explanations about how people behave and live their lives. We should be sceptical, though, about any explanations of social and cultural life that reduce human behaviour simply to biological phenomena.[1]

Despite earlier conceptions, race itself as a definable biological entity is thought by many in the scientific community today to be largely a "fiction," as Smedley and Smedley (2005) observe, but race as a social problem, they argue, is very real. The idea that there are different classes, or races, of humans, such as black, white, or yellow, has long been seen as a fallacy in biological terms. What is more accurate is that there exists a continuum of phenotypical characteristics in the *Homo sapiens* population. The most identifiable, such as skin colour, range across many populations and areas of the world. The darkness or lightness of one's skin is based on melanin content, and this phenomenon ranges over many shades and degrees.

This inability to make biological sense out of the concept of race has led many to suggest that it is merely a social construct that is used for discriminatory and prejudicial purposes. Physical characteristics are reified in various ways in order to justify the isolation of certain groups, and thus make such people more of a target for discriminatory practices, as suggested in Gravlee's (2009) study of "How Race Becomes Biology," which are then transmuted into forms of social inequality. This idea that race does not really have a biological foundation has led Helleiner (2000), in her study of Irish Travellers (also referred to as Tinkers or Gypsies), to utilize the phrase "same race racism." She demonstrates that racism does not necessarily involve people of different colour, since the Travellers in Ireland have long been a target of racism and assimilative state settlement policies. Helleiner explores the ongoing realities of Traveller life by focusing on local and national anti-Traveller discourse, which is linked to legitimating and reproducing other social inequalities, including those of class, gender, and generation.

Traveller collective identity and culture is, in part, shaped by the oppressive forces of racism, thus illuminating the manner in which "Irish racism [points] to its articulation with other forms of social inequality" (Helleiner 2000: 9). Even at the national level in Ireland, a country not normally associated with racism, discriminatory practices in the state's institutional framework, as Lentin (2007) argues, are at the basis of restrictive immigration and employment policies. Similarly, other contemporary studies of racism in Europe (e.g., Goodey 2007) examine what Gorodzeisky and Semyonov (2009) refer to as "terms of exclusion," which pertain to the "admission and allocation of rights to immigrants."

In concluding her ethnography of Irish Travellers, Helleiner (2000) states that racism must be understood "within local, national, and increasingly globalized arenas structured by unequal power relations" (p. 241). Many scholars are apt to agree that, above all else, racism is primarily a political phenomenon, and this perspective has a fairly long history. Baker (1978: 316) has argued that "race relations are essentially group power contests." Ruth Benedict (1960: 148) shared this point of view, declaring, "Racism remains ... merely another instance of the persecution of minorities for the advantage of those in power."

In *The Anatomy of Racism*, Hughes and Kallen (1974: 105) state, "Racism, in the context of majority-minority relations, is a political tool, wielded by the dominant ethnic group to justify the status quo and rationalize the disability to which the minority group is subject." Furthermore, "in addition to its sociological and political nature, racism has been fostered by a range of factors such as the individual's need for scapegoats, the propensity for ethnocentrism, and the search for security, stability, and simplicity; in the latter regard, racism acts as a classificatory tool, carving up, categorizing, and thus simplifying the social universe" (Barrett 1987: 342). In sum, while many disparate factors can be used to explain racism, it is the power dimension of racism that appears to have the greatest explanatory punch.

The Violent Suppression of Aboriginal Resistance

There is no doubt many Canadians who would object to a racist characterization of their country. To call a person a racist would seem to be the worst sort of insult, because racism runs counter to one's notions of fairness and equality. They would point to our charity at the international level, to our favourable immigration policies, to our universal health care programs and social support systems, to our role in international peacekeeping, or, in Ontario, to the Human Rights Commission (William 2006). These are all, no doubt, valid to a certain degree, but we are also a very wealthy nation and can afford such benevolence. What matters more is how we actually think about our fellow Canadians who are disadvantaged – is this "charity" extended out of brotherly love, or can it be accounted for in a more calculating manner, perhaps not consciously designed, but nonetheless, one that keeps certain groups such as Aboriginal peoples and immigrants under control.

There will also be those among us who would see in the *Report of the Ipperwash Inquiry* evidence of intolerant altitudes that would be judged to be idiosyncratic; ones not attributable to the wider Canadian populace. Premier Mike Harris, one might say, in rebuttal to racist charges, was an ambitious politician from North Bay who has probably harboured racist attitudes to First Nations people his whole life – as if the mere fact of association with Aboriginal populations is apt to make one prone to such negative ways of thinking. How, then, do we account for the shocking communications of the OPP officers themselves, surely not all of them grew up in the north?

One could point to the Aboriginal demonstrators themselves, call them troublemakers, mention that they were not elected members of their communities, and therefore deserve to be treated as the ruffians that they are. What is missing in this rationalization is the larger picture in which the First Nations have been suppressed for so long that political mobilization appears to be their only viable alternative. Take the military base at Camp Ipperwash as an example. There were no political negotiations involved when the land on which the base was situated was taken away from the Kettle and Stony Point First Nation. Under the War Measures Act, the government of Canada felt justified in making such a move, for the public good, as the was a war on. However, the removal of the land from Aboriginal control in 1942 came with a promise that it would be returned after the war ended, but this never happened in spite of repeated effort and requests from the Aboriginal owners.

To band members themselves, it had become obvious that the compliant, obsequious approach of their elected chief and council was proving ineffective in restoring the land to their use and control. In other words, more attention-getting actions were necessary. It is hard to blame them, since the alternative of engaging in court action would have been prohibitively expensive, and beyond their means – so using the news media to make their grievances known seemed an effective manoeuvre. The same applies to the occupation of Ipperwash Provincial Park. The First Nation was basically swindled out of this highly valuable beachfront property by land developers and the high-pressure tactics of an Indian agent. There were sacred burial sites on the property, making it a culturally sensitive spot as well. When the Aboriginal protesters of the Kettle and Stony Point First Nation had, over a half-century, exhausted available avenues with no results, they no doubt felt they had no choice but to take matters into their own hands, by provoking an event that would get media attention.

Keep in mind that the activists chose a date for their occupation of Ipperwash Provincial Park when the tourists and campers had left after the Labour Day weekend, thereby minimizing any potential harm to members of the general public. The occupation was not formally sanctioned by the elected band council, and it is possible this fact provided the motivation for the rough treatment of the protesters by the OPP. Nevertheless, avenues for negotiations were available and they were not used. The response to the occupation was brutal. Armed and heavily protected officers overpowered the Aboriginal protesters, armed with little more than sticks and stones, with the result that one of them, Dudley George, was shot and killed. Irreparable harm was done to the reputation of the OPP, and by implication all of the government agencies involved, up to the Ontario Premier's Office. One could consider that racism and cultural intolerance are an endemic or systemic fact of the Canadian state system.

Could the confrontation at Ipperwash be regarded as an isolated incident, the treatment of which could perhaps be justified because of its idiosyncratic nature? The answer unfortunately is "absolutely not!" Canadians have to become aware that there has been a certain "sanitizing" of their history that has been going on for as long as we have had schools in this country. Schoolbooks books portray an Indigenous population happily hunting and fishing in the first chapter, then the Aboriginals just seem to disappear as the Plains of Abraham, Confederation, the construction of railways, and so on take centre stage. Certainly, it is not widely advertised that the Canadian government has played a very active role is suppressing First Nations' pleas for increased autonomy, for increased Aboriginal rights, and for attention to the issues involved with the loss of their land through treaties and other initiatives.

Although they are ostensibly citizens like the rest of Canada's population, First Nations people were denied the right to vote in federal elections until 1960. Their cultural practices were suppressed in ongoing acts of malfeasance, such as the British Columbian Pre-emption Act of 1870, the outlawing of the potlatch in the 1880s, and the prohibition of Aboriginal political groups in 1927. By the 1960s, there were confrontations over the loss of Aboriginal lands at Anicinabe Park near Kenora, followed by well-publicized acts of civil disobedience at Oka, Gustafsen Lake, Burnt Church, and Caledonia, among many other such events. In this light, the occupation at Ipperwash Provincial Park and the treatment of the First Nation protesters by the OPP could hardly be regarded as an isolated incident.

The scenario leading up to the occupation of Ipperwash Provincial Park would also appear to be a common pattern that underlies virtually all of the other acts of resistance just mentioned. First there was the large-scale removal of hundreds of acres of land from Aboriginal control under the guise of treaties and other land surrenders. Then there was the sequestering of Aboriginal populations on reserves or other limited tracts of property, usually devoid of useful natural resources by which traditional subsistence patterns could continue in an effective, life-sustaining manner. Next were the appeals to the federal government that the treaties should be reviewed because of discrepancies between what was in the written documents and the memories of signatory elders. In other cases, appeals were made for the negotiation of treaties over the large areas of land never ceded, such as in British Columbia, Quebec, and the Arctic. Most of these requests were ignored, by each successive government through the years.

Finally, confrontational approaches emerged in the 1960s, in which a younger generation of Aboriginal leaders was willing to stand up to the oppression of the politicians, police, and army. The results of these confrontations were mostly tragic, resulting in some cases in a loss of life and an ever-increasing cycle of violence. Eventually, but not always, the federal government stepped in because of all the adverse publicity, and it made cash "awards" to the Aboriginal participants – but did little else to restore an atmosphere of good will and justice. The appearance is that these cash settlements were made in a begrudging manner, with the implication that the Aboriginal civil disobedience did not really have any merit in the first place, but that the cash was distributed simply as a mechanism to quell dissent.

The unfortunate aspect of these cash dispersals is that they do little to alleviate the root causes of the discontent. They do not address First Nations poverty, unemployment, or inadequate housing. No mechanisms have been put in place by which First Nations' disputes could be resolved in an amicable manner without resort to the violence that so often characterizes these recent confrontations. There appears to be little by way of "cultural sensitivity" training given to front-line OPP and army personnel who probably regard the Aboriginal activists as "the enemy." In such a state of awareness, or lack of it, the authorities are apt to see themselves as legitimately using an exercise of force to quell what are regarded to be illegal acts. However, it would be far more effective if the police and army staff were to have an informed knowledge of Aboriginal rights, treaties, and their historical role that underlies these situations of political mobilization. With this knowledge, the OPP might be more likely to try to contain violence, rather than provoke it. The police might be used as facilitators in a negotiation process.

Policy Recommendations concerning Aboriginal Resistance

The foregoing discussion of police involvement in Aboriginal protests and confrontations suggests the following recommendations for policy in order to ameliorate conflict:

1 Police should be briefed as fully as possible about the reasons for Aboriginal acts of protests in which they are involved. Especially important would be information, as in the case of Ipperwash and Oka, where such protests concern burial sites or other locations considered sacred by First Nations people which could lead to a heightened sense of emotion on the protesters' part and an intense desire to protect these areas at all costs.

2 Aboriginal persons with training in negotiation and mediation, who are capable of serving as a buffer between police and protesters, and as a means of furthering communication between the two conflicting parties, should be utilized whenever possible in First Nations confrontations.

3 Police who are involved in Aboriginal protests are advised to wear attire as is customary when on normal duty, and they should be armed as they would in everyday situations, unless there is verifiable and concrete information that Aboriginal protesters are themselves armed. The Ipperwash case highlights the tragic results of a reliance on misinformation and hearsay reports.

4 It is highly advisable that "on the ground" involvement by qualified government officials who have expertise in land claims negotiations take part in Aboriginal protests as a means of diffusing tensions and creating an atmosphere in which there is an expectation of immanent government action on particular claims. Such involvement by government officials would also have the tendency to remove the Aboriginal protest from the criminal realm to that of civil litigation.

5 The protest site should be isolated in such a way that the situation is not further aggravated by persons not directly involved in an Aboriginal dispute, such as townspeople or even other Aboriginal people who have arrived from distant places "to give their support" to local protests. Such additional individuals tend to unnecessarily increase tension and magnify a local dispute into a much larger arena, making it virtually impossible to resolve. In other words, the smaller the crowd, and the more specific the dispute, the more effectively such situations can be managed.

Aboriginal Policy as an Exercise of Choice?

A conclusion of the present study of Ipperwash and other related matters of government Aboriginal policy should lead one to regard such policy as a problem of exercising choice. A prevalent perspective in government circles is that the problems of Aboriginal policy in Canada are primarily ones of enlarging the avenue of choice for First Nations people, especially in economic matters.

In *Creating Choices: Rethinking Aboriginal Policy*, a publication of the C.D. Howe Institute,[2] the argument is made that "no matter where they live, Aboriginals and their children should have options that are as broad and attractive as those available to other Canadians" (Richards 2006: 128). Certainly, the sentiment expressed here is a laudable one, for who could argue against such goals, but is an equality of choice at this point in time a realistic option?

The problem with choices is that they are only as good as the alternatives available from which one has the ability to choose. All choices have constraints or parameters associated with them that limit any available course of action. There are also the "opportunity costs" of choice making, meaning that choosing one path usually prohibits the following of other, possibly better, options. Above all, our choices are constrained by scarce resources and the competing ends to which these choices are applied.

As far as Aboriginal policy in Canada is concerned, there are social, economic, and political constraints and opportunities. Unfortunately, the political structure in which Aboriginal life is situated is primarily a restrictive one, often predicated on the constraints imposed by the Indian Act. The legislation serves more to inhibit initiative in the Aboriginal status community than it does to encourage opportunities. Breaking out of these shackles has been difficult, as the Sechelt band found when it faced opposition even from the Assembly of First Nations in its attempt to form a municipal form of government outside the stipulations of the Indian Act (Etkin 1988).

Economic opportunities are restricted by a myriad of factors, including distance from markets, difficulties in raising capital on reserves, a largely untrained labour force, and problems of an economy of small scale because of the small local populations. Social problems stem from discrimination that prejudices a movement towards equal opportunity. Politically, as we observe in the Ipperwash case, government representatives see the Aboriginal community as a problem to be dealt with, rather than as neighbours in need of help.

The whole of Canadian history, from an Indigenous perspective, has been one in which the Aboriginal population has been shunted into increasingly smaller tracts of land, with a very limited resource base. Under these circumstances, how can we talk about choices for Aboriginal peoples, when the "system" is so unfavourably stacked against them? On practically every socio-economic scale that one could imagine – employment, health care, education, incarceration rates, local income generation – Aboriginal peoples are much lower or higher, depending on the scale, than other Canadians. Does this mean that the plight of Aboriginal Canadians is a consequence of bad choices they have made? No, the answer is that whatever resources they might have used to better themselves have been largely stripped away from them by treaties and other questionable practices that have consistently worked against their advantage.

When Aboriginal peoples become fed up with this "inequity of opportunity," when they engage in acts of political mobilization to make their plight more widely known, what happens? More times than not, the first reaction of government, whether provincial or federal, is to call in the police and armed forces to suppress the particular event in progress. Violence escalates under such circumstances, leading to such regrettable situations as Oka and Ipperwash.

Why are not more reasonable options tried initially? What is wrong with reasoned dialogue and negotiations? Why does such dialogue only seem to take place after a confrontation turns violent and anger reaches a fever pitch? There is much to be learned from the *Report of the Iperwash Inquiry* (Linden 2007) in terms of preventing the needless loss of life, but will anybody listen, or is it all business as usual until the next time?

The Systemic Nature of Racial Oppression

Systemic racism refers to discriminatory practices that pervade a sociocultural system as a whole and that place certain groups at a disadvantage in the distribution of valued assets such as status, economic resources, and political positions. In this regard, is Canada a racist society? Does the Ipperwash Inquiry prove that it is? It is certainly evident that there are Canadians who hold racially oppressive attitudes, some of which are directed towards First Nations people and some that are directed towards other minorities as well. As Bolaria and Li (1988) argue in *Racial Oppression in Canada*, "Many Canadians have little idea of what constitutes race and racism, let alone what constitutes racial antagonism. Many misconceptions of race appear in Canadian society, ranging from outright bigotry to racial idealism. These misconceptions permeate many aspects of society in Canada; they cannot be dismissed as the isolated ideas of misinformed individuals. Like other dominant ideas, the roots of racist ideology are grounded in the daily experiences of people, and in the practice of social institutions" (p. 13).

Many Canadians would see their country as comprised of those with moderate views, favourably predisposed to minorities and ethnic populations. They would also view racists as neo-fascist, misanthropic people, thugs and nut cases who are probably in the vast minority. Yet, in a study of the right wing in Canada, such as the Ku Klux Klan, the Western Guard, and other white-supremacist organizations, Barrett (1987: vii) concludes that the racist appears quite ordinary, except for an extremity of view about those who are different from themselves: "Certainly that type [thugs and mentally disturbed people] exists, but much more numerous are those who can be described as solidly middle class – reasonably well-educated, often well-travelled, intelligent and thoughtful, but racists none the less. In other words, these people are not so different from the average Canadian citizen."

As far as the systemic aspects of discrimination towards Aboriginal peoples in Canada are concerned, one might begin to examine the social, economic, and political institutions that place them in a disadvantaged position. Many would point immediately to the Indian Act as an example of federal legislation that keeps the Aboriginal population in a state of dependency and marginality. Frideres (1988b: 76), for instance, describes the relationship between institutional structures and economic deprivation of which the Indian Act is a central piece of legislation, as follows: "The Indian Act continues to regulate every aspect of the lives of Native people. For example, until recently, a registered female Indian who married a non-Indian male lost her status while a non-Indian female who married an Indian becomes a status Indian.[3] The effects of the Act were and are devastating for personal autonomy and group morale, as well as for traditional Native political and social organization."

Henry and Tator (1985: 322), experts on racism in Canada, offer a particularly trenchant commentary on Canada's treatment of its Aboriginal population: "No group has suffered more seriously from racism than our native people, and Canada's discriminatory treatment of them has been widely documented. The history of the relationship between native and white Canadians has been characterized by exploitation and the denial of the most fundamental rights and freedoms, including the annihilation of native people's culture, land, and sovereignty."

Whether Canadians want to recognize it or not, there is an abundance of social scientific literature such as that presented by Henry and Tator (1985) that suggests quite unequivocally that Native people in this country are subject to a form of racism that has become intrinsic to the structure of Canadian society, such as forces that systematically deny employment and adequate housing to Natives.

According to Peter Carstens (1971), a retired University of Toronto professor who was raised in South Africa, the reserve system in Canada is the counterpart of the apartheid system formerly existing in his home country. Many Canadians were, no doubt, embarrassed when Bishop Desmond Tutu visited the Sandy Lake Reserve, in northwestern Ontario, where he was shown the dilapidated housing of the First Nations residents. He exclaimed, on the basis of this visit, that he had seen very few cases this bad even in his home of South Africa. In an obvious attempt to cover up the political damage of this unfavourable comparison, as I recall, Eric Malling a short time later on the CBC's *Fifth Estate* suggested that the Aboriginal population of northern Ontario had staged the Tutu visit for media purposes. The denial concerning the deplorable living conditions of Aboriginal life in the north is thereby allowed to continue, and the government continues to avoid providing adequate housing on reserves.

A few houses might be built, but when media attention lessons, funds for additional programs dry up. This is an example of what has been termed by one researcher as "mock change": "Governmental programs set up to instil a sense of independence and self-reliance among native peoples are discontinued just when it appears that they might be successful. The government makes a show of consulting with native peoples, thus putting them momentarily off guard, but introduces legislation exactly the opposite of what was requested by native people" (Barrett 1984: 190).

In the matter of systemic or institutional racism, the difference between the United States and Canada is that in American society it is Blacks not Aboriginals who have been the primary targets of oppression. Levin and Levin (1982: 30) explain, "Native Americans might have qualified for that dubious distinction were it not for the fact that they were pushed aside, ignored, exploited, and even annihilated without the need to resort to complex justifications." In Canada, the Aboriginal populace is larger on a per capita basis than in the United States, and therefore, their relative socio-economic importance is greater. However, the "complex justifications" that the Levins refer to are probably not a whole lot different in the two countries, it is just their relative importance that differs.

In other words, as far as the institutional structures that promote oppressive and discriminatory practices are concerned, the First Nations people in Canada suffer from a fate similar to their American Black counterparts, especially when it comes to equality in housing, education, employment, and health care. For example, in David Stymeist's (1975) previously discussed study of a mixed white-Aboriginal community in northwestern Ontario, he arrived at the conclusion that First Nations people are kept handy as a source of cheap summer labour, but they are not allowed into the social fabric of the community. He identifies how crucial the economic importance of the surrounding Native population is to the viability of the town's economy. The labour provided by the Native population as tourist guides, firefighters, and seasonal railroad employees contributes to the economic viability of the stores, restaurants, and hotels of the town. Similarly, in the nearby Rainy River area of northwestern Ontario, recent research on white-Aboriginal community relations has arrived at similar conclusions by referring to such relations as an example of "Canadian Apartheid" (Denis 2011, 2012).

These sorts of economic relationships, in which a disadvantaged First Nations population is one of the underpinnings of a town's stability and social infrastructure, is what Blalock (1982: 38–41) has described as the "inequitable exchanges involving minorities." These inequitable exchanges promote the economic ascendency of a dominant group but keep another at a depressed state. Frideres (1988b: 71–100) argues that

First Nations people in Canada suffer from economic deprivation because of institutional structures that have led to a high degree of dependency, which in turn, forces them into a position of marginality.

This relationship of dependency was fostered by an assimilationist governmental policy, "to the extent that they [Aboriginal people] would become wage earners and domestic consumers of various goods produced by capitalist entrepreneurs" (Frideres 1988b: 88). Richards's (2006) proposal of "creating choices" as a mechanism for alleviating the depressed socio-economic condition of Canada's Aboriginal population, therefore, would probably have little of the salubrious effects that he suggests until there are corresponding changes in the systemic or institutional structures that work to disadvantage certain minority sectors of the population while benefiting others in the dominant class who profit from such situations.

As Stymiest (1975) argues for the northern "Crow Lake" community, the main socio-economic problem is the structured system of inequality. First Nations people are prevented from becoming permanent residents because they are prohibited from securing rental accommodations (places are rented only by word of mouth, and are not advertised in newspapers), or employment, or otherwise participating in the socio-economic life of the town. He finds that the concept of "ethnicity" does little to explain Crow Lake's characteristics, which are better understood as a matter of race prejudice. "I suggest," Stymeist writes, "that active discrimination against Native people largely prevented them from taking a full and active part in the social life of the town ... for a Native person locked into this system, the hypocrisy of bureaucratic agencies and the violence and prejudice of the local white society become two omnipresent and inescapable forces" (pp. 9, 93–4). It is probable that the people of the Kettle and Stony Point First Nation would be all too familiar with these "two omnipresent and inescapable forces."

Conclusion

The *Report of the Ipperwash Inquiry* (Linden 2007) is a most salient document because of what it reveals about the management of Aboriginal acts of civil disobedience in Canada. The report informs us about the attitudes of politicians and law enforcement officers concerning demonstrations for Aboriginal rights. As the material that is presented in this book apply illustrates, negative attitudes towards First Nation societies have a very long history in Canada, and the policies enacted by successive federal and provincial government have served more to suppress legitimate Aboriginal rights and claims than they have to solve the issues stemming from them.

As the Ipperwash Inquiry demonstrates, such intransigent attitudes continue even today, with little hope that the impoverished conditions of First Nations communities will change any time soon. It would appear that the government is only willing to act when Aboriginal acts of resistance are elevated to an extreme condition, with a loss of life, for example, and then the resulting measures are largely ones of appeasement, rather than attempts to enact meaningful, perdurable change in housing, employment, and legal claims. One wonders, however, about the sincerity of our elected representatives. For example, the event launching the *Report of the Royal Commission on Aboriginal Peoples*, the most expensive Royal Commission in Canadian history, which cost taxpayers $63 million and produced four hundred recommendations, did not even merit a meeting with the prime minister to discuss the details. Given that the RCAP report was initiated, in large part, in response to the Oka Crisis of 1990, when Aboriginal frustrations were at their highest levels in decades, one could have expected more than just silence. Thus, many Aboriginal peoples are apt to justifiably feel that Canadians, as a whole, do not regard First Nations issues to be very important.

The Ipperwash Inquiry was also an expensive affair, costing $13.3 million, and it produced one hundred recommendations. Although the Ontario Provincial Police have made some changes to their procedures when handling Aboriginal civil disobedience, the Ontario government has not yet addressed in any meaningful way the suggestions and proposals made by the Hon. Sidney Linden (2007). The cynic would submit that it is easy for the government to spend taxpayers' dollars to diffuse a troubling situation, such as Oka or Ipperwash, with the hope that such matters will eventually fade from the public's memory. Surely, though, this approach is hardly an effective utilization of public funds and an insult to the many dozens of people who presented thoughtful testimony.

The problem with such a laissez-faire attitude is that it only serves to aggravate matters further. More Aboriginal protests, demonstrations, and occupations are inevitable, given the sizeable backlog of unresolved land claims and the endemic poverty on Native reserves. Furthermore, by not paying attention to the recommendations of public inquiries, politicians are sending a message that Aboriginal issues are essentially trivial matters, not to be taken seriously.

This is an unfortunate and irresponsible message to convey because the issues are important, not just to First Nations peoples, but to all Canadians. The issues are important because the injustices suffered by one group in society are the potential injustices that we can all expect, under the right circumstances, to suffer as well. One can be sure that Dudley George did not expect to be shot by an OPP officer on that fateful September evening in 1995. He had just joined fellow members of his community to protest what they felt was discriminatory treatment. However, it behooves all of us to valorize the sacrifice Dudley George made in the same manner that we have honoured the sacrifices of other Canadians who have given their lives, in different times and places, to preserve justice and equality in Canada.

Chapter Eight

Institutional Racism in Canada

No matter whether the dimension is time, place, or social class, racism has been endemic in Canada ... the degree, scope, and persistence of the phenomenon leads to a single conclusion: racism in Canada has been institutionalized.
                                    – Stanley R. Barrett, *Is God a Racist?* (1987: 307)

It is possible to end our racial nightmare together.
                            – Phil Fontaine, National Chief of the Assembly of First Nations
                                                        (*CBC News*, 11 June 2008)

Most Canadians are justifiably proud of their country and what has been achieved in its first century and a half. Canadians can point to their official government policy of multiculturalism and its tolerant immigration policy. They can also point to the Canadian Charter of Rights and Freedoms (1982) and its explicit recognition of Aboriginal rights. Moreover, it is true that the present prime minister, Stephen Harper, issued a public apology in the House of Commons, on 11 June 2008, stating that the government's "policy of assimilation was wrong, has caused great harm, and has no place in our country ... The Government of Canada sincerely apologizes and asks the forgiveness of the aboriginal peoples of this country for failing them so profoundly. We are sorry." Aboriginal leaders reacted to the prime minister's apology with guarded optimism, but also with trepidation. They have heard such ameliorative initiatives from the government in the past, in particular, during the Trudeau-Chrétien era, which were subsequently turned against them. Assembly of First Nations National Chief Phil Fontaine observed, "The attempts to erase our identities hurt us deeply. But it

also hurt all Canadians and impoverished the character of our nation ...
it is possible to end our racial nightmare together" (*CBC News*, 11 June
2008).

The reason for Chief Fontaine's trepidation is, no doubt, due to the
fact that politicians can say anything, at any time, as appeasement
mechanisms. What really counts, in Chief Fontaine's mind, would be
the government policies that would serve to reverse decades of abuse
and oppression. Seemingly ingrained negative attitudes towards Aboriginal peoples by the larger Canadian population are not so easily
erased.

The Characteristics of Institutional Racism

The initial use of the term *institutional racism* is commonly associated
with the Black American political activist Stokely Carmichael in the
1960s. In what is widely credited to be the first attempt to define the
term, Carmichael and Hamilton (1967: 112) argue, "Institutional racism ... is less overt, far more subtle, less identifiable in terms of *specific*
individuals committing the acts. But it is no less destructive of human
life. [It] originates in the operation of established and respected forces
in the society, and thus receives far less public condemnation" (original emphasis). The latter part of this quote is highly significant and
bears repeating; institutional racism "originates in the operation of *established* and *respected* forces in the society" (emphasis added). Thus, to
understand the dynamics and characteristics of institutional racism, it
is necessary to adopt a critical perspective on the nature of politics and
society in general (Gillborn 2008: 27–8).

Shirley Better (2008: xv–xvi) describes institutional racism as a "2000-
pound elephant." She writes, "As we explore the ramifications of institutional racism, we will discover that it is analogous to a 2000-pound
elephant residing in one's living room. Everyone in the house is dis-
gusted with the elephant taking over the living room ... Nevertheless, everyone in the household continues to act as if the elephant is
not there. Why is this? ... no one in the house has the political will to
force the elephant to leave. And it never will leave until someone in the
house develops the courage to acknowledge the beast's existence and
create an action plan to rid the house of it."

This analogy is particularly a propos because institutional racism is
so embedded in our social institutions – and in the attitudes of people
in power – that it seems not to exist at all. Better points out that "it

is exceedingly difficult for us to control our institutions which, being products of their history, cannot but perpetuate practices which advantage the typical white and handicap the typical minority person" (p. 13). Similarly, Rangasamy (2004: 27) argues, "Institutional racism is rooted in history. It is a symptom of fundamental maladjustments in the interactions of culturally and ethnically differentiated. beings." Institutional racism is an important social problem that should be informed by research and that deserves appropriate academic analysis. "Only then," Rangasamy suggests, "can the wealth of good work and good intentions be founded on an understanding which effectively addresses the cultural problems that underlie institutional racism" (ibid.).

The dominant group in society has historically justified its rule and continued to exploit those in the minority population by building into the society's social, economic, and political institutions ideologies and practices that have had the tendency to support and justify this domination. All manner of social institutions are involved including schools, newspapers and other media, welfare agencies, businesses, city councils, and the criminal justice system. The domination that perpetuates institutional racism, therefore, is largely in the hands of enlightened persons who produce the inequalities. In sum, institutional racism can be defined as "those patterns, procedures, practices, and policies that operate within social institutions so as to consistently penalize, disadvantage, and exploit individuals who are members of non-white racial/ethnic groups" (Better 2008: 19).

Satzewich, in his book *Racism and Social Inequality in Canada*, identifies three forms of institutional racism (1998: 39–44). "The concept of institutional racism," he suggests, "refers to circumstances in which social practices and institutions are guided by racist ideas" (p. 39). In the first form, "there are circumstances where certain exclusionary practices are derived from a set of racist ideas, but where those practices are no longer guided by those ideas" (ibid.). An example of this form of institutional racism, Satzewich submits, would be the programs whereby seasonal workers from the Caribbean enter Canada to work in Ontario's fruit and vegetable industry. Initially, these programs were justified on the racist idea that such workers were suited for the strenuous labour under the hot Ontario sun, but were not suitable as permanent immigrants. The programs continue today, but racist ideas are no longer used to justify them.

In the second form of institutional racism, "there are circumstances where a racist discourse is modified in such a way that the explicitly

racist content is eliminated, but the new words carry the original meaning" (p. 39). Satzewich's example of this form is the Immigration Act.
Early versions of the Canadian Immigration Act allowed the federal
government to prohibit the entry of immigrants for such reasons as na-
tionality, ethnicity, or geographical area of origin, for peculiar customs,
habits, or modes of life, or purported inability to become readily as-
similated. Today, there are no explicit references to race in the criteria
for immigration, and the Canadian government has abandoned race as
a basis for exclusion.

In the third form of institutional racism, "there are circumstances
where institutional practices are based on apparently universalistic and
non-racist rules, standards and procedure, but where those standards
may in turn have negative effects for certain minority groups" (p. 41).
Satzewich elaborates here, describing circumstances and practices that
could be referred to as institutional racism, for example, certain weight
and/or height requirements as employment criteria, which have the effect of excluding members of some ethnic groups, for example, Asians,
from securing employment in police forces or fire departments. Other
forms of institutional racism could be based on overly inflated educational requirements for what are essentially non-technical jobs, or the
use of word-of-mouth recruiting, which serves to place members of certain groups at a disadvantage when scarce resources are distributed.

Economic privilege is one of the most important underpinnings of
institutional racism. Wealthy groups have profited the dominant group
through the maintenance of racism. The enslavement of Africans in
America is a particularly striking historical example of this sort of economic domination in which slavery increased the profits of white plan-
tation owners. Economic privileging of the dominant group can also be
seen in the plight of the First Nations of America, who were removed
from their lands with little or no compensation in return. Removal of
the Indigenous populations from their ancestral lands opened up possibilities for European settlers, as homesteaders, who profited from farm-
land purchased for small sums or taken by force.

Employment is a significant area in which institutional racism oper-
ates. Agocs and Jain (2001) undertook a study for the Canadian Race
Relations Foundation of the prevalence of systemic racism in employment in this country. They found that the "analysis of human rights
cases in Canada involving employment-related complaints on grounds
of race found an increase in the number of cases at the federal level
from 1980 to 1998 ... Dismissal, refusal to hire, and harassment were

amongst the most prevalent complaints [of those interviewed]" (p. iii). As far as Aboriginal workers were concerned, "the salary gap between them and the general Canadian workforce widened despite a steady increase in their representation" (p. 3).

Agocs and Jain analysed 119 Canadian human rights cases, from 1980 to 1998, involving racially discriminatory behaviour in the area of employment. They found "that racial discrimination in employment is a serious problem that prevents the efficient operation of the labour market and causes significant losses for the national economy in terms of underutilized human resources as well as the personal suffering and loss of fair opportunities to a large segment of the [Canadian] society" (p. 16). They concede that "this phenomenon is complex and multidimentional" (ibid.) and suggest that an understanding of the cultural and social aspects of discrimination is needed in addition to its economic aspects.

Aside from employment and other economic aspects, educational perspectives have been the subject of scrutiny with regard to institutional racism (see, e.g., Law, Phillips, and Turney 2004; Chesler, Lewis, and Crowfoot 2005; Gillborn 2008; Davies and Guppy 1998). Gillborn (2008) points out that members of education departments have a tendency, privately at least, to equate discussions of racism with a question of semantics, "as if racism were merely a *word* rather than a structured, recurrent and deeply embedded *reality*" (p. 127, original emphasis). He also suggests that educators, while frequently using the language of "race," often fail to adopt a critical perspective "that seeks relentlessly to get beneath the rhetoric of legal and public policy debates to expose the material racist inequities that are created and sustained behind an inclusive and progressive façade" (p. 28). In other words, it is one thing to "pay lip service" to racial injustice in the classrooms of the nation under the guise of a liberal education system, but it is quite another to engage in a determined and consistent critique of the very institutions in society that perpetuate the inequities that are so freely criticized.

In an article entitled "Race and Canadian Education," Davies and Guppy (1998: 131) observe, "History shows unquestioned examples of racism in Canadian education. Almost from the outset, European settlers deemed Aboriginal culture to be inferior and set out to 'civilize' the indigenous population ... Schools can promote or erode cultural identities, and they have become a prime institutional arena for waging these cultural wars." Davies and Guppy point to such historical examples as the early missionaries' overly zealous promotion of Christianity, the residential boarding schools for Aboriginal children, segregated schools for the children of Chinese immigrants in British Columbia during the 1920s, and the separate schools for Blacks in southwestern Ontario and Nova Scotia until the 1960s. These examples suggest that racial minorities in Canada experienced dislocation from their existing cultural and social traditions through the school system, cultural degradation, and possible exclusion from opportunities in the mainstream society.

In his article entitled "Institutional Racism in the Academy?" Pilkington (2004: 20–1) notes that although police forces have begun to pay attention to race, especially since the 1980s, "the same cannot be said of the academy's response. Until very recently, no connection was made between the transition from an elite to a mass system of higher education which produced an increasingly diverse student population, and the growing proportion from minority ethnic communities ... The lack of attention paid to race and ethnicity in relation to higher education is therefore extraordinary."

Sharma (2004) looks at the problem of multiculturalism in school systems, which ostensibly means living with difference, but whose purposes "do not reflect existing ideological conflicts – they are constitutive of its ambivalent political praxis" (p. 105). What Sharma suggests is that multiculturalism "persists in its marginality, especially for those schools in 'all white areas,' as cultural diversity has been defined as of relevance only to other ethnic groups" (p 111). It is common in schools to use non-white children as a multicultural resource, which has resulted in a situation such that "an exegesis of the politics of whiteness has never been explored ... Failing to examine the culture of whiteness within the liberal tradition of multicultural education has not been an oversight but an outcome of its own reductive conception of culture" (pp. 111–12).

There have been educational leaders who may be credited with championing multicultural initiatives; nonetheless, as Chesler, Lewis, and Crowfoot (2005: 216) argue, "Affirmative action and other means of increasing diversity and approaching racial justice in organizational policies and practices were not initiated primarily by higher education institutions themselves." Racial justice has resulted from the civil rights movement and various other external pressures applied by the courts, the federal government, and community advocates. They submit that since the mid-1990s there are universities and colleges that have substantially slowed the progress towards greater racial diversity.

Chesler et al. cite a substantial number of examples of institutional racism in higher education (pp. 16–19). Although their primary focus is higher education in the United States, their examples can probably be found in many other countries as well, with an intellectual rationale and justification for racism provided by early university scholars. In the nineteenth century, for example, scientific racism treated slavery as a "benign institution" and promoted belief in the inherent biological inferiority of people of colour. By the twentieth century, people of colour able to attend institutions of higher education were able to enrol only in segregated institutions. When segregated schools became less common, many people of colour continued to attend them because of the negative experiences of many students in predominantly white male institutions. Black-only colleges were an attraction also because of the presence of faculty role models who shared the students' race so that, in many cases, such colleges and universities were less racist and thus less of a systemic barrier to higher educational achievement.

Chesler et al. (p. 19) sum up their discussion of institutional racism in higher education with their finding that "the legacy of racism in higher education organizations ... pervades the curriculum, pedagogy, structure of departments and disciplines, formal and informal relationships among participants, and decision making about hiring, promotion, and retention." In other words, there are few aspects of higher education not influenced in some manner or other by the taint of institutional racism. To counteract these pervasive trends, Law et al. (2004) offer an "antiracist toolkit" for tackling institutional racism in higher education. This toolkit contains suggestions on achieving race equality and employment in higher education, student recruitment and support, issues pertaining to teaching and learning, research on ethnicity and racism, and other initiatives relevant to antiracist actions.

Policing is an important area of concern as it relates to discrimination and institutional racism, especially pertaining to the highly controversial issue of racial profiling (see, e.g., Glover 2009, Tator and Henry 2006, Gumbhir 2007, Tanovich 2006). For example, Tanovich (2006: 1) argues, "The colour of justice in Canada is White. The unequal impact of our criminal justice system begins with police surveillance. If you are not White, you face a much greater risk of attracting the attention of law enforcement officials in public spaces such as the highway, street, border, or airport ... The evidence suggests that ... increased police surveillance is triggered by appearance, not behavior."

In 1995, the Ontario Commission on Systemic Racism in the Ontario Criminal Justice System released its report (Ontario 1995; see also Satzewich 1998: 177–200). The Commission asked the question of Ontario residents: "Do you think that there is racism in the criminal justice system?" The Commission then conducted various surveys and consultations to elicit answers to this question. Throughout the province, public forums were held in urban centres in order that Ontario residents could share their views on this issue. Various members of the criminal justice system were surveyed including police officers, judges, lawyers, and parole board members. The surveys focused on Metro Toronto rather than all of Ontario because of the high concentration of racial minorities living in this city, thereby leaving open for criticism the possibility that the opinions of certain sectors of the population were overrepresented and not representative of what the average person thinks.

The Commission concluded that a large proportion of Black Torontonians appear to have little confidence that the criminal justice system delivers justice equally. This is a view shared by many White and Asian residents of Toronto, as well. A widely held opinion, which emerged from the interviews and survey data, is that the criminal justice system in Ontario comprises two sectors: one for the majority group, that is, people with money and connections, and the other for members of racial minorities. The Commission reported that many people in the province of Ontario believe that discrimination is common in the justice system.

Of particular interest to our focus in this book, on the shooting of Aboriginal activists such as Dudley George, is the presentation in Chapter 11 of the Commission's report entitled "Systemic Responses to Police Shootings" (Ontario 1995: 377–90), where it is stated:

No incidents involving the criminal justice system generate as much public outcry, especially in the black community, as police shootings of civilians. In the past two decades [1975–1995], the number and circumstances of police shootings in Ontario have convinced many black Ontarians that they are disproportionately vulnerable to police violence. They conclude that the police are quicker to use their guns against black people and that the shootings are unduly harsh responses to the incidents under investigation. The resulting deaths and injuries have also come to represent the ultimate manifestation of daily discrimination and harassment that many black people experience, especially in interactions with police. In short, the shootings are perceived not as isolated incidents, but as tragedies that affect the entire black community – and as a reflection of the destructive force of systemic racism. (p. 377)

There would be those who might be tempted to suggest, as noted above, that police shootings of members of racial and ethnic minorities are isolated events, while others would argue that such shootings are a result of a systemic process of racial profiling that discriminates unfairly against Blacks, Aboriginals, Asians, and other minority peoples. Racial profiling is, therefore, an important area of discussion pertaining to the characteristics of systemic discrimination in the criminal justice system.

Gumbhir (2007: 16–17) gives the following definition: "Racial profiling is defined as any police-initiated action that relies on race, ethnicity, or national origin rather than the behaviour of an individual or information that leads the police to a particular individual who has been identified as being, or having been, engaged in criminal activity." This definition rests on the idea that it is the use of racial or ethnic stereotypes in officer decision making that is the cause of differential treatment. For example, Holbert and Rose (2004) suggest that such stereotypes are possibly related to the overt racial prejudices of the individual police officers themselves. As evidence for this position, about 25 per cent of the officers in the Holbert and Rose study reported their belief that racial or ethnic biases and prejudices influenced the work of other officers in their treatment of minority suspects (p. 104).

It is important to note, however, that Gumbhir (2007) bases his definition on the contrast between racial profiling – the use of ethnic or racial stereotypes in an officer's decision making – with what is commonly regarded as acceptable tactics of law enforcement – using a suspect's behaviour or known information on crimes as the basis for an arrest or detention. Behaviour associated with the former, that is, racial profiling, includes such practices as police targeting minorities for contacts, such as frequent "stop and frisk" practices; police initiating contacts with minorities for minor reasons, such as minority members being pulled over for vehicle stops involving trivial or obscure equipment or moving violations; police initiating contacts with minorities because of suspicious circumstances as opposed to actual violations of the law; and police using force more frequently in contacts involving minorities (pp. 10–13). Gumbhir concludes that "institutional racism and associated discriminatory practices are generally embedded in the laws, rules, policies, norms, and standard practices of an institution, and can manifest itself [sic] in discrimination in a number of ways" (p. 55).

In the introduction to his book, *Systemic Racism: A Theory of Oppression*, Feagin (2006: 2) asks, "What are the distinctive social worlds that have been created by racial oppression over several centuries?" He answers this question with reference to U.S. society by arguing that because racism is more than "racial prejudice and individual bigotry ... [but] material, social, and ideological reality that is well-embedded in major [social, economic, and political] institutions" (ibid.), it is systemic to society as a whole. Similarly, Glover (2009: 66) makes the assertion that "all racial-ethnic relationships and events need to be contextualized within this systemic understanding of racial oppression. The *everydayness* of racial profiling is critical to understanding the cumulative racial processes and effects that manifest in social institutions such as the criminal justice system" (original emphasis).

Processes of racial profiling can be situated within the realm of institutional racism because there is a "recurring exercise of power" that is necessary for the operation of racial oppression (Feagan 2006: 21). Since racial minorities tend to be overrepresented in traffic stops and associated events, it is the regularity of racial profiling as a social phenomenon that is particularly troublesome in its discriminatory aspects. In this regard, "systemic racism," as Glover (2009: 66) argues, "is also appropriate as a theoretical guide because of its emphasis on the separating, distancing, and alienating relations that emerge under racial systems ... Clearly, racial profiling processes emerge from these radicalized ideas, stereotypes, and inclinations at social control via the legal realm." These "racial profiling processes" are also responsible for generating, in Feagin's (2006: 25) terms, the "recurring and habitual discriminatory actions" that are manifested in the routine activities of social institutions.

Tator and Henry's (2006) study, entitled *Racial Profiling in Canada*, which they subtitle *Challenging the Myth of "a Few Bad Apples,"* is an important contribution to understanding the relationship between the criminal justice system, policing, and racial and ethnic minorities. Their central argument reads as follows: "The first crucial element in racial profiling is its links to the practices of racialization – practices that can be seen to operate in virtually every sector of society. Racialization is part of a broader process that inferiorizes and excludes groups in the population ...the discourses around criminal acts by particular minority groups depend on essentialized and stereotypical thinking" (pp. 8–9). Moreover, "racialization begins with ideology, which is then filtered through the everyday micro-interactions and discourses of police, security officers, judges, journalists and editors, educators, politicians, and bureaucrats, among others" (p. 9).

Tator and Henry contend that people of colour and Aboriginals are seen in the criminal justice system to be "problem people" or, in their terms, "bad apples," in need of special scrutiny by the police because there is an a priori expectation on the part of law enforcement officers that such people are troublemakers. That Aboriginal and coloured people are overrepresented in prisons, or tend to be charged with offences to a greater extent than other Canadian citizens, would appear to be a sort of self-fulfilling prophecy.

According to Correction Canada's statistics, for example, Aboriginal adults are incarcerated over six times more often than anyone else. Aboriginal people form less than 5 per cent of the total Canadian population, yet account for 17 per cent of all federal inmates. In Saskatchewan, Aboriginal people are incarcerated at almost ten times the overall provincial rate (Smith 2006: 81). Aboriginal people are also subjected to greater scrutiny than other citizens, and to a greater numbers of charges, which probably goes some distance in accounting for these alarming statistics. Such overall incarceration rates can then be used as a justification for continuing the profiling of Aboriginal people, in a seemingly endless cycle of detentions, arrests, and incarcerations.

Racial profiling is based, to some extent, on the negative stereotypes of First Nations people that are part of the larger North American culture. Ponting (1998: 279–82) has studied the impact of stereotyping on First Nations individuals, especially in terms of the role of public opinion that is supportive of negative stereotypes. These stereotypes emanate from a myriad of sources. Stereotypes about "Indians" were once prominent in school textbooks and in the many Hollywood western-style "cowboy and Indian" movies. Such movies tend to promote a negative stereotypical view of Aboriginal people as uncivilized, bloodthirsty, and wagon-burning, wild savages. Other sources include the geographical segregation of Indian reserves, which serve to isolate contact with the larger Canadian society. There is the persisting stereotype of the "drunken Indian," which is problematic in promoting a more positive view of Aboriginal persons. Ponting submits, "Even though stereotypes are often false or contain only a kernel of truth, where they persist great harm is done to native people, especially to their identity. Furthermore, even stereotypes which are no longer part of popular culture still exert a debilitating influence on subsequent generations of Native people" (p. 279).

Media including as newspapers, radio, and television play a role in perpetuating racial stereotypes, since the media are a powerful force for disseminating images and ideas. To a large extent, the media "inform our beliefs, values, and behaviours" (Tator and Henry 2006: 51). Although the media are capable of depicting a range of democratic values, such as freedom, fairness, and equality, the media can also reinforce negative racist stereotypes. This is particularly the case in the coverage of crime and immigration in which ethnocentric judgments are made. For example, Feagin (2010: 109) reports on research of television news in Los Angeles, where it was "found that black residents were more likely to be portrayed as criminals and less likely to be portrayed as victims than white residents. Again black suspects were overrepresented relative to their actual arrest rates, while the opposite was true for white suspects." This research suggests that media imagery such as that portrayed on Los Angeles television news is likely to influence the way many whites view their chances of being crime victims, in addition to the way they might decide on the guilt or innocence if serving on juries in cases involving Black defendants. Similarly, it is apparent that First Nations people, in particular, are singled out in the media as "problem people," who require a disproportionate amount of political attention and economic resources, or who are making unacceptable demands on society. Tator and Henry (2006: 54) conclude, "Racialized images and ideas embedded in popular culture and other social institutions fuel moral panic among the White dominant culture. Moral panic thus becomes the vehicle of the dominant ideology; as such, it marginalizes, inferiorizes, and stigmatizes people of colour."

Writing about the role of the media in the context of policing, Martin (2007: 258–9) argues, "A crisis in governance becomes a matter of public concern when a ruling or a judgement has considerable media interest, such as a ruling on a controversial subject. A minority of these cases generate sufficient challenge to legitimacy that special responses evolve or are called upon, such as public inquiries, legislative changes, or reforms to modes of civilian review, often driven by community and media pressures." In other words, the media can become a powerful force not just in disseminating "news," but in shaping the very social and political stories they are covering. The news media are capable of playing a role in determining, certainly partially, the outcome of events, or at least the images that the public retains of them.

Furthermore, the media can help shape the public's perceptions of ongoing police investigations. Manning (2008: 317) points out that "there is a [media] bias *toward* investigating crimes involving favoured victims – the aged and infirm, 'the respectables' especially women (or at least 'deserving' women, small children seen as innocent, and very high status community leaders" (original emphasis). Those deemed less worthy – e.g., drug users, homosexuals, or prostitutes – are apt to experience less media coverage and attention. "Along with discrimination based on preferred victims," Manning argues, "the level of effort may relate also to preferred crimes – as defined politically or within the occupational culture" (ibid.).

As far as the involvement of minority and ethnic group members in the criminal justice system is concerned, Charles Smith (2006: 80–5) has written on the long history of racialized policies towards Aboriginal peoples, especially in the context of race-based inequality, which has undermined Aboriginal social, economic, and political self-sufficiency. The comparatively high incarceration rate for Aboriginal people in Canadian prisons has been commented on in the *Report of the Royal Commission on Aboriginal Peoples* (1996). The suspicious deaths of Aboriginal persons who were detained by police officers have also been the subject of public inquiries.

The Manitoba government, for example, called the Aboriginal Justice Inquiry of Manitoba, on 13 April 1988, to investigate the circumstances surrounding the deaths of two Aboriginal persons: the police shooting of John Joseph (J.J.) Harper in 1988 and the murder of Helen Betty Osborne, in 1971, by local white youths in The Pas – but for which a trial was held only in 1987. On 9 March 1988, J.J. Harper was shot and killed by a Winnipeg police officer for no apparent reason, other than he was an Aboriginal man walking down the street. J.J. Harper was the executive director of the Island Lake Tribal Council and a prominent leader in the Manitoba Aboriginal community. On the evening of his death, Harper was detained by police officers investigating a stolen vehicle. Harper refused to identify himself, and when an officer grabbed Harper's arm a scuffle ensued during which Harper was shot. The inquiry was unable to determine what happened once the men were on the ground; however, the commissioners indicated, contrary to the officer's claim, that "Harper never had any significant control over [his] revolver" (Tanovich 2006: 154).

The commissioners concluded that race was the reason that J.J. Harper was stopped by the officer: "We believe that he decided to stop and question Harper simply because Harper was a male Aboriginal person in his path. We are unable to find any other reasonable explanation for his being stopped. We do not accept [the officer's] explanation. It is clearly a retroactive attempt to justify stopping Harper. We believe that [he] had no basis to connect him to any crime in the area and that his refusal or unwillingness to permit Harper to pass freely was ... racially motivated" (in ibid.). It is noteworthy that, in this case, the police officer was never criminally charged, nor did he lose his job over the shooting of J.J. Harper.

Subsequent additional cases in western Canada would suggest that racial profiling of Aboriginal men in Saskatoon, Saskatchewan, has also been the basis for several inquiries after some of these men died during encounters with police. A prominent case involves the death of Neil Stonechild in Saskatoon (Green 2011). In the fall of 1990, the body of Neil Stonechild, an Aboriginal teenager, was found in a field just outside the city. He had suffered injuries and marks on his body caused by handcuffs. It was reported that Stonechild was last seen in the back of a police cruiser. An inquiry was ordered in 2003 to investigate his death, and a subsequent report issued by Justice David Wright determined that two police officers had Neil Stonechild in their custody before he died and that they attempted to conceal this fact in their testimony before the inquiry. Justice Wright concluded that the "self-protective and defensive" attitudes of policing authorities resulted in an incompetent investigation, years of indifference, and a police service that failed to "lift a finger to inquire into the merits of the complaints against its members" (in Tator and Henry 2006: 199).

Further similar cases of mistreatment of Aboriginal people in Saskatchewan at the hands of police officers have come to light. For example, the body of Lloyd Dusthorn was found in January 2000: he had frozen to death outside his apartment after he had been in police custody (Smith 2006: 82). That same month, the body of Rodney Naistus was found on the outskirts of Saskatoon near the Queen Elizabeth II Power Station (ibid.). The same power station was also the site of the discovery of the frozen body of Lawrence Wegner, a social work student, who apparently had just previous to his death been pursued by the police (ibid.). Another man, Darrel Night, claimed that he had been dropped off by the police south of the city on a bitterly cold night, but he survived by seeking help at a nearby power station; subsequently, two Saskatoon police officers were found guilty of unlawful confinement in the Darrel Night case and were sentenced to eight months in jail (ibid.).

The preceding discussion aptly illustrates the pervasive nature of institutional racism and discrimination. It is found in practically all areas of society, in policing and the criminal justice system, the news media, schooling and other aspects of education such as teaching and curriculum, religious bodies, and employment and economic sectors, in addition to politicians and government policies at the federal and provincial levels towards Aboriginal peoples and members of other ethnic and minority groups. Although such overt expressions of institutional racism that were found historically in the past are not as evident today, some would argue that such racialized practices, attitudes, and ideas have just moved into more subtle and less recognizable realms, but nonetheless still exist embedded in society's institutions.

What these situations and cases discussed above would suggest is that it is particularly difficult to eliminate the links of racism to power and privilege in society. What we are referring to here are the institutionalized links of racial oppression emanating from the media, the police, and the state, which are discussed now specifically in relation to the Ipperwash Inquiry.[1]

The Media

Miller's (2005, 2007) informative critical analysis of the media coverage of the Ipperwash story presents a step-by-step account of how events are framed by journalists for public consumption. First, there was the implicit assumption that it was Aboriginal protesters who had fired at police officers, rather than the other way around, which served to instil in the public's mind an image of the First Nations occupiers of Ipperwash Provincial Park as thugs and troublemakers. From then on, with each succeeding newspaper article, the issue focused quite squarely on the confrontation between activists and the Ontario Provincial Police. What was lost rather quickly in all of this rush to blame the Aboriginal protesters was the real story, which was the history of betrayal through which the Stony Point community was dispossessed of their traditional territory through treaties, unscrupulous Indian agents, and the federal government. What is startling about this transformation from a story about land claims to one of political mobilization is that not one member of the media was actually there on 6 September 1995, to personally witness what transpired on that fateful night.

It was almost as if firsthand observation was unnecessary, as negative opinions had already between formed, prejudicing a fair account of the shooting of Dudley George before the fact. Attitudes, psychologists tell us, precede behaviour. In this instance, the old adage of not letting the facts get in the way of a good story would appear to have been patently true. It would take more than a decade of Aboriginal agitation to initiate a public inquiry, the testimony of dozens of witness, and millions of dollars of government money spent to reveal the actual facts, which were, of course, in direct opposition to the initial media assumptions. Even faced with the incontrovertible evidence that an OPP officer had shot Dudley George in what was, essentially, "cold blood," there are still Canadians who insist on various web pages and in letters to the editors of newspapers that it is the police who have suffered injustice.

Some did speak out against this impartial coverage and demanded that the Aboriginal side of the story be investigated. There was a story in the *New York Times* in which the land claims aspect was studied. However, these examples were by far in the minority, according to Miller's meticulous examination of news coverage stories. Of course, it is hard to tell in all of this without more rigorous research how culpable the Canadian public actually is in seeing Aboriginal activists as troublemakers, on the one hand, or as legitimate land claims protesters, on the other. It is not possible to gauge, for example, if the few articles criticizing the media's preoccupation with a negative image of Aboriginal occupiers to the neglect of the land claims side of the events represent a true percentage of Canadians holding this view, or whether the larger public, as reflected in the preponderance of negative media coverage holds a view of Aboriginal protesters as miscreants. In other words, when it comes to Aboriginal protests in this country, it certainly could be made a profitable area of new research if the extent to which the media serves to form public opinion on these matters, or if the media simply reflects it, was made a focal point of scientific investigation so that we could start to get to the truth of these matters.

Whatever the case, whether such research would reveal a tendency one way or the other, there is no doubt, as evidenced by Miller's study (2005) that the media would appear to be predisposed to a negative stance on Aboriginal issues. It cannot be forgotten, whatever such research might reveal, that the media, nonetheless, play a powerful role in shaping public opinion, which is especially the case when it comes to the portrayal of Aboriginals, Blacks, Asians, Jews, and members of other racial and ethnic minorities. The issue about whether the media shape public opinion, or simply reflect it, has been of some interest in the social scientific literature. In Britain, for example, Bagley (1973) concluded that the press has a profound and largely negative influence on race relations. In their book, *Racism and the Mass Media*, Hartmann and

Husband (1974: 146) have argued that the media not only reflect public attitudes regarding racial matters, but also play a significant role in shaping them as well.

The media tend to increase rather than decrease white hostility towards non-whites, as Barrett's (1987: 318–21) study of the right wing in Canada points out. An ongoing criticism of the media is that reporters and journalists permit themselves to be manipulated by racists. Racists may provide a "good story," but the representatives of antiracist organizations are not invited to offer a rebuttal of such stories or editorial commentary. The adage that any press is good press seems to fulfil racists' need for attention, so any mention of an anti-Aboriginal perspective tends not only to inflame cultural and racial insensitivities but also to promote such causes.

What is perplexing, given Canadians' policy of multiculturalism on the national stage, is why this continual deluge of hate in the media towards Aboriginal land claims, protests, and occupations does not eventually stiffen the attitudes of the general populace against such intolerant perspectives. Is it that average Canadians do not care enough to speak out against such intolerance, are they not educated enough about such matters, or possibly, do they harbour more racial negativity than is commonly thought to exist in this country? Whatever the answer, it is abundantly evident that the media have a free rein to publish the most outlandish and inaccurate diatribes against Aboriginal peoples in this country with absolute impunity.

The Police

Some social scientists assert that racism is essentially an exercise in power, or more specifically, a contest over power (see Baker 1978: 316; Barrett 2002: 59; Carter and Virdee 2008: 661–79; Hughes and Kallen 1974: 105). In this conceptual scheme, power is seen as a fundamental factor, but power does not exhaust the explanations of racism. What follows from this position is that since racism is largely an expression of power, which whites tend to monopolize, it is mostly whites that are racists. This view also coincides with a conventional Marxist perspective, which sees racism as a by-product of a class struggle in which workers are divided along colour lines to the benefit of the owners of the means of production.

If we accept the argument that racism and power are at least linked, then a broader understanding of these aspects would likely involve an examination of the sources of power and authority in society and who controls them. In this regard, Cardinal Carter noted, in a 1979 report on tensions between the police and minorities in Toronto, that "perhaps nothing in all my research was more universal than a sense of frustration about real or fancied injustice and harassment at the hands of police officers" (in Barrett 1987: 321). In another study, Roach (1980: 27) concludes that racial prejudice among policemen is even a much more serious problem than among the larger citizenry because it is the police who control the legitimate exercise of force and power in society and, therefore, are able to act out their prejudices on innocent victims.[2]

A more recent study by Stults and Baumer (2007) argues that, in a racial context, police force size is an important factor in exacerbating conflicts. A frequently noted correlation is that the police-to-citizen ratio is much greater in racial and minority group settings than in other social contexts. The impression is that the police in such settings expect more crimes to be committed. This is especially true when the police officers are of one racial group (usually white) and the other citizens are of a different (minority) group. The suggestion is that increasing the number of minority group members in police forces offsets the sense of antagonism and potential conflict between the police and members of minority groups.

The charge that police have the prerogative to arbitrarily use their discretionary power in a prejudicial manner when it comes to arresting or detaining for questioning members of minority groups is also a particularly sensitive one when it comes to the practice of racial profiling. The Ontario Human Rights Commission (OHRC 2003) reported on the human costs of racial profiling, and in response, the Ontario government issued a warning to OPP Commissioner Fantino to deal with the issue of profiling (*Toronto Star*, 11 Dec. 2003).

Among several problems cited in the Ontario Human Rights Commission's report (2003) with regard to racial profiling is the observation that it is too security-centred. However, "the OHRC framing of racial profiling is problematic ... [because they] have produced a report that is more befuddling than enlightening, more cautious than critical, more politically expedient than analytically sound" (William 2006: 7). With regard to the security issues of racial profiling, as far as police involvement in relations with minority groups is concerned, detention on "reasonable suspicion" is at the root of much of the trouble.

For an article entitled "Police Racism," Lea (1986: 160) interviewed a former English chief constable, who stated, "There is no limitation on police discretion. Only reasonable suspicion is required, and this can be interpreted very loosely." Similarly, a former chief of the Minneapolis Police Department, Anthony Bouza (1990: 6), observed in his book entitled *The Police Mystique* that "the borders of action are laced with stretchable legal concepts like reasonable suspicion, probable cause, questionable circumstances, and articulate grounds. It doesn't take the skills of a sophist to construct a justification for aggressive actions within those parameters."

The concern is that the rather nebulous concept of *reasonable suspicion* could be used as a rationalization for abusing the rights of minority group members because, say, among other things, "they are in neighbourhoods where they do not belong." Readers might remember the news story of the Black Harvard professor who was attempting to deal with a jammed doorlock to his home and who was subsequently arrested on suspicion of unlawful entry because a passer-by called 911, thinking that the professor "looked out of place" in the up-scale neighbourhood. "They should know their place." "Don't step out of line." This is the language of oppression.

Aboriginal people in Canada express frustration all the time about being detained because of this principle of "reasonable suspicion." The feeling is that in racially mixed communities there is a police bias because the police are much quicker to detain or arrest Aboriginal persons suspected of committing a crime than non-Aboriginals exhibiting similar behaviours. Whyte (2008: 116) explains, "Beyond the issue of the level of the formal police practices of detaining and charging, Aboriginal people complain about being treated disrespectfully and, at times, abusively; they complain about being under constant suspicion; and they complain that police do not conduct serious and thorough investigations of crimes committed against them."

The police claim that such criticisms against them are unfounded, because there are no hard and fast rules that can be used in all circumstances, so there are times when they must use their own judgment. They point out that police officers are frequently thrust into situations that are conflict-ridden in the first place, or whose parameters and ground rules are inherently ambiguous, such as Aboriginal acts of civil disobedience, with little in the way of guidelines according to which they might conduct themselves. The Ipperwash confrontation was an example in which the information coming their way was full of contradictions and often faulty. The OPP was told by a member of the Stony Point First Nation that the protesters were armed with AK-47s and other firearms. Police officers were also given directives from an Ontario government cabinet that appeared to have acted in haste. They did not take up an outside offer of an opportunity for negotiation. All in all, the OPP claim that they were not equipped to engage the protesters in any way other than the manner in which they proceeded on the evening of 6 September 1995.

We can gather from this position that the role of the police officer is grounded in contradiction. The contradiction stems, on the one hand, from the fact that a chain of command exists that may be flawed and subject to misinformation. On the other hand, an officer is sworn to uphold the law, which is at times an ambiguous exercise, especially when it comes to managing Aboriginal land claims and treaty rights, making their behaviour in these circumstances unpredictable.

Yet, if the Ipperwash occupation is any example, one can only conclude that some members of the OPP are flawed by racist inclinations. It would appear that Acting Sergeant Ken Deane's shooting of Dudley George was a spontaneous act, albeit happening under mitigating circumstances, for example, the prior information given to the police regarding firearms and the generally heightened emotions of the moment. However, other action by OPP officers would appear to have been based on premeditated racist attitudes. How else does one explain the recorded verbal outrage by Sergeant Korosec when he referred to a "big, fat, fuck Indian" if we do not see such comments as profoundly racist? The production of inflammatory T-shirts and related paraphernalia by OPP officers can only be understood to be acts of premeditated vehemence towards the Aboriginal population.

OPP Inspector Carson admitted to the Ipperwash Inquiry that these comments were "not to be tolerated," and he considered such statements to be racist (Linden 2007: 29). Commissioner Linden agreed and summed up his findings in the following manner: "The most obvious instance of racism and cultural insensitivity was heard in the comments made by members of the OPP intelligence team on September 5, 1995 – one day before the shooting ... There is no place for racial taunts or slurs of any type by police officers. Not only are such comments counterproductive to the efforts of police officers in their role as peacekeepers, they are contrary to professional standards, and they can lead to violence" (pp. 28–9). Violence is what the OPP should be trying to prevent; the police should not be exacerbating or initiating it.

In sum, it is apparent that the role of the police regarding racism is an ambiguous one. It must be remembered that the role of the police is essentially a conservative one designed largely to maintain the status quo. As such, the police are opposed to all groups, whether on the extreme right or left, that present a challenge to their authority when it comes to their monopolization of the use of force in society. A contradiction thus exists in the police's role in combatting racism because there are sectors of society that are flawed by racist inclinations and that have become institutionalized over time. The police are in an inadequate position to eradicate such attitudes. They are hardly in a position to take on this challenge since certain racist inclinations are found in the very fabric and structures of the state itself.

The State

A state is comprised of a complex interrelationship of roles, statuses, and institutions organized in a hierarchical structure. Power, prestige, wealth, and influence accrue to the upper echelons of such a structure. States monopolize or otherwise control the use of force and authority, and states will usually attempt to counteract any challenges to their authority within a circumscribed geopolitical setting.[3] In this context, we can regard the government of Ontario as having many of the characteristics of a state, but is not a state per se because it answers to a larger, more encompassing political unit, which is the federal government of Canada.

In historical terms, the first Black slave in Canada was brought to New France in 1608, and by 1760 the number of slaves in New France exceeded four thousand (Frideres 1976: 137). Slavery actually lasted longer in Canada than it did in the northern United States. With the passing of the Emancipation Act by the British Parliament in 1833, slavery was officially abolished in Canada, although racism was not eliminated. In 1849, racially segregated schools were legalized in Ontario (Barrett 1987: 300). More than fifteen thousand Chinese were brought into Canada by 1855 to work on the Canadian Pacific Railway, and in 1885, a head tax of $50 was established to discourage further Chinese immigration (Bolaria and Li 1988: 86); by 1903, this head tax was increased to $500 (Kallen 1982: 140). There was a race riot in Vancouver in 1907, when Japanese and Chinese immigrants were attacked by whites (Bolaria and Li 1988: 128).

How can we regard the efforts of the Canadian state in confronting racism in more modern times? In the area of immigration policy, there have been efforts to rid the country of its most blatant bigotry, although

Frideres (1976: 137) argues that until 1962 Canada had an explicit and formal racist immigration policy. Until 1953, "climatic suitability" was still formally included in the Immigration Act, and it was used to bar people from non-Western countries from coming to Canada. As Kallen (1982: 140) has stated, "A racist immigration policy is one of the most invidious techniques utilized by those in power to guarantee their ethnic ascendency in any society." In more recent years, there has been removal of conditions that favour Anglo-Saxon entry, and there has been a corresponding increase in Third World immigration, although there are Canadians who feel that this change will lead to racial problems in Canada.

There has also been an effort to prosecute prominent antisemites such as Ernst Zundel and James Keegstra. During the 1920s, the Ku Klux Klan was a powerful force, and in the period between the two world wars, various fascist and Nazi parties took root in Canada. Since the Second World War, there has been a steady increase in right-wing activity such as the Western Guard and Aryan Nations, to name only two of dozens of such extremist and white-supremacist organizations.

Most Canadians would probably hardly recognize the names of even a few of these groups, and they would not be familiar with their ideals and organizational structures. One could argue that one of the reasons for this imperceptibility of racist groups is that the people who belong to them are not the vocally vociferous or confrontational sort of people one would imagine holding extremist views. But, contrary to what most people would imagine, the members of such organizations blend well into the general population, are reasonably well educated, usually middle class, intelligent, and mild mannered, yet racist nonetheless.

Another reason that bigots often do not stand out is because, whether Canadians admit it or not, the views of the right-wing organizations are often not so different from the views that many others hold. Many Canadians think that immigrants are taking valuable jobs away from more deserving citizens, that Jews are evil, money-grabbing people, or that Aboriginals are treated with kid gloves and receive far more attention from the government than they deserve. If you do not think that this is true, then why was there so little outcry from the Canadian populace when Dudley George was shot, or when the many derogatory articles began to appear in Canadian newspaper denigrating attempts by First Nations people to reclaim land unjustly taken away from them?

The conclusion that would appear inevitable, when presented with the facts, is that white extremists are not so different from the average

Canadian citizen. Indeed, as Barrett (1987: 355) concludes, after an exhaustive study of extremism in this country, "Canada is unexceptional in both its right-wing tendencies and its tolerance ... the radical right's racist thrust [is not] incompatible with the nation's wider setting and institutions."

This conclusion makes intelligible the overt acts of racism and intolerant attitudes revealed in this study of the Ipperwash protest and occupation. Intolerance of First Nations people is found at the very apex of Ontario society, from the inner workings of the provincial government, and it percolates down through the rank and file of the police, and among the local citizenry. In a wider historical perspective, government policy acts to suppress Aboriginal peoples and take away their land. The protectionist policy, under British colonial rule was paternalistic in nature, based on the assumption that Aboriginals were childlike and needed to be looked after, which was one of the justifications for seizing their land and forcing them onto reserves. By the time of Canadian Confederation, the reigning policy was an assimilationist one, based on the idea that primitive, heathen cultures should be eliminated and First Nations people should be forced into the fabric of Canadian society. Residential schools were established to force children into a Christian mould, away from their parental and community influences, and many of these children were subjected to the worst forms of sexual and physical abuse. Later, by the 1960s, the Trudeau government embarked on a termination policy, in an attempt to do away with "the Indian problem" once and for all at the federal government level. This included termination of special Indian status, such as eliminating Indian women from band rolls who married non-status males. The intent of the 1969 White Paper (Canada 1969) was to eliminate the entire reserve system that gave special status to Aboriginal people.

If the Canadian government can be seen to share complicity in the suppression of certain minorities, such as Aboriginal peoples, what can be said about state-driven "anti-racism" initiatives? For the cynically minded, who see in such endeavours another measure of control by the state apparatus, this issue of control is one of the reasons the Ontario Human Rights Commission has come under severe criticism for its handling of the racial profiling issue (OHRC 2003). William (2006), for one, suggests that racial profiling is not justified because it is too "security-centered." He explains: "In Canada, specifically, where the discourse of racial tolerance has far more currency than that of racial justice and where the preferred mode of crisis containment is the production and issuance of commissioned reports, the scope of (ostensibly) progressive state action tends to be tightly circumscribed. What this means, then, is that a significant discrepancy exists between, on the one hand, what needs to be done (if the aim is to mount uncompromising challenges to racism), and on the other hand, what the state is actually willing to do" (p. 2).

These various commissions that deal with human rights could be seen as the "management" of race relations by the state. An oppressed group of workers is an integral part of capitalist economies. Racism tends to weaken organized labour by dividing the solidarity of unions and other organizations of the working class, while in turn, strengthening the position of the companies that hire them. However, a continual fragmenting of the working class could lead to anarchy and work disruptions of various sorts, so from the perspective of employers, a balance is needed between these two movements of cohesion and fragmentation.

The state has an interest in not allowing racism to undermine its legitimacy. The result of these contradictory forces – racism that divides and worker organizations that provide cohesion – is that the state steps in to promulgate public policies whose apparent ideals are to promote racial equality and social order without having to overhaul the basic structure and processes by which the very inequality that the state is attempting to undermine is created and allowed to continue. Thus, the state is seen to give the impression that it is combatting racism, while at the same time allowing the basic underlying processes that are responsible for racism to continue essentially unabated.

A case can be made for viewing Canadian human rights commissions in this light. The federal government began to establish the Canadian Human Rights Commission in 1978, and since then various provinces have established their own respective commissions. Such commissions face a daunting task in regulating racial harmony, as it did not take very much time before the commissions became centres of dispute involving individual grievances about racial discrimination. The victims of racial discrimination were usually allotted a token monetary compensation, thus establishing a precedent in which the human rights commissions were forced to adopt an intermediary role between victim and offender, with the result that the larger structural aspects of racism in Canada remained largely unexamined in the process. What this discussion suggests is that the state establishes various policies to contain the most detrimental effects of racism, to "manage" the spread and magnitude of racism through various "buffer" institutions, commissions, and public inquiries.

We wait in abeyance for a government response to the recommendations of the Ipperwash Inquiry. We wait to see if the aim of the government's initiation of the Inquiry was simply one of "containment," or if, as those with a view towards social justice would hope, our government has the courage to mount its own "uncompromising challenges to racism." Such placatory measures as the commissioned reports of the Ipperwash Inquiry (Linden 2007) or the Royal Commission on Aboriginal Peoples (1996) serve to mollify anger stemming from racial injustice, however, "from the point of view of the state, the best racial policy is one which gives the appearance of change without changing the status quo" (Bolaria and Li 1988: 39). Only time will tell if such cynicism is warranted.

A Policy of Respect, Justice, and Tolerance

Throughout the history of Canadian policy and that of its British predecessor towards the Aboriginal inhabitants of this country, several orientations have predominated – protectionism, assimilation, and termination. Each policy has failed to achieve its objectives because in one way or another each one is a policy of suppression. These policies were not designed to promote growth, initiative, or development in the First Nation populations of Canada, because the result of these policies has been to impoverish, marginalize, and isolate Aboriginal peoples. It is also evident that a "single" national policy will never be very effective or useful until the development of Aboriginal policy begins to take into account the cultural, social, historical, and linguistic diversity of Canada's original peoples.

Moreover, it is evident from the material presented in the foregoing study that Aboriginal peoples in Canada have to combat a prodigious presence that keeps them as subject people. There are certainly racist attitudes in Canadian society that work to their detriment, but an even more omnipotent presence is the very apparatus of the status itself that keeps perpetuating the deleterious consequences that those politicians, academics, and liberal thinkers so decry.

There is a problem, therefore, with recent studies of Aboriginal policy, which are no doubt well-meaning but essentially misplaced, for example, Richards's (2006) *Creating Choices: Rethinking Aboriginal Policy*. Richards, writing for the C.D. Howe thinktank, would have us believe that if only Aboriginal people became better educated and made better choices in their lives, their problems of inadequate health care, high unemployment, deplorable housing conditions, and other such issues, would eventually solve themselves.

The question here is on what basis are these supposedly better choices to be made? Choices are made from alternative sources of action – so what are the different courses of action available to First Nations people? Richards seems to ignore the fact that it is the very institutions of Canadian society itself that perpetuate these depressing problems, and no amount of "correct" choice making is likely to alter this fact. I wonder if Richards has ever lived in an Aboriginal community and observed first-hand the depressing human problems that are so cavalierly discussed and in such a remote manner under the rubric of "public policy?"[4] I strongly believe that it is imperative that those engaged in the Aboriginal policy field, and who feel qualified to suggest programs of action, need to see the problems on a first-hand basis, over an extended period – not at a remote distance, from a desk in Ottawa.

Were this the case, one would be less likely to suggest that the problems in Canadian Aboriginal communities stem from improper choices. On the ground level, it is evident that there is almost a complete lack of resources that could be used to design alternative courses of action. As far as the matter of a better-educated Aboriginal population is concerned, I certainly am not against education per se, but in the face of inadequate opportunities to apply this education, the result is apt to be even more discouragement and frustration than already exist. Education needs to be harnessed with opportunities to be effective.

These expanded opportunities are only going to come from an expansion in the availability of resources, and for the most part, this means a larger land base. It is, therefore, contingent on the federal and the provincial governments to deal effectively and in a more expeditious manner with the hundreds of land claims at present before the courts and various land commissions. It is inexcusable that First Nations people should have to wait for decades, or even generations, to have land returned to them that was sold illegally or simply taken away from them, as in the Ipperwash case. How can anyone blame the Stony and Kettle Point community, after waiting since 1945, in the case of the Camp Ipperwash military base, until the 1990s for the promised return of their land not to take matters into their own hands?

The same holds largely true for the Ipperwash Provincial Park, land removed from Aboriginal ownership by an unscrupulous Indian agent and a local land developer in the 1920s. Did anyone in government seem to care that the Ipperwash Provincial Park property contained an Aboriginal cemetery, or about the hard feelings that creating a park on such land would cause? And how did the Ontario government react to this occupation in 1995? Did politicians say among themselves, "Let's look into this and see if they have a case." The answer is no; instead, a heavily armed police force was quickly mobilized to confront the protesters, one of whom was shot to death.

Unfortunately, Ipperwash is not an isolated incident. It is apparent that the real government policy, when it comes to Aboriginal acts of political mobilization, is to use excessive force, rather than a policy of negotiation, to resolve land claims issues. The large question here: is this approach acceptable to Canadians, especially given our assumed mantle of tolerance and understanding? The more conservative elements of Canadian society would probably see the present work as just more pro-Aboriginal propaganda promulgated by a liberal academic. It is, therefore, contingent on those who have a nose for injustice to speak out, in the popular press and other venues of the media. To remain silent is to suggest passive agreement with the suppressive stance towards the Aboriginal population of this country, and so, because of this passivity, to become complicit partners in their suppression.

When Prime Minister Stephen Harper made his historic apology, in 2008 in the House of Commons, for the ills inflicted on the Aboriginal population of this country, Beverley Jacobs, president of the Native Women's Association of Canada, whose grandmother had been beaten and sexually abused in a residential school, said that the government's word must be followed by clear action: "We've given thanks to you for your apology. But in return, the Native Women's Association wants respect" (*CBC News*, 11 June 2008). The plea made by Beverley Jacobs is for a culture of respect, one that replaces the existing one of intolerance and injustice. Of course, only time will tell if Harper's statement is a cynical attempt to curry votes, or if there is a genuine reorientation of government attitudes in its relationship with Aboriginal peoples. Many enlightened Canadians hope that the latter approach predominates in the future and that confrontation as a mechanism of dispute resolution is replaced with one of respect and good will.

Summary of Aboriginal Issues

The use of the term *tragic* in the title of this book as a reference to Canada's Aboriginal policy is not meant to evoke a sense of alarm, or even one of sympathy, but to point to the evident fact that, although this country is one of the wealthiest nations on earth, its Aboriginal population continues to exist in what are basically Third World conditions. The latest census report (Canada 2008) reveals in the starkest manner possible the deplorable nature of these conditions. The unemployment rate for all of Canada, in 2006, was 6.6 per cent, but 13.3 per cent for First Nations people, and 18.2 per cent for the Inuit. In other words, the unemployment rate for Aboriginal people is two to three times the national average.

Employment incomes are low, comparatively. When both full-time and part-time incomes are combined, the Aboriginal average annual income ($27,838) is 23.3 per cent lower than the all-Canadian average ($36,301). One can presume that these averages reflect a smaller number of employment sources in Aboriginal communities as opposed to other Canadian centres. There are other related factors, such as the greater distance from markets that tend to characterize Aboriginal communities, many of which are situated in isolated, rural areas.

If higher education is seen as a means to increase income levels, the picture here is not encouraging, as the all-Canadian average population with university degrees (15.7%) is over twice that of the Aboriginal average (7.1%). In terms of the wider educational perspective, the average number of people with certificates, diplomas, and degrees in the all-Canadian population (76.2%) is 14 per cent higher than the Aboriginal average (62.2%). Possibly, there is less incentive in Aboriginal communities to better educational achievement when such a high unemployment rate exists, and for which there are fewer employment opportunities than exist for other Canadians.

All of these economic problems will, no doubt, be exacerbated by a growing Aboriginal population. Over the decade of 1996–2006, the Aboriginal population growth rate (45%) was more than five times the national average (8%). The fertility rate for Aboriginal women (2.6 children) is also significantly higher than for non-Aboriginal women (1.5). Not surprisingly, these population growth and fertility rates are reflected in the higher proportion of children (under 15 years of age) in Aboriginal families (50.5%) versus in Canadian families overall (37.3%).

The conclusion to be drawn here should be rather obvious, that is, that whatever social and economic problems currently exist in the Aboriginal population in the future will only get worse. When just over 50 per cent of Aboriginal families have children under 15 years of age, this will, no doubt, result in an increasing demand on educational, health care, and other related facilities. Employment opportunities will also have to be increased substantially just to keep pace with the Aboriginal growth rate, regardless of attempts to increase employment levels so as to reduce the already high unemployment rate.

Since the Canadian government is responsible for producing these figures, one can only presume that government officials are as aware of these Aboriginal socio-economic conditions as anyone else who wishes to look at them. The most important concerns are about what sorts of government initiatives will serve to alleviate the existing social and economic problems. The tragedy of Canadian government Aboriginal policy is that after nearly a century and a half we still have such appalling inequities in employment, incomes, and education, not to mention housing, health care, and other factors not discussed here.

No doubt the problem would be even worse than it is if a substantial (60%) and increasing proportion of the First Nations population had not forsaken their home reserves for an urban environment. However, this is not a sustainable solution because studies of the urban Native population (Anderson and Denis 2003, Dosman 1972: 47–9) suggest that Aboriginal people who migrate to the city often lack the training and educational background that would allow them to be successful in an urban environment, although the Metis more than First Nations people or the Inuit would appear to have greater chances of a successful urban adaptation. The pressure on existing employment and health resources in the Aboriginal community may be alleviated somewhat by an off-reserve demographic pattern, but these moves only result in an increase in the social assistance rolls of the city.

Is the answer to be found in a better set of choices being made by Aboriginal residents, as the C.D Howe Institute study suggests (Richards 2006)? There is no doubt that a more effective allocation of existing resources, both at the federal government and local levels, would save costs that could then be channelled into new programs of change. However, as indicated previously, choice making can pertain only to the resources at hand, those that *can* be used to make improvements. If existing resources are already stretched to the limit, as they must be for most Aboriginal communities, then more effective choice making is almost beside the point without a corresponding increase in available resources.

So the problem, it is suggested here, is not so much one of making the right choices, but of finding ways to do the following: (1) increase the pool of existing resources and (2) improve the manner in which these resources might be allocated to areas of need. For many Aboriginal communities, the manner in which the existing resource base could be increased is by extending the land base in some manner. It should come as no surprise, then, that most disputes that Aboriginal people have with the government concern traditional lands that have been removed from Aboriginal control by treaties, surrenders, and various other land deals, most of which greatly diminished the resource base of the community. Some of these lands were taken away by unscrupulous means, by manipulative Indian agents, or by expropriations by non-Aboriginal authorities.

It is no wonder that most of the confrontations that have taken place between Aboriginal dissidents and Canadian authorities have, as their root cause, issues pertaining to lost land and resources. One of the main reasons for taking the Ipperwash Inquiry as a case study of Aboriginal policy in Canada is to illustrate the frustrations of Aboriginal peoples who have seen their resource base shrink decade after decade. Government inaction, such as that illustrated by the promised return of the Camp Ipperwash military base, only heightens the sense that government representatives are not acting on one's behalf, but are part of the problem. When protests take place, and there are attempts to suppress these by armed confrontations, this only serves to reinforce a belief on the part of Aboriginal peoples that the government is not interested in resolving these many long-standing disputes.

There is little doubt that members of such armed forces as the Royal Canadian Mounted Police or the Ontario Provincial Police are not well equipped to handle Aboriginal civil disobedience. The police lack the means to negotiate land claims disputes, since they see their job as one of containing whatever violence takes place. Unfortunately, police tactics can contribute to increasing the level of violence, even if this is done inadvertently. Government officials are also at fault, because they do not give clear instructions to the police, or they fail to provide the negotiators who have the ability to dissipate the frustration that leads to violent confrontations.

The overall problem, it could be reasonably argued, lies with the history of government Aboriginal policy, which over the past century and a half has been demonstrably ineffective. Aside from three or four periods of government policy characterized as protectionism, assimilation, or termination, there have been four pivotal turning points at which government action could have made a difference. The first of these turning points occurred just after the Second World War, with the 1951 revisions to the Indian Act. As a result of the publicity surrounding

Aboriginal soldiers and their contribution to the war effort, the general Canadian public was sympathetic to Aboriginal people, especially their involuntary enfranchisement and lack of the right to vote.

The Joint Senate-House Committee on Indian Affairs, in 1948, called for a complete overhaul of the Indian Act, the ending of discrimination against Aboriginal peoples, the granting of full citizenship, and an expanded political role for Aboriginal women (Canada 1948). However, the revised Indian Act (1951) fell far short of these objectives. Several of the more punitive aspects of the previous Indian Act were removed, for example, the prohibition of the potlatch, which had been on the legal books since the 1880s, and the onerous ban on political organizations beyond the local reserve level, which had been instituted in 1927. Aside from a few other minor modifications, the 1951 Indian Act remained essentially the same in form and content as its earlier 1876 version. The extension of the right to vote in federal elections for status Indians took another nine years to implement, becoming law in 1960.

The second major opportunity to improve Aboriginal-government relationships took place in the 1960s. The Hawthorn Report (1966–67) was based on a large-scale research initiative conducted in over fifty Aboriginal communities. Dozens of recommendations were made regarding educational, social, political, and policy matters, including the famous "citizens plus" proposal. The federal government responded with the White Paper in 1969, which called for the repeal of the Indian Act, the abolition of the Department of Indian Affairs, and the transfer of Aboriginal responsibilities to provincial governments.

Aboriginal leaders in Canada were dumbfounded by this response. The consultation meetings held across the country in 1968–9 suggested that the federal government had an honest desire to hear the concerns of Aboriginal people and that it would initiate programs that meet with their approval. Instead, the government did the exact opposite; instead of strengthening the Indian Affairs structure and handing over more control to Aboriginal peoples, as suggested in the Indian Chiefs of Alberta (1970) document, the federal government appeared to have completely abrogated its responsibility in a most callous and insensitive manner.

The third opportunity to enact significant change occurred with the Royal Commission on Aboriginal Peoples (1996). This Commission was prompted by the outcry over the Oka Crisis of 1990, took four years to complete, cost $63 million, and heard 3,500 witnesses. Some four hundred recommendations were proposed in the five published volumes, ranging over almost every conceivable aspect of Aboriginal life in Canada. In response, the Department of Indian Affairs produced the report entitled *Gathering Strength: Canada's Aboriginal Action Plan* (Canada 1998), which did not directly comment on any of the RCAP's recommendations, but did comment on certain vague generalities, for example, the need to facilitate consultation, community building, and the promotion of Aboriginal self-government initiatives. When the prime minister was invited to comment on the RCAP's recommendations by attending an all-chiefs conference, he declined the offer, citing prior commitments.

The fourth opportunity pertains to the more recent Ipperwash Inquiry (Linden 2007), initiated eight years after the shooting of Dudley George in September 1995. The Ipperwash Inquiry, with its hundred recommendations, had a more limited scope than the RCAP investigation: however, its implications for Aboriginal-government relations are probably just as important. It is still too early to comment on what the Ontario government's response might be to the Ipperwash recommendations, yet at the time of the writing of the present study almost six years have passed without any official comment.

This is not to suggest that there have not been any significant results of the Inquiry. Certainly, the OPP's *Framework for Police Preparedness for Aboriginal Critical Incidents* (2006) is noteworthy and holds much promise in reducing conflict during protests and confrontations. The wording of the document, such as "building positive trusting relationships ... consulting with community leaders ... [and] encouraging people to come together" (p. 5) would appear to indicate a willingness on the part of police officials to conduct their roles with sensitivity and discretion.

The worst fear among Aboriginal leaders is that this is just another public relations document written by the advertising agents of Bay Street. As with Prime Minister Harper's apparently sincere apology in the House of Commons, words are just words, and are essentially meaningless unless followed up with corresponding actions and behaviour. What needs to be addressed is a much more fundamental problem in Canadian society regarding the racist and culturally insensitive attitudes not only of the average citizen, but of those in power. It will be a long time before Aboriginal people forget about Premier Mike Harris's alleged use of expletives in reference to the Ipperwash Provincial Park protesters, or the abusive profanity caught on tape used by OPP officers at the time.

Probably the most important lesson of the Ipperwash Inquiry is that it is a reminder to all Canadians who believe in working towards a tolerant society how entrenched racist attitudes are in Canada. Such attitudes have become institutionalized in the media, the police, and the very state structures installed to protect against the proliferation of misanthropic ideals. We need to hear from our leaders that the ideals espoused in the Canadian Charter of Rights and Freedoms are the values that will prevail over those who promote hatred and intolerance.

Concluding Remarks on Aboriginal Resistance

Next summer, and the summer after that, groups of Aboriginal people will gather in dissent by barricading a highway, occupying a government office, or camping out in a provincial park. It will not take long for the local non-Aboriginal people to begin grumbling that the police and politicians always treat the Aboriginal population "with kid gloves," remarking that "you and I couldn't get away with that sort of behaviour – we'd end up in jail real quick!" There is apparently little sympathy for Aboriginal acts of resistance among the Euro-Canadian population, who complain that Aboriginal civil disobedience costs them jobs and a loss of valuable tourist income. The irony is that their local town is probably built on land previously occupied and owned by ancestors of the present-day Aboriginal population, and obtained by the whites at little or no expense – and this is most likely lost on the non-Aboriginal complainers.

The Aboriginal people themselves probably do not like to attract such negative attention to themselves but see no other way to make their situation known, or to bring about government action. "If they don't protest; nobody notices," is the refrain. But government officials apparently do notice. They appear on local television, saying that the protest situation is well in hand – "there are land claims commissions set up to handle these sorts of disputes," they might say, not mentioning that it might take ten or maybe twenty years, or even several generations before particular land claims cases are dealt with, if ever.

Eventually, if the confrontation becomes troublesome enough, the police are called in. There might be rumours that the Aboriginal protesters have firearms, which may or may not be the case, since no one on the government side is sure about what the activists want or about their defensive position. In any event, the police will arrive well equipped with the latest firearms and body armour. The protesters may throw a few rocks and brandish sticks or baseball bats, make threatening gestures to the police. In unfortunate circumstances, the police will discharge their firearms, perhaps killing a protester. In any ensuing investigation, it will be hard to determine who fired at whom, or who actually shot the protester. The police complain that they don't have enough training for this sort of situation: "Why," they might ask, "are we placed in harm's way in what is essentially a matter of civil litigation?"

The police have a point, of course; they have wives (or husbands) and children as well to look after, so they blame the politicians. The politicians want to look good to the public media, by taking a hard stance on an apparently unruly and unlawful Aboriginal act of civil disobedience. On the inside, though, to the protesters, the politicians make appeasing gestures: "We'll get right on this, as soon as Parliament convenes after the summer holidays; you'll be a top priority."

The activists have heard all this before. They know its all part of a game: "we protest, the police are called in (we hope no one is killed), and the politicians play a game of 'piggy-in-the middle.'" Meanwhile, not much gets done. Before long, activists who were energetic in their youth, now sit grey-haired on the sidelines, brushing the smoke of sweet grass around the gathering. There may be the odd white person who takes an interest in what is going on – they wonder why so little changes, when so much of the taxpayers' money is apparently being thrown at Aboriginal issues.

If the government is working so diligently at solving "the Indian problem," over so many successive governments going back in history, why, one might ask, is the Aboriginal unemployment rate today over twice the national average (three time the average for the Inuit)? Why are earnings for Aboriginal workers over $10,000 less per year than the national average? Why is an Aboriginal person twice as likely not to have a university degree? Then there are the troubling statistics on inadequate housing, roads, health care facilities, and other infrastructural problems in Aboriginal communities.

After a particularly alarming protest, such as Oka or Ipperwash, a public inquiry is apt to be called: "We'll get to the bottom of this," the politicians will exclaim. Millions of dollars will be spent, much of it on expensive hotel rooms, meals, and air travel. Years later, an elaborate report will be released with much fanfare in the media and a myriad of recommendations to remedy "the Indian problem." The premier of a province, the prime minister of Canada, or a Minister of Aboriginal

Affairs will be asked to join a panel with Aboriginal leaders to discuss what the government plans are to implement any of the recommendations. None of the politicians will show up, begging off with more pressing concerns. The inquiry reports will gather dust in the basement of university and government library shelves.

A strong argument could be made that these enduring problems will never be solved because of the 2,000-pound elephant in the room that takes up so much space, but is nonetheless apparently invisible to practically everyone except the persons who suffer from oppression. In other words, these problems are the result of the very institutional structures of society itself. As Tator and Henry (2006: 206) argue, the problem is the result of "racism that consists of policies and practices, entrenched in established institutions that result in the exclusion or advancement of specific groups of people." The truth of the matter is that the problems faced by Aboriginal peoples are the result of a persistent, endemic, institutionalized history of discriminatory policy and practice that has denied to the First Nations people of Canada an equitable share of the nation's resources, wealth, and opportunities.

The policy of successive Canadian governments, since the very founding of this country, has served to marginalize the Aboriginal population, geographically on remote reserves and other out-of-the-way places, so that they do not have equal access to the economic and political institutions of Canadian society that are enjoyed by the rest of the population. Aboriginal societies have been denigrated, suppressed, and forced into assimilative processes by a Eurocentric policy that has been maintained by oppressive systems of colonialism and racism. Is it little wonder, then, that Aboriginal people engage in acts of resistance against such forces?

Aboriginal people today may form a relatively small percentage of the overall Canadian population, yet they continue to demand that attention be given to their grievances. They continue to push back against the almost overwhelming hegemonic economic, political, and cultural forms exerting pressure on them by the Canadian state. In terms of how it treats its Aboriginal population, Canada is hardly the shining example of racial equality, tolerance, and justice that it prides itself in being on the world stage.

Appendix:
Socio-economic Conditions of
the Canadian Aboriginal Population

Figure 1. Total Aboriginal population in Canada, 1996–2011.

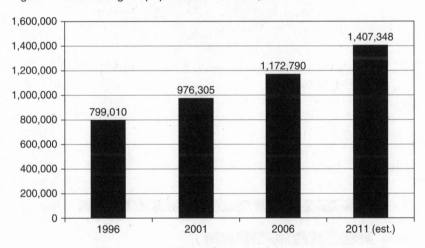

Source: Statistics Canada, Census of Population, 1996, 2001, 2006 (Canada 2008).

Figure 2. Aboriginal population in 2006 by category:
First Nations, Metis, Inuit. First Nations comprises
status (564,870, 81%) and non-status (133,155,
19%) persons. Other means persons who reported
belonging to more than one Aboriginal group.

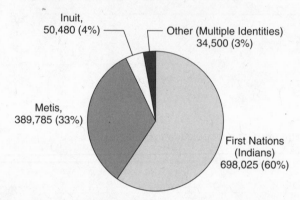

Inuit,
50,480 (4%)

Other (Multiple Identities)
34,500 (3%)

Metis,
389,785 (33%)

First Nations
(Indians)
698,025 (60%)

Source: Statistics Canada, Census of Population, 2006
(Canada 2008).

Figure 3. Aboriginal population by province, 2006.

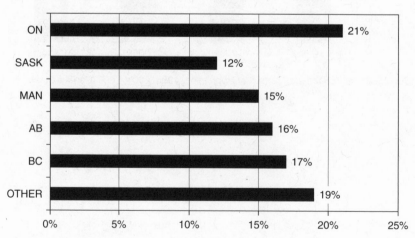

Source: Statistics Canada, Census of Population in Canada, 2006 (Canada 2008).

Figure 4. Family composition, all Canada and Aboriginal, 2006. Number of family persons (i.e., households with at least one adult and at least one child under 15 years of age): all Canada, 26,113,390; Aboriginal, 1,425,875.

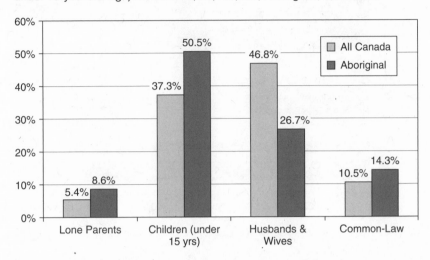

Source: Statistics Canada, Census of Population, 2006 (Canada 2008).

Figure 5. Unemployment rate, all Canada and Aboriginal (%), 2006.

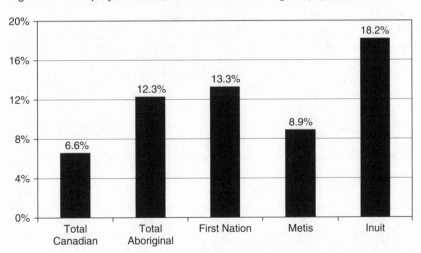

Source: Statistics Canada, Census of Population, 2006 (Canada 2008).

Figure 6. Average annual employment income, full-time and part-time, all Canada and Aboriginal, 2006.

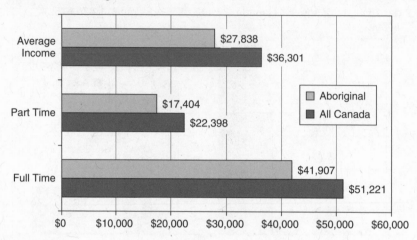

Source: Statistics Canada, Census of Population, 2006 (Canada 2008).

Table 1. Labour force (15 years and older) by category of worker, 2006.

	All Canada	n %	Aboriginal	n %
Wage earners	14,816,208	87.9	703,515	92.1
Self-employed	1,993,715	11.8	58,865	7.7
Unpaid family worker	51,265	0.3	1,580	0.2
Total	16,861,185	100	763,795	100

Source: Statistics Canada, Census of Population 2006 (Canada 2008).

Table 2. Educational characteristics, all Canada and Aboriginal, 2006.

	All Canadan	%	Aboriginal	%
No certificate, diploma, or degree	6,098,325	23.8	447,500	37.8
Certificate, diploma, or degree	19,565,895	76.2	735,000	62.2
Total	25,664,220	100	1,182,500	100
Degree				
Bachelor	2,981,460	11.6	67,345	5.7
Master	866,980	3.4	14,550	1.2
Doctorate	176,945	0.7	272	0.2
Total	4,025,385	15.7	84,615	7.1

Source: Statistics Canada, Census of Population, 2006 (Canada 2008)

Notes

1. Introduction

1   There were no news reporters at the scene of Dudley George's death, nor at the confrontation at Ipperwash Provincial Park. Subsequent news coverage was based on interviews conducted with OPP officers and not with any of the Aboriginal protesters themselves.
2   There is a broad swath of territory in northern Ontario centring more or less along the Albany River where the Aboriginal population speaks a mixture of Cree and Ojibway. In any event, both languages are closely related to one another and are almost mutually intelligible.

2. Aboriginal Policy in Canada

1   A much more in-depth commentary was subsequently published by Beverley Jacobs in *Canadian Woman Studies* (2008). In particular, she notes, "Most Canadians became a little educated on June 11, 2008 about the assimilationist policy of the Canadian government. Being that this is one of the most troubling 'black marks' against Canada, every Canadian person should be knowledgeable that the human rights violations that occurred against Aboriginal children is as a result of Canada's genocidal policies" (p. 225).

3. The Nature of Aboriginal Rights

1   The literature on the fur trade in Canada is diverse and extensive. The classic work is Harold Innis's *The Fur Trade in Canada: An Introduction to Canadian Economic History* (1970 [1930]). For the relationship between

Aboriginal First Nations and the Hudson's Bay Company, consult Arthur J. Ray and Donald Freeman, *"Give Us Good Measure": An Economic Analysis of Relations between the Indians and the Hudson's Bay Company before 1763* (1978); Arthur J. Ray, *Indians and the Fur Trade: Their Roles as Trappers, Hunters, and Middlemen in the Lands Southwest of Hudson Bay, 1660–1870* (1970); Charles A. Bishop, *The Northern Ojibwa and the Fur Trade: An Historical and Ecological Study* (1974); Shepard Krech III, ed., *The Subarctic Fur Trade: Native Social and Economic Adaptations* (1984); and Colin Yerbury, *The Subarctic Indians and the Fur Trade, 1680–1860* (1986). The general tenor of this body of literature is that Aboriginal hunters and trappers of the northern forests were not, as commonly perceived, hapless victims of global economic processes, but were often able to negotiate from a position of strength.

2   The text of the Royal Proclamation of 1763 can be found in Asch (1984: 112–14).

3   Jennifer Brown (1980: 220) states, in *Strangers in Blood*, "It is clear that the community lives of the different categories of fur trade progeny came to differ widely. Some remained enmeshed in Indian life. Some preserved no shared communal existence; patrifocality [a marriage residence pattern whereby the married couple live with the husband's relatives] led to their mobility, dispersal, and assimilation into larger white communities."

4   Speaking of the Mistassini Cree system of land tenure, Tanner (2005 [1979]: 183–4) remarks, "The early historical data presents us with a contradictory picture of Algonkian land ownership, and other contradictions arise when we look at the present-day situation ... There are at least two possible ways of explaining these contradictions in the evidence, and of determining how we are to understand the significance of hunting territories. One way would be to assume that the contradictions indicate a conflict within Mistassini society between a relatively new idea of land as property, which has yet to take hold firmly ... The alternative approach is to assume that there is only one system of land tenure, but that it is not based on and is in conflict with European notions of fixed tracts of land."

5   There is a long history of this sort of homestead pre-emption system in Canada that was meant to encourage settlers to make improvements (clear fields, build barns and houses) to Crown lands after which they were sold the property for a nominal fee per acre. Commenting on the British Columbia Pre-emption Act of 1870, Patterson (1972: 163) writes, "In order to discourage Indians, a series of requirements was laid down which

conflicted with Indian practice in the use of land. Pre-emptors were required to clear a stated amount of land over a five-year period and to bring a portion of this land under cultivation. It may be that this was a calculated step, based on knowledge of Indian use of land as a range for hunting, fishing, and gathering of wild fruits, vegetables, and roots, rather than for agriculture or domestication of animals."

6 Moss (1985: 684–5) notes, "No consultation or negotiation of land claims had been anticipated by the Quebec government, even though the province has a statutory obligation, under the Boundaries Extension Act of 1912, to deal with the Indian title of those native people living in the newly added territory ... Requests by the Crees and the Inuit to negotiate a cessation of their property interest, as well as some form of compensation for the loss of hunting and other economic rights, were ignored by the provincial government."

7 The "Paypom document" is an original set of notes made for Chief Powasson at the signing of the 1873 treaty between the Ojibways and the government of Canada, at Lake of the Woods, consisting of eighteen points with the names August Nolin and Joseph Nolin written at the bottom. Historically, this document emerged under peculiar circumstances. Elder Paypom explains how he obtained the document:

> Linde was a photographer and a friend to the Indian people. One day, about 40 or 50 years ago, he told me he had a paper and the Government wanted to buy it from him. He said they would give him $5,000 for it. But he wanted me to have it, "for your children" he said.
>
> That winter I saved all the money from my trapline ... I saved my money and in the spring I gave it to Linde. He moved south, but he sent me a parcel in the mail. He sent it like a parcel of clothes so nobody would suspect it was the treaty [i.e., document].
>
> The notation below appears in pencil on the back of the original.
>
> This copy was given to me in 1906 by chief Powasson at Bukety – the Northwest Angle- Lake of the woods.
>
> (signed)
> C.C. Linde
> (Source: Grand Council Treaty # 3, www.gct3.net/wp-content).

8 The Supreme Court made no decision on the land dispute, insisting that another trial was necessary. However, for the first time, the Court directly addressed the issue of Aboriginal title.

4. The Politics of Resistance and Confrontation

1   The Ojibway Warrior Society probably had its origins about the time of the Dakota Sioux incursions into Anishinabe territory in the Lake of the Woods region in the first half of the nineteenth century; thus, place names like Sioux Lookout, north of Kenora, and Warroad, Minnesota. Ritzen-thaler (1978: 744) explains, "Ordinarily, it was small-scale warfare ... The common pattern was for a warrior to invite a number of other warriors to join him in a war party that he would lead. Upon completion of the raid, the war party was dissolved." The incident at Kenora's Anicinabe Park would appear to have been of a similarly spontaneous nature.

2   Note the other instances in which the Assembly of First Nations, or its forerunner the National Indian Brotherhood, has not supported particular Aboriginal causes because it felt that larger issues were more important, for example, the Lavell-Bedard case (1973), Bill C-31 (1985), or the Sechelt initiative (1986).

3   Archaeologists have established that the St. Lawrence Iroquois were an independent group of Iroquois people, of whom many were dispersed between the visits of Cartier and Champlain, probably in wars with the Hurons of the Trent River system in the mid-sixteenth century. Village sites of the St. Lawrence Iroquois were situated along the upper St. Lawrence Valley of southern Quebec, eastern Ontario, and adjacent New York State (Wright 1972: 86–90). Thus, the claim that the Iroquois were not Indigenous to the area of Oka, Quebec, is not supported by existing archaeological evidence.

5. The Ipperwash Confrontation

1   Although every attempt is made in this chapter to portray the events and situations described herein as accurately as possible, the reader should be aware that the writer himself was not a witness to these events. The details described here are a précis or compilation from evidence presented to the Ipperwash Inquiry. As such, readers are encouraged to read the original accounts presented in the *Report of the Ipperwash Inquiry* for further details (Linden 2007).

2   Anthony O'Brien (Dudley) George was born in Sarnia, Ontario, on 17 March 1957.

3   The Aboriginal groups referred to as Chippewas, Ojibways, and Saulteaux are closely related First Nations whose members were living in a fairly compact area in the mid-seventeenth century. As such, there has

never been a single, distinctive name for these groups as a whole. Ojibway speakers commonly refer to themselves as *Anishinabe*, meaning "the people" or "the human beings." The term *Chippewa* tends to be the preferred spelling for groups living in the United States and southern Ontario, while *Ojibway* (or Ojibwa, Ojibwe), meaning "moccasins puckered up," has more of a northern Canadian usage. *Saulteaux* refers to the First Nations living at Sault Sainte Marie in the mid-seventeen century, with the term *Soto* used in southern Manitoba for those who later migrated there. *Bungi*, meaning "give me 'a little,'" is used in the Prairie Provinces. *Mississauga* refers to a First Nation having its origins on the northern end of Lake Huron near the Mississagi River, and for a while was used for all Ojibway people of southern Ontario; however, today its usage is more restricted to the residents of the New Credit Reserve (Rogers 1978: 768). In the *Handbook of Indians of Canada* (Hodge 1971 [1913]: 96–100), dozens of terms are listed as synonymous with Chippewa or Ojibway, but most of these are clan designations, such as the Amikwa ("beaver"), or the Nikikouek ("otter"). In addition, there are many other names used to refer to the Chippewas in the languages of such tribes as the Huron ("Kwa'yatha"), Mohawk ("Tewa'kenha"), or Assiniboine ("Wah'kah'towah").

4   Kettle Point is the name for the unusual spherical boulders that erode from the underlying Devonian shale beds along the shores of Lake Huron. These boulders or "kettles" have always been considered a local natural wonder, and they are not found at any other Canadian location. Stony Point derives its name from an outcropping of flintbeds that have been quarried by the First Nations people for thousands of years. According to the Kettle and Stony Point Historical Claims Research Office, the trade in flint found its way along Indigenous trade routes forming links to many other Aboriginal communities (Gulewitsch 1995: 1–2).

5   The *Report of the Ipperwash Inquiry* (Linden 2007) uses both "Stoney Point" and "Stony Point," often employing both of these terms on the same page. It is not known if the writer(s) of this report were aware of this inconsistency, or whether these two terms were regarded as synonymous or interchangeable with one another. The present work uses only "Stony Point" because that is the only usage employed by the Chippewas themselves (see Gulewitsch 1995).

6   The Stony Point Reserve was "two miles square at the River aux Sable which empties into Lake Huron" (Gordon 1996).

7   A Ministry of Natural Resources memo from 1972 claims that there was no evidence of a burial mound; however, a later memo by the same agency cautions that the 1972 methodology "does not agree with current

archaeological survey standards." There are also many government letters from the 1930s mentioning finding graves on the site, in addition to the park superintendent's wife's report of finding bones in the park in 1950 (Linden 2007: 59).

8 The promise states: "if, at the termination of the war, no further use of the area is required by the Department of National Defence negotiations will be entered into with the Department of Indian Affairs to transfer the lands back to the Indians at a reasonable price determined by mutual agreement" (Koehler 1996).

9 Royal Canadian Army Cadets. After the summer of 1993, the cadet camp was no longer used because of the growing unrest and the occupation of an adjacent piece of land. The summer training facilities were subsequently moved to CFB Borden.

10 In March 1992, the Standing Senate Committee on Aboriginal Peoples recommended in its tabled report that the appropriated land be returned to its former Aboriginal inhabitants. The report also indicated that the federal government's reasons for continuing to occupy the land were "spurious and without substance" (see, e.g., Gordon 1996, Hamilton 1998, Steckley and Cummins 2008: 205).

11 The issue over Premiere Harris's denial once again became an object of public attention in February 2006, when CTV aired a television movie called *One Dead Indian*, which was based on a book by the same name written by Peter Edwards, a *Toronto Star* reporter (Edwards 2003). Premier Harris's alleged use of the f-word in reference to the Aboriginal protesters of Ipperwash Provincial Park was part of the testimony given by ex-Attorney General Charles Harnick heard on 16 February 2006 (Peterson 2008). On the date of the release of the Ipperwash Inquiry Report, Mike Harris referred to the Ipperwash allegations as "malicious and petty" (*CBC News*, 31 May 2007).

12 As stated in the *Report of the Ipperwash Inquiry*, "a fundamental problem was that the information about guns was not authenticated or verified by OPP intelligence officers" (Linden 2007: 56). Gerald George's description of the different firearms was recorded in a notebook by Detective Constable Dew, who referred to Gerald George as an "anonymous source." Band Councillor Gerald George apparently was also the source of other misinformation when it was reported to the OPP that damage had been done to his car by a group of park occupiers. The damage to the councillor's car was by a rock thrown by one of the occupiers who took exception to an article the councillor had written disapproving of the occupation. A rumour was also started that the occupiers had smashed the vehicle of a female

driver using a baseball bat, but according to the Ipperwash Report, Justice
Sidney Linden found this information false and misleading, as indicated
by a transcript of his comments before the Inquiry on 19 September 2007.

13 In an ironic twist of fate, OPP negotiator Sergeant Margaret Eve, who
had attempted to negotiate with the Aboriginal protesters back in 1995,
and was present when Dudley George was shot, was hit by a transport
truck on Highway 401 near Chatham, Ontario, in June 2000, when a truck
swerved off the road into the path of four police officers. The truck driver,
as was Acting Sergeant Ken Deane, was found guilty of criminal negligence causing death. In another incident, in October 2000 – four months
after the death of Sergeant Eve – OPP Inspector Dale Linton, the officer
who activated Deane's unit the night Dudley George was shot, was killed
in a single-vehicle crash near Smith Falls, Ontario; to this day, it is not
known why Inspector Linton swerved off the road and crashed his car. According to one theory, falling into the subversive plot category, the three
vehicular deaths are part of an OPP cover-up instigated by former Premier
Mike Harris. Although this theory is totally unsubstantiated, of course,
its logic goes like this: "The OPP had a lot to lose from the Ipperwash Inquiry. The OPP's reputation had been permanently tarnished by the death
of Dudley George in 1995 and lives could be permanently ruined if certain witnesses explained what really happened ... The OPP members in
question also had previous stains on the record from racist issues, so it's
conceivable that ... some hit man working for Mike Harris is another possibility for the cop-killer in question" (www.lilith-ezine.com/articles/
canada/ontarioCop-Killer-in-Ontaro).

14 In addition, three other roles are listed: (1) maintain contacts within Aboriginal communities throughout the province; (2) remain current on Aboriginal issues; (3) provide informed advice to OPP Executive and incident
commanders regarding Aboriginal issues (Ontario Provincial Police 2006:
3). The reader is requested to consult the complete *Framework* document,
as no attempt is made here to effectively summarize or discuss all of the
pertinent points raised therein.

15 See also Mark Vandermass, "Canada at the Crossroads: The Ipperwash
Legacy," a speech given at the Caledonia Lions Hall, 10 June 2007. This is
the sort of speech given across Ontario whose intent is to inflame anti-Native opinion. In this particular diatribe, the belief is expressed that "OPP
Two Tier Justice policies are based on the false premise that native people
have no-self-control, that they are incapable of obeying the law, that they
and their children are willing to live in a lawless world ruled by criminals
who take what they want, when they want. For more than 15 years the

OPP has been sacrificing the well-being of law-abiding people – both native and non-native – for the benefit of sociopaths and demagogues" (2007: 5).
16 Henry and Tator (2000), in *Racist Discourse in Canada's English Print Media*, identify and discuss a number of discourses pertaining to denial, equal opportunity, blame the victim, and white victimization, among others.
17 See also Miller's follow-up article in the *Toronto Star* (29 June 2007), in which he asks, "We always learn best from our mistakes. By ignoring Linden's report, are the media going to learn anything from Ipperwash?"

6. Ipperwash Inquiry Recommendations

1 For our purposes in this chapter, unless otherwise noted, the discussion of the *Report of the Ipperwash Inquiry* (Linden 2007) focuses on the "Executive Summary," an abridged version of the final report comprising the "Investigation and Findings, Volume 1," "Policy Analysis, Volume 2," and "Recommendations."
2 It could be suggested that the Winnipeg General Strike of 1919 and the manner in which the Conservative government handled that affair contributed to the Conservatives' resounding defeat in the 1921 election. The succeeding Liberal government, no doubt fearing a further labour backlash, enacted labour reforms proposed by the Royal Commission. In addition, one of the strike leaders, J.S. Woodsworth, went on to found the Co-operative Commonwealth Federation (CCF), predecessor of the New Democratic Party (NDP) of Tommy Douglas.
3 The use of the term *attorn* in the OPP Association submission (2006: 46) is puzzling since it means to "transfer" in some sense, such as its alternative form "attorney" meaning to act on one's behalf, i.e., to transfer authority. Perhaps the meaning intended, given the context, is to acknowledge the police as a higher authority, such as in acknowledging a new landlord.
4 In June 2007, a stand-alone Ministry of Aboriginal Affairs was created, replacing the Ontario Secretariat of Aboriginal Affairs. Its website (www.aboriginalaffairs.gov.on.ca) has a section on current land claims and related negotiations.

7. Ipperwash as Racial Oppression

1 The theoretical orientation known as sociobiology owes much of its modern popularity to E.O. Wilson (1978). Sociobiology is perhaps best placed in the long-standing "nature versus nurture" debate, with the

understanding that neither side provides a complete explanation for human social and cultural life.

2 The C.D. Howe Institute, with its head office in Toronto, Ontario, has an extensive research and publication agenda. It describes itself as a "national, non-partisan, non-profit research organization that aims to improve Canadians' standard of living by fostering sound economic and social policy" (see www.cdhowe.org).

3 Bill C-31 was passed in 1985 eliminating these marriage stipulations, and supposedly, the discrimination against Aboriginal women on the basis of gender (see Hedican 2008b: 226–9). However, prior to 1972–73, minor unmarried children were automatically enfranchised (had their Indian status taken away) with their mothers. Since that time, minors are enfranchised only when the parents request it and the request is approved by the Department of Indian Affairs. In the period 1968–88 more than 13,000 Indians lost their legal status under various provisions of the Indian Act (Hedican 2008b: 226–9).

8. Institutional Racism in Canada

1 I am particularly indebted to Stan Barrett for our discussions of these issues in an Aboriginal context, and his explication of the links between power, privilege, and racism in a wider context (Barrett 1987, 2002).

2 Although certain policemen may hold racist attitudes towards members of minority groups, a related issue concerns the number of individual policemen in right-wing or white supremacist organizations. There are no doubt policemen who hold very conservative ideas, but this does not necessarily mean that they will ultimately join right-wing organizations. As Barrett (1987: 322) concludes, "what has been remarkable about Canada is that so few policemen have been formal members of the right wing."

3 Force is the exercise of power and control. Authority is the legitimate use of force. Thus, force may be legitimated or not, while authority comes from some generally accepted use of influence by a particular sector of society.

4 The author's own long-term fieldwork among the Anishinabe of northwestern Ontario is described in the following books: *The Ogoki River Guides* (Hedican 1986), *Up in Nipigon Country* (Hedican 2001), *Applied Anthropology in Canada* (Hedican 2008b), and *Social Anthropology: Canadian Perspectives on Culture and Society* (Hedican 2012).

References

Aboriginal Justice Implementation Commission (Manitoba). 2009. *Final Report.* www.ajic.mb.ca.

Adams, H. 1989. *Prison of Grass: Canada from a Native Point of View.* Saskatoon: Fifth House Publishers.

Agocs, C., and H. Jain. 2001. *Systemic Racism in Employment in Canada: Diagnosing Systemic Racism in Organizational Culture.* Toronto: Canadian Race Relations Foundation.

Alcantara, C. 2007. "Explaining Aboriginal Treaty Negotiation Outcomes in Canada: The Cases of the Inuit and the Innu in Labrador." *Canadian Journal of Political Science* 40 (1): 185–207. http://dx.doi.org/10.1 017/ S0008423907070060.

Alfred, T. 2011. "Colonial Stains on Our Existence." In *Racism, Colonialism and Indigeneity in Canada,* ed. M.J. Cannon and L. Sunseri. Oxford: Oxford University Press.

Alfred, T., and J. Corntassel. 2011. "Being Indigenous: Resurgences against Contemporary Colonialism." In *Racism, Colonialism and Indigeneity in Canada,* ed. M.J. Cannon and L. Sunseri. Oxford: Oxford University Press.

Allahar, A. 1998. "Race and Racism: Strategies of Resistance." In *Racism and Social Inequality in Canada: Concepts, Controversies and Strategies of Resistance,* ed. V. Satzewich. Toronto: Thompson Educational.

Amnesty International Canada. 2008. "Open Letter: Ontario's Duty to Ensure Rights Are Upheld in Police Response to Indigenous Protest." 12 Nov. www.amnesty.ca/resource_center/news/view. Accessed 2 Feb. 2010.

Anderson, C., and C. Denis. 2003. "Urban Natives and the Nation: Before and After the Royal Commission on Aboriginal Peoples." *Canadian Review of Sociology and Anthropology/La Revue Canadienne de Sociologie et d'Anthropologie* 40 (4): 373–90. http://dx.doi.org/10.1111/j.1755-618X.2003.tb00253.x.

Anderson, M.C., and C. Robertson. 2007. "The 'Bended Elbow' News, Kenora 1974: How a Small Town Newspaper Promoted Colonization." *American Indian Quarterly* 31 (3): 410–40. http://dx.doi.org/10.1353/aiq.2007.0027.

Anderssen, E. 1998. "Nunavut to a Welfare Case." *Globe and Mail*. 5 June.

Armitage, P., and J.C. Kennedy. 1989. "Redbaiting and Racism on Our Frontier: Military Expansion in Labrador and Quebec." *Canadian Review of Sociology and Anthropology/La Revue Canadienne de Sociologie et d'Anthropologie* 26 (5): 798–817.

Asch, M. 1984. *Home and Native Land: Aboriginal Rights and the Canadian Constitution*. London: Methuen.

Asch, M. 2000. "First Nations and the Derivation of Canada's Underlying Title: Comparing Perspectives on Legal Ideology." In *Aboriginal Rights and Self-Government*, ed. C. Cook and J.D. Lindau. Montreal and Kingston: McGill-Queen's University Press.

Asch, M. 2001a. "Aboriginal Rights." In *International Encyclopedia of the Social and Behavioural Sciences*, ed. P. Baltes and N. Smelser. Oxford: Pergamon. http://dx.doi.org/10.1016/B0-08-043076-7/02842-4.

Asch, M. 2001b. "Indigenous Self-Determination and Applied Anthropology in Canada: Finding a Place to Stand." *Anthropologica* 43 (2): 201–9. http://dx.doi.org/10.2307/25606035.

Asch, M. 2002. "From Terra Nullius to Affirmation: Reconciling Aboriginal Rights with the Canadian Constitution." *Canadian Journal of Law and Society* 17 (2): 23–9.

Asch, M., ed. 1997. *Aboriginal and Treaty Rights in Canada: Essays on Law, Equality, and Respect for Difference*. Vancouver: UBC Press.

Ashini, D. 1990. "David Confronts Goliath: The Innu of Ungava versus the NATO Alliance." In *Drumbeat: Anger and Renewal in Indian Country*, ed. B. Richardson. Toronto: Summerhill.

Bagley, C. 1973. "Race Relations and the Press: An Empirical Analysis." *Race* 15 (1): 59–89. http://dx.doi.org/10.1177/030639687301500104.

Baker, D. 1978. "Race and Power: Comparative Approaches to the Analysis of Race Relations." *Ethnic and Racial Studies* 1 (3): 316–35. http://dx.doi.org/10.1080/01419870.1978.9993236.

Balikci, A. 1970. *The Netsilik Eskimo*. Prospect Heights, IL: Waveland Press.

Banton, M. 1977. *The Idea of Race*. London: Tavistock.

Barrett, S.R. 1984. *The Rebirth of Anthropological Theory*. Toronto: University of Toronto Press.

Barrett, S.R. 1987. *Is God a Racist? The Right Wing in Canada*. Toronto: University of Toronto Press.

Barrett, S.R. 2002. *Culture Meets Power*. Westport, CN: Praeger.

Bashir, B., and W. Kymlicka. 2008. "Introduction: Struggles for Inclusion and Reconciliation in Modern Democracies." In *The Politics of Reconciliation in Multicultural Societies*, ed. W. Kymlicka and B. Bashir. Oxford: Oxford University Press.

Battiste, M., and S. Henderson. 2011. "Eurocentrism and the European Ethnographic Tradition." In *Racism, Colonialism, and Indigeneity in Canada*, ed. M.J. Cannon and L. Sunseri. Oxford: Oxford University Press.

B.C. Treaty Commission. 1999. *A Lay Person's Guide to Delgamuukw*. Vancouver: Author. www.bctreaty.net.

Beare, M.E. 2008. "Shouting Innocence from the Highest Rooftop." In *Honouring Social Justice*, ed. M.E. Beare. Toronto: University of Toronto Press.

Belanger, Y.D. 2010. *Ways of Knowing: Native Studies in Canada*. Toronto: Nelson Education.

Bell, C., and M. Asch. 1997. "Challenging Assumptions: The Impact of Precedent in Aboriginal Rights Litigation." In *Aboriginal and Treaty Rights in Canada*, ed. M. Asch. Vancouver: UBC Press.

Bemis, S.F. 1962. *Jay's Treaty: A Study in Commerce and Diplomacy*. New Haven, CT: Yale University Press.

Benedict, R. 1960. *Race: Science and Politics*. New York: Viking.

Berger, T.R. 1977. *Northern Frontier, Northern Homeland: Report of the Mackenzie Valley Pipeline Inquiry*. 2 vols. Ottawa: Supply and Services Canada.

Berger, T.R. 1983. "Native Rights and Self-Determination." *Canadian Journal of Native Studies* 3 (2): 363–75.

Berkhofer, R.F. 1978. *The White Man's Indian*. New York: Random House.

Better, S. 2008. *Institutional Racism: Theory and Strategies for Social Change*. New York: Rowman and Littlefield.

Billig, M. 1979. *Psychology, Racism and Fascism*. Birmingham: Searchlight Booklet.

Blalock, H.M. 1982. *Race and Ethnic Relations*. Englewood Cliffs, NJ: Prentice-Hall.

Bock, P.K. 1966. *The Micmac Indians of Restigouche: History and Contemporary Description*. Ottawa: National Museum of Canada.

Bolaria, B.S., and P.S. Li. 1988. *Racial Oppression in Canada*. Toronto: Garamond.

Borrows, J. 1994. "Traditional Contemporary Equality: The Effect of the Charter on First Nations Politics." *University of New Brunswick Law Journal* 43: 19–48.

Borrows, J. 1996. "With or without You: First Nations Law (in Canada)." *McGill Law Journal/Revue de Droit de McGill* 41 (3): 630–65.

Borrows, J. 2002. *Recovering Canada: The Resurgence of Indigenous Law*. Toronto: University of Toronto Press.

Borrows, J. 2010. *Canada's Indigenous Constitution.* Toronto: University of Toronto Press.

Bouza, A. 1990. *The Police Mystique: An Insider's Look at Cops, Crime, and the Criminal Justice System.* New York: Plenum.

Brown, J.S.H. 1980. *Strangers in Blood: Fur Trade Company Families in Indian Country.* Vancouver: UBC Press. http://dx.doi.org/10.2307/1183555.

Bueckert, D. 2003. "Mercury Poisoning Issue Back 30 Years Later, Disease Signs Present in Indians." *Toronto Star.* 28 July.

Burstein, P. 2008. "Sentencing Acts of Civil Disobedience: Separating Villains and Heroes." In *Honouring Social Justice,* ed. M.E. Beare. Toronto: University of Toronto Press.

Cairns, A.C. 2000. *Citizens Plus: Aboriginal Peoples and the Canadian State.* Vancouver: UBC Press.

Calder v. The Attorney General of British Columbia. [1973]. S.C.R. 313.

Calverley, D. 2006. "The Impact of the Hudson's Bay Company on the Creation of Treaty Number Nine." *Ontario History* 98 (1): 30–51.

Campbell, M. 1973. *Halfbreed.* Toronto: McClelland and Stewart.

Canada. 1948. Special Joint Committee of the Senate and the House of Commons Appointed to Examine and Consider the Indian Act. *Minutes of Proceedings and Evidence, 28 May 1946–21 June 1948.* Ottawa: King's Printer.

Canada. 1969. *Statement of the Government of Canada on Indian Policy, 1969.* (White Paper.). Ottawa: Queen's Printer.

Canada. 1970. *Official Consolidation of the Indian Act.* Ottawa: Queen's Printer.

Canada. 1971 [1891]. *Indian Treaties and Surrenders.* (Coles Reprint.). Ottawa: Queen's Printer.

Canada. 1975. *Indian Claims in Canada.* Ottawa: Indian Claims Commission.

Canada. 1982. *Constitution Act.* Ottawa: Queen's Printer.

Canada. 1983. *Indian Self-Government in Canada: Report of the Special Committee.* Ottawa: Queen's Printer.

Canada. 1985. *Living Treaties: Lasting Agreements. Report of the Task Force to Review Comprehensive Claims Policy.* Ottawa: Department of Indian and Northern Development.

Canada. 1998. *Gathering Strength: Canada's Aboriginal Action Plan.* Ottawa: Ministry of Supply and Services.

Canada. 2003. *Urban Aboriginal Youth: An Action Plan for Change.* Sixth Report, Hon. Thelma Chalifoux, Chair. Ottawa: Standing Senate Committee on Aboriginal Peoples.

Canada. 2005. *Urban Aboriginal Strategy Pilot Projects Formative Evaluation: Final Report.* Ottawa: Aboriginal Affairs and Northern Development.

Canada. 2008. *Aboriginal Peoples of Canada, 2006 Census*. Cat. No.92–593-XCB. Ottawa: Statistics Canada.

Cannon, M.J., and L. Sunseri, eds. 2011. *Racism, Colonialism, and Indigeneity in Canada*. Oxford: Oxford University Press.

Cardinal, H. 1969. *The Unjust Society: The Tragedy of Canada's Indians*. Edmonton: M.G. Hurtig.

Carmichael, S., and C.V. Hamilton. 1967. *Black Power: The Politics of Liberation in America*. New York: Random House.

Carstens, P. 1971. "Coercion and Change." In *Canadian Society*, ed. R. Ossenberg. Scarborough, ON: Prentice-Hall.

Carter, B., and S. Virdee. 2008. "Racism and the Sociological Imagination." *British Journal of Sociology* 59 (4): 661–79. http://dx.doi.org/10.1111/j.1468-4446.2008.00214.x.

CBC News. 2000. "Oka Crisis Ottawa's Fault: Ciaccia." 10 July.

CBC News. 2004. "The Marshall Decision." 9 May.

CBC News. 2006. "Harris Denies Using Profanity over Native Protest." 14 Feb.

CBC News. 2006. "Ontario Buys Site of Disputed Caledonia Claim." 16 June.

CBC News. 2007. "George Family Braces for Ipperwash Inquiry Report." 31 May.

CBC News. 2007. "Ipperwash Allegations 'Malicious and Petty, Harris says." 31 May.

CBC News. 2007. "Ipperwash Inquiry Spreads Blame for George's Death." 31 May.

CBC News. 2008. "Federal Commission: Truth and Reconciliation." 16 May.

CBC News. 2008. "Aboriginal Leaders Look to Future after Historic Apology." 11 June. www.cbc.ca/canada/story/2008/06/11/apology/future. Accessed 8 March 2009.

CBC News. 2008. "Chairman Quits Troubled Residential-School Commission." 20 Oct.

CBC News. 2009. "Border Authorities Shut Down Akwesasne Crossing." 1 June. www.cbc.ca/canada/montreal/story/2009/06/01/akwesassne-guards-border-guns. Accessed 8 March 2009.

Chesler, M., A. Lewis, and J. Crowfoot. 2005. *Challenging Racism in Higher Education: Promoting Justice*. New York: Rowman and Littlefield.

Chiefs of Ontario. 2006. *A Framework for Police Preparedness for Aboriginal Critical Incidents: Critical Response*. www.attorneygeneral.jus.gov.on.ca/.../Chiefs_of_Ontario-Framework.

Christie, G. 2007. "Police-Government Relations in the Context of State-Aboriginal Relations." In *Police and Government Relations: Who's Calling the Shots?* ed. M.E. Beare and T. Murray. Toronto: University of Toronto Press.

Ciaccia, J. 2000. *The Oka Crisis: A Mirror of the Soul*. Dorval, QC: Maren.

Coates, K. 2000. *The Marshall Decision and Native Rights*. Montreal and Kingston: McGill-Queen's University Press.

Cox, K. 1990a. "Innu Fighting Back on Challenges to Traditional Lifestyle." *Globe and Mail*. 12 Feb.

Cox, K. 1990b. "NATO Rejects Goose Bay for Base, Innu Protesters Claim Victory." *Globe and Mail*. 22 May.

Cox, K. 2000. "Native Lobster Fishery Ends but Dispute Doesn't." *Globe and Mail*. 7 Oct.

Coyle, M. 2005. Ipperwash Inquiry Consultation on Draft Paper: "Addressing Aboriginal Land and Treaty Rights in Ontario: An Analysis of Past Policies and Options for the Future." 4 Feb. Toronto. Copy in author's possesseion.

Culhane, D. 1998. *The Pleasure of the Crown: Anthropology, Law, and First Nations*. Vancouver: Talonbooks.

Cumming, P.A. 1973. "Indian Rights: Means of Settling as Vital as End." *Globe and Mail*. 21 Feb.

Cumming, P.A., and N.H. Mickenberg, eds. 1972. *Native Rights in Canada*. 2nd ed. Toronto: Indian-Eskimo Association of Canada.

Dakota Ojibway Police Service. 2009. www.dops.org.

Dalton, J.E. 2006. "Aboriginal Self-Determination in Canada: Protections Afforded by the Judiciary and Government." *Canadian Journal of Law and Society* 21 (1): 11–37. http://dx.doi.org/10.1353/jls.2006.0034.

Daly, R. 2005. *Our Box Was Full: An Ethnography for the Delgamuukw Plaintiffs*. Vancouver: UBC Press.

Darnell, R. 2000. "Canadian Anthropologists, the First Nations and Canada's Self-Image at the Millennium." *Anthropologica* 42 (2): 165–74.

Daugherty, W.E. 1985. *Treaty 3 Research Report (1873)*. Ottawa: Indian and Northern Affairs.

Davies, S., and N. Guppy. 1998. "Race and Canadian Education." In *Racism and Social Inequality in Canada: Concepts, Controversies and Strategies of Resistance*, ed. V. Satzewich. Toronto: Thompson Educational.

Delgamuukw v. R. [1997]. 3 S.C.R. 1010.

Denis, J. 2011. *Canadian Apartheid: Boundaries and Bridges in Aboriginal-White Relations*. Doctoral Dissertation, Department of Sociology, Harvard University.

Denis, J. 2012. "Transforming Meanings and Group Positions: Tactics and Framing in Anishinaabe-White Relations in Northwestern Ontario, Canada." *Ethnic and Racial Studies* 35 (3): 453–70. http://dx.doi.org/10.1080/01419870.2011.589525.

Dewbury, A. 2007. "The American School of Scientific Racism in Early American Anthropology." *Histories of Anthropology Annual* 3 (1): 121–47. http://dx.doi.org/10.1353/haa.0.0026.

Dickason, O.P. 2009. *Canada's First Nations.* Oxford: Oxford University Press.

Doern, B. 1967. "The Role of Royal Commissions in the General Policy Process and in Federal-Provincial Relations." *Canadian Public Administration* 10 (4): 417–33. http://dx.doi.org/10.1111/j.1754-7121.1967.tb00994.x.

Doerr, A.D. 1975. "The Dilemma of Indian Policy in Canada." *Quarterly of Canadian Studies* 3 (4): 198–207.

Dosman, E. 1972. *Indians: The Urban Dilemma.* Toronto: McClelland and Stewart.

Doxtader, E. 2003. "Reconciliation: A Theoretical Conception." *Quarterly Journal of Speech* 89 (4): 267–92. http://dx.doi.org/10.1080/0033563032000160954.

Doxtator, D. 2011. "'The Idea of 'Indianness' and Once Upon a Time: The Role of Indians in History." In *Racism, Colonialism, and Indigeneity in Canada,* ed. M.J. Cannon and L. Sunseri. Oxford: Oxford University Press.

Driben, P. 1983. "The Nature of Métis Claims." *Canadian Journal of Native Studies* 3 (1): 183–96.

du Plessis, V., R. Bestiri, R.D. Bollman, and H. Clemenson. 2002. *Definitions of "Rural."* Ottawa: Statistics Canada.

Dunk, T.W. 2007. *It's a Working Man's Town: Male Working-Class Culture.* Montreal and Kingston: McGill-Queen's University Press.

Dyck, N. 1991. *What Is the Indian "Problem": Tutelage and Resistance in Canadian Indian Administration.* St. John's: Memorial University of Newfoundland.

Dyck, N. 1997. "Tutelage, Resistance and Co-optation in Canadian Indian Administration." *Canadian Review of Sociology and Anthropology/La Revue Canadienne de Sociologie et d'Anthropologie* 34 (3): 333–48. http://dx.doi.org/10.1111/j.1755-618X.1997.tb00212. x.

Edwards, P. 2003. *One Dead Indian: The Premier, the Police and the Ipperwash Crisis.* Toronto: Stoddard.

Etkin, C.E. 1988. "The Sechelt Indian Band: An Analysis of a New Form of Native Self-Government." *Canadian Journal of Native Studies* 8 (1): 73–105.

Fabian, J. 1993. "Crossing and Patrolling: Thoughts on Anthropology and Boundaries." *Culture (Canadian Ethnology Society)* 13 (1): 49–54.

Fanon, F. 1963. *The Wretched of the Earth.* New York: Grove Press.

Fanon, F. 2010. *Racist America: Roots, Current Realities, and Future Reparations.* New York: Routledge.

Farnsworth, C. 1995. "Ipperwash Military Reserve, Ont." *New York Times.* 27 Aug.

Feagin, J.R. 2006. *Systemic Racism: A Theory of Oppression*. New York: Routledge.

Feit, H.A. 1973. "The Ethno-Ecology of the Waswanipi Cree; or How Hunters Can Manage Their Resources." In *Cultural Ecology*, ed. B. Cox. Toronto: McClelland and Stewart.

Feit, H.A. 1991. "Anthropology and Current Social Issues: The Judgement on the Gitksan-Wet'suwet'en." *Canadian Anthropology Society Newsletter* 19 (2): 7–9.

Feit, H.A. 2004. "Hunting and the Quest for Power: The James Bay Cree and Whiteman Development." In *Native Peoples: The Canadian Experience*, ed. R.B. Morrison and C.R. Wilson. Don Mills, ON: Oxford University Press.

Ferguson, R. 2007. "Caledonia Protests Greet Bryant." *Toronto Star*. 26 Nov.

Franks, C.E.S. 2000. "Rights and Self-Government for Canada's Aboriginal Peoples." In *Aboriginal Rights and Self-Government*, ed. C. Cook and J.D. Lindau. Montreal and Kingston: McGill-Queen's University Press.

Frideres, J.S. 1976. "Racism in Canada: Alive and Well." *Western Canadian Journal of Anthropology* 6 (4): 124–45.

Frideres, J.S. 1988a. *Native Peoples in Canada: Contemporary Conflicts*. 3rd ed. Scarborough, ON: Prentice-Hall.

Frideres, J.S. 1988b. "Institutional Structures and Economic Deprivation: Native People in Canada." In *Racial Oppression in Canada*, ed. B.S. Bolaria and P.S. Li. Toronto: Garamond.

Frideres, J.S. 1996. "The Royal Commission on Aboriginal Peoples: The Route to Self-Government?" *Canadian Journal of Native Studies* 16 (2): 247–66.

Frideres, J.S. 1998. *Aboriginal Peoples in Canada: Contemporary Conflicts*. 5th ed. Scarborough, ON: Prentice-Hall.

Frideres, J.S., and R. Gadacz. 2008. *Aboriginal Peoples in Canada*. 8th ed. Toronto: Prentice-Hall.

Fudge, J., and E. Tucker. 2004. *Labour before the Law: The Regulation of Workers' Collective Action in Canada, 1900–1948*. Toronto: University of Toronto Press.

Gobel Azoulay, K. 2006. "Reflections on 'Race' and the Biologization of Difference." *Patterns of Prejudice* 40 (4–5): 353–79. http://dx.doi.org/10.1080/00313220601020098.

Gillborn, D. 2008. *Racism and Education: Coincidence or Conspiracy?* New York: Routledge.

Gilroy, P. 2001. *Against Race: Imagining Political Culture beyond the Color Line*. Cambridge, MA: Harvard University Press.

Globe and Mail. 1986. "Canadian Indians Must Face Massive Obstacles in Path." 20 May.

Globe and Mail. 1990. "Innu Chief Warns Government." 2 Oct.

Globe and Mail. 2001. "Ottawa, Natives Reach Compromise on Fishing." 23 April.

Globe and Mail. 2006. "Caledonia Barricades Go Back Up." 22 May.

Glover, K.S. 2009. *Racial Profiling: Research, Racism, and Resistance.* New York: Rowman and Littlefield.

Goddard, J. 1991. *Last Stand of the Lubicon Cree.* Vancouver: Douglas and McIntyre.

Goodey, J. 2007. "Racist Violence in Europe: Challenges for Official Data Collection." *Ethnic and Racial Studies* 30 (4): 570–89. http://dx.doi.org/10.1080/01419870701356007.

Gordon, T.H. 1996. "Trial Date Set for Stoney Point Members Charged in Defence of Traditional Territory." *Prison News Service* 54 (Spring).

Gorodzeisky, A., and M. Semyonov. 2009. "Terms of Exclusion: Public Views towards Admission and Allocation of Rights to Immigrants in European Countries." *Ethnic and Racial Studies* 32 (3): 401–23. http://dx.doi.org/10.1080/01419870802245851.

Grand Council Treaty #3. n.d. *The Paypom Treaty.* www.gct3.net/wp-content. Accessed 7 April 2010.

Gravlee, C.C. 2009. "How Race Becomes Biology: Embodiment of Social Inequality." *American Journal of Physical Anthropology* 139 (1): 47–57. http://dx.doi.org/10.1002/ajpa.20983.

Gravlee, C.C., and E. Sweet. 2008. "Race, Ethnicity, and Racism in Medical Anthropology, 1977–2002." *Medical Anthropology Quarterly* 22 (1): 27–51. http://dx.doi.org/10.1111/j.1 548-1387.2008.00002.x.

Green, J. 2011. "From Stonechild to Social Cohesion: Antiracist Challenges for Saskatchewan." In *Racism, Colonialism, and Indigeneity in Canada*, ed. M.J. Cannon and L. Sunseri. Oxford: Oxford University Press.

Guerin v. R. [1984]. 2 S.C.R. 335.

Gulewitsch, V.A. 1995. *The Chippewas of Kettle and Stony Point: A Brief History.* Forest, ON: Kettle and Stony Point First Nations Historical Claims Research Office.

Gumbhir, V.K. 2007. *But Is It Racial Profiling? Policing, Pretext Stops, and the Color of Suspicion.* New York: LFB Scholarly Publishing.

Haig-Brown, C., and D.A. Nock, eds. 2006. *With Good Intentions: Euro-Canadian and Aboriginal Relations in Colonial Canada.* Vancouver: UBC Press.

Halifax Daily News. 2001. "Fishing for Lobster." 3 June.

Hamilton, G. 2000. "Burnt Church Votes to End Fall Fishery Early." *National Post.* 20 Sept.

Hamilton, J. 1998. "Ipperwash Protesters Sent to Jail, Natives Angered over 'Injustice.'" *London Free Press.* 4 April.

Harper, Prime Minister S. 2008. *Text of Prime Minister Harper's Apology.* 11 June. www.fns.bc.ca

Hartmann, P., and C. Husband. 1974. *Racism and the Mass Media.* London: Davis-Poynter.

Hatch, J.B. 2008. *Race and Reconciliation: Redressing Wounds of Injury.* New York: Lexington Books.

Hawthorn, H.B., ed. 1966–67. *A Survey of the Contemporary Indians of Canada.* Ottawa: Queen's Printer.

Hedican, E.J. 1986. *The Ogoki River Guides: Emergent Leadership among the Northern Ojibwa.* Waterloo, ON: Wilfrid Laurier University Press.

Hedican, E.J. 1990. "On the Rail-Line in Northwestern Ontario: Non-Reserve Housing and Community Change." *Canadian Journal of Native Studies* 19 (1): 15–32.

Hedican, E.J. 2001. *Up in Nipigon Country: Anthropology as a Personal Experience.* Halifax: Fernwood.

Hedican, E.J. 2008a. "The Ipperwash Inquiry and the Tragic Death of Dudley George." *Canadian Journal of Native Studies* 28 (1): 159–73.

Hedican, E.J. 2008b. *Applied Anthropology in Canada: Understanding Aboriginal Issues.* 2nd ed. Toronto: University of Toronto Press.

Hedican, E.J. 2012. *Social Anthropology: Canadian Perspectives on Culture and Society.* Toronto: Canadian Scholars' Press.

Helleiner, J. 2000. *Irish Travellers: Racism and the Politics of Culture.* Toronto: University of Toronto Press.

Henriksen, G. 1973. *Hunters in the Barrens: The Naskapi on the Edge of the White Man's World.* St. John's: Institute of Social and Economic Research, Memorial University of Newfoundland.

Henry, F., and C. Tator. 1985. "Racism in Canada: Social Myths and Strategies for Change." In *Ethnicity and Ethnic Relations in Canada,* ed. R.M. Bienvenue and J.E. Goldstein. Toronto: Butterworths.

Henry, F., and C. Tator. 2000. *Racist Discourse in Canada's English Print Media.* Toronto: Canadian Race Relations Foundation.

Hodge, F.W. 1971 [1913]. *Handbook of Indians of Canada.* Ottawa: King's Printer. (Coles Reprint).

Hodgins, B.W., and J. Benidickson. 1989. *The Temagami Experience: Recreation, Resources, and Aboriginal Rights in the Northern Ontario Wilderness.* Toronto: University of Toronto Press.

Hodgins, B W., U. Lischke, and D. McNab. 2003. *Blockades and Resistance: Studies in Actions of Peace and the Temagami Blockades of 1988–89.* Waterloo, ON: Wilfrid Laurier University Press.

Holbert, S., and L. Rose. 2004. *The Color of Guilt and Innocence: Racial Profiling and Police Practices in America*. San Ramon, CA: Page Marque.

Hughes, D., and E. Kallen. 1974. *The Anatomy of Racism*. Montreal: Harvest House.

Hume, S. 1991. "Judge Prefers Dusty Documents to Oral Truth." *Proactive: Society of Applied Anthropology in Canada* 10 (1): 31–2.

Hutchins, P.W. 2010. "Power and Principle: State-Indigenous Relations across Time and Space." In *Aboriginal Title and Indigenous Peoples*, ed. L.A. Knafla and H. Westra. Vancouver: UBC Press.

Indian Chiefs of Alberta. 1970. *Citizens Plus: A Presentation of the Indian Chiefs of Alberta to the Right Honourable P.E. Trudeau, June 1970*. Edmonton: Indian Association of Alberta.

Isaac, B. 2006. "Proto-Racism in Graeco-Roman Antiquity." *World Archaeology* 38 (1): 32–47. http://dx.doi.org/10.1080/00438240500509819.

Jacobs, B. 2008. "Response to Canada's Apology to Residential School Survivors." *Canadian Woman Studies* 26 (3–4): 223–5.

Jacobson, E.M. 1975. *Bended Elbow: Kenora Ontario Talks Back*. Kenora, ON: Central Publications.

Johnston, C.M. 1964. *The Valley of the Six Nations*. Toronto: University of Toronto Press.

Jahoda, G. 2009. "Intra-European Racism in Nineteenth-Century Anthropology." *History and Anthropology* 20 (1): 37–56. http://dx.doi.org/10.1080/02757200802654258.

Kallen, E. 1982. *Ethnicity and Human Rights in Canada*. Toronto: Gage.

Knafla, L.A. 2010. "'This Is Our Land': Aboriginal Title at Customary and Common Law Contexts." In *Aboriginal Title and Indigenous Peoples*, ed. L.A. Knafla and H. Westra. Vancouver: UBC Press.

Koehler, H.P. 1996. "Stoney Point Peoples Support." 26 March. www.exucu-link.com/~hkoeler/stonsups.html.

Kymlicka, W. 1997. *The Rights of Minority Cultures*. New York: Oxford University Press.

Kymlicka, W. 2007. *Multicultural Odysseys: Navigating the New International Politics of Diversity*. New York: Oxford University Press.

Kymlicka, W., and B. Bashir, eds. 2008. *The Politics of Reconciliation in Multicultural Societies*. New York: Oxford University Press.

Lackenbauer, P.W. 2007. *Battle Grounds: The Canadian Military and Aboriginal Lands*. Vancouver: UBC Press.

Lambertus, S. 2004. *Wartime Images, Peacetime Wounds: The Media and the Gustafsen Lake Standoff*. Toronto: University of Toronto Press.

LaRocque, E. 2010. *When the Other Is Me: Native Resistance Discourse 1850–1990*. Winnipeg: University of Manitoba Press.

Larsen, T. 1983. "Negotiating Identity: The Micmacs of Nova Scotia." In *The Politics of Indianness: Case Studies of Native Ethnopolitics in Canada*, ed. A. Tanner. St. John's: Memorial University of Newfoundland.

LaViolette, F.E. 1973. *The Struggle for Survival: Indian Cultures and the Protestant Ethic in British Columbia*. Toronto: University of Toronto Press.

Law, I., D. Phillips, and L. Turney. 2004. "Tackling Institutional Racism in Higher Education: An Antiracist Toolkit." In *Institutional Racism in Higher Education*. ed. I. Law, D. Phillips, and L. Turney. Stoke-on-Trent: Trentham Books.

Lawrence, B. 2011. "Rewriting Histories of the Land: Colonization and Indigenous Resistance in Canada." In *Racism, Colonization, and Indigeneity in Canada*, ed. M.J. Cannon and L. Sunseri. Oxford: Oxford University Press.

Lawrence, B., and E. Dua. 2005. "Decolonizing Antiracism." *Social Justice* (San Francisco) 32 (4): 120–43.

Lea, J. 1986. "Police Racism: Some Theories and Their Policy Implications." In *Confronting Crime*, ed. R. Matthews and J. Young. Beverly Hills, CA: Sage.

Legere, A. 1998. "An Assessment of Recent Political Development in Nunavut: The Challenges and Dilemmas of Inuit Self-Government." *Canadian Journal of Native Studies* 18: 271–99.

Lentin, R. 2007. "Ireland: Racial State and Crisis Racism." *Ethnic and Racial Studies* 30 (4): 610–27. http://dx.doi.org/10.1080/01419870701356023.

Leslie, J.E., and R. Maguire. 1978. *The Historical Development of the Indian Act*. Ottawa: Indian and Northern Affairs.

Letkemann, P.G. 2005. "Reclaiming Aboriginal Justice, Identity, and Community." *Canadian Review of Sociology and Anthropology/La Revue Canadienne de Sociologie et d'Anthropologie* 42 (2): 233–5.

Levin, J., and W. Levin. 1982. *The Functions of Discrimination and Prejudice*. New York: Harper and Row.

Linden, Hon. Sidney B. 2007. *Report of the Ipperwash Inquiry*. Toronto: Publications Ontario.

London Free Press. 1995. "Two Versions of the Same Event: Who Fired the First Shot?" 8 Sept.

London Free Press. 2007. "Law and Order." Cartoon. 26 May.

London Free Press. 2009. "Ipperwash Park to Re-Open in 2010." 28 May.

Long, J.S. 2006. "How the Commissioners Explained Treaty Number 9 to the Ojibway and Cree in 1905." *Ontario History* 98 (1): 1–29.

MacFarlane, R.O. 1938. "British Indian Policy in Nova Scotia to 1760." *Canadian Historical Review* 19: 154–67.

Macklem, P. 1997. "The Impact of Treaty 9 on Natural Resource Development in Northern Ontario." In *Aboriginal and Treaty Rights in Canada*, ed. M. Asch. Vancouver: UBC Press.

Madden, J. 2008. "The Métis Nation's Self-Government Agenda: Issues and Options for the Future." In *Métis-Crown Relations: Rights, Identity, Jurisdiction, and Governance*, ed. F. Wilson and M. Mallet. Toronto: Irwin Law.

Mahoney, J. 1999. "On a Frosty Northern Night, Nunavut Is Born." *Globe and Mail*. 1 April.

Manning, P.K. 2008. "Shadows of the Case." In *Honouring Justice*, ed. M.E. Beare. Toronto: University of Toronto Press.

Marshall, Chief D., Sr. 1990. "The Mi'kmaq: The Covenant Chain." In *Drumbeat: Anger and Renewal in Indian Country*, ed. B. Richardson. Toronto: Summerhill.

Martin, D. 2007. "Accountability Mechanisms: Legal Sites of Executive-Police Relations: Core Principles in a Canadian Context." In *Police and Government Relations: Who's Calling the Shots?* ed. M.E. Beare and T. Murray. Toronto: University of Toronto Press.

Martin-Hill, D. 2008. *The Lubicon Lake Nation: Indigenous Knowledge and Power*. Toronto: University of Toronto Press.

Mathewson, G. 1995. "FOREST – The Cops Are Everywhere." *Sarnia Observer*. 13 Sept.

McGee, H.F., Jr. 1984. *The Native Peoples of Atlantic Canada: A History of Indian-European Relations*. Ottawa: Carleton University Press.

McNeil, K. 1990. "The Temagami Indian Land Claim: Loosening the Judicial Strait-jacket." In *Temagami: A Debate on Wilderness*, ed. M. Bray and A. Thomson. Toronto: Dundurn Press.

McNeil, K. 2010. "The Sources and Content of Indigenous Land Rights in Australia and Canada: A Critical Comparison." In *Aboriginal Title and Indigenous Peoples*, ed. L.A. Knafla and H. Westra. Vancouver: UBC Press.

Mevorach, K.G. 2007. "Race, Racism, and Academic Complicity." *American Ethnologist* 34 (2): 238–41. http://dx.doi.org/10.1525/ae.2007.34.2.238.

Michalenko, G., and R. Suffling. 1982. "Social Impact Assessment in Northern Ontario: The Reed Paper Controversy." In *Indian SIA: The Social Impact Assessment of Rapid Resource Development on Native Peoples*, ed. C. Geisler, R. Green, D. Usner, and P.C. West. Ann Arbor: University of Michigan Press.

Miller, J. 2005. *Ipperwash and the Media: A Critical Analysis of How the Story Was Covered*. Report Submitted to the Aboriginal Legal Services of Toronto. www.attorneygeneral.jus.gov.on.ca.

Miller, J. 2007. "Media Failed to Deliver on Ipperwash." *Toronto Star*. 29 June.

Milloy, M.J. 1995. "Whose 'Law' and Whose 'Order'? The Siege at Gustafsen Lake." *McGill Daily*. 7 Sept.

Mitchell, M., Grand Chief. 1990. "Akwesasne: An Unbroken Assertion of Sovereignty." In *Drumbeat: Anger and Renewal in Indian Country*, ed. B. Richardson. Toronto: Summerhill.

Morison, S.E. 1972. *Samuel de Champlain: Father of New France*. Boston: Little, Brown.

Morris, Hon. A. 1979 [1880]. *The Treaties of Canada with the Indians of Manitoba and the North-West Territories*. (Cole reprint.) Toronto: Belfords, Clarke.

Moss, W. 1985. "The Implementation of the James Bay and Northern Quebec Agreement." In *Aboriginal Peoples and the Law: Indian, Metis and Inuit Rights in Canada*, ed. B.W. Morse. Ottawa: Carleton University Press.

Mullings, L. 2005. "Interrogating Racism: Towards an Antiracist Anthropology." *Annual Review of Anthropology* 34 (1): 667–93. http://dx.doi.org/10.1146/annurev. anthro.32.061002.093435.

National Post. 2007. "Native Violence Becomes Blameless." 2 June.

National Post. 2007. "For Natives, a Legal Free-for-All." 2 June.

Neizen, R. 2004. *A World beyond Difference: Cultural Identity in the Age of Globalization*. Oxford: Blackwell.

Nettheim, G. 2007. "The Influence of Canadian and International Law on the Evolution of Australian Aboriginal Title." In *Let Right Be Done: Aboriginal Title, the Calder Case, and the Future of Indigenous Rights*, ed. H. Foster, H. Raven, and J. Webber. Vancouver: UBC Press.

Nicholas, A. 1970. "New Brunswick Indians – Conservative Militants." In *The Only Good Indian: Essays by Canadian Indians*, ed. Waubageshig. Toronto: New Press.

Nishnawbe-Aski Police Service. 2009. "Thunder Bay Drug Seizure." 16 July. www.naps.ca.

Ohler, S. 1999. "Nunavut Born with High Hopes, Big Challenges." *National Post*. 1 April.

Ontario. 1995. Commission on Systemic Racism in the Ontario Criminal Justice System. *Report of the Commission on Systemic Racism in the Ontario Criminal Justice System*. Toronto: Queen's Printer.

Ontario Human Rights Commission (OHRC). 2003. *Paying the Price: The Human Costs of Racial Profiling*. Toronto: OHRC.

Ontario Provincial Police (OPP). 2006. *A Framework for Police Preparedness for Aboriginal Critical Incidents*. 23 Jan. Ontario Government Documents. Collection. www.archives.gov.on.ca/english/collections.

Ontario Provincial Police Association (OPPA). 2006. *Submissions to the Ipperwash Inquiry*. Paliare Roland Rosenberg Rothstein LLP. 28 July.

Ontario [Attorney General] v. *Bear Island Foundation*. [1991]. 2 S.C.R. 570.

Patterson, E.P. 1972. *The Canadian Indian: A History since 1500*. Don Mills, ON: Collier-Macmillan.

Penikett, T. 2006. *Reconciliation: First Nations Treaty Making in British Columbia*. Toronto: Douglas and McIntyre.

Petersen, K. 2008. "Land & Jail: Ipperwash, Official Racism and the Future of Ontario." 23 Sept. www.dominionpaper.ca/articles.

Philpott, D. 2006. "Beyond Politics as Usual: Is Reconciliation Compatible with Liberalism?" In *The Politics of Past Evil: Religion, Reconciliation, and the Dilemmas of Transitional Justice*, ed. D. Philpott. Notre Dame, IN: University of Notre Dame Press.

Pilkington, A. 2004. "Institutional Racism in the Academy? Comparing the Police and University in Midshire." In *Institutional Racism in Higher Education*, ed. I. Law, D. Philips, and L. Turney. Stoke-on-Trent: Trentham Books.

Platiel, R. 1996. "Significant Differences Seen between Native Standoffs." *Globe and Mail*. 29 Aug.

Ponting, J.R. 1998. "Racism and Stereotyping of First Nations." In *Racism and Social Inequality in Canada: Concepts, Controversies and Strategies of Resistance*, ed. V. Satzewich. Toronto: Thompson Educational.

Potts, Chief G. 1990. "Teme-Augama Anishnabai: Last Ditch Defence of a Priceless Homeland." In *Drumbeat: Anger and Renewal in Indian Country*, ed. B. Richardson. Toronto: Summerhill.

Pue, W.W. 2007. "Comment on: The Oversight of Executive-Police Relations in Canada: The Constitution, the Courts, Administrative process, and Democratic Governance." In *Police and Government Relations: Who's Calling the Shots?* ed. M.E. Beare and T. Murray. Toronto: University of Toronto Press.

Quimby, G.I. 1967. *Indian Life in the Upper Great Lakes, 11,000 B.C. to A.D. 1800*. Chicago: University of Chicago Press.

Rainforest Action Network (RAN). 2007. "Grassy Narrows Blockade 5th Anniversary." 12 Dec. http://understory.ran.org/2007/12/12/grassy-narrows-blockade-5th-anniversay/.

Rangasamy, J. 2004. "Understanding Institutional Racism: Reflections from Linguistic Anthropology." In *Institutional Racism in Higher Education*, ed. I. Law, D. Phillips, and L. Turney. Staffordshire: Trentham Books.

Ray, A.J. 2010. "From the U.S. Indian Claims Commission Cases to *Delgamuukw*: Facts, Theories, and Evidence in North American Land Claims." In *Aboriginal Title and Indigenous Peoples*, ed. L.A. Knafla and H. Westra. Vancouver: UBC Press.

Redbird, D. 1980. *We Are Métis: A Métis View of the Development of Canadian Native People*. Toronto: Ontario Métis and Non-Status Indian Association.

Richards, J. 2006. *Creating Choices: Rethinking Aboriginal Policy.* Ottawa: C.D. Howe Institute.

Richardson, B. 1990. "Wrestling with the Canadian System: A Decade of Lubicon Frustration." In *Drumbeat: Anger and Renewal in Indian Country,* ed. B. Richardson. Toronto: Summerhill.

Ritzenthaler, R.E. 1978. "Southwestern Chippewa." In *Northeast: Handbook of North American Indians,* vol. 15, ed. B. Trigger. Washington, DC: Smithsonian Institution.

Roach, K. 2007. "The Overview: Four Models of Police-Governance Relations." In *Police and Government Relations: Who's Calling the Shots?* ed. M.E. Beare and T. Murray. Toronto: University of Toronto Press.

Robinson, A. 2005. *Ta'n Teli-ktlamsitasit (Ways of Believing): Mi'kmaw Religion in Eskasoni, Nova Scotia.* Toronto: Pearson Prentice-Hall.

Rogers, E.S. 1966. *Subsistence Areas of the Cree-Ojibwa of the Eastern Subarctic: A Preliminary Study.* Ottawa: National Museum of Canada.

Rogers, E.S. 1978. "Southeastern Ojibwa." In *Northeast: Handbook of North American Indians,* vol. 15, ed. B. Trigger. Washington, DC: Smithsonian Institution.

Rogers, E.S. 1981. "History of Ethnological Research in the Subarctic Shield and Mackenzie Valley." In *Subarctic: Handbook of North American Indians,* vol. 6, ed. J. Helm. Washington, DC: Smithsonian Institution.

Rogers, E.S., and F. Tobobundung. 1975. "Parry Island Farmers: A Period of Change in the Way of Life of the Algonkians of Southern Ontario." *Mercury Series Paper* 31: 247–366. Ottawa: National Museum of Canada, Ethnology Division.

Royal Commission on Aboriginal Peoples (RCAP) (Canada). 1996. *Report of the Royal Commission on Aboriginal Peoples.* Ottawa: Canada Communication Group.

Russell, P.H. 2005. *Recognizing Aboriginal Title: The Mabo Case and Indigenous Resistance to English-Settler Colonization.* Toronto: University of Toronto Press.

R. v. Bernard. [2005]. 2 S.C.R. 220.

R. v. Gladstone. [1996]. 2 S.C.R. 723.

R. v. Kapp. [2008]. 2 S.C.R. 483.

R. v. Marshall. [1999]. 3 S.C.R. 456.

R. v. Marshall. [2005] 2 S.C.R. 220.

R. v. Sparrow. [1990]. 1 S.C.R. 1075.

R. v. Van Der Peet. [1996]. 2 S.C.R. 507.

Ryan, J. 1988. "Economic Development and Innu Settlement: The Establishment of Sheshatshit." *Canadian Journal of Native Studies* 8 (1): 1–25.

Sanders, D. 1985. "Aboriginal Rights: The Search for Recognition in International Law." In *The Quest for Justice*, ed. M. Bolt, J. Long, and L. Little Bear. Toronto: University of Toronto Press.

Satzewich, V. 1998. "Racism in Justice." In *Racism and Social Inequality in Canada: Concepts, Controversies and Strategies of Resistance*, ed. V. Satzewich. Toronto: Thompson Educational.

Sawchuck, J. 1978. *The Metis of Manitoba: Reformulation of an Ethnic Identity*. Toronto: Peter Martin.

Sawchuck, J. 1982. "Some Early Influences on Metis Political Organization." *Culture* 2 (3): 85–91.

Scheffel, D.Z. 2000. "The Post-Anthropological Indian: Canada's New Images of Aboriginality in the Age of Repossession." *Anthropologica* 42 (2): 175–87.

Schmalz, P.S. 1991. *The Ojibwa of Southern Ontario*. Toronto: University of Toronto Press.

Shanklin, E. 2000. "Representations of Race and Racism in American Anthropology." *Current Anthropology* 41 (1): 99–103. http://dx.doi.org/10.1086/300105.

Sharma, N., and C. Wright. 2008–9. "Decolonizing Resistance, Challenging Colonial States." *Social Justice* (San Francisco) 35 (3): 120–38.

Sharma, S. 2004. "Transforming the Curriculum? The Problem with Multiculuralism." In *Institutional Racism in Higher Education*, ed. I. Law, D. Philips, and L. Turney. Staffordshire: Trentham Books.

Smedley, A., and B.D. Smedley. 2005. "Race as Biology Is Fiction, Racism as a Social Problem Is Real: Anthropological and Historical Perspectives on the Social Construction of Race." *American Psychologist* 60 (1): 16–26. http://dx.doi.org/10.1037/0003-066X.60.1.16.

Smith, C.C. 2006. "Racial Profiling in Canada, the United States, and the United Kingdom." In *Racial Profiling in Canada: Challenging the Myth of "a Few Bad Apples,"* ed. C. Tator and F. Henry. Toronto: University of Toronto Press.

Smith, J. 1988. "Canada: The Lubicon Lake Cree." *Cultural Survival Quarterly* 11 (3): 61–2.

St. Catherine's Milling and Lumber Co. v. R. [1888]. 14 App. Cas. 46 (J.C.P.C.).

Steckley, J.I., and B.D. Cummins. 2008. *Full Circle: Canada's First Nations*. Toronto: Pearson Education Canada.

Stepan, N. 1982. *The Idea of Race in Science*. London: Macmillan.

Stults, B.J., and E.P. Baumer. 2007. "Racial Context and Police Force Size: Evaluating the Empirical Validity of the Minority Threat Perspective." *American Journal of Sociology* 113 (2): 507–46. http://dx.doi.org/10.1086/518906.

Stymeist, D.H. 1975. *Ethnics and Indians: Social Relations in a Northwestern Ontario Town*. Toronto: Peter Martin.

Sudbury Star. 2007. "Ipperwash Inquiry Folly: It's Inconceivable that Natives Were Found to Have No Part in the Problems." 6 June.

Surtees, R.T. 1969. "The Development of an Indian Reserve Policy in Canada." *Ontario History* 61: 87–98.

Surtees, R.T. 1982. *Canadian Indian Policy.* Bloomington: Indiana University Press.

Tanner, A. 1986. "The New Hunting Territory Debate: An Introduction to Some Unresolved Issues." *Anthropologica* 28 (1/2): 19–36. http://dx.doi.org/10.2307/25605191.

Tanner, A. 2005 [1979]. *Bringing Home Animals: Religious Ideology and Mode of Production of the Mistassini Cree Hunters.* London: Palgrave Macmillan.

Tanovich, D.M. 2006. *The Colour of Justice: Policing Race in Canada.* Toronto: Irwin Law.

Tator, C., and F. Henry, eds. 2006. *Racial Profiling in Canada: Challenging the Myth of "a Few Bad Apples."* Toronto: University of Toronto Press.

Telegraph Journal (New Brunswick). 2002. "Fishermen Hope for Calm Autumn: Communities Optimistic that Burnt Church Deal Will End Tensions on Miramichi Bay." 24 Aug.

Times-News (Thunder Bay). 1975. "Book on Anicinabe Park Siege, Alcohol Sparks Uproar in Kenora." 23 April.

Times-News (Thunder Bay). 1975."Occupation at Anicinabe Park Won't Recur." 15 April.

Times-News (Thunder Bay). 1975. "Davis Presented Indians' Problems." 1 May.

Toronto Star. 2003. "Province to Fantino: Deal with Profiling." 11 Dec.

Toronto Star. 2006. "Attempted Murder in Caledonia." 12 June.

Toronto Star. 2007. "Canada Votes against U.N. Aboriginal Declaration." 13 Sept.

Toronto Star. 2007. "Builder, 52, Hurt in Caledonia Home Clash." 14 Sept.

Toronto Star. 2007. "Ipperwash Land Returned to Indians." 21 Dec.

Toronto Star. 2008. "Seeking Truth about Lost Children." 29 May.

Toronto Star. 2008. "Protest Prompts Abitibi Pullout: Negotiations with Band Would Take too Long, Forestry Giant Says." 5 June.

Toronto Star. 2008. "OPP Forgets Lessons of Ipperwash: Fantino's Threats Ignored Emphasis on Negotiation and Building Trust during Aboriginal Occupations." 30 July.

Treaty 7 Elders and Tribal Council. 1996. *The True Spirit and Original Intent of Treaty 7.* Montreal and Kingston: McGill-Queen's University Press.

Tully, J. 2000. "A Just Relationship between Aboriginal and Non-Aboriginal Peoples of Canada." In *Aboriginal Rights and Self-Government*, ed. C. Cook and J.D. Lindau. Montreal and Kingston: McGill-Queen's University Press.

Tully, J. 2008. *Public Philosophy in a New Key: Democracy and Civic Freedom.* Cambridge: Cambridge University Press.

Upton, L.F.S. 1975. "Colonists and Micmacs." *Journal of Canadian Studies/Revue d'Etudes Canadiennes* 10: 44–50.

Upton, L.F.S. 1979. *Micmacs and Colonists: Indian-White Relations in the Maritime Provinces, 1713–1867.* Vancouver: UBC Press.

Vandermass, M. 2007. *The Ipperwash Papers.* www.ipperwashpapers.ca.

Vandermass, M. 2007. "Canada at the Crossroads: The Ipperwash Legacy." Speech delivered at the Caledonia Lions Hall. 10 June.

Voyageur, C., and B. Calliou. 2011. "Aboriginal Economic Development and the Struggle for Self-Government." In *Racism, Colonialism, and Indigeneity in Canada,* ed. M.J. Cannon and L. Sunseri. Oxford: Oxford University Press.

Wadden, M. 2001. *Nitassinan: The Innu Struggle to Reclaim Their Homeland.* Vancouver: Douglas and McIntyre.

Walter, M.D. 2008. "The Jurisprudence of Reconciliation: Aboriginal Rights in Canada." In *The Politics of Reconciliation in Multicultural Societies,* ed. W. Kymlicka and B. Bashir. Oxford: Oxford University Press.

Weaver, S.M. 1981. *Making Canadian Indian Policy: The Hidden Agenda 1968–1970.* Toronto: University of Toronto Press.

Weaver, T. 1985. "Anthropology as a Policy Science." *Human Organization* 82: 95–103, 197–205.

Whyte, J.D. 2008. "Developmental and Legal Perspectives on Aboriginal Justice Administration." In *Moving towards Justice: Legal Traditions and Aboriginal Justice,* ed. J.D. Whyte. Saskatoon: Purich.

Wilkes, R. 2004. "A Systematic Approach to Studying Indigenous Politics: Band-Level Mobilization in Canada, 1981–2000." *Social Science Journal* 41 (3): 447–57. http://dx.doi.org/10.1016/j.soscij.2004.04.007.

William, C.J. 2006. "Obscurantism in Action: How the Ontario Human Rights Commission Frames Racial Profiling." *Canadian Ethnic Studies* 38 (2): 1–18.

Williams, T., and K. Murray. 2007. "Comment on: Police-Government Relations in the Context of State-Aboriginal Relations." In *Police and Government Relations: Who's Calling the Shots?* ed. M.E. Beare and T. Murray. Toronto: University of Toronto Press.

Wilson, E.O. 1978. *Sociobiology: The New Synthesis.* Cambridge, MA: Harvard university Press.

Wright, J.V. 1972. *Ontario Prehistory: An Eleven-Thousand-Year Archaeological Outline.* Ottawa: National Museums of Canada.

York, G., and L. Pindera. 1991. *People of the Pines: The Warriors and the Legacy of Oka.* Toronto: Little, Brown.

Index